WOMEN AND HUMAN DEVELOPMENT

In this major book Martha Nussbaum, one of the most innovative and influential philosophical voices of our time, proposes a new kind of feminism that is genuinely international, argues for an ethical underpinning to all thought about development planning and public policy, and dramatically moves beyond the abstractions of economists and philosophers to embed thought about justice in the concrete reality of the struggles of poor women.

In much of the world today women are less well nourished than men, less healthy, and more vulnerable to physical violence and sexual abuse. Martha Nussbaum argues that international political and economic thought must be sensitive to gender difference as a problem of justice, and that feminist thought must begin to focus on the problems of women in the third world. Taking as her point of departure the predicament of poor women in India, she shows how philosophy should undergird basic constitutional principles that should be respected and implemented by all governments, and used as a comparative measure of quality of life across nations.

The account is based on the idea of human capabilities: what people are actually capable of doing or becoming in the real world. This approach is then defended against the charge that all universals are bound to be insensitive to regional and cultural specificity. Martha Nussbaum also argues that it is an approach superior to the preference-based approaches prevalent in contemporary economics. Two final chapters consider the particular problems that arise when sex equality clashes with the claims of religion or family.

This is a vividly written book that is rich in narrative examples. It offers a radically fresh account of how we should understand the "quality of life" in a nation, and how we should think about the basic minimum that all governments should provide for their citizens. Moreover, it calls for a new international focus to feminism, and shows through concrete detail how philosophical arguments about justice really do connect with the practical concerns of public policy.

Martha C. Nussbaum is Ernst Freund Distinguished Professor of Law and Ethics at the University of Chicago, appointed in the Philosophy Department, the Law School, the Divinity School, and the College. She is an Associate in the Classics Department, an Affiliate of the Committee for Southern Asian Studies, and a member of the Board of the Committee on Gender Studies.

THE JOHN ROBERT SEELEY LECTURES

The John Robert Seeley lectures have been established by the University of Cambridge as a biennial lecture series in social and political studies, sponsored jointly by the Faculty of History and the University Press. The Seeley lectures provide a unique forum for distinguished scholars of international reputation to address, in an accessible manner, themes of broad and topical interest in social and political studies. Subsequent to their public delivery in Cambridge the University Press publishes suitably modified versions of each set of lectures. Professor James Tully of McGill University delivered the inaugural series of Seeley lectures in 1994 on the theme of *Constitutionalism in an Age of Diversity*. Professor Jeremy Waldron of Columbia University gave a series in 1996 on *The Dignity of Legislation*; in 1998, Professor Martha Nussbaum of The University of Chicago delivered the latest series, on *Feminist Internationalism*. Professor Joseph Raz of the University of Oxford will deliver his series in 2000.

WOMEN AND HUMAN DEVELOPMENT

The Capabilities Approach

MARTHA C. NUSSBAUM

The University of Chicago

CAMBRIDGE
UNIVERSITY PRESS

CAMBRIDGE UNIVERSITY PRESS
Cambridge, New York, Melbourne, Madrid, Cape Town, Singapore, São Paulo, Delhi

Cambridge University Press
32 Avenue of the Americas, New York, NY 10013-2473, USA

www.cambridge.org
Information on this title: www.cambridge.org/9780521003858

First published 2000
13th printing 2008

Printed in the United States of America

A catalog record for this publication is available from the British Library.

ISBN 978-0-521-66086-0 hardback
ISBN 978-0-521-00385-8 paperback

In Memory of Sara Nussbaum
1912–1999

We come from our family's house to live in our husband's house. If we mention *our* name in this house, they say, "Oh, that is *another* family." Yet when it comes to working, they say, "What you earn is ours, because you are in *this* family's house," or "because you are working on *this* family's land." Let the land be registered in our names, so that we will not always feel like we are in someone else's family.

Santokbehn, agricultural laborer, Ahmedabad

In your joint family, I am known as the second daughter-in-law. All these years I have known myself as no more than that. Today, after fifteen years, as I stand alone by the sea, I know that I have another identity, which is my relationship with the universe and its creator. That gives me the courage to write this letter as myself, not as the second daughter-in-law of your family. . . .

I am not one to die easily. That is what I want to say in this letter.

Rabindranath Tagore, "Letter from a Wife" (1914)

On the roads I have had banyan trees planted, which will give shade to beasts and men. I have had mango groves planted and I have had wells dug and rest houses built every nine miles . . . And I have had many watering places made everywhere for the use of beasts and men . . . This benefit is important . . . I have done these things in order that my people might conform to *Dhamma* [moral law].

Ashoka, emperor, third century B.C. (edict translated by Romila Thapar)

We not only want a piece of the pie, we also want to choose the flavor, and to know how to make it ourselves.

Ela Bhatt, founder, Self-Employed Women's Association (SEWA) (1992)

CONTENTS

PREFACE

This study of human capabilities as the basis for fundamental political principles focuses on the lives of women in developing countries. That is obviously only one area where this approach might be used to think about political principles; my discussion will allude to some of its other implications. Even within the study of women, this account deals with only some of the issues that might be addressed in a more exhaustive treatment of the capabilities approach. Thus religion and the family receive detailed treatment, while other equally important topics, such as property rights and education, do not.

In another way as well the present account is narrow: it presents the capabilities approach for a broad interdisciplinary audience, with a view to shaping public policy. Because my version of this approach is philosophical and would offer nothing if stripped of its philosophical arguments, those arguments are here, but sometimes in a brief and compressed form. Many philosophical issues that deserve detailed analysis – in particular, issues of justification, realism, and objectivity – are only sketched (although I have given some of them more detailed treatment in articles cited in the notes).

Finally, I discuss only my own version of the capabilities approach. I do not spend time on its historical antecedents in Aristotle and Marx, or on relatives such as Mill's Aristotelian view of human flourishing, the writings of the Yugoslav humanist Marxists, and various forms of modern Thomism. Nor do I even engage in detailed analysis of the writings of Amartya Sen, the pioneer of the capabilities approach in economics. Finally, I do not address the by-now extensive economic literature debating various aspects of the capabilities approach and the measures used in the *Human Development Reports*.

These omissions reflect a long-term strategy. In this book I aim to present a single clear line of feminist argument, accessible to a wide variety of readers. Over the long term, I intend to produce a much more compendious and scholastic book on capabilities that will discuss all the topics I omit here. That book (I hope) will answer many questions philosophers will have about aspects of the present book, and other more technical questions that economists regard as salient. It will also address a wider range of specific political problems. The present book is to that book as a 10K race is to a marathon: it is complete in itself, it has a beginning and an end, but it doesn't require as much stamina either of the reader or of the author. I believe that enough is said about my views on the most salient contested issues to convey the approaches that I would favor. Nonetheless, I ask readers eager for fuller discussions in some areas to wait for the marathon.

Chicago
February 1999

ACKNOWLEDGMENTS

The work that ultimately became this project began in 1986, when I became a research advisor at the World Institute for Development Economics Research (WIDER) in Helsinki, an institute of the United Nations University. Before this, like most American academics, I had lived a relatively insular life. I was ill-educated about the problems of developing countries and, more generally, about non-Western traditions and ways of life. My office neighbors from Sri Lanka and India could talk easily about Sophocles and Aristotle, but I had absolutely nothing to say about the *Mahabharata*, or about Buddhist ethics. Although my work was beginning to focus on social justice, I had thought relatively little about problems of global justice. Nor had feminist philosophy been a particular focus of my work. My eight years at WIDER (in residence for one month every summer) transformed my work, making me aware of urgent problems and convincing me that philosophy had a contribution to make toward their solution. I also began to see that the peculiar combination of philosophical concerns I had brought to WIDER might actually be an asset rather than a liability. The ancient Greek philosophers contended with the misery of people whose living standard more closely approximated that of present-day India than that of the United States or Europe; their proposals have, in some respects, great pertinence to the diagnosis and amelioration of problems in developing countries. And Aristotle's insistence on the ethical importance of a vivid perception of concrete circumstances had its own contribution to make, I felt, to a field that is frequently so preoccupied with formal modeling and abstract theorizing that it fails to come to grips with the daily reality of poor people's lives.

For his help during the early years of this work, I owe great thanks to Lal Jayawardena, WIDER's director, who believed in the strange idea that philosophy should be brought to bear on the foundations of development economics. Above all I am grateful to Amartya Sen, who helped to formulate the project, and whose work has been, and continues to be, a source of insight and inspiration, especially for the way it combines a passion for justice with a love of reason. Stephen and Frédérique Marglin provoked me to respond to their attacks on universalism, thus getting me started on that aspect of the present project. As I formulated my ideas during the WIDER years, I also received tremendous help from Martha Alter Chen, David Crocker, Jean Drèze, Jonathan Glover, Valentine Moghadam, Nkiru Nzegwu, Onora O'Neill, Siddiq Osmani, Hilary and Ruth Anna Putnam, John Roemer, Margarita Valdés, Roop Rekha Verma, and the other participants in our three conferences. As I developed the views further in a series of articles, I was especially grateful for the encouragement and the criticisms of John Rawls, Henry Richardson, Cass Sunstein, and Paul Weithman. My own sense of the issues and their urgency took shape, too, through time spent with the other members of the Sen family: Amita, Indrani, Kabir, Picco, Tumpa, and Babu. I am grateful to Amita for many keen observations about modernity and tradition, and about the situation of India's women, and to Babu for comments on the lecture drafts.

In March 1997 I went to India to look at women's development projects, because I wanted to write a book that would be real and concrete rather than abstract, and because I knew that I knew too little to talk about the problems of poor working women in a country other than my own. I had to hear about the problems from them. This was not my first visit to India, but it was the first in which I had focused on learning as much as I could about women's development projects. My greatest thanks are due to Martha Alter Chen, who orchestrated the entire visit and put me in touch with people whom I never would have been able to meet without her. The daughter of American Christian missionaries, Chen grew up in India, and now divides her time between India and the United States; she is as close to being a fully bicultural person as an American can be, and her unique insight into issues of human aspiration across boundaries has been extremely important to me as I developed these ideas. Her sure-footed knowledge, linguistic mastery, expertise in fieldwork, and personal warmth made easy and exhilarating days that were different from any days I had ever spent, going around with credit-union collectors in the slums of Kolaba in the hundred-degree heat, visiting a squatters' settlement in Trivandrum in the thick March humidity, seeing the daily operations of the Self-Employed Women's Association (SEWA) bank and union. Because I knew that Marty is committed, in her work, to letting the voices of poor women speak and to writing books that are above all their own, I knew I could trust her to help me learn. Though I am still in many respects a neophyte, she did more than I can ever adequately thank her for.

I returned to India in December 1998, visiting still more projects in other regions; once again I am grateful to Martha Chen for her help and advice, and also to Bina Agarwal and Leela Gulati for their recommendations and to Bina for invaluable help with travel and contacts.

I am especially grateful, too, to people with whom I met in various regions for their kind assistance and their generosity with their time. In connection with the 1997 trip, I owe thanks to Ela Bhatt, Renana Jhabvala, and Mirai Chatterjee of SEWA in Ahmedabad; to Leela Gulati, who showed me the field site for her study of working women in Trivandrum, and whose wonderful work on the daily lives of poor women has been one of my greatest inspirations; to Yedla Padmavathi, who accompanied me during my visit to a desert work site outside Mahabubnagar, and whose work with the Mahila Samakhya Project, a national government-run project promoting women's empowerment through education, showed me new dimensions of the difficulty of effecting change, in regions that almost totally lack basic infrastructure and schools. I am grateful, too, to all the staff at the Mahabubnagar field station for spending so much time telling me about their work. Indira Jaising of the Lawyers' Collective gave me advice and insight about personal laws and other aspects of the legal scene. Abha Bhaiya, of the Jagori women's project, helped me learn about initiatives on domestic violence and other issues of bodily integrity. Prema Purao, director of the Annapurna Mahila Mandel, met with me in Bombay to describe her work with poor self-employed women; I am most grateful to the staff for taking me along on a loan-collection visit to one of their work sites. Sheela Patel helped me understand projects for homeless pavement dwellers in Bombay. Sudha Murali of UNICEF helped me to learn about current problems of child labor in Andhra Pradesh. Ritu Menon, of the feminist publishing house Kali for Women in Delhi, was extremely generous, setting up a lecture for me to try out some of these ideas, and introducing me to many people. I was most grateful, too, to a number of fine economists and other social scientists who met with me and gave me advice about India, including Bina Agarwal, Praful Bidwai, Veena Das, Devaki Jain, Zoya Hasan, Tanika Sarkar, Romila Thapar, and Patricia Uberoi. Antara Dev Sen (Picco) was, as always, an insightful commentator and a warm friend.

In connection with the 1998 trip, I owe special thanks to Ginny Srivastava, Bhanwar Singh Chandana, and Nan Lal Pandey of Astha, a nongovernmental organization in Udaipur, Rajasthan, that works with women, especially tribal women, in rural areas, helping them to improve their economic situation through cottage industries and political action; to Sarda Jain in Jaipur, who helped me see some of the activities in that region (conducted by Vishaka and other local organizations) concerned with female education. In Bihar, I owe thanks to Viji Srinivasan, founder of Adithi, a nongovernmental organization that organizes many different projects in the areas of female education and economic empowerment, for taking me with her on a visit to project sites in Muzaffarpur and other parts of northern Bihar; to Sita Narasimhan for illuminating discussion on that same trip; to Dolly and the other peer educators in Muzaffarpur for telling me about their work with other daughters of sex workers; to Asma (a singer and sex worker) for challenging me, making me think hard about the differences in capability between her life and mine. In West Bengal, I wish to thank the department of philosophy at Vishva-Bharati University in Santinketan, and especially Maya Das, Bijoy Mukherjee, and Asha Mukherjee for their hospitality when I lectured there and their valuable comments; in Calcutta, the program in women's studies at Jadavpur University, where I lectured, and Sheftali Moitra, Anuradha Chanda, and Jasodhara Bagchi for organizing the event. Thanks also to Amiya Kumar Bagchi and Jasodhara Bagchi for hospitality and helpful comments; and above all, to Amita Sen for her warmth, her hospitality, and for her generosity in talking with me about the history of Tagore's educational ideas.

For comments on earlier drafts of the lectures I am extremely grateful to Bina Agarwal, Jeremy David Bendik-Keymer, Homi Bhabha, Joshua Cohen, Thomas D'Andrea, John Deigh, David Estlund, Mary Kimura, Andrew Koppelman, Richard Kraut, Angelika Krebs, Charles

Larmore, Catharine MacKinnon, Michelle Mason, Jeremy Mynott, Uma Narayan, Susan Moller Okin, Herlinde Pauer-Studer, Eric Posner, Richard Posner, Mark Ramseyer, Henry Richardson, Stephen Schulhofer, David Strauss, Cass Sunstein, Susan Wolf, and an anonymous referee. Sonia Katyal provided invaluable research assistance and productive comments; conversing with her about her bicultural experience was another source of insight. I am extremely grateful to Amartya Sen, Quentin Skinner, and Gareth Stedman Jones for their warm hospitality and their helpful comments during my stay in Cambridge, and to Jasodhara Bagchi, Diemut Bubeck, and Frances Olsen for other valuable comments. In addition to presenting the lectures as Seeley Lectures at Cambridge University, I presented three of the lectures as Thalheimer Lectures at Johns Hopkins University, two as Hesburgh Lectures at the University of Notre Dame, three at Northwestern University, two at Stanford University, and individual lectures at the University of Arizona, Tufts University, the University of Michigan, the University of Illinois at Chicago, the University of Pennsylvania, the Law-Philosophy Group at the University of Chicago, the Institut für die Wissenschaften vom Menschen in Vienna, Creighton University, the UCLA Legal Theory Workshop, the Human Development Workshop at the University of Chicago, a seminar on Human Rights in a Multicultural World at the National Center for the Humanities, the Wittgenstein Symposium in Kirchberg-am-Wechsel, Austria, Wayne State University in Detroit, Mercer University, Rice University, the Australian National University, and Harvard University. I am grateful to Sudhir Anand, Julia Annas, Richard Arneson, Daniel Brudney, Mary Ann Case, Juan Cole, Cioran Cronin, Norman Daniels, Steve Darwall, John Deigh, Richard Epstein, Sam Freeman, Alvin Goldman, David Golove, Robert Goodin, Mitu Gulati, Barbara Herman, Stanley Hoffman, Frances Kamm, Kenneth Karst, Erin Kelly, Elizabeth Kiss, Anthony Laden, Jane Mansbridge, Charles Mills, Christopher Morris, David Owen, Jack Sammons, Jerome Schneewind, Thomas Scanlon, Seana Shiffrin, Larry Temkin, Lori Watson, and Paul Weithman, among others, for their most helpful comments on those occasions. I feel lucky that so many people have helped me, and I have tried to make the arguments better in response to their suggestions and questions.

Chapter 2 was delivered at the Jean Hampton Memorial Conference at the University of Arizona at Tucson, November 1997, and it is dedicated to her memory. Before her tragic and untimely death from a stroke at the age of forty-two, Jean, a graduate student at Harvard while I was teaching there, and a fellow member of a discussion group there on the relationship between feminism and philosophy, was one of this country's leading moral philosophers. Her contribution to feminist thought was very important for its insistence on the worth of the social contract tradition for feminists. Her tough-mindedness, humor, creativity, and commitment to rationality live in her remarkable books and articles, which will continue to be an inspiration to feminists and to anyone who wants to think about justice.

During the final days of work on this manuscript, I had the good fortune to present it as a seminar at the Bunting Institute of Radcliffe College, Harvard University. The seminar was designed to bring non-academic professional women back for a week-long immersion in an academic topic; participants included lawyers, bankers, doctors, a foundation director, a psychoanalyst, a director of family support services for the U.S. Air Force, an insurance executive, and a director of an M.B.A. exchange program; their countries of residence included Switzerland, France, and Romania, as well as the United States. Their intelligence, their practical experience, and the sheer sense of reality they brought to the academic discussions were very moving to me, and made me think better about some of my ways of presenting ideas. They also confirmed my preference for women's collectives as both supporters of women's capabilities and incubators of good thought about women's problems. (I guess it could be the closest I've ever come in my own life to the sense of group solidarity that animates so many of the self-descriptions of Indian women in this book.) I am extremely grateful to Rita Brock, director of the Bunting Institute, for having the idea and for designing a wonderful interchange; to Mim Nelson for encouraging us all to lift weights instead of taking a coffee break; and above all to Sondra Albano, Kay Boulware-Miller, Mary Brandt, Margaret Eagle, Renee Grohl, Silvia Gsell-Fessler, Judith Melin, Claire O'Brien, Patricia Peterson, Ellen Poss, Cherie Taylor, Maria Tedesco, and Avivah Wittenberg-Cox for the friendship and illumination they gave me and, I hope, will in the future.

Above all, I am grateful to the working women in India who took time from their work to speak with an ignorant stranger through interpreters, often welcoming me into their homes and introducing me to their families. Their lives are the reality in this book; I hope and believe that it is possible to write a kind of philosophy that doesn't efface that reality.

For research support I am grateful to the Shure Fund and to the Elsie O. and Philip D. Sang Faculty Fund of the University of Chicago Law School.

This book is dedicated to a woman for whom I had and have deep admiration and love. Sara Nussbaum, my late mother-in-law, was born in Galicia and moved to Vienna at the age of two. She was educated at the University of Vienna, where she received a Ph.D. in German and English literature. A gifted student, she attended Friedrich Waismann's seminar and was present on the day Moritz Schlick was shot. She left Vienna shortly before the Anschluss, with her husband Nathan Nussbaum, a second-generation American who had come to Vienna to study medicine. She worked for the U.S. Censors' Bureau during the war, as a translator of German prisoners' letters, and she taught in the public schools. Although she later abandoned formal career plans to focus on raising her four children, she remained a passionate intellectual and lover of the arts. She often came to hear philosophy lectures, and even sometimes attended the meetings of the American Philosophical Association. She was a warm and extraordinary person, so alive that it is very difficult to conceive of her not being alive. She died on February 3, 1999, at the age of eighty-seven.

INTRODUCTION

Feminism and International Development

I. DEVELOPMENT AND SEX EQUALITY

Women in much of the world lack support for fundamental functions of a human life. They are less well nourished than men, less healthy, more vulnerable to physical violence and sexual abuse. They are much less likely than men to be literate, and still less likely to have preprofessional or technical education. Should they attempt to enter the workplace, they face greater obstacles, including intimidation from family or spouse, sex discrimination in hiring, and sexual harassment in the workplace – all, frequently, without effective legal recourse. Similar obstacles often impede their effective participation in political life. In many nations women are not full equals under the law: they do not have the same property rights as men, the same rights to make a contract, the same rights of association, mobility, and religious liberty.[1] Burdened, often, with the "double day" of taxing employment and full responsibility for housework and child care, they lack opportunities for play and for the cultivation of their imaginative and cognitive faculties. All these factors take their toll on emotional well-being: women have fewer opportunities than men to live free from fear and to enjoy rewarding types of love – especially when, as often happens, they are married without choice in childhood and have no recourse from bad marriages. In all these ways, unequal social and political circumstances give women unequal human capabilities.

---

1 For examples of these inequalities, see Chapter 3, and my "Religion and Women's Human Rights," in Paul Weithman, ed., *Religion and Contemporary Liberalism* (Notre Dame: University of Notre Dame Press, 1997), 93–137, also in Nussbaum, *Sex and Social Justice* (New York: Oxford University Press, 1999).

I

One might sum all this up by saying that all too often women are not treated as ends in their own right, persons with a dignity that deserves respect from laws and institutions. Instead, they are treated as mere instruments of the ends of others – reproducers, caregivers, sexual outlets, agents of a family's general prosperity. Sometimes this instrumental value is strongly positive; sometimes it may actually be negative. A girl child's natal family frequently treats her as dispensable, seeing that she will leave anyhow and will not support parents in their old age. Along the way to her inevitable departure she will involve the family in the considerable expense of a dowry and wedding festivities. What use would it be, then, to care for her health and education in the same way that one would care for a boy's? What wonder, that the birth of a girl is often an occasion for sorrow rather than for rejoicing? As the old Indian proverb puts it, "A daughter born / To husband or death / She's already gone."

Nor is the marital home likely to be a place of end-like respect for such a daughter, although here her instrumental value may become positive. Her in-laws are likely to see her as a mere adjunct of a beloved son, a means to (especially male) grandchildren, an addition to the number of household workers, perhaps as a device to extract money in dowry payments from her parents. Even when she is not abused, she is unlikely to be treated with warmth, nor is her education likely to be fostered. Should her husband prove kind, he can be a buffer between her and the demands of his parents. Should he prove unkind, the woman is likely to have no recourse from abuse in the marital family, and no good exit options. Her natal family will probably refuse to have her back, she probably has no employment-related skills, and the law is not very interested in her predicament. Should the husband die, her situation is likely to become still worse, given the stigma attached to widowhood in many parts of the world. A tool whose purpose is gone: that is what a widow is, and that's rather like being dead.

These are not rare cases of unusual crime, but common realities. According to the *Human Development Report 1997* of the United Nations Development Programme, there is no country that treats its women as well as its men, according to a complex measure that includes life expectancy, wealth, and education.[2] Developing countries,

---

2 *Human Development Report 1997*, United Nations Development Programme (Oxford and New York: Oxford University Press, 1997), 39.

however, present especially urgent problems. Gender inequality is strongly correlated with poverty.[3] When poverty combines with gender inequality, the result is acute failure of central human capabilities. In the developing countries as a whole, there are 60% more women than men among illiterate adults; the female school enrollment rate even at the primary level is 13% lower than that of males; and female wages are only three-fourths of male wages. We do not yet have reliable statistics for rape, domestic violence, and sexual harassment, because in many countries little attention is paid to domestic violence and sexual harassment, rape within marriage is not counted as a crime, and even stranger-rape is so rarely punished that many women are deterred from reporting the crime.[4]

If we turn to the very basic area of health and nutrition, there is pervasive evidence of discrimination against females in many nations of the developing world. Researchers standardly claim that where equal nutrition and health care are present, women live, on average, slightly longer than men: thus, we would expect a sex ratio of something like 102.2 women to 100 men (the actual sex ratio of sub-Saharan Africa).[5]

---

3 The four countries ranking lowest in the gender-adjusted development index (GDI) (Sierra Leone, Niger, Burkina Faso, and Mali) also rank lowest in the Human Poverty Index (HPI), a complex measure (see 126–7) including low life expectancy, deprivation in education, malnutrition, and lack of access to safe water and health services; among the four developing countries ranking highest in the HPI, three (Costa Rica, Singapore, and Trinidad and Tobago) also rank among the highest in the GDI: see *1997 Report*, 39.

4 On India, see the special report on rape in *India Abroad*, July 10, 1998. According to recent statistics, one woman is raped every 54 minutes in India, and rape cases increased 32% between 1990 and 1997. Even if some of this increase is due to more reporting, it is unlikely that all is, because there are many deterrents to reporting. A woman's sexual history and social class is sure to be used against her in court, medical evidence is rarely taken promptly, police typically delay in processing complaints, and therefore convictions are extremely difficult to secure. Penile penetration is still a necessary element of rape in Indian law, and thus cases involving forced oral sex, for example, cannot be prosecuted as rape. Rape cases are also expensive to prosecute, and there is currently no free legal aid for rape victims. In a sample of 105 cases of rape that actually went to court (in a study conducted by Sakshi, a Delhi-based NGO) only 17 resulted in convictions.

5 Sub-Saharan Africa was chosen as the "baseline" because it might be thought inappropriate to compare developed to developing countries. Europe and North America have an even higher ratio of women to men: about 105/100. Sub-Saharan Africa's relatively high female/male ratio, compared to other parts of the developing world, is very likely explained by the central role women play in productive economic activity, which gives women a claim to food in time of scarcity. For a classic study of this issue, see Esther Boserup, *Women's Role in Economic Development* (New York: St. Martin's Press, 1970; second edition Aldershot: Gower Publishing, 1986). For a set of valuable re-

Many countries have a far lower sex ratio: India's, for example, is 92.7 women to 100 men, the lowest sex ratio since the census began early in this century. If we study such ratios and ask the question, "How many more women than are now present in Country C would be there if C had the same sex ratio as sub-Saharan Africa?" we get a figure that economist Amartya Sen has graphically called the number of "missing women." There are many millions of missing women in the world today.[6] Using this rough index, the number of missing women in Southeast Asia is 2.4 million, in Latin America 4.4, in North Africa 2.4, in Iran 1.4, in China 44.0, in Bangladesh 3.7, in India 36.7, in Pakistan 5.2, in West Asia 4.3. If we now consider the ratio of the number of missing women to the number of actual women in a country, we get, for Pakistan 12.9%, India 9.5%, Bangladesh 8.7%, China 8.6%, Iran 8.5%, West Asia 7.8%, North Africa 3.9%, Latin America 2.2%, Southeast Asia 1.2%. In India, not only is the mortality differential especially sharp among children (girls dying in far greater numbers than boys), the higher mortality rate of women compared to men applies to all age groups until the late thirties.[7]

Women, in short, lack essential support for leading lives that are fully human. This lack of support is frequently caused by their being women. Thus, even when they live in a constitutional democracy such as India, where they are equals in theory, they are second-class citizens in reality.

II. THE CAPABILITIES APPROACH: AN OVERVIEW

I shall argue that international political and economic thought should be feminist, attentive (among other things) to the special problems women face because of sex in more or less every nation in the world, problems without an understanding of which general issues of poverty and development cannot be well confronted. An approach to interna-

sponses to Boserup's work, see *Persistent Inequalities*, ed. Irene Tinker (New York: Oxford University Press, 1990).

6 The statistics in this paragraph are taken from Jean Drèze and Amartya Sen, *Hunger and Public Action* (Oxford: Clarendon Press, 1989) and Drèze and Sen, *India: Economic Development and Social Opportunity* (Delhi: Oxford University Press, 1995), Chapter 7. Sen's estimated total number of missing women is one hundred million; the *India* chapter discusses alternative estimates.

7 See Drèze and Sen, *Hunger*, 52.

tional development should be assessed for its ability to recognize these problems and to make recommendations for their solution. I shall propose and defend one such approach, one that seems to me to do better in this area than other prominent alternatives. The approach is philosophical, and I shall try to show why we need philosophical theorizing in order to approach these problems well.[8] It is also based on a universalist account of central human functions, closely allied to a form of political liberalism; one of my primary tasks will be to defend this type of universalism as a valuable basis from which to approach the problems of women in the developing world.

The aim of the project as a whole is to provide the philosophical underpinning for an account of basic constitutional principles that should be respected and implemented by the governments of all nations, as a bare minimum of what respect for human dignity requires. (Issues of implementation are complex, and I shall give these separate discussion in section VII of this chapter.) I shall argue that the best approach to this idea of a basic social minimum is provided by an approach that focuses on *human capabilities*, that is, what people are actually able to do and to be – in a way informed by an intuitive idea of a life that is worthy of the dignity of the human being. I shall identify a list of *central human capabilities*, setting them in the context of a type of *political liberalism* that makes them specifically political goals and presents them in a manner free of any specific metaphysical grounding. In this way, I argue, the capabilities can be the object of an *overlapping consensus* among people who otherwise have very different comprehensive conceptions of the good.[9] And I shall argue that the capabilities in question should be pursued for each and every person, treating each as an end and none as a mere tool of the ends of others: thus I adopt a *principle of each person's capability*, based on a *principle of each person as end*. Women have all too often been treated as the supporters of

8 On this see my "Public Philosophy and International Feminism," *Ethics* 108 (1998), 770–804; "Why Practice Needs Ethical Theory: Particularism, Principle, and Bad Behavior," forthcoming in *The Path of the Law in the Twentieth Century*, ed. S. Burton, Cambridge University Press; and "Still Worthy of Praise: A Response to Richard A. Posner, The Problematics of Moral and Legal Theory," *Harvard Law Review* 111 (1998), 1776–95.

9 The terms "political liberalism," "overlapping consensus," and "comprehensive conception" are used as by John Rawls in *Political Liberalism* (expanded paperback edition, New York: Columbia University Press, 1996), hereinafter PL.

the ends of others, rather than as ends in their own right; thus this principle has particular critical force with regard to women's lives. Finally, my approach uses the idea of a *threshold level of each capability*, beneath which it is held that truly human functioning is not available to citizens; the social goal should be understood in terms of getting citizens above this capability threshold.

The capabilities approach has another related, and weaker, use. It specifies a space within which *comparisons of life quality* (how well people are doing) are most revealingly made among nations. Used in this way, it is a rival to other standard measures, such as GNP per capita and utility. This role for the conception is significant, since we are not likely to make progress toward a good conception of the social minimum if we do not first get the space of comparison right. And we may use the approach in this weaker way, to compare one nation to another, even when we are unwilling to go further and use the approach as the philosophical basis for fundamental constitutional principles establishing a social minimum or threshold. On the other hand, the comparative use of capabilities is ultimately not much use without a determinate normative conception that will tell us what to make of what we find in our comparative study. Most conceptions of quality of life measurement in development economics are implicitly harnessed to a normative theory of the proper social goal (wealth maximization, utility maximization, etc.), and this one is explicitly so harnessed. The primary task of my argument will be to move beyond the merely comparative use of capabilities to the construction of a normative political proposal that is a partial theory of justice. (The reasons for saying that it is not a complete theory of justice will be presented in section IV.)

The capabilities approach is fully universal: the capabilities in question are important for each and every citizen, in each and every nation, and each is to be treated as an end. Women in developing nations are important to the project in two ways: as people who suffer pervasively from acute capability failure, and also as people whose situation provides an interesting test of this and other approaches, showing us the problems they solve or fail to solve. Defects in standard GNP- and utility-based approaches can be well understood by keeping the problems of such women in view; but of course women's problems are urgent in their own right, and it may be hoped that a focus on them will help compensate for earlier neglect of sex equality in development economics and in the international human rights movement.

This project is somewhat unusual in feminist political philosophy because of its focus on developing countries. Such a focus, already common in feminist economic thought and feminist activism, is becoming more common in feminist philosophy, and rightly so. Feminist philosophy, I believe, should increasingly focus on the urgent needs and interests of women in the developing world, whose concrete material and social contexts must be well understood, in dialogue with them, before adequate recommendations for improvement can be made. This international focus will not require feminist political philosophy to turn away from its traditional themes, such as employment discrimination, domestic violence, sexual harassment, and the reform of rape law; these are all as central to women in developing countries as to Western women. But feminist philosophy will have to add new topics to its agenda if it is to approach the developing world in a productive way; among these topics are hunger and nutrition, literacy, land rights, the right to seek employment outside the home, child marriage, and child labor. (Some of these topics are also essential in framing a philosophical approach to the lives of poor women in wealthier nations.) In general, it seems right that problems of poor working women in both developing and developed nations should increasingly hold the center of the scene, and that problems peculiar to middle-class women should give way to these.

Feminist philosophy has frequently been skeptical of universal normative approaches. I shall argue that it is possible to describe a framework for such a feminist practice of philosophy that is strongly universalist, committed to cross-cultural norms of justice, equality, and rights, and at the same time sensitive to local particularity, and to the many ways in which circumstances shape not only options but also beliefs and preferences. I shall argue that a universalist feminism need not be insensitive to difference or imperialistic, and that a particular type of universalism, framed in terms of general human powers and their development, offers us in fact the best framework within which to locate our thoughts about difference.

In the first chapter, I map out and defend an approach to the foundation of basic political principles using the idea of human capability.

I argue that this approach yields a form of universalism that is sensitive to pluralism and cultural difference; in this way it enables us to answer the most powerful objections to cross-cultural universals. I also explain the relationship of my approach to various forms of liberalism and defend a form of political liberalism in connection with the capabilities idea. I then explain the relationship of this approach to the idea of fundamental human rights. And I offer an account of the relationship between political justification and political implementation.

But to display the attractive features of a conception is only one small part of the task of justification. In the second chapter, I take on one further part of that task by arguing that this approach is superior to approaches based on subjective welfarism, the idea that each person's perceived well-being should be the basis for social choice. Welfarist conceptions are ubiquitous and highly influential in economics and therefore in development; so it seems important, both philosophically and practically, to think clearly about the relationship between the capabilities view and welfarism. I shall argue that the problem of preference-deformation makes a welfarist approach unacceptable as the basis for a normative theory of political principles; we need a substantive account of central political goods, of the sort the capabilities approach gives us. Recognizing the phenomenon of adaptive preference-formation does not entail an unacceptable type of paternalism, if this recognition is combined with a version of political liberalism and a focus on capabilities (not actual functions) as political goals. But the welfarist approach, by showing respect for human desire, gets something right: and I shall try to say what that something is, contrasting my capabilities approach with Platonist accounts of the human good.

The third and fourth chapters investigate two specific problem areas that have particular salience for women's lives. There are several such areas that one might fruitfully pursue. Education and property would be obvious choices, as would rape, domestic violence, and sexual harassment.[10] I have chosen religion and the family, both because of their

10 On education, see Drèze and Sen, *India*, Chapter 6; on land rights, see Bina Agarwal, *A Field of One's Own: Gender and Land Rights in South Asia* (Cambridge: Cambridge University Press, 1994); on sexual harassment, see my "The Modesty of Mrs. Bajaj: India's Problematic Route to Sexual Harassment Law," in a volume on sexual harassment ed. Reva Siegel and Catharine MacKinnon, forthcoming from Yale University Press.

complexity (in a way, they include all the others) and because they raise complicated problems of a distinctively philosophical kind. The chapter on religion analyzes conflicts between religion and sex equality, developing a strategy for dealing politically and legally with such conflicts. I argue that any good approach to this problem must balance recognition of religion's importance in the human search for meaning (including women's search) against a critical scrutiny of religion when it threatens valuable areas of human functioning. Here the tradition of U.S. constitutional law provides helpful insights, which can be suitably adapted to the problems of pluralistic democracies in the developing world; most of the materials for my solution are already present in the Indian Constitution. Chapter 4, finally, tackles the difficult question of family love and care, asking how, if at all, it is possible to retain the idea that women have value as givers of love and care while promoting political goals of full equality and family justice. Tackling this problem requires, first, giving an adequate philosophical account of love (or at least the general outlines of one), and then examining the social and political origins of that apparently "natural" entity, the family.

I focus throughout on the case of India, a nation in which women suffer great inequalities despite a promising constitutional tradition. Some writings about women and development pull in thinly described examples from many different cultures, without setting any of them in a deep or rich context. I feel that this is unwise; we cannot really see the meaning of an incident or a law without setting it in its context and history. By focusing on India, I can write on the basis of personal observation and familiarity, as well as study, and I am able to assess scholarly debates in a way that I could not had I tried to cover a wider area. The best way of thinking about the relationship between the political ideal presented here in connection with India and its wider application was suggested by Jawaharlal Nehru, in these famous words:

The service of India means the service of the millions who suffer. It means the ending of poverty and ignorance and disease and inequality of opportunity. The ambition of the greatest man of our generation has been to wipe every tear from every eye. That may be beyond us, but as long as there are tears and suffering, so long our work will not be over . . . Those dreams are for India, but they are also for the world, for all the nations and people are too closely knit together today for any one of them to imagine that it can live apart. Peace has been said to be indivisible; so is freedom, so is prosperity now, and so also is disaster in this One World that can no longer be split into isolated fragments.[11]

Similarly, this ideal political proposal takes its orientation from the example of India, but pertains to all nations.

I am doubly an outsider vis-à-vis the places about which I write, that is, both a foreigner and a middle-class person. But most Indian scholarship about India is also the work of foreigners in at least some sense, that is, people who live middle-class lives that are not remotely like the lives about which they write. (So too is most American scholarship about poverty and welfare reform.) I believe that through curiosity and determination one can surmount these hurdles – especially if one listens to what people say. Maybe at times a foreigner can maintain, too, a helpful type of neutrality amid the cultural, religious, and political debates in which any scholar living in India is bound to be enmeshed. Certainly one is sometimes more warmly received as an unimplicated foreigner than as an upper-class person from the person's own culture. I would not find the warm and trusting reception I found in working-class homes in India, were I to walk one block from my office into the Woodlawn area (a poor African-American neighborhood) that borders the prosperous university community. In a situation of entrenched inequality, being a neighbor can be an epistemological problem.

This is a philosophical project, whose aim is to develop a particular type of normative philosophical theory. I am not an empirical social scientist, nor is this book intended as the record of sustained empirical research. But I do attempt to be responsive to empirical facts and to what I have seen. I believe that philosophical theorizing has practical political value, and that its place cannot be filled by other more empirical types of inquiry. Part of theory's practical value lies in its abstract and systematic character. Feminists who disparage abstraction in a global way are, I believe, very unwise to do so. Without abstraction of some sort, there could be no thought or speech; and the type of abstraction characteristic of the tradition of political philosophy has great value, so long as it is tethered in the right way to a sense of what is relevant in reality (something that has not always been the case).[12]

11 Speech delivered in the Constituent Assembly, New Delhi, August 14, 1947, on the eve of Independence.
12 See my "The Feminist Critique of Liberalism," a Lindley Lecture published in pamphlet form by the University of Kansas Press, and in Nussbaum, *Sex and Social Justice*.

Some feminist philosophy, particularly the type influenced by postmodernist literary theory, has involved a type of abstraction that turns the mind away from reality, and that does not help us see or understand real women's lives better. A focus on real cases and on empirical facts can help us to identify the salient features that a political theory should not efface or ignore. So I have tried to write in a way that is responsive to reality and that helps the reader imagine the relevant reality, however theoretical my ultimate aims. I shall therefore begin my argument, in section IV, by presenting two accounts of particular lives that I have encountered, which should help us to see the salient problems and how they bear on one another. These lives will provide an illustrative focus for many of the concrete discussions in subsequent chapters.[13] In section V I shall set these particular lives against the background of a more general factual account of some of the problems facing women in today's India.

III. THE CAPABILITIES APPROACH: SEN AND NUSSBAUM

Before we can begin the argument, however, the capabilities approach must be introduced from a different perspective. For, as will emerge more fully from the concrete discussions in Chapters 1 and 2, an approach based on functioning and capability was pioneered in development economics by Amartya Sen. My own version of the approach derives from a period of collaboration with Sen at the World Institute for Development Economics Research beginning in 1986, when we recognized that ideas I had been pursuing in the context of Aristotle scholarship had a striking resemblance to ideas that he had for some years been pursuing in economics. It might therefore be assumed that we agree on all the matters to be discussed here, and controversial proposals in the present argument might be attributed to Sen, who has enough

---

13 Different examples will be used in Chapter 3. Vasanti seems little interested in religion; although Jayamma prays regularly, religion has not played a major role in shaping her circumstances. Religious law has played a relatively small role in both lives. Both, moreover, are Hindu, and my aim is to investigate tensions among the religions, as they bear on sex equality. Finally, the religion issue requires a focus on law, and thus a selection of examples from among significant legal cases.

arguments on his hands already. It therefore seems important to try to describe what is and is not common to our respective approaches.

Sen's primary use of the notion of capability is to indicate a space within which comparisons of quality of life (or, as he sometimes says, standard of living) are most fruitfully made. Instead of asking about people's satisfactions, or how much in the way of resources they are able to command, we ask, instead, about what they are actually able to do or to be. Sen has also insisted that it is in the space of capabilities that questions about social equality and inequality are best raised.

I agree wholeheartedly with Sen's claims about the capability space, and with the arguments he has used to support them, many of which will be replicated here. But my goal in this book is to go beyond the merely comparative use of the capability space to articulate an account of how capabilities, together with the idea of a threshold level of capabilities, can provide a basis for central constitutional principles that citizens have a right to demand from their governments. The notion of a threshold is more important in my account than the notion of full capability equality: as I argue, we may reasonably defer questions about what we shall do when all citizens are above the threshold, given that this already imposes a taxing and nowhere-realized standard. Thus my proposal is intended to be compatible with several different accounts of distribution above the threshold; it is consequently a partial, rather than a complete, theory of just distribution. Sen nowhere uses the idea of a threshold. I do not think he has stated whether he would actually favor complete capability equality; to the extent that his proposal is open-ended on this point, he and I may be in substantial agreement.

Another area of strong agreement is in the important role we both give to the political liberties. Sen has explicitly endorsed the Rawlsian priority of liberty. My view holds that all the capabilities are equally fundamental, and does not announce a lexical ordering among them. But insofar as we both argue strenuously that economic needs should not be met by denying liberty, we are in complete agreement.

Finally, we are in agreement in stressing that the capabilities we strive for should be understood to be valuable for each and every person, and that it is the capability of each that we should consider, when we ask how nations are doing. Sen has never announced anything so explicit as my *principle of each person's capability*, but his criticism of organic models of the family, for example, makes it perfectly clear that he supports this emphasis on treating each person as an end.

My approach, however, departs from Sen's in several significant ways. First of all, although Sen and I are in strong agreement about the poverty of cultural relativism and the need for universal norms in the development policy arena, he has never produced explicit arguments against relativism, apart from historical arguments about non-Western cultures that show the descriptive inadequacy of many anti-universalist approaches. It is reasonably clear that he agrees with the way in which I would answer what, in Chapter 1, I call the *argument from culture*, by stressing that cultures are scenes of debate and contestation. But it is less clear whether he would endorse the other replies to relativist arguments that I present in Chapter 1, although he is in sympathy with their general spirit.

Nor has Sen ever attempted to ground the capabilities approach in the Marxian/Aristotelian idea of truly human functioning that plays a central role in my argument. Although he occasionally alludes both to Marx and to Aristotle in articulating the approach, it is unclear to me whether those thinkers played a central role in shaping his conception; insofar as they did, it was probably in an indirect way, through their role in shaping a climate of debate on the left in India. Thus the arguments about which lives are worthy of the dignity of the human being, and about the waste and tragedy involved in the blighting of human powers – and, in addition, all discussions of philosophical justification – should be understood to have no assent from him, though that does not mean that he disagrees with them either.

Most importantly, Sen has never made a list of the central capabilities. He gives lots of examples, and the Human Development Reports organize things in ways that correspond to at least some of the items on my list. But the idea of actually making the list and describing its use in generating political principles is not his, and he should not be taken as endorsing either the project or its specific contents.

Other distinctions introduced in my account – for example, the definitions of the three types of capabilities (basic, internal, combined) – have no parallel in Sen, although in his treatment of examples he sometimes makes similar points. The idea that capability, not functioning, is the appropriate political goal is an idea he sometimes supports through examples, but he has never endorsed it as a general theoretical point.

My own treatment of this question is closely linked to my articulation of the list as a basis for a specifically political conception and a specifically political overlapping consensus. Sen has never yet discussed the contrast between comprehensive and political liberalism, and it is unclear which type of liberalism he would actually favor. On religion his position is complex. At times he inclines toward what, in Chapter 3, I identify as secular humanist feminism; but in writing about the Indian situation he has supported the type of secularism that now prevails, which gives the religions a large political role.

One set of distinctions prominently used by Sen is absent in my own version of the capabilities approach. This is the distinction between well-being and agency, which, together with the distinction between freedom and achievement, structures much of his recent writing about capabilities. I agree with Sen that the concepts introduced by these distinctions are important: but I believe that all the important distinctions can be captured as aspects of the capability/function distinction. When we think of health, for example, we should distinguish between the capability or opportunity to be healthy and actual healthy functioning: a society might make the first available and also give individuals the freedom not to choose the relevant functioning. But I am not sure that any extra clarity is added by using a well-being/agency distinction here: healthy functioning is itself a way of being active, not just a passive state of satisfaction. Although Sen would surely agree with this, I fear that the Utilitarian associations of the idea of "well-being" may cause some readers to suppose that he is imagining a way of enjoying well-being that does not involve active doing and being. I would therefore prefer to dissociate my own terminology more strongly from that of the Utilitarian tradition, and I do not think that any important philosophical issues are blurred by sticking to a simpler set of distinctions (along with the distinctions among levels of capability discussed above).

On the relationship between rights and capabilities we have a modest disagreement, connected to a larger one that does not touch the present project. Sen, who defends a complex non-Utilitarian form of consequentialism, has criticized the view that rights should be understood as supplying side-constraints. I defend a version of that view, putting the central capabilities in the place of rights: central capabilities may not be infringed upon to pursue other types of social advantage.

In substance, however, our views are very close, because I also give an analysis of rights that differs from the one he uses in attacking the claim that rights supply side-constraints. (See Chapter 1, section VI.)

Finally, the narrative method I sometimes employ, with its implicit emphasis on the political importance of the imagination and the emotions, is not something about which Sen has ever written one way or another. My own views on that topic, which I have developed at length elsewhere, should certainly not be attributed to him. To that narrative material I now turn.

IV. TWO WOMEN TRYING TO FLOURISH

Ahmedabad, in Gujarat, is the textile mill city where Mahatma Gandhi organized labor in accordance with his principles of nonviolent resistance. Tourists visit it for its textile museum and its Gandhi ashram. But today it attracts attention, too, as the home of another resistance movement: the Self-Employed Women's Association (SEWA), with more than 50,000 members, which for over twenty years has been helping female workers in the informal sector to improve their living conditions through credit, education, and a labor union. (In India a very large proportion of the labor force works in what is called the "informal sector" – meaning cottage industries, agricultural labor, and various types of self-employment. Among working women, 94% are self-employed.)[14] On one side of the polluted river that bisects the city is the shabby old building where SEWA was first established, now used as offices for staff. On the other side are the education offices and the SEWA bank, newly housed in a marble office building. All the customers and all the employees are women. Women like to say, "This bank is like our mother's place" – because, says SEWA's founder Ela Bhatt, a woman's mother takes her seriously, keeps her secrets, and helps her solve her problems.[15]

14 See Kalima Rose, *Where Women Are Leaders: The SEWA Movement in India* (Delhi: Vistaar, 1992), 17, and personal communication, Ela Bhatt, March 1997. SEWA prefers the term "self-employed" to the term "informal sector," on the ground that it gives dignity and positive status to people who might otherwise be regarded as marginal to economic activity. Rose notes that 55% of the work force in Ahmedabad and 50% in Calcutta and Bombay are self-employed.
15 Bhatt, interview, May 1988, reproduced in Rose, *Where Women Are Leaders*, 172–4.

Vasanti sits on the floor in the meeting room of the old office building.[16] A tiny dark woman in her early thirties, she wears an attractive electric blue sari, and her long hair is wound neatly into a bun on the top of her head. Soft and round, she seems more comfortable sitting than walking. Her teeth are uneven and discolored, but otherwise she looks to be in reasonable health. My colleague Martha Chen tells me later she is a Rajput, that is, of good (Hindu) caste; I've never figured out how one would know that.[17] She has come with her older (and lower-caste)[18] friend Kokila, maker of clay pots and a janitor at the local conference hall, a tall fiery community organizer who helps the police identify cases of domestic violence. Vasanti speaks quietly, looking down often as she speaks, but there is animation in her eyes.

Vasanti's husband was a gambler and an alcoholic. He used the household money to get drunk, and when he ran out of that money he got a vasectomy in order to take the cash incentive payment offered by the local government. So Vasanti has no children to help her. Eventually, as her husband became physically abusive, she could live with him no longer and returned to her own family. Her father, who used to make Singer sewing machine parts, has died, but her brothers run an auto parts business in what used to be his shop. Using a machine that had once been her father's, and living in the shop itself, sleeping on the floor, at first she earned a small income making eyeholes for the hooks on sari tops. Her brothers got her a lawyer to take her husband to court for maintenance – quite an unusual step for someone in her economic class – but the case has dragged on for years with no conclusion in sight. Meanwhile, her brothers also gave her a loan to get the ma-

---

16 Throughout our conversation, Vasanti referred to herself, and was referred to, as Vasantibehn, following Gujarati custom.

17 Indicia would typically include name, style of speech, and, in a limited way, occupation. But, given changing economic opportunities, many of which do not map onto traditional caste occupations, norms of what it's proper to do for upper caste men have shifted considerably (as the occupations of Vasanti's father and brother illustrate). Women are more frequently restricted by caste norms of propriety. Thus Uma Narayan observes (in correspondence) that in her mother's generation upper-caste women did not engage in paid work – or if they did, driven by economic necessity, they tried to conceal it from their relatives. Today this is less an issue.

18 Kokila, a lower-caste Hindu, told us that she used to live in an "integrated" Hindu-Muslim area; she moved away to a purely Hindu area as religious tensions escalated in the city.

chine that rolls the edges of the sari; but she didn't like being dependent on them, since they are married and have children, and may not want to support her much longer. With the help of SEWA, therefore, she got a bank loan of her own to pay back the brothers, and by now she has paid back almost all of the SEWA loan. She now earns 500 rupees a month, a decent living.[19] She has two savings accounts, and is eager to get more involved in the SEWA union. Usually, she says, women lack unity, and rich women take advantage of poor women. In SEWA, by contrast, she has found a sense of community. She clearly finds pleasure in the company of Kokila, a woman of very different social class and temperament.

By now, Vasanti is animated; she is looking us straight in the eye, and her voice is strong and clear.[20] Women in India have a lot of pain, she says. And I, I have had quite a lot of sorrow in my life. But from the pain, our strength is born. Now that we are doing better ourselves, we want to do some good for other women, to feel that we are good human beings.

Jayamma stands outside her hut in the ovenlike heat of a late March day in Trivandrum, in Kerala, at the southern tip of India.[21] The first thing you notice about her is the straightness of her back, and the muscular strength of her movements. Her teeth are falling out, her eyesight seems clouded, and her hair is thin – but she could be a captain of the regiment, ordering her troops into battle. It doesn't surprise me that her history speaks of fierce quarrels with her children and her

19 The amount of maintenance allotted to destitute women under the Criminal Procedure Code (see Chapter 3) was Rs. 180 per month in 1986.
20 The first day of the typical SEWA education program for future union and bank leaders is occupied by getting each woman to look straight at the group leader and say her name. The process is videotaped, and women grow accustomed to looking at themselves. Eventually, though with considerable difficulty, they are all able to overcome norms of modesty and deference and to state their names publicly.
21 Unlike Vasanti, Jayamma has been examined previously in the development economics literature. See the chapter "Jayamma, the Brick Worker," in Leela Gulati, *Profiles in Female Poverty: A Study of Five Poor Working Women in Kerala* (Delhi: Hindustan Publishing Company, 1981), and Leela Gulati and Mitu Gulati, "Female Labour in the Unorganised Sector: The Brick Worker Revisited," *Economic and Political Weekly*, May 3, 1997, 968–71, also scheduled for publication in Martha Chen, ed., *Widows and Social Responsibility* (Delhi: Sage, forthcoming). I am very grateful to Leela Gulati for introducing me to Jayamma and her family and for translating.

neighbors. Her jaw juts out as she chews tobacco. An Ezhava – a lower but not "scheduled" (Hindu) caste[22] – Jayamma loses out in two ways, lacking good social standing but ineligible for the affirmative action programs established by government for the lowest castes. She still lives in a squatters' colony on some government land on the outskirts of Trivandrum. Although I am told that I am seeing the worst poverty in all Trivandrum, given Kerala's generally high living standard the colony seems relatively prosperous compared to poor areas in Bombay and some rural areas. The huts in the settlement are clean and cool, solidly walled, some with mud, some with brick, decorated with photos and children's artwork; some of them command a stunning view of a lake covered with water hyacinth. Many have toilets, provided by a local government program; both water and electricity reach the settlement reliably. Although the settlers were originally squatters, by now they have some property rights in the land. The bus stops right outside, on a well-maintained road; there is a hospital not far away; and there's a cheerful primary school in the settlement itself. Older children all seem to be enrolled in school: clean and proud in their school uniforms, looking healthy and well nourished, they escort visitors around the settlement. (In many regions of India, there simply aren't any schools, and basic utilities are unreliable.)

For approximately forty-five years, until her recent retirement, Jayamma went every day to the brick kiln and spent eight hours a day carrying bricks on her head, 500 to 700 bricks per day. (She never earned more than five rupees a day, and employment depended upon the weather.) Jayamma balanced a plank on her head, stacked twenty bricks at a time on the plank, and then walked rapidly, balancing the bricks by the strength of her neck, to the kiln, where she then had to unload the bricks without twisting her neck, handing them two by two to the man who loads the kiln. Men in the brick industry typically do this sort of heavy labor for a while, and then graduate to the skilled (but less arduous) tasks of brick molding and kiln loading, which they can continue into middle and advanced ages. Those jobs pay up to twice as much, though they are less dangerous and lighter. Women are

---

22 The two largest religious groups in Kerala are Hindus and Christians. Kerala (formerly the princely states of Travancore and Cochin) was once also the home of India's largest Jewish community, but most of those Jews have since emigrated.

never considered for these promotions and are never permitted to learn the skills involved. Like most small businesses in India, the brick kiln is defined as a cottage industry and thus its workers are not protected by any union. All workers are badly paid, but women suffer special disabilities. Nonetheless, they cling to the work because it offers regular employment, unlike construction and agriculture; kilns also typically employ children of workers, so Jayamma could take her children to work with her. She feels she has a bad deal, but she doesn't see any way of changing it.

Thus, in her middle sixties, no longer able to perform the physically taxing job of brick carrying, Jayamma has no employment to fall back on. Her husband never supported the family much anyway, and now he has died; in his old age she lost a lot of work time nursing him. She is unwilling to become a domestic servant, because in her community such work is considered shameful and degrading. Jayamma adds a political explanation: "As a servant, your alliance is with a class that is your enemy." A widow, she is unable to collect a widows' pension from the government: the village office told her that she was ineligible because she has able-bodied sons, although in fact her sons refuse to support her. Males in this region are unreliable contributors to the care and maintenance of aged relatives; only one of Jayamma's sons lives in the region at all. At the same time, during their childhood she invested more in her sons than in her daughters – so her daughters, who are more willing to help her, have very restricted skills and opportunities. There is one exception: one of her granddaughters actually has a nursing diploma, through affirmative action programs in education aimed at the lowest castes (her mother married a Pulaya man). But corruption in the hospital system means that she would have to pay Rs. 2,500 upfront money to have a chance at a nursing job. So this tall, proud, beautiful woman sits at home all day doing housework; she keeps the nursing diploma in a box, and shows it sadly to visitors.

Despite all these reversals (and others), Jayamma is tough, defiant, and healthy. She doesn't seem interested in talking, but she shows her visitors around, and makes sure that they are offered lime juice and water.

Vasanti and Jayamma have very different lives. One is on the poor edges of the lower middle class, and one is at the very bottom of the economic ladder.[23] Vasanti has five times the income that Jayamma had at her employment peak. Jayamma could never hope to have a bank loan, since she has no security (her property rights in the land would need to be established in court, at some cost), and the very idea of two savings accounts is far beyond her. But in many ways their lives reveal similar patterns, patterns extremely common among women in India and in much of the developing world. Both have been raised in a nation in which women are formally the equals of men, with equal political rights and nominally equal social and employment opportunities. (Discrimination on the basis of sex is outlawed by the Indian Constitution itself.) And both suffer to some extent from general problems of poverty that are not caused exclusively by their being women. Both, however, have also suffered from deprivations that do arise from sex discrimination, and sex discrimination is such a pervasive factor in these women's experience of poverty that it would be wrong to say that any aspect of their poverty is fully understandable without taking it into account. Jayamma's entire life as a worker has been defined by the rigid stratification of the sexes in the brick industry, and by the fact that women in the lower classes rarely get opportunities for formal education and higher skill development. (Men don't always get these chances either, but if any child in the family does, it is almost certain to be a male, for several reasons: males in fact have greater economic opportunities; daughters' income typically belongs to their conjugal, not their natal, family; and in some regions and classes it is thought shameful to depend on one's daughters.)[24] Vasanti has been held up by different,

---

23 Not the social ladder: Jayamma was furious that her daughter married a Pulaya man, even though it meant government benefits for the family.

24 Notice that this asymmetry of expectation is built into law itself: the government of Kerala gives widows' pensions to women with able-bodied daughters, but not to those with able-bodied sons – even though in Kerala, where many communities are matrilineal and some of these are also matrilocal, it is more likely than in most of India that daughters will in fact remain close to their natal home. (Sardamoni, a leading historian of Kerala, tells me in conversation that she has concluded that customs of matriliny and matrilocal residence date back to the eleventh century. Among the communities that are not matrilocal, some are duolocal – the men do not reside with their wives – and others are "avunculocal," that is, residing near the matrilineal kin of the husband; see Agarwal, *A Field of One's Own*, 141, 505.) Notice, too, that although these three reasons make unequal education of girls seem rational from the parents' point of view, the practice of unequal education persists even when these factors are less in evidence. Women in Kerala frequently support their mothers and males frequently don't; and yet Jayamma too took the traditional course, educating only her sons. The one case of

more middle-class pressures: early marriage, the restriction of a married woman to a domestic role, her lack of formal education and of training for any useful occupation. Obviously a very intelligent and resourceful woman, she didn't have a chance to make her way into a really middle-class job, since she is illiterate.

Both live in a world in which women are profoundly dependent upon males, and in which males often take their responsibilities lightly. Jayamma's husband usually used up all his income (not large in any case) on tobacco, drink, and meals out for himself, leaving it to Jayamma not only to do all the housework after her backbreaking day, but also to provide the core financial support for children and house. This is a common Kerala pattern, which Jayamma's sons have imitated. Vasanti's husband exhibited a depressingly common pattern: alcoholism and domestic violence – problems pervasive enough (and combined often enough with one another) to have caused the state of Gujarat to pass alcohol prohibition, in response to pressures from women's groups. He didn't do much to support her, and he even deprived her of children who might have supported her by his clever stratagem of getting drunk on vasectomy money (revealing a dark face of a state program that was supposed to make things better for women). In order to leave him, she had to become the dependent of yet other men – though in this instance her brothers proved unusually helpful, both getting her a lawyer and giving her the loan that eventually enabled her to stand on her feet. Although she clearly has a good legal case for maintenance, the inefficiency of the somewhat Dickensian legal system has not served her well. Both women, finally, have been severely limited by their lack of education, a lack that is explained at least in part by their sex.

The problems faced by Jayamma and Vasanti are particular to the social situation of women in particular caste and regional circumstances in India. One cannot understand Jayamma's choices and constraints without understanding, at many different levels of specificity and generality, how she is socially placed: what it means to be an

equal female education in Leela Gulati's study in Trivandrum involved a family with two daughters and no sons – and, in addition, an unusually home-involved and hard-working husband. Their daughters were finishing high school at the time of the study (1981). More recently, government has taken a strong hand, promoting female primary education through a system of free school lunches; by now there is almost universal literacy among adolescents of both sexes.

Ezhava rather than a Pulaya, what it means that she lives in Kerala rather than some other state, what it means that she is in the city rather than a rural area, what it means that she is Hindu in Kerala rather than Christian,[25] why she prays every evening and why she thinks it matters, and, of course, what it means more generally that she was born in India rather than in Europe or the U.S. One cannot understand Vasanti without understanding the double bind of being both upper-caste – with lots of rules limiting what it's proper to do – and very poor, with few opportunities to do nice proper things that bring in a living.[26] One also cannot understand her story without knowing about family planning programs in Gujarat, the progress of the SEWA movement, the background Gandhian tradition of self-sufficiency on which the Gujarati women's movement draws, and many other highly particular things. No doubt all this particularity shapes the inner life of each woman, in ways that it is hard for an outsider to begin to understand.

On the other hand, in this highly concrete set of circumstances, in some ways so unlike the circumstances of poor working women in the U.S., are two recognizable and imaginable women, with problems not altogether and unrecognizably different from problems of many women (and many poor people generally) in many parts of the world. In Jayamma's tenacity and feistiness, Vasanti's desire to serve the community and to show that she is a good human being, the intense desire of both women for independence and economic self-sufficiency, Jayamma's complex pride in her family, Vasanti's affection for her female friends, the desire of both to have some money and property in their own names, in general in their search for competence and mastery and control over the conditions of their lives – we see efforts common to women in many parts of the world. The body that labors is in a sense the same body all over the world, and its needs for food and nutrition and health care are the same – so it is not too surprising that the female manual laborer in Trivandrum is in many ways comparable to a female manual laborer in Alabama or Chicago, that she doesn't seem to have

---

25 For example, the Christian churches in Kerala strongly oppose family planning, and this does have a serious effect on their poorest followers: see the difficult story of Sara the fish vendor, in Gulati, *Profiles*.

26 Thus the advantage of her actual employment is clearly that it can be carried on at home, without going out and dealing with men, and without being in a partly male workplace.

an utterly alien consciousness or an identity unrecognizably strange, strange though the circumstances are in which her efforts and her consciousness take root. Similarly, the body that gets beaten is in a sense the same all over the world, concrete though the circumstances of domestic violence are in each society. Even what is most apparently strange in the circumstances of each is also, at another level, not so unfamiliar. We find it pretty odd that the brick kiln makes women do all the heavy jobs and then pays them less – but many forms of sex discrimination in employment exhibit similar forms of irrationality;[27] we find it odd that Jayamma seems to accept this as the way things are, and yet we know that women suffering from discrimination have not always been able to organize to fight against inequality. Again, the fact that Vasanti did not go to school again seems odd, but the more general idea that women are basically wives and mothers and that men are workers in the outside world is not in the least unfamiliar. The fact that she does not even seem to want to go to school is not so surprising either, or the sign of an alien consciousness, given that she does not see any signs of a better way of life that she could enjoy by becoming educated. (As we shall see, many women in the SEWA organization become literate quickly enough – when they see women serving as bank tellers and union organizers, and using literacy to better their lives.)

Indeed, the biggest obstacle for a Western feminist philosopher in thinking about these lives may the specific details and dynamics of their poverty more than their foreignness: Western feminist philosophy has not typically focused on getting loans, learning to read, and buying a sewing machine, although such a focus is common in feminist politics and in other academic disciplines such as development economics and political science. The very idea that crucial choices would be made (as in Jayamma's household) about who gets to have milk in tea and who only sugar, is a fact that feminist philosophers may find more difficult to comprehend than the the big facts of location and political organi-

---

27 Strictly speaking, we would need to ask more questions before we could conclude that the arrangement is, in an economic sense, irrational: we would need, for example, to know a lot more about other employment opportunities available to men and women. Furthermore, it is possible that even if the arrangement is irrational, all things considered, it was rational at one time – for example, because of the need to compete for male laborers against other trades – and has been maintained because of habit and male power.

zation and religion. (Most American philosophers probably are not aware – I certainly was not – that the amount of sugar that goes into tea costs less than the amount of milk that goes into tea – I would not begin to count pennies to the extent that is common in poor households the world over.)[28] This feminist philosophical project therefore needs to begin by orienting the reader in a general way to the situation of women (especially poor women) in India.

V. INDIA: SEX EQUALITY IN THEORY, NOT IN REALITY

The situation of women in India is an extraordinarily difficult topic to introduce, since there is probably no nation in the world with greater internal diversity and plurality. In what follows I shall be describing some of those differences (of caste, religion, regional background, wealth and class, and still others). But there are some very basic facts that should be borne in mind in what follows.

India celebrated the fiftieth anniversary of its independence from Britain on August 15, 1997. It is the world's largest democracy, with a population of 846.3 million. It is a constitutional parliamentary democracy, with a written account of Fundamental Rights that includes the abolition of untouchability and an elaborate set of equality and nondiscrimination provisions. Its legal system is in some respects similar to (and modeled on) that of the U.S., combining a basically common-law tradition with the constraints of a written constitution. Its Supreme Court, like ours, is the ultimate interpreter of the Fundamental Rights, and frequently uses U.S. constitutional jurisprudence (and legal writings) as sources of precedent. (For example, most of the privacy jurisprudence that is by now so controversial in the U.S. has been incorporated into Indian constitutional law, through a very similar understanding of substantive due process.)

India's Constitution is a very woman-friendly document. The right of nondiscrimination on the basis of sex is guaranteed in the list of justiciable Fundamental Rights, as is the right to the equal protection

28 In that sense, Western women are, in Indian terms, more like men: Gulati's research on poor women in Kerala has shown that these women are much more accurate when estimating the cost of a meal they have eaten than men are.

of the laws – which, as in the U.S., has been interpreted to be incompatible with systematic gender-based hierarchy. Article 21, which states that no citizen shall be deprived of "life or liberty" without due process of law, has been interpreted as entailing the full range of privacy-right judgments involved in U.S. cases such as *Griswold v. Connecticut* and *Roe v. Wade*, and this privacy right has been used to call into question the Victorian law mandating "restitution of conjugal rights" when a wife has left the conjugal home.[29] Especially interesting is the fact that the framers explicitly state that nondiscrimination is compatible with systematic programs of affirmative action aimed at bettering the lot of deprived groups: thus the principle of affirmative action, for both gender and caste, is written into the Constitution itself. India has never understood equality in the bare formal way that has sometimes prevailed in American law: there has been a shared understanding that equality has material and institutional prerequisites, and that it is best understood to require the elimination of systematic hierarchies of all kinds. (Article 17 abolishes untouchability: "its practice in any form is forbidden.")[30]

India has a uniform code of criminal law, in most respects a relic of the Victorian colonial period. Some aspects of this Victorian code have recently been used by feminists to make progress on women's issues. For example, a Victorian law regarding modesty has been used to win a (problematic) victory in a case of sexual harassment.[31] But the code's Victorian understanding of women (as either modest or depraved) is ultimately a barrier to full sex equality. Indian feminists have made some progress in the area of rape law, where consent under threat of violence now no longer counts as consent. In a creative and innovative reform that goes beyond U.S. accomplishments, rape in police custody has been sharply deterred by shifting the burden of proof in such cases to the defendant. But some of the most important accomplishments of American rape reform (for example, not allowing questioning about the woman's prior sexual experience) remain to be achieved in India.

---

29 See my *Sex and Social Justice*, Introduction, for a discussion of this issue; a lower court declared the remedy of restitution unconstitutional, citing the right to privacy as well as equal protection; but the Supreme Court overruled the judgment, and the remedy (in the Hindu legal system) was retained.
30 For more discussion of constitutional issues, see Chapter 3.
31 See my "The Modesty of Mrs. Bajaj."

There is one tremendous structural difference between India and the U.S. where their legal systems are concerned. India has no uniform code of civil law (even within each region). With the exception of commercial law, which was uniformly codified on a nationwide basis by the British and has remained so, civil law remains the province of the various religious systems of law, Hindu, Muslim, Parsi, and Christian.[32] There are some individual secular laws of property, marriage, and divorce, but they do not form a system, and, for reasons to be discussed in Chapter 3, it is not so easy for individuals to avail themselves of them, once they are classified in one of the religious systems. Cases may be appealed from the religious systems to the secular courts, but the lines of authority are extremely unclear, and much difficulty thus ensues.

To turn from law to economics, India is on the whole an extremely poor nation, ranking number 138 out of the 175 nations of the world on the Human Development Index of the 1997 *Human Development Report*. As I have mentioned, this measure includes three components: longevity (measured by life expectancy at birth), knowledge (measured by adult literacy and mean years of schooling), and income (using the Atkinson formulation for the utility of income, which assumes diminishing returns as income rises).[33] The average life expectancy at birth is 61.3[34] (as opposed to nearly 80 in the U.S., Canada, Japan, and most of Europe), and infant mortality is high, at 74 per 1,000 live births (although this represents a great decline from 165 per 1,000 in 1960). Women do even worse than men in basic nutrition and health. The sex ratio has not even reached 1/1 at any time since measurements began in the early twentieth century. From a high of 97 women to 100 men in 1901, the ratio dropped steadily, reaching a low of around 93/100 in 1971; after a slight rise, it declined again even further, reaching 92.7/100 in 1991.[35] Experts in health and nutrition generally attribute this uneven ratio to differential nutrition of boys

---

32 See Chapter 3 for discussion of the development of these systems of personal law. Sikhs are defined as Hindus for legal purposes, although many resent this. Members of religions such as Judaism that have no separate legal system use the secular laws.
33 The aggregation involves a complex weighting process described in the 1991 report.
34 Data are from 1994.
35 For these and other statistics, see J. Drèze and A. Sen, *India: Economic Development and Social Opportunity*.

and girls and to unequal health care, rather than primarily to active infanticide, but there is strong evidence of infanticide in some areas.[36] This hypothesis is confirmed by the presence of considerable regional differences. Kerala, for example, has more women than men; other regions, for example Uttar Pradesh, Bihar, and Rajasthan, do far worse. Bihar as a whole has a sex ratio of 90/100, and in one rural area where a reliable head count has been performed by a careful NGO, the astonishing figure of 75/100 was the result.[37] There is also increasing evidence of sex-selective abortion: a recent study by the Indian Association of Women's Studies estimates that 10,000 female fetuses are aborted every year.[38] Life chances in India generally are far from equal to those in the developed world, but women clearly face unequal obstacles.

In education, the male-female gap is even more striking: in 1991, adult literacy rates for women were as low as 39%, as against 64% for men. (In China, the figures are 68% for women and 87% for men.)[39] Such statistics are hard to interpret, since local governments tend to be boastful, and since it is hard to establish a clear measure of literacy: and yet what is unambiguously clear is that, despite the fact that education is a state responsibility, India has done extremely badly in basic education across the board, and even worse in basic education for women – far worse, clearly, than China, which began with comparable problems. Nor does this seem to be a necessary or unbreakable pattern, since some otherwise poor regions have done extremely well. Kerala, Jayamma's state, has an adult literacy rate of 90% and near-universal literacy among adolescent boys and girls. This remarkable record is the outcome of more than a hundred years of concerted public action,[40]

36 Personal communication, Viji Srinivasan of Adithi, who tells me of the evidence of infanticide uncovered by members of her organization in Northern Bihar, where the sex ratio is as low as 75/100.
37 Personal communication, Viji Srinivasan of Adithi. The region was the Sitamarhi district near the Nepalese border, where Adithi has found widespread evidence of female infanticide.
38 *India Abroad*, July 10, 1998, p. 31.
39 These figures are from Drèze and Sen, *India*. The HDR for 1997 gives, as 1994 data, the figures 36.1 for females and 64.5 for males in India, and 70.9 (females) and 89.6 (males) in China.
40 V. K. Ramachandran, "Kerala's Development Achievements," in J. Drèze and A. Sen, *Indian Development: Selected Regional Perspectives* (Oxford and Delhi: Oxford University Press, 1996).

involving both the state and the general public, and building on a long (partly Jesuit-inspired) tradition of education that goes back to the eighteenth century. But Kerala is very unusual. Although all Indian states have laws making primary education compulsory, these laws have little relation to reality. Many regions utterly lack schools of any kind, just as they frequently lack reliable electricity, medical services, water, and decent roads; many local functionaries are corrupt, and so teachers in many regions accept pay but never even show up in the region where they are supposed to be teaching. In some rural areas, the female literacy rate is as low as 5%.[41] The national government, though well-intentioned, has done little to fill these gaps, although some adult education programs have been established in some of the poorer states, and many nongovernmental organizations run both adult education programs and after-work programs for working girls.[42] Recently a constitutional amendment has been introduced that would make the right to education a justiciable fundamental right.[43] It may be hoped that the passage of this amendment will goad government into acting more aggressively on its good intentions.

Child labor compounds the problem. Large numbers of poor families, especially rural families, depend on the work performed by their children. Children often begin working as early as age five or six, herding animals, and a large proportion are at work during the day by the age of twelve. Although this situation affects both male and female children, females suffer disproportionately, since their housework is frequently thought crucial to sustaining a household where the mother, like Jayamma, performs long days of manual labor. In general, if only one child in a family can be sent to school, it is far more likely that a poor family will choose a boy. Despite pressures against child labor from foreign entities such as the World Bank, from domestic political action, and from national and international agencies, the national government has been reluctant to intervene actively, because so many poor

41 Personal communication, Sarda Jain, Jaipur, Rajasthan.
42 See the detailed report in Archana Mehendale, "Compulsory Primary Education in India: The Legal Framework," *From the Lawyers Collective* 13 (April 1998), 4–12. I am grateful to Viji Srinivasan, Sarda Jain, and Ginny Srivastava for giving me valuable information about nongovernmental education programs in Bihar and Rajasthan.
43 Amendment 83, to be inserted in the Fundamental Rights section of the Constitution as Article 21a. See the full text of the amendment in *From the Lawyers Collective* 13 (April 1998), 10.

families depend on it for their very survival. Many nongovernmental organizations have been reluctant to take an unequivocal stand against child labor under present conditions; they prefer to provide supplementary after-hours schooling for working children, to help working children acquire some small property and savings, and to teach them how to work for social change. One group I visited in rural Bihar, for example, provided basic education for girls who spend their days herding goats, helped the group save to buy their own goats, and showed them how women in other regions had been able to resist the dowry system that is such a large part of what constructs the unequal worth of female life. In the present situation, all this is much more helpful than getting the truant officer (if one existed) to force the girls to stop work and go to school.

Any approach to women's situation in India must begin from such facts, understanding that it is not simply a matter of waving a wand and saying even "universal compulsory primary education." Far less is it realistic at this point, in most regions, to hold out more advanced goals, such as secondary education for both boys and girls. Any attempt to improve women's quality of life faces harsh economic realities. Nonetheless, it is also striking how certain regions, above all Kerala, have been able to make great strides despite these realities. One impressively successful program has been the school lunch program, which makes sending children to school economically more advantageous to many families than using them as child labor.

Women face many other obstacles to fully equal citizenship. Child marriage, although illegal, is a very common reality, especially in some regions where it is traditional.[44] Laws against it are not enforced, and it pervasively shapes the trajectory of a girl's life. In Rajasthan, for example, girls I visited with the organization Vishaka were already married by the age of eight or nine; thus, although they had not yet moved into their husband's home, they saw that as their inevitable future, and this awareness of themselves as small wives shaped their

---

44 Child marriage is common in parts of Rajasthan, Madhya Pradesh, and Uttar Pradesh. For a good popular treatment of this issue, see John F. Burns, "Though Illegal, Child Marriage Is Popular in Part of India," *New York Times*, May 1998. Burns studied a group of child marriages in Rajasthan, focusing on a ceremony in which the bride was four and the groom twelve. Under law, eighteen is the minimum age for women and twenty-one for men.

attitudes toward education, dress, and especially play – they were un-willing to race around and enjoy childhood, in the manner of boy children. (The protective attitude of their families toward their purity exacerbates this situation: they are rarely permitted to play outside.)

Domestic violence is so pervasive that three states have adopted al-cohol prohibition laws in response to women's lobbying; and yet, as Vasanti and Kokila's story shows, police do not aggressively investigate this crime, nor is rape within marriage even illegal.[45] Virtually no women's shelters exist anywhere in India. As I have mentioned, rape is badly dealt with under the current legal system, and the number of rapes appears to be on the rise. It is easy to find cases where acquittal was secured on the ground that the woman was of low caste, or "im-modest," even when there is ample evidence of forcible rape in the particular instance.[46]

Rape is also used as a weapon against women crusading for political change. In 1993 Bhanwari Devi, a member of Rajasthan state's Sathin movement for women's welfare, was campaigning against child mar-riage when she was gang-raped by men from a community that sup-ports this practice. Because the men were influential community lead-ers, police refused to register the case until it was too late to perform the necessary medical examination; a lower court in Jaipur acquitted all the accused. Although Bhanwari appealed this judgment and the Rajasthan High Court agreed in 1996 to hear her appeal, arguments in the case have not yet been heard.

India has also seen an apparent increase in the sexual abuse of chil-dren: statistics suggest a 23.4 percent rise in the number of such cases between 1992 and 1995, but it is believed that most cases still go un-reported, particularly when they occur within families.[47] Some notori-ous child-abuse cases involve boys, but estimates suggest that two girl children are raped every day.[48]

45 See Sumeet Malik, "Marital Rape," *From the Lawyers Collective* 13 (January 1998), 13–15.
46 For a rundown of recent cases, see Hutokshi Rustomfram and Sanjoy Ghose, "Rape: When Victim Is Seen as Villain," *India Abroad*, July 10, 1998; also "Torment over Terror: The Vithura Rape Case," *From the Lawyers Collective* 13 (January 1998), 4–12.
47 See "Growing Child Abuse a Worrying Social Phenomenon," *India Abroad*, July 10, 1998, p. 32.
48 Statistics from the Indian Association of Women's Studies, meeting in Pune, July 1998.

VI. SAMENESS AND DIFFERENCE

We should do as much as we can to master these and many other facts that construct the circumstances within which women like Vasanti and Jayamma attempt to flourish. These circumstances affect the inner lives of people, not just their external options: what they hope for, what they love, what they fear, as well as what they are able to do. Neither Vasanti nor Jayamma even thinks about getting a college degree – that would be totally alien to their sense of what is possible for them, and there would be no point in even entertaining the thought, however strong-willed, able, and determined they are. By contrast, Meeghan D., a cashier at the Hyde Park Co-op who sometimes rings up my groceries, is finishing her B.A. at Roosevelt College while working full time, and has already been accepted for graduate study in social science at Howard University. She doesn't know how easy it will be to get a job to support herself in Washington, but she says, "It doesn't matter. I'll make it somehow." This both is and is not similar to the determination and strength of both Vasanti and Jayamma. We should not underrate the extent to which such differences in options construct differences in thought; neither, however, should we overrate these differences, thinking of them as creating an Indian "essence" that is utterly incomprehensible to other imaginations. Certain basic aspirations to human flourishing are recognizable across differences of class and context, however crucial it remains to understand how context shapes both choice and aspiration.

There are obtuse ways of thinking across cultural boundaries. Some of these ways were characteristic of colonialism all over the world, which typically assumed that the ways of the colonial power were progressive and enlightened, the ways of the colonized people primitive. Such mistaken judgments can still be found today, even among feminists, who sometimes characterize developing cultures as uniformly reactionary and their own as progressive, neglecting the history of sexism in the West and of progressive traditions in the "East." Such blindness to complexity has made many sensitive thinkers skeptical about all forms of universalism; but of course universalism need not have these defects, and universal values may even be necessary for an adequate critique of colonialism itself.

Other forms of obtuse universalizing can be found in the current global economy, where it is sometimes assumed that people are all simply rational agents in the global market, seeking to maximize utility whatever their traditions or context. It is because such approaches seem obtuse – neglecting tradition and context and their role in constructing desire and preference, neglecting the many different conceptions of the good that citizens of different nations have and their urgent need to be able to live in accordance with these conceptions – that many sensitive thinkers feel all universalizing approaches are bound to be obtuse, and mere accomplices of a baneful globalizing process. Such thinkers see before them the prospect of a world in which all interesting differences, all the rich texture of value, have been flattened out, and we all go to McDonald's together. But the fact that some universal approaches are obtuse does not indict them all. Pluralism and respect for difference are themselves universal values that are not everywhere observed; they require a normative articulation and defense, and that is one of the things I hope to provide in this project. More generally, in a time of rapid globalization, when non-moral interests are bringing us together across national boundaries, we have an especially urgent need to reflect about the moral norms that can also, and more appropriately, unite us, providing constraints on the utility-enhancing choices nations may make. If utility is inadequate as a source of basic political principles in a pluralistic nation – as I believe it clearly is – this hardly means that there are no cross-cultural sources of such basic principles, or that they cannot command a broad consensus among the nations. Seeking such norms is an urgent task; if we do not seek them, we will be governed, without the input of our own critical reflection, by interests and processes that very likely could not withstand the scrutiny of ethical argument.

Critical moral principles are especially urgent when we consider women's situation, as particularly vulnerable people in a time of rapid economic change. If we consider each person as worthy of regard, as an end and not just a means, we cannot in any simple way praise Gujarat's rapid economic growth, which has left many powerless people behind and caused many self-employed women to lose their livelihoods. (The traditional lace-making industry is under threat from factory-made lace, and there are many political controversies over how to resolve this problem.) Economic growth, furthermore, does not by itself improve the situation with regard to literacy and health care:[49] so there are issues affecting all citizens that are left in a state of relative neglect when growth becomes the sole target. On the other hand, we should also not demonize the pursuit of economic growth, which does play a role in the well-being of citizens. Kerala, with its union-inspired wage controls, has driven many employers out of the region and caused unnecessarily high unemployment; these failures are not necessary correlates of its positive achievements in health and education, and they have made people's lives worse.

In short, we need to ask what politics should be pursuing for each and every citizen, before we can think well about economic change. We need to ask what constraints there ought to be on economic growth, what the economy is supposed to be doing for people, and what all citizens are entitled to by virtue of being human. That citizens such as Vasanti and Jayamma should be able to live with a full menu of opportunities and liberties, and thus be able to have lives that are worthy of the dignity of human beings: this political goal should constrain all economic choices. Justice takes priority in social reflection; contrary to what some economists think, it is not simply what you mention "when you have nothing else to say."[50] Considerations of justice for women have been disproportionately silenced in many debates about international development; it is only fitting, then, that they should be a central focus of a project aimed at constructing basic political principles for all.

49 This is a central thesis of Drèze and Sen, *India*.
50 Law student, University of Chicago Law School, quoting an unnamed faculty member's instruction to students.

I

IN DEFENSE OF
UNIVERSAL VALUES

I found myself beautiful as a free human mind.

> Mrinal, in Rabindranath Tagore's "Letter from a Wife"[1]

It is obvious that the *human* eye gratifies itself in a way different from the crude, non-human eye; the human *ear* different from the crude ear, etc. . . . The *sense* caught up in crude practical need has only a *restricted* sense. For the starving man, it is not the human form of food that exists, but only its abstract being as food; it could just as well be there in its crudest form, and it would be impossible to say wherein this feeding activity differs from that of *animals*.

> Marx, *Economic and Philosophical Manuscripts of 1844*

I. CHALLENGES TO CROSS-CULTURAL NORMS

An international feminism that is going to have any bite quickly gets involved in making normative recommendations that cross boundaries of culture, nation, religion, race, and class. It will therefore need to find descriptive and normative concepts adequate to that task.[2] I shall argue

---

1 Published in Bengali in 1914; translated by Kalpana Bardhan in Bardhan, ed., *Of Women, Outcastes, Peasants, and Rebels: A Selection of Bengali Short Stories* (Berkeley: University of California Press, 1990), 96–109.

2 For earlier articulations of my views on capabilities see "Nature, Function, and Capability: Aristotle on Political Distribution," *Oxford Studies in Ancient Philosophy*, Supplementary Volume I: 1988, 145–84, hereinafter NFC; "Aristotelian Social Democracy," in *Liberalism and the Good*, ed. R. B. Douglass et al. (New York: Routledge, 1990), 203–52, hereinafter ASD; "Non-Relative Virtues: An Aristotelian Approach," in *The Quality of Life*, ed. M. Nussbaum and A. Sen (Oxford: Clarendon Press, 1993), hereinafter NRV, volume hereinafter QL; "Aristotle on Human Nature and the Foundations of Ethics," in *World, Mind and Ethics: Essays on the Ethical Philosophy of Bernard Williams*, ed. J. E. J. Altham and Ross Harrison (Cambridge: Cambridge Uni-

that certain universal norms of human capability should be central for political purposes in thinking about basic political principles that can provide the underpinning for a set of constitutional guarantees in all nations. I shall also argue that these norms are legitimately used in making comparisons across nations, asking how well they are doing relative to one another in promoting human quality of life. My project, then, commits itself from the start to making cross-cultural comparisons and to developing a defensible set of cross-cultural categories. This enterprise is fraught with peril, both intellectual and political. Where do these categories come from, it will be asked. And how can they be justified as appropriate ones for lives in which those categories themselves are not explicitly recognized? The suspicion uneasily grows that the theorist is imposing something on people who surely have their own ideas of what is right and proper. And this suspicion grates all the more unpleasantly when we remind ourselves that theorists often come from nations that have been oppressors, or from classes in poorer nations that are themselves relatively privileged. Isn't all this philosophizing, then, simply one more exercise in colonial or class domination?

Now of course no normative political theory uses terms that are straightforwardly those of ordinary daily life. If it did, it probably could not perform its special task as theory, which involves the systematization and critical scrutiny of thoughts and perceptions that in daily life are frequently jumbled and unexamined. For this task theory needs overarching analytical concepts that may not be familiar in daily conversation, although the theorist should be able to show that they correspond to reality and help us scrutinize it. Germans of the eighteenth century did not walk around talking about "the kingdom of ends," nor did Greeks of the fourth century B.C. speak readily of "a disposition lying in a mean." Some thinkers hold that all philosophical theorizing

versity Press, 1995), 86–131, hereinafter HN; "Human Functioning and Social Justice: In Defense of Aristotelian Essentialism," *Political Theory* 20 (1992), 202–46, hereinafter HF; "Human Capabilities, Female Human Beings," in *Women, Culture, and Development*, ed. M. Nussbaum and J. Glover (Oxford: Clarendon Press, 1995), 61–104, paper hereinafter HC, volume hereinafter WCD; "The Good as Discipline, the Good as Freedom," in *Ethics of Consumption: The Good Life, Justice, and Global Stewardship*, ed. David A. Crocker and Toby Linden (Lanham, MD: Rowman and Littlefield, 1997), 312–411, hereinafter GDGF; "Women and Cultural Universals," Chapter 1 in Nussbaum, *Sex and Social Justice* (New York: Oxford University Press, 1999), 29–54, hereinafter WC; and "Capabilities and Human Rights," *Fordham Law Review* 66 (1997), 273–300, hereinafter CHR.

in ethics is suspect just on that account, that we would all be better off without these departures from the language of the everyday.[3] Though I cannot argue the point fully here, I am convinced that this wholesale assault on theory is deeply mistaken, and that the systematic arguments of theory have an important practical function to play in sorting out our confused thoughts, criticizing unjust social realities, and preventing the sort of self-deceptive rationalizing that frequently makes us collaborators with injustice. It's perfectly obvious, too, that theory has great practical value for ordinary nonphilosophical people, giving them a framework in which to view what is happening to them and a set of concepts with which to criticize abuses that otherwise might have lurked nameless in the background of life. Jayamma's use of the Marxian language of class struggle – whether one endorses it or not – is just one obvious example of this point, and Kerala would hardly be governed, as it is, by a (democratic) Communist government unless those concepts were seen by lots of people as doing something valuable for them in their daily lives. Whatever one may say against Marxism in the developing world, it is hard to denounce it for practical irrelevance.

But even if one defends theory as valuable for practice, it may still be problematic to use concepts that originate in one culture to describe and assess realities in another – and all the more problematic if the culture described has been colonized and oppressed by the describer's culture. Such a history does not, of course, imply that the particular describer has colluded with colonization and oppression; she may be a determined critic of colonialism, just as an indigenous woman may be a supporter of it.[4] Despite this fact, however, any attempt by interna-

---

3 Some aspects of this view are suggested by Bernard Williams in his books *Making Sense of Humanity, Ethics and the Limits of Philosophy,* etc.; see my discussion in *Ethics* 107 (1997), 526–29, and in "Why Practice Needs Ethical Theory: Particularism, Principle, and Bad Behavior," forthcoming in *The Path of the Law in the Twentieth Century,* ed. S. Burton (Cambridge: Cambridge University Press, 1999). But Williams makes a distinction between moral theory and political/legal theory in more recent writings, suggesting that the latter may be valuable even when the former is not; in this he differs from more extreme antitheorists, such as Annette Baier in philosophy and Richard Posner in law. See "Why Practice" on Baier, and, on Posner, "Still Worthy of Praise: Comments on Richard Posner's 'The Problematics of Legal and Moral Theory,' " *Harvard Law Review* 111 (1998), 1776–95.
4 For an account of Western women who supported Indian nationalism, see Kumari Jayawardena, *The White Woman's Other Burden: Western Women and South Asia during*

tional feminists today to use a universal language of justice, human rights, or human functioning to assess lives like those of Vasanti and Jayamma is bound to encounter charges of Westernizing and colonizing – even when the universal categories are introduced by feminists who live and work within the nation in question. For, it is commonly said, such women are alienated from their culture, and are faddishly aping a Western political agenda. The minute they become critics, it is said, they cease to belong to their own culture and become puppets of the Western elite.[5]

Interestingly, such charges were less frequently made against Marxism, which was usually understood to have powerful indigenous roots in people's experience of economic exploitation, although the theory itself was obviously created within elite Western culture, using its cultural resources. Sometimes accusations of "Westernizing" are made today against those who struggle for democracy and political liberties in totalitarian societies – but we usually know to greet such accusers with skepticism, asking whose interests are served by branding those concepts as alien Western intrusions into a culture's traditions. For example, when the autocratic Singaporean leader Lee Kuan Yew proclaimed that the concept of freedom is alien to Asian culture, he did find some support, but he also encountered vigorous criticism.[6] But when feminists appeal to notions of equality and liberty – even when those notions are actually included in the constitutions of the nations in which they live, as they are, for example, in the Indian Constitution – they are

British Rule (New York and London: Routledge, 1995); she shows that the Western women shared many of the viewpoints taken by Indian women, and that in both cases there was a multiplicity of perspectives. On the role of David Hare and Drinkwater Bethune in the Bengal Renaissance, see "Introduction" in Kalpana Bardhan, *Of Women, Outcastes*, 43. Hare, who came to Calcutta in 1800 as a watch trader, set up schools for boys beginning in 1816, and Hindu College in 1817, which became the renowned Presidency College in 1855. When he died of cholera, five thousand Indians followed his hearse. Susobhan Sarkar writes, "His statue on the lawn of the Presidency College is surely the one monument to a foreigner in the city which even the most fanatic of nationalists would not dream of removing," in A. Gupta, ed., *Studies in the Bengal Renaissance* (Jadavpur, Calcutta: The National Council of Education, 1958), 28.

5 See the excellent discussion of these attacks in the essay "Contesting Cultures" in Uma Narayan, *Dislocating Cultures: Identities, Traditions, and Third World Feminism* (New York: Routledge, 1997).
6 See, for example, Amartya Sen, "Human Right and Asian Values," *The New Republic*, July 14/21, 1997, pp. 33–41.

frequently accused of Westernizing and of insufficient respect for their own cultures, as if there had been no human suffering, no reasons for discontent, and no criticism before aliens invaded the peaceful landscape. We should ask whose interests are served by this nostalgic image of a happy harmonious culture, and whose resistance and misery are being effaced. Describing her mother's difficult life, Indian feminist philosopher Uma Narayan writes, "One thing I want to say to all who would dismiss my feminist criticisms of my culture, using my 'Westernization' as a lash, is that my mother's pain too has rustled among the pages of all those books I have read that partly constitute my 'Westernization,' and has crept into all the suitcases I have ever packed for my several exiles." This same pain is evident in the united voice of protest that has emerged from international women's meetings such as those in Vienna and Beijing, where a remarkable degree of agreement has been found across cultures concerning fundamental rights for women.

In one way, then, the charge of "Westernizing" looks like a shady political stratagem, aimed at discrediting forces that are pressing for change. Surely opponents who claim that women were all happy in India before Western ideas came along to disrupt them hardly deserve the time of day. They are ignoring tremendous chunks of reality, including indigenous movements for women's education, for the end of *purdah*, for women's political participation, that gained strength straight through the nineteenth and early twentieth centuries in both Hindu and Muslim traditions, in some ways running ahead of British and U.S. feminist movements.[7] Similarly out of touch with reality is any opponent who denies, in the 1990s, that the ideas of political liberty, sex equality, and nondiscrimination are Indian ideas – for such a per-

7 For two good overviews, see Barbara Metcalf, "Reading and Writing about Muslim Women in British India," and Faisal Fatehali Devji, "Gender and the Politics of Space: The Movement for Women's Reform, 1857–1900," both in Zoya Hasan, ed., *Forging Identities: Gender, Communities and the State in India* (Delhi: Kali for Women, and Boulder, Co: Westview Press, 1994), 1–21 and 22–37; also Imtiaz Ahmad, ed., *Modernization and Social Change among Muslims in India* (Delhi: Manohar, 1983). For the special situation of Bengal, which developed progressive educational ideas somewhat earlier than other regions, under the influence of the reforms of Rammohun Roy and the Brahmo movement, see Bardhan, "Introduction," 4–11 and 42; and Susobhan Sarkar, *On the Bengal Renaissance* (Calcutta: Papyrus, 1979). In both East and West Bengal, schools for girls were well established by 1850, and Bethune College, which opened in 1849, in 1888 became the first college in India to teach women through the M.A. level.

son is simply saying that India should not have the Constitution it does have, one that was adopted, ultimately, by overwhelming consensus despite the sharp political divisions that existed and continue to exist. It is perfectly clear, fifty years later, that no proposal to repeal any of the enumerated Fundamental Rights would find any serious political support. (Indeed, movement is in the opposite direction, with a broadly supported proposal to add to the list of justiciable Fundamental Rights the right to free and compulsory primary education for all children from ages six to fourteen.)[8] So the opponent seems to be saying that even though the Founders took women's equality and other basic liberties seriously enough to fight to get them into the Constitution, even though their freedom struggle prominently used the language of "inalienable rights,"[9] these ideas were just alien colonial ideas. What an implausible and condescending story to tell about Nehru and his fellow freedom fighters – all nothing but dupes of colonial powers, even when they thought that had risked their lives for independence and were writing a constitution for an independent India! This objection, then, shows such ignorance of Indian history and Indian law that it should not be taken seriously; only ill-informed and guilt-ridden Westerners are likely even to entertain it. How absurd, too, to take credit for sex equality as an American idea when America has not been able to pass an equal rights amendment, something that India did in 1951, and when the Indian goal of equality of opportunity, unlike its American counterpart, has been consistently understood to be incompatible with systematic social hierarchies of all kinds.[10]

On the other hand, when we make a concrete proposal for a universal framework to assess women's quality of life, we will face a somewhat more respectable form of this objection that does deserve to be seriously answered. For it will be suggested that the particular categories we choose are likely to reflect our own immersion in a particular theoretical tradition and may be, in some respects, quite the wrong

---

8 See Introduction, section IV.
9 See Jawaharlal Nehru, *An Autobiography* (Delhi: Oxford University Press, 1936, centenary edition 1989), Appendix A, "Pledge Taken on Independence Day, January 26, 1930": "We believe that it is the inalienable right of the Indian people, as of any other people, to have freedom and to enjoy the fruits of their toil and have the necessities of life, so that they may have full opportunities of growth" (612).
10 See Introduction, section IV.

ones for the assessment of Indian lives. We need to ask, then, whether it is appropriate to use a universal framework at all, rather than a plurality of different though related frameworks. And we also need to ask whether the framework we propose, if a single universal one, is sufficiently flexible to enable us to do justice to the human variety we find.

This challenge is serious because international development projects have often gone wrong through insufficient attunement to cultural variety and particularity. When, for example, development workers proceed on the (typically Western) assumption that nuclear families are the primary units of personal solidarity and that women relate to other women primarily as members of heterosexual couples, existing traditions of female solidarity and group membership, often highly productive for economic development, are ignored.[11] Even where there are few local traditions of female group solidarity and women are to a great extent cut off from the company of other nonfamily women, an approach based on the Western-style nuclear family ignores fruitful possibilities for change that can be created by constructing local women's collectives, a strategy that development projects in India and Bangladesh have successfully exploited.[12] Again, if Western feminists speak of Indian issues such as *sati* and dowry deaths, they will do so productively only if they understand the issues fully in their historical and cultural contexts.[13] Similarly, if they offer criticisms of Hindu or Islamic traditions regarding women, they will be both wrong and offensive if they neglect the variety and complexity of those traditions,

11 On the role of such assumptions in undermining African development projects, see Nkiru Nzegwu, "Recovering Igbo Traditions: A Case for Indigenous Women's Organizations in Development," in WCD, 444–66.
12 See Martha Alter Chen, *A Quiet Revolution: Women in Transition in Rural Bangladesh* (Cambridge, MA: Schenkman, 1983), describing women's collectives organized by the Bangladesh Rural Advancement Committee (BRAC); see also Chen, "A Matter of Survival: Women's Right to Employment in India and Bangladesh," in WCD, 37–57. Another such project is the Mahila Samakhya Project created by the government of India to create women's collectives in four regions of the country, teaching women how to mobilize to demand their rights from local government and from their employers. Similar techniques of female group solidarity are employed by SEWA (see Introduction) and other women's employment/credit groups. This issue will be further discussed in Chapter 4.
13 See "Cross-Cultural Connections, Border-Crossings, and 'Death by Culture,' " in Uma Narayan, *Dislocating Cultures: Identities, Traditions, and Third World Feminism* (New York and London: Routledge, 1997), 41–80.

equating them with their most stridently misogynistic elements.[14] In general, any productive feminism must be attentive to the issues that people really face and to the actual history of these issues, which is likely to be complex.

But it is one thing to say that we need local knowledge to understand the problems women face, or to direct our attention to some aspects of human life that middle-class people tend to take for granted. It is quite another matter to claim that certain very general values, such as the dignity of the person, the integrity of the body, basic political rights and liberties, basic economic opportunities, and so forth, are not appropriate norms to be used in assessing women's lives in developing countries. How might one argue this more contentious point?

II. THREE ARGUMENTS: CULTURE, DIVERSITY, PATERNALISM

As I have said, the claim that there is a global difference between Western and Eastern values, and that Indian culture (to focus on that example) simply does not value the rights and liberties cherished by the West, is not a serious contender. But when we propose a universal framework to assess women's quality of life, we face three more respectable arguments that deserve to be seriously answered.

The first is an *argument from culture*. A more subtle and sincere version of the anti-Westernizing argument, it says that Indian culture contains, in both Hindu and Muslim traditions, powerful norms of female modesty, deference, obedience, and self-sacrifice that have defined women's lives for centuries. We should not assume without argument that those are bad norms, incapable of constructing good and flourishing lives for women. Western women are not so happy, the objector adds, with their high divorce rate and their exhausting careerism. Feminists condescend to third-world women when they assume that only lives like their own can be fruitful.

My full answer to this point will emerge from the proposal I shall make, which certainly does not preclude any woman's choice to lead a traditional life, so long as she does so with certain economic and political opportunities firmly in place. Indeed, my proposal protects spaces

14 See Chapter 3.

within which women may make such choices, and in which parents may teach the value of their traditions to their children. But we should also note that the objector, once again, oversimplifies tradition, ignoring countertraditions of female defiance and strength, ignoring women's protests against harmful traditions, and in general forgetting to ask women themselves what they think of these norms, which are typically purveyed, in tradition, through male texts and the authority of male religious and cultural leaders, against a background of women's almost total economic and political disempowerment. We should say, first, that if divorce and career difficulties are painful, as they surely are, they are a lot less painful than being unable to work when one is starving because one will be beaten if one goes outdoors, or being unable to leave an abusive marriage because of illiteracy and lack of employable skills.[15] Traditions of modesty and purity have often relegated women to such substandard lives, against their wills. Neither Vasanti nor Jayamma comes close to defending such traditions, since both are preoccupied with the struggle for survival, and both have no choice but to work outside the home in ways that would be considered immodest for more prosperous women – although in Vasanti's case, caste norms do constrain the types of labor she can perform. Uma Narayan, however, does describe a traditional upbringing, in a well-off middle-class Bombay family, in which she was told by her mother never to question adult male authority, and taught norms of female submissiveness, silence, and innocence – all the while hearing from the same unhappy mother a constant stream of highly articulate protest against the misery such confining traditions had caused. Is it any wonder, she asks, that she understood her tradition as a Janus-faced one, with two quite different female voices – the silence of subservience and the turbulent voice of protest? "The shape your 'silence' took," she addresses her mother, "is in part what has incited me to speech."[16] It would be mistaken to describe only the public norm as Indian tradition, ignoring the protest.

Even when women appear to be satisfied with such customs, we should probe more deeply. If someone who has no property rights

15 For the first case, a common one in upwardly mobile Hindu castes, see Martha A. Chen, "A Matter of Survival," in WCD. The second very common pattern is exemplified in Vasanti's life; it will be further discussed in Chapter 4.
16 Narayan, 7.

under the law, who has had no formal education, who has no legal right of divorce, who will very likely be beaten if she seeks employment outside the home, says that she endorses traditions of modesty, purity, and self-abnegation, it is not clear that we should consider this the last word on the matter (as Chapter 2 will argue). Women's development groups typically encounter resistance initially, because women are afraid that change will make things worse. A group of women I met in a desert area of Andhra Pradesh, about ninety minutes by jeep from Mahabubnagar, told me that they had initially resisted participating in the government project, called Mahila Samakhya, aimed at the construction of women's collectives. They thought that it would be a waste of time, changing nothing; and they were afraid that their husbands would react harshly, because the husbands initially told them that the collectives were just an excuse to spend time talking and not working. But over time they began to see that many advantages could be gained by collective discussion and action: now they get the health visitor to come more regularly, they demand that the teacher show up. Men welcome these changes too, and they gain new respect for their wives, seeing them articulating their demands with clarity and winning concessions from local government. Traditions of deference that once seemed good have quickly ceased to seem so. Nor did these women cherish traditions of purity. One elderly toothless woman told me that she had recently gone with a group to Delhi and had been struck by the extent of women's seclusion in the North: she says that the women there are not really like women, but more like "sheep and buffaloes": they just peep out of their houses and don't take any action in the world. Without any theoretical perspective, this illiterate woman articulated the idea that seclusion is incompatible with fully human functioning.[17] What she liked in the North, she said, was that she saw a woman driving a truck and another repairing a pump: this showed her what they could do in their village. This is an entirely typical story in women's development groups, and it should make us reflect before we conclude that women without options really endorse the lives they lead.[18]

---

17 These women had never practiced purdah, so their reaction in this instance was not a criticism of their own local tradition. But similar refutations of local norms are common: see Chen, *A Quiet Revolution.*

18 For a group of similar stories, see Chen, *A Quiet Revolution.*

Female protest against unfair treatment by males is, moreover, a very old theme in Indian tradition, going straight back to Draupadi's eloquent protest against sexual harassment in *Mahabharata*, book 2, when, lost by one of her Pandava husbands[19] in a dice game, she is dragged by her hair into the hall and undressed by the winners, who gloat and call her a slave. She gains justice in a miraculous way: her sari keeps growing new yards of cloth, so that she remains fully clothed no matter how eagerly they try to undress her. This story serves, in fact, as a touchstone for the women of SEWA, who invoke it to compare the struggles of their founder Ela Bhatt (a deeply religious woman) against the humiliating treatment she suffered at the hands of male labor-union leaders.[20] This, too, is Indian tradition, as is the more general idea of human dignity that underlies the story.

And if Draupadi's protest against sexual violence may seem in some ways a confirmation of deep-seated customs of female purity,[21] there are other even more radical norms of female independence in the Hindu tradition. Mrinal, the heroine of Rabindranath Tagore's story "Letter from a Wife," declares her independence from her husband in a way

19 Draupadi has five husbands (the Pandava brothers). She is described as "supremely happy with her five heroic husbands, as is the river Sarasvati with her elephants." For further discussion of this complex incident, see Chapter 3, note 1, where the failure to question Draupadi's status as property is discussed. Only one of the husbands questions the dice game itself on grounds of the damage done to Draupadi.

20 See Rose, *Where Women Are Leaders*, 83–4, and 74–82, describing Bhatt's ouster from the National Labor Association and her humiliating treatment at a national meeting. The conflict arose over an issue of caste closely related to women's struggle against hierarchy: Bhatt opposed all compromise on the issue of affirmative action for lower castes in medical schools, out of concern for the lack of medical treatment for lower-caste women in rural areas, whom higher-caste doctors are not interested in treating. Bhatt (the Brahmin daughter of a judge, who married a lower-caste man) compared her own experience to that of Draupadi, saying "I felt like I was being stripped in front of the people I had respected most, with no one speaking up for me." Significantly, the SEWA version of the story has Draupadi prevail by praying to Krishna, whereas in the original epic she prevails by appealing to the idea of Law. Presumably Bhatt had not gotten very far through Law, and judged that a higher power was more likely to be on her side.

21 A pervasive problem in Indian legal feminism is the need to fight for feminist goals, for example protections against sexual harassment, using notions of female modesty and purity that are in some ways inimical to women's progress, and are actually legacies of Victorian British law-making. See my "The Modesty of Mrs. Bajaj: India's Problematic Route to Sexual Harassment Law," forthcoming in a volume on sexual harassment, ed. Reva Siegel and Catharine MacKinnon, Yale University Press.

that expresses the ideas of nineteenth- and early twentieth-century Bengali humanist thought;[22] and of course Tagore's fiction is obsessed with the damage done by ossified custom to the human search for self-expression and love. But such thoughts are not confined to Bengali modernity. The Bengal Renaissance was based not only on independent moral argument but also on a close interpretation of aspects of Hindu tradition; it called on Hindus to reject contemporary superstitions and rigid rules in order to return to what is finest in the tradition.[23] And Mrinal explicitly invokes a historical paradigm: Meerabai, the sixteenth-century Rajput queen who left her marriage and her royal status to become a singer, performing "joyfully rebellious songs." "Meerabai too," she tells her husband, "was a woman like me."[24]

Such critical thinking is old in the Muslim tradition as well. In 1905, Muslim feminist Rokeya Sakhawat Hossain mocked the seclusion of women in her fantasy *The Sultana's Dream*, whose characters maintain that, since men are the dangerous ones, they are the ones who should be shut up in purdah:

'Where are the men?' I asked her.

'In their proper places, where they ought to be.'

[The Sultana tells her that in her country it is women who are secluded.]

'But, dear Sultana, how unfair it is to shut in the harmless women and let loose the men . . . Suppose some lunatics escape from the asylum and begin to do all sorts of mischief to men, horses, and other creatures: in that case what will your countrymen do?'

'They will try to capture them and put them back into their asylum.'

'And you do not think it wise to keep sane people inside an asylum and let loose the insane?'

'Of course not!' said I, laughing lightly.

'As a matter of fact, in your country this very thing is done! Men, who do

---

22 Especially influential for Tagore (1861–1941) is the thought of Bengali thinker and social reformer Rammohun Roy (1772–1833). On the Bengal Renaissance, see Kalpana Bardhan, "Introduction," in *Of Women, Outcastes*, 4–8, 42–4; and Susobhan Sarkar, *On the Bengal Renaissance*.

23 See Bardhan, 42, discussing Rammohun Roy, who based his campaign against *sati* on religious texts; and Iswarchandra Vidyasagar (1820–92), who used his scriptural knowledge to campaign against child marriage and polygamy and for widow remarriage.

24 "Letter from a Wife," trans. Kalpana Bardhan, in *Of Women, Outcastes*, 109.

or at least are capable of doing no end of mischief, are let loose and the innocent women shut up in the zenana! . . . You have neglected the duty you owe to yourselves, and you have lost your natural rights by shutting your eyes to your own interests.'[25]

This articulate protest relies on a long tradition of thought about sex equality within the Indian Muslim tradition, and defines that tradition further.[26] By now, such norms of self-cultivation and rights-seeking have caused widespread reexamination of the basis of norms of female deference; women have urged other women to ask what is really important in the tradition, and whether the really important features justify seclusion and veiling.[27]

At times, in fact, it may be the uncritical veneration of the past that is more "foreign," the voice of protest that is more "indigenous" or "authentic," if such terms have any meaning at all. Chinese women I met at a 1995 conference on feminism in Beijing[28] reacted to a paper praising Confucian values of care as good norms for feminists by saying, "That was a Western paper. She would not have said that had she not come from Hong Kong" (as indeed the young speaker did). What they meant was that for her the traditions could look beautiful, since she had never had to live in the world they constructed. For them, Confucian values were living excuses for sex discrimination in employment and other things they didn't value at all. This is also the way many Indian women, though by no means all, view the norms of the "good" or "pure" woman to which traditionalist Hindu and Muslim leaders are currently giving enormous emphasis, construing control over female sexuality as a central aspect of cultural continuity.[29]

We should also remember that the equation of the entirety of a

25 Rokeya Sakhawat Hossain, *Sultana's Dream and Selections from The Secluded Ones*, ed. and trans. by Roushan Jahan (New York: Feminist Press of the City University of New York, 1988).
26 This of course does not imply that the tradition as a whole is one of sex equality: obviously enough, strong inequalities in property rights, divorce rights, and other important rights have been deeply rooted in the Muslim legal tradition: see Chapter 3 of this volume, and the discussion in Agarwal, *A Field of One's Own*, Chapter 5.
27 For further discussion of internal debate in the religious traditions, see Chapter 3.
28 This was not the large Beijing meeting in August 1995, but a small academic conference sponsored by the Ford Foundation in June 1995.
29 See Elizabeth A. Mann, "Education, Money, and the Role of Women in Maintaining Minority Identity," and Huma Ahmed-Ghosh, "Preserving Identity: A Case Study of Palitpur," in Hasan, ed., *Forging*, 130–67, 169–87.

culture with old or change-resistant elements is frequently a ploy of imperialism and chauvinism. The British in India harped continually on elements of Indian culture that they could easily portray as retrograde; they sought to identify these as "Indian culture," and critical values (especially those favoring women's progress) as British importations. Historically this was untrue; but it served in the minds of many to justify domination. At the same time, the British actively promoted antiscientific elements in Indian culture in order to prevent a development of science and technology in India that would threaten their continued hegemony. As Nehru was later to put it, the British encouraged "the disruptive, obscurantist, reactionary, sectarian, and opportunist elements in the country."[30] It would be a grave mistake on the part of the foreign observer to endorse this British construction as the way things are concerning what is "Indian."

More generally, we should say that any story that attributes to India only a single set of cultural norms, even for women, is bound to be bizarrely inadequate. Few American feminists make such generalizations about "American culture" – or, insofar as they do, they are well aware that the culture contains much besides the norms they attack (including, of course, themselves). They don't conclude that the existence of reactionary elements in American tradition makes their own critique improper. But India is probably the most diverse single nation in the world, if there is any such coherent notion. With seventeen official national languages, four prominently institutionalized religions with their own legal systems (and other smaller religious groups), huge regional differences and differences of class and caste, differences between urban and rural, differences between matrilineal and patrilineal traditions, between secularism and religiosity, between rationalism and mysticism – all these would have to be included in any adequate story of the stock of tradition out of which Indian women may select their norms. As Indira Karamcheti writes, "Neither I nor anyone else can deliver a representative, authentic Third-world woman to academia or elsewhere. Even in India, there is no such thing as *the* Indian woman – there are only Indian women. And the individuals are far more interesting than any assumed stories of authenticity."[31]

30 Nehru, *Autobiography*, 449.
31 In "The Graves of Academe," in *Our Feet Walk the Sky*.

Another more general point should be stressed: Cultures are dynamic, and change is a very basic element in all of them. Contrasts between Western and non-Western societies often depict Western cultures as dynamic, critical, modernizing, while Eastern cultures are identified with their oldest elements, as if these do not change or encounter contestation. Looking at the relationship between her grandmother's way of life and her own, Narayan comments, "I find it impossible to describe 'our traditional way of life' without seeing *change* as a constitutive element, affecting transformations that become 'invisible' in their taken-for-grantedness."[32] Criticism too is profoundly indigenous to virtually all cultures,[33] but to none more so than to the culture of India, that extremely argumentative nation.[34] To cite just one famous and typical example, Bengali religious thinker Rammohun Roy, imagining the horrors of death, singles out as especially terrible the fact that "everyone will contest your views, and you will not be able to reply."[35] This too is Indian culture. When a Bengali-Finnish couple I know discuss where they would like to live, he cannot imagine why anyone would like to wander alone in the forest, and she cannot see why anyone would want to sit in a crowded cafe all day arguing.

One might try to refurbish the argument from culture by an appeal to the idea of cultural relativism: the idea, that is, that normative criteria must come from within the society to which they are applied. I believe such an attempted salvage operation would be totally unsuccessful. As a descriptive thesis about how people really do make moral judgments, relativism is clearly false. People are resourceful borrowers of ideas. The ideas of Marxism, which originated in the British Library, have influenced conduct in Cuba, China, and Cambodia. The ideas of democracy, which are not original to China, are by now extremely important Chinese ideas. The ideas of Christianity, which originated in

32 Narayan, 26.
33 For one fascinating example of this point, together with a general critique of communitarian fantasies of cultural peace and homogeneity, see Fred Kniss, *Disquiet in the Land: Cultural Conflict in American Mennonite Communities* (New Brunswick: Rutgers University Press, 1997).
34 For a general discussion, with many references, see M. Nussbaum and Amartya Sen, "Internal Criticism and Indian Rationalist Traditions," in *Relativism: Interpretation and Confrontation*, ed. Michael Krausz (Notre Dame: University of Notre Dame Press, 1989), 299–325.
35 Cited by Amartya Sen, in speech at the conference on The Challenge of Modern Democracy, The University of Chicago, April 1998.

a dissident sect of Judaism in a small part of Asia Minor, have by now influenced conduct in every region of the globe, as have the ideas of Islam. As Aristotle said, "In general, people seek not the way of their ancestors, but the good."[36]

As a normative thesis about how we should make moral judgments, relativism has several problems. First, it has no bite in the modern world, where the ideas of every culture turn up inside every other, through the internet and the media. The ideas of feminism, of democracy, of egalitarian welfarism, are now "inside" every known society. Many forms of moral relativism, especially those deriving from the cultural anthropology of a previous era, use an unrealistic notion of culture. They imagine homogeneity where there is really diversity, agreement or submission where there is really contestation.[37] My observations about India apply here: there is little that is not "internal" to India, once we get a sufficiently complex idea of its traditions. Second, it is not obvious why we should think the normative relativist thesis true. Why should we follow the local ideas, rather than the best ideas we can find? Finally, normative relativism is self-subverting: for, in asking us to defer to local norms, it asks us to defer to norms that in most cases are strongly nonrelativistic. Most local traditions take themselves to be absolutely, not relatively, true. So in asking us to follow the local, relativism asks us not to follow relativism.

Many people, in particular students, confuse relativism with the toleration of diversity, and find relativism attractive on the ground that it shows respect for the ways of others. But of course it does no such thing. Most cultures have exhibited considerable intolerance of diversity over the ages, as well as at least some respect for diversity. By making each tradition the last word, we deprive ourselves of any more general norm of toleration or respect that could help us limit the intolerance of cultures. Once we see this, our interest in being relativists should rapidly diminish.

The cultural argument fails; nor can it be rescued by an appeal to moral relativism. At this point, however, two other objections to universal

36 Aristotle, *Politics*, 1269a3–4.
37 This error sprang from methodological error: for often the anthropologist selected a single "native informant" and built the picture of the culture on this basis.

values need to be heard. I shall call them the *argument from the good of diversity*, and the *argument from paternalism*.

The argument from the *good of diversity* reminds us that our world is rich in part because we don't all agree on a single set of categories, but speak many different languages of value. Just as we think the world's different languages have worth and beauty, and that it's a bad thing, diminishing the expressive resources of human life generally, when any language ceases to exist, so too we may think that each cultural system has a distinctive beauty, and that it would be an impoverished world if everyone took on the value system of America.

Here we must be careful to distinguish two claims the objector might be making. She might be claiming that diversity is good as such; or she might simply be saying that there are problems with the value system of America, and that it would therefore be too bad if the rest of the world emulated our materialism and aggressiveness. This second claim, of course, doesn't yet say anything against universal values, it just suggests that their content should be critical of some American values. So the real challenge to our enterprise lies in the first claim. To meet it we must ask how far cultural diversity really is like linguistic diversity. The trouble with the analogy is that languages, as such, do not harm people, and cultural practices frequently do. We could think that Cornish or Breton should be preserved, without thinking the same about domestic violence, or absolute monarchy, or genital mutilation. Nehru put the point well in criticizing Gandhi's sympathy for antiquated feudal practices of land tenure that seem oppressive to tenants. Invoking Thomas Paine's criticism of Burke, Nehru wrote, " 'He pities the plumage, but forgets the dying bird.' " And then he added: "Gandhiji certainly never forgets the dying bird. But why so much insistence on the plumage?"[38]

In the end, then, the objection doesn't undermine the search for universal values, it requires it: for what it invites us to ask is, whether the cultural values in question are among the ones worth preserving, or possibly part of what is killing the bird. And to ask this entails at least a very general universal framework of assessment, one that will tell us what is and is not beyond the pale, what is and is not implicated in killing the bird. I will be offering just such a very general framework,

38 Nehru, *Autobiography*, 534.

one that allows a great deal of latitude for diversity, but one that also sets up some general benchmarks that will tell us when we are better off letting a practice die out. Traditional practices like the division of labor at Jayamma's brick kiln site, or Vasanti's husband's highly traditional practice of wife beating, are not worth preserving simply because they are there, or because they are old; to make a case for preserving them, we have to assess the contribution they make against the harm they do. And this requires a set of values that gives us a critical purchase on cultural particulars. So the argument gives us good reasons to preserve types of diversity that are compatible with human dignity and other basic values; but it does not undermine and even supports our search for a general universal framework of critical assessment.

We might add that it is not clear that there is interesting diversity exemplified in the practices of male dominance that feminists have most contested. Getting beaten up and being malnourished have depressing similarities everywhere; denials of land rights, political voice, and employment opportunities do also. Insofar as there is diversity worth preserving in the various cultures, it is perhaps not in traditions of sex hierarchy, any more than in traditions of slavery, that we should search for it.

Finally, we have the *argument from paternalism*. This argument says that when we use a set of universal norms as benchmarks for the world's various societies, telling people what is good for them, we show too little respect for people's freedom as agents (and, in a related way, their role as democratic citizens). People are the best judges of what is good for them, and if we prevent people from acting on their own choices, we treat them like children. This is an important point, and one that any viable cross-cultural proposal should bear firmly in mind. That is why the whole of my second chapter will be devoted to the role of actual preferences in the choice of basic political principles. But we can say already that a commitment to respecting people's choices hardly seems incompatible with the endorsement of universal values. Indeed, it appears to endorse explicitly at least one universal value, the value of having the opportunity to think and choose for oneself. Thinking about paternalism gives us a strong reason to respect the variety of ways citizens actually choose to lead their lives in a pluralistic society, and therefore to prefer a form of universalism that is compatible with freedom and choice of the most significant sorts. But religious toleration, associative freedom, and the other major liberties are themselves universal values. They require a universalist account for their recognition and their protection against those who don't want other people to make choices for themselves.

The issue of paternalism arises in different ways when we think about a national state's relation to its citizens, and when we think about the relationship between a system of international law to the various national states. The latter relationship raises complex issues of accountability, and even strong universalists about rights may legitimately worry about the democratic credentials of international human rights bodies, when they seek to enforce norms against democratically accountable nation states. I shall return to the issue of accountability later in this chapter (section VII), discussing the role of the nation state in securing capabilities for all citizens. For now, I shall focus on the first issue, that of a nation state's treatment of groups within the nation whose traditional practices that treat women unequally. Thinking of this problem, then, we can insist that universal norms of religious toleration, freedom of association, and the other liberties are essential in order to prevent illiberal subgroups from threatening legitimate forms of pluralism. India remains a highly pluralistic society only because it has committed itself to a menu of fundamental rights and liberties; to the extent that those liberties are in jeopardy for some citizens, pluralism in India is acutely in jeopardy.

We can make a further claim: many existing value systems are themselves highly paternalistic, particularly toward women. They tell them what to do, claiming that they are promoting women's good. They treat women as unequal under the law, as lacking full civil capacity, as not having the property rights, associative liberties, and employment rights of males. When we encounter a system like this, as we certainly do in India, in the form not only of traditional practices but also of the various religious systems of personal law, it is in one sense paternalistic to say, sorry, that is unacceptable under the universal norms of equality and liberty that the state would like to defend. To say that is to tell people how to conduct their lives with one another, in a way that may run counter to their actual desires. In that way, any bill of rights is "paternalistic," vis-à-vis families, or groups, or practices, or even pieces of legislation, that treat people with insufficient or unequal respect, if paternalism means simply telling people that they cannot behave in some way that they have traditionally behaved and want to behave. The Indian Constitution is in that sense "paternalistic," when it tells people that it is from now on illegal to treat women as unequal in matters of property and civil capacity, or to discriminate against people on grounds of caste or sex. More generally, any system of law is "paternalistic," keeping some people from doing some things that they want to do. But that is hardly a good argument against the rule of law, or, more generally, against opposing the attempts of some people to tyrannize over others. These cases are different from classically controversial cases of paternalism (such as seat-belt and helmet laws) because there are issues of justice involved: people are being harmed; the freedom of some to pursue their good is interfering with the legitimate pursuits of others. We dislike paternalism, insofar as we do, because there is something else that we like, namely each person's liberty of choice in fundamental matters. It is fully consistent to reject some forms of paternalism while supporting those that underwrite these central values, on an equal basis. Even strong opponents of paternalism with respect to private choices that do not harm others, such as John Stuart Mill, have countenanced state interference as soon as the conduct does harm others; and Mill clearly thought that many forms of traditional sex hierarchy fell afoul of the "harm principle."[39]

Beyond this, we should note that the various liberties of choice have material preconditions, in whose absence there is merely a simulacrum of choice. Jayamma in a sense had the choice to go to school, but the economic circumstances of her life made this impossible. Nothing told Vasanti she couldn't have economic independence from her brothers; but in the absence of the SEWA bank the independence she now enjoys would not have been available to her. Children in the desert areas of Andhra Pradesh[40] have the right to go to school – but there aren't any

39 See *The Subjection of Women*, ed. S. M. Okin (Indianapolis: Hackett, 1988), objecting to the failure to prosecute rape within marriage, the unequal legal conditions of marriage, etc. See also David Dyzenhaus, "John Stuart Mill and the Harm of Pornography," in *Mill's* On Liberty: *Critical Essays*, ed. Gerald Dworkin (Lanham: Rowman and Littlefield, 1997), 31–54, arguing that there is a strong Millean case to be made for some legal regulation of pornography.

40 Technically speaking, these areas are designated "semiarid": only certain areas of Rajasthan are called "desert." However, in my personal experience these areas are indis-

WOMEN AND HUMAN DEVELOPMENT

functioning schools or teachers in many areas, since the corrupt local government does not ensure that teachers show up. All citizens of India have the right to exercise their religion freely, on an equal basis; the Constitution says so. But in an area torn by communal violence, where police are either impotent or corrupt, where rape in police custody is generally agreed to be widespread,[41] it doesn't mean a whole lot to point to the Constitution. All women in India have equal rights under the Constitution; but in the absence of effective enforcement of laws against rape[42] and Supreme Court guidelines on sexual harassment,[43] and in the absence of programs targeted at increasing female literacy, economic empowerment, and employment opportunities, those rights are not real to them. As a recent report on laws addressing violence against women puts it, "For the vast majority of Indian women, these statutes are meaningless . . . Lack of basic knowledge about the law and procedures, delays and insensitivity of the judicial system, the cost involved in getting justice have all contributed to this."[44]

In short, liberty is not just a matter of having rights on paper, it requires being in a position to exercise those rights. And this requires material and institutional resources, including legal and social acceptance of the legitimacy of women's claims. The state that is going to guarantee people rights effectively is going to have to take a stand about more than the importance of these basic rights themselves. It will

tinguishable from areas of the U.S. (e.g., in California and Nevada) that are called "desert."

41 In the law of rape in India, the burden of proof has recently been shifted for police-custody rape accusations: there is a presumption of guilt if the accused is a civil servant: see Introduction, section V. The reason for this change is to deter police misconduct by ensuring that police will not be alone with female prisoners, but will keep witnesses around to testify to their conduct. Obviously this will work only if the relevant parties do not collude to protect one another.

42 On the increasing rate of reported rape and the extreme difficulties in securing convictions, see the good account in "Rape: When Victim Is Seen as Villain," lead feature (with a number of different related articles) in *India Abroad*, Friday, July 10, 1998, pp. 1, 30–34.

43 For discussion of the Supreme Court guidelines and other legal developments, see my "The Modesty of Mrs. Bajaj."

44 *India Abroad* (note 42), p. 34, citing report by United Nations Population Fund. According to a recent study by the Delhi-based NGO Sakshi, 68% of judges surveyed felt that "provocative" clothes are an invitation to sexual assault, and 55% felt that the moral character of a woman is relevant in a sexual assault case.

have to take a stand on the distribution of wealth and income, the distribution of property rights, access to the legal system, in short, on the use of resources to guarantee to citizens what John Rawls has called the "fair value" of the various liberties – for example, by raising revenue through taxation in sufficient quantity to make schools available to all, or by supplying free legal assistance to impoverished defendants or victims. That requires yet more universalism and in a sense paternalism, meaning interference with activities that some people choose; but we could hardly say that those rural children, living in a state of virtual anarchy, are free to do as they wish.

In this instance, we may note that, far from being a Western imposition, such redistributive measures are more clearly supported by the Indian tradition than by the American, where affirmative action and even redistributive taxation are frequently viewed as unacceptably paternalistic. The Indian constitutional tradition, by contrast, holds that policies needed to promote full civic equality by redistribution and affirmative action are fully compatible with liberty and nondiscrimination.

The argument from paternalism indicates, then, that we should prefer a universal normative account that allows people plenty of liberty to pursue their own conceptions of value, within limits set by the protection of the equal worth of the liberties of others. It gives us no good reason to reject all universal accounts, and some strong reasons to construct one, including in our account not only the liberties themselves, but also forms of economic empowerment that are crucial to making the liberties truly available.

The argument suggests one thing more: that the account we search for should preserve liberties and opportunities for each and every person, taken one by one, respecting each of them as an end, rather than simply as the agent or supporter of the ends of others. The idea that the individual person should be the focus of political thought has sometimes been given dismissive treatment by feminists, on the grounds that it implies neglect for care and community and involves a male Western bias toward self-sufficiency and competition, as opposed to cooperation and love. We could argue for a long time over whether particular Western liberal theorists are indeed guilty of neglecting cooperation, community, and love. I believe that a lot of what communitarian thinkers have said in criticism of figures such as Rawls and Kant, and even Mill, is mistaken.[45] But we need not pursue that issue here; we need only notice that there is a type of focus on the individual person as such that requires no particular metaphysical tradition, and no bias against love and care. It arises naturally from the recognition that each person has just one life to live, not more than one; that the food on A's plate does not magically nourish the stomach of B; that the pleasure felt in C's body does not make the pain experienced by D less painful; that the income generated by E's economic activity does not help to feed and shelter F; in general, that one person's exceeding happiness and liberty does not magically make another person happy or free. Programs aimed at raising general or average well-being do not improve the situation of the least well-off, unless they go to work directly to improve the quality of those people's lives. If we combine this observation with the thought, which all feminists share in some form, that each person is valuable and worthy of respect as an end, we must conclude that we should look not just to the total or the average, but to the functioning of each and every person.[46] We may call this the *principle of each person as end.*

It has been claimed by Veena Das that even this very intuitive idea that each person has her own dignity and that questions of well-being should be considered one by one, rather than in the aggregate, is a Western intrusion: Indian women are simply unable to form the concept of their own personal well-being as distinct from the well-being of family members.[47] If Das simply means that Indian women frequently judge sacrifice for the family to be a good thing, and frequently subordinate their own well-being to the well-being of others, it is plausible enough, but hardly an objection to the type of political focus on the individual that I have recommended; there is no incompatibility be-

---

45 For some examples, see my "The Feminist Critique of Liberalism," *Sex and Social Justice,* 55–80.
46 For this interpretation of individualism, see further "The Feminist Critique of Liberalism."
47 Veena Das and Ralph Nicholas, " 'Welfare' and 'Well-Being' in South Asian Societies," ACLS-SSRC Joint Committee on South Asia (New York: Social Science Research Council, 1981); although this paper has been circulated as a pamphlet, Das has never published it. For a contrary view, see Agarwal, *A Field of One's Own,* 422–38, and " 'Bargaining' and Gender Relations: Within and Beyond the Household," *Feminist Economics* 3 (1997), 1–51.

tween the idea that politics should treat each person as an end and the idea that some people may choose to make sacrifices for others. If, however, Das really means to say that Indian women cannot distinguish their own hunger from the hunger of a child or a husband, cannot really distinguish their own body and its health from someone else's body and its health, then she does not have a leg to stand on. Jayamma certainly in some ways puts others first and herself second. She takes sugar in her tea, for example, while she allows her husband and her children to take the more expensive milk. But even in that act she is distinguishing her own well-being from that of others; in general, she budgets the family accounts with intense awareness of the separateness of the various family members, asking how much shall be spent on each one. She is well aware, too, of exactly how much labor she performs with her own body, and all too clearly aware that it is her own body doing that brick carrying, not the body of some male fellow laborer who has been happily promoted into brick molding. When she is denied her own pension on the grounds that she has able-bodied sons, furthermore, she is outraged: she has a right to something for herself, regardless of what children she does or does not have. It is difficult to believe that Das has not had many conversations with Indian women in her own social class that emphasize the tensions between a woman's well-being and the well-being of someone else. But extremely poor people are likely to be especially keenly aware of the separateness of each person's well-being – for hunger and hard physical labor are great reminders that one is oneself and not someone else. Bengali author Manik Bandyopadhyay put it this way, in his short story "A Female Problem at a Low Level":

A slum girl and daughter of a laborer cannot mentally depend on her father or brother, like the daughters of the babu families who even as grown women see individual disaster in any family mishap. She is used to fending for herself, relying on her own wits.[48]

On this account, the perception of the organic connectedness of interests in the family is more likely to be an upper-middle-class (*babu*) mode of consciousness, alien to those who are really struggling to sur-

48 In Kalpana Bardhan, ed., *Of Women, Outcastes*, 155.

vive. (Has Das, not at all from a peasant background, mistaken her own background for a special "Indian essence"?)

One might, of course, come to accept religious beliefs, in particular Buddhist beliefs, that do hold that people aren't really separate individuals at all, and that the whole idea that objects and people are distinct from one another is an illusion. But first of all, Buddhist metaphysics is hardly typical of non-Western religion as a whole; many traditions take the individual very seriously as the locus of purity, self-discipline, and spiritual achievement. Buddhism, furthermore, self-consciously portrays itself as a radical critique of ordinary practices, and as making demands that take people, in meditation, far away from the world of physical objects they must continue to inhabit in their daily lives. So a political focus on the individual is not insulting or unfair even to Buddhists, since it is meant to supply a basis for politics in the daily world, not in the world of enlightened meditation and reflection. The Buddhist can accept the appropriateness of relieving the suffering of bodies one by one, even though she believes that at some level bodies as such are an illusion, and that the more correct description of the goal would be to minimize the quantity of suffering in the world as a whole.[49]

If we agree that citizens are all worthy of concern and respect, and grant that they live separate lives in the sense just characterized, then we ought to conclude that politics should not treat people as agents or supporters of other people, whose mission in the world is to execute someone else's plan of life. It should treat each of them as ends, as sources of agency and worth in their own right, with their own plans to make and their own lives to live, therefore as deserving of all necessary support for their equal opportunity to be such agents. To treat everyone as an end we will have to take a stand on some values that will be made central for political purposes, and we will have to take a stand against some very common ways of treating women – as childlike, as incompetent in matters of property and contract, as mere ad-

---

49 On the close relationship between Buddhist and Utilitarian ideas of aggregation, see Damien Keown, *The Nature of Buddhist Ethics* (New York: St. Martin's Press, 1992), Chapter 7, "Buddhism and Utilitarianism." The idea of reducing suffering plays a central role in Buddhist political discourse, but usually not in its more severe metaphysical form, in which the sufferings of individuals would be treated simply as elements in a global total. The stricter form might have radical implications for policies, such as public provision of health care, that most Buddhists would agree in supporting.

juncts of a family line, as reproducers and care givers rather than as having their own lives to live. But when we take a stand in this way, that should not raise the charge of paternalism in its classic form, since we do so in order to treat each and every citizen as an end and permit all citizens to search for the good in their own ways.

III. DEFECTS OF STANDARD ECONOMIC APPROACHES

Let me recapitulate. The *argument from culture* reminded us that we should leave space for women who may wish to choose a traditional hierarchical way of life. But it said nothing against using a universal account to criticize unjust cultural practices; indeed, we were reminded that the activity of criticism is deeply internal to Indian culture itself. More generally, cultures are dynamic and full of contestation. The *argument from the good of diversity* told us something important about any proposal we should endorse: that it ought to provide spaces in which valuably different forms of human activity can flourish. We should not stamp out diversity, or even put it at risk, without a very strong reason. But in light of the fact that some traditional practices are harmful and evil, and some actively hostile to other elements of a diverse culture, we are forced by our interest in diversity itself to develop a set of criteria against which to assess the practices we find, asking which are acceptable and worth preserving, and which are not. As for the *argument from paternalism*, it nudges us strongly in the direction of what might be called *political* rather than *comprehensive liberalism,* in the sense that it urges us to respect the many different conceptions of the good citizens may have and to foster a political climate in which they will each be able to pursue the good (whether religious or ethical) according to their own lights, so long as they do no harm to others. In other words, we want universals that are facilitative rather than tyrannical,[50] that create spaces for choice rather than dragooning people into a desired total mode of functioning. But understood at its best, the paternalism argument is not an argument against cross-cultural universals. For it is all about respect for the dignity of

50 For the charge that international human rights norms are tyrannical, see Wendy Brown, *States of Injury: Power and Freedom in Late Modernity* (Princeton: Princeton University Press,1995). As will be evident in section VI, I dispute this claim.

persons as choosers. This respect requires us to defend universally a wide range of liberties, plus their material conditions; and it requires us to respect persons as separate ends, in a way that reflects our acknowledgment of the empirical fact of bodily separateness, asking how each and every life can have the preconditions of liberty and self-determination.

We have some good reasons already, then, to think that universal values are not just acceptable, but badly needed, if we really are to show respect for all citizens in a pluralistic society. But we can now approach this question from another direction, by looking at the three most prominent approaches, in international development work, to assessing a nation or region's quality of life. For the defects of these approaches, both in general and as approaches to the situation of poor women in developing countries, give us yet more reason to turn to a universal normative account for the philosophical underpinning of basic political principles. (I assume that if an account fails at the less demanding normative task of telling us how well people in a given country are doing, it must fail, a fortiori, at the more demanding task of providing a normative account of a basic social minimum of life quality.)

The most prominent approach to quality of life assessment used to be simply to ask about GNP per capita, treating the maximization of this figure as the most appropriate social goal and basis for cross-cultural comparison. It has by now become obvious that this approach is not very illuminating, because it does not even ask about the distribution of wealth and income, and countries with similar aggregate figures can exhibit great distributional variations. In Charles Dickens's *Hard Times*, circus girl Sissy Jupe is asked by her economics teacher to imagine that her schoolroom is a nation, "and in this Nation are fifty millions of money." Next, she is asked to say whether this isn't a prosperous nation, and whether she herself isn't in "a thriving state." Sissy replies, in tears of confusion, that she doesn't see how she can answer the question until she knows "who has got the money, and whether any of it is mine." But that, as she soon learns "is not in the figures" – and so it was not, for a long part of the subject's history. Sissy's intuitive sense of the distinctness of one person from another informs her that aggregate data aren't enough for a normative assessment of how a nation is doing: we need to know how each one is doing, considering each as a separate life.

Sissy's critique was incomplete. In addition to distributional information, we also need information about important goods that are not always well correlated with wealth and income – such as life expectancy, infant mortality, educational opportunities, employment opportunities, political liberties, the quality of race and gender relations. Countries that do very well on GNP per capita have often done egregiously badly on one of these other distinct goods: think of South Africa under apartheid, or Singapore under its extremely constraining political regime. And, of particular importance for our project, countries with similar GNP performance often exhibit great variation in various aspects of gender equality. Thus Pakistan, Zimbabwe, and Honduras have almost exactly the same GNP per capita, while the female literacy rate is 23% in Pakistan, 60% in Zimbabwe, and 71.6% in Honduras; the proportion of income earned by women is 20% in Pakistan, 24% in Honduras, and 35% in Zimbabwe. India and Kenya have the same GNP per capita, while the female literacy rate is 36% in India and 67.8% in Kenya; the earned income share that goes to women is 25.7% in India and 42% in Kenya.[51] Seeing what is absent from the GNP account nudges us sharply in the direction of mapping out basic goods in a universal way, so that we can use a list of basic goods to compare quality of life more fruitfully across societies.

Suppose, instead, we take a more straightforwardly utilitarian approach, asking about the total or average utility of the population, as measured by expressions of satisfaction. Here again, we run into the problem of respect for the separate person – for an aggregate figure doesn't tell us where the top and the bottom are. In that sense, it doesn't tell us "who has got the money, and whether any of it is mine" any more than does the crude GNP approach. Suppose a majority of citizens of Andhra Pradesh express satisfaction with their educational opportunities in a hypothetical poll: such a result does not give us the information that things are disastrously bad out in the desert areas, where there are often no functioning schools at all. We could imagine getting a similar average satisfaction figure in Kerala, where the bottom is far better situated.[52] Nor, of course, does such an aggregate inform us about the different views of men and women, and it can conceal an

---

51 *Human Development Report 1997* (Oxford and New York: Oxford University Press, 1997).
52 This might be so, for example, if middle and upper classes were dissatisfied with the system of higher education.

extremely bad situation for women within a total or average that looks pretty good. We may or may not want to improve the lot of the worst off, or of women; but we certainly shouldn't make decisions without knowing how they are doing. Average utility is an imprecise number, which does not tell us enough about different types of people and their relative social placement. This makes it an especially bad approach when we are selecting basic political principles with a commitment to treat each person as an end; this problem is all the worse when we focus on the situation of women, whose placement in a hierarchy of power is a critical part of any good description.

What is more, utilitarians typically aggregate not only across distinct lives but also across distinct elements of lives. Thus, within the total or average utility will lie information about liberty, about economic well-being, about health, about education. But these are all separate goods, which to some extent vary independently[53] and there are reasons to think that they all matter, that we should not give up one of them simply to achieve an especially large amount of another. A central argument used by John Rawls against utilitarianism has been that because of its commitment to trade-offs among diverse goods, it offers insufficient protection for political and religious liberty. It encourages trade-offs between those goods and others, in order to produce the largest social total (or average).[54] Once again, this will create problems for thinking well about marginalized or deprived people, for whom some of the opportunities that utilitarianism puts at risk may have an especially urgent importance.

There is a further problem with the reliance on utility. This is, that it does not even include all the relevant information. One thing we want to know is how individuals feel about what is happening to them, whether dissatisfied or satisfied. But we also want to know what they are actually able to do and to be. Suppose Jayamma were to say on our poll that she feels satisfied with her educational attainment (which is nil), on the grounds that it is just right for the type of labor she has been performing all her life, and that she doesn't see what point there would be in learning superfluous skills. Well, that is a plausible reply.

---

53 For one compelling argument about this, see the regional comparisons in Drèze and Sen, *India*, and its companion volume of comparative regional studies.
54 Rawls, *A Theory of Justice* (Cambridge, MA: Harvard University Press, 1971), hereinafter TJ, 156–73, discussing average utility and its difficulties.

But in a sense it begs some questions: for had Jayamma had more education, she would have had different options, and the skills would not have been superfluous. She thinks them so because of habit, because she is not used to seeing any woman of her class and generation go to school, and maybe also because it's human not to cry over spilt milk, but rather to adjust your sights to the kind of life you actually can have. Because this question is so important, I shall discuss it at length in Chapter 2, arguing that this conditioned satisfaction does not give the government of Kerala reasons not to promote the education of girls in the poorest areas, as it most aggressively has. Debating this issue well certainly requires looking at people's satisfaction and dissatisfaction; but it will also require using everything known about the connections between education and population control, education and political empowerment, education and employment opportunities. Confining our inquiry to the space of utility prevents us, then, from using information that is highly relevant to the question before us.

Thinking about the defects of utilitarian approaches to development pushes us, then, in the direction of a substantive account of certain central abilities and opportunities, as the relevant space within which to make comparisons of quality of life across societies, and as the relevant benchmark to use in asking what a given society has or has not done for its citizens. Our critique suggests that such a list will contain a plurality of distinct items, and that it will not treat these items as simply offering different amounts of a single homogenous good. Nor will the assessment focus solely on how people feel about their relation to these goods; it should look, as well, for information about what they are actually able to do and to be.

Before we turn to the third major approach to quality of life assessment, we should mention a variant on the utilitarian approach that has had enormous influence on modeling and information gathering the world over: Gary Becker's model of the family. Becker does think (for descriptive, not normative, purposes) that the goal of the family as unit is the maximization of utility, and that utility (construed as the satisfaction of preference or desire) is the relevant space of comparison when we are asking how families (and, presumably, larger groups such as nations) are doing. But inside the family he takes a different line. The family, he holds, should be understood as a group held together by motives of altruism. In particular, the head of the household is assumed to be a beneficent altruist who will adequately distribute resources and opportunities to the family's members.[55] The upshot of this assumption is that we need not ask how each and every individual in the family is doing, even with regard to utility: we need only ask about the whole, and assume that the distribution has been altruistic. For this reason, development workers influenced by Becker's model have typically sought information about households, rather than about individual household members; it is difficult to find data, for example, on how widows in India are doing, since in the data they usually appear as members of a household headed by someone else. Although Becker's model itself has only descriptive and predictive purposes, when used by others in this way it has clear normative implications: for we can hardly make things better for widows unless we can first of all attend to them as distinct persons, and ask how they are doing.

Becker made an immensely valuable contribution when he put the whole question of the family on the agenda of the economics profession. But his model is inadequate in some crucial ways. It assumes a picture of the family that is romance more than reality. In real life, as Becker acknowledges, families contain all sorts of struggles over resources and opportunities. Some family members get milk in their tea, some only sugar; some go to school and some do not; some get life-sustaining health care and some do not. Vasanti's husband beat her and used his government money to go get drunk. Jayamma's husband contributed very little to household income, since he used most of his own wages on drink and meals out for himself. Vasanti's brothers got some education and the opportunity to take over their father's business, while she was married off young, with no education or skills to fall back on in hard times. In Jayamma's house, it was standard for females to get less food than males, and much less protein; and the question of schooling for girls did not even arise. Becker is interested in such conflicts, and tries to address them: but the theoretical resources of his model are insufficient to the task. Becker has recently stated that other motives, such as anger and guilt, need to be added to the model.[56] But

55 Becker, *A Treatise on the Family* (Cambridge, MA: Harvard University Press, 1981, second edition 1991).
56 "The Economic Way of Looking at Behavior," Nobel address, 1992, in *The Essence of Becker*, ed. Ramón Febrero and Pedro S. Schwartz (Stanford: Hoover Institution,

even with such changes, a model based on utility, with commitments to aggregation across lives, will prove an inadequate basis for the selection of normative principles. Far more revealing are conflict-based models that treat each family member as separate throughout.[57] The new "bargaining model" of the family has marked advantages over the more organic approach (as we will see further in Chapter 4).

Like the GNP and utility-maximizing approaches (and indeed as a variant of the latter), the Becker model fails to provide an adequate basis for normative thinking in large part because it is not individualistic enough: it does not look at people one by one to see how each one is doing. This would not be a good way to proceed even if the assumption about the head of the household were true: for seeing other family members as recipients of the largesse of a beneficent altruist is not the same thing as seeing them as agents, each with a life to live, deserving of both respect and resources. But it is even more inadequate when we acknowledge that heads of households do not allow all family members what they need, and are sometimes quite indifferent to their well-being. To the extent that women often acquiesce in such schemes and adapt their preferences accordingly, the Becker model may provide correct predictions; but once we recognize how unreliable preferences are as a guide to justice and social choice, we must conclude that it provides a bad basis for normative thought. We need to ask not just what family members feel about their situations, but what they are actually able to do and to be.

Distinctly more promising is our third major alternative, an approach that looks at a group of basic resources and then asks about their distribution, advancing criteria for a fair social allocation. The most famous such approach is that of John Rawls, who, in *A Theory*

1995), 648: "Many economists, including me, have excessively relied on altruism to tie together the interests of family members." He mentions guilt, affection, obligation, anger, and fear of physical abuse as factors that need to be taken into account.

57 See A. Sen, "Gender and Cooperative Conflicts," in I. Tinker, ed., *Persistent Inequalities* (New York: Oxford University Press, 1990), 123–49; Partha Dasgupta, *An Inquiry into Well-Being and Destitution* (Oxford: Clarendon Press, 1993), Chapter 11. For other useful examples of bargaining approaches, see Agarwal, *A Field of One's Own* and "Bargaining"; Shelly Lundberg and Robert A. Pollak, "Bargaining and Distribution in Marriage," *Journal of Economic Perspectives* 10 (1996), 139–58; L. Chen, E. Huq, and S. D'Souza, "Sex Bias in the Family Allocation of Food and Health Care in Rural Bangladesh," *Population and Development Review* 7 (1981), 55–70.

of Justice and subsequent works, has advanced a list of the "primary goods," items that all rational individuals, regardless of their more comprehensive plans of life, would desire as prerequisites for carrying out those plans.[58] Rawls's list is heterogeneous. It includes liberties, opportunities, and powers, which are capacities of citizens in their social environment.[59] Structurally similar is the social basis of self-respect, a feature of society in relation to the powers of persons; Rawls calls this "the most important of the primary goods."[60] At the same time, however, the list includes thing-like items, above all wealth and income, and these items have a particularly central role on the list, since they are used to define the class of the least well-off.[61] The basic idea is that, whatever else citizens pursue, they should be able to arrive at a working political consensus about the central importance of these basic resources and about some rough criteria for their fair distribution. There are special issues about how Rawls models the family, which will be addressed in Chapter 4. At this point I shall concentrate on some general features of Rawls's approach to primary goods, mentioning the household only where it seems important for the treatment of that issue.

Rawls's approach is very promising in terms of all our concerns so

---

58 Rawls, TJ, 62–65, 90–95, 396–7. More recently, Rawls has qualified his view of primary goods by stating that they are to be seen not as all-purpose means, but as the needs of citizens understood from a political point of view, in connection with the development and expression of their "moral powers." He has stressed that the account of the moral powers (of forming and revising a life plan) is itself one important part of the political theory of the good: see Rawls, PL, 178–90.
59 More recently, Rawls has added freedom of movement and the free choice of occupation: PL, 181.
60 Rawls, TJ, 396, 440.
61 Rawls, TJ, 97: "[T]aking these individuals as specified by levels of income and wealth, I assume that these primary social goods are sufficiently correlated with those of power and authority to avoid an index problem . . . On the whole, this assumption seems safe enough for our purposes." The problem is all the greater when we recognize that Rawls's parties are heads of households who bargain, Becker-fashion, on behalf of the entire household; and yet the relation between the income/wealth of a household and women's powers and opportunities may be highly insecure. Self-respect may be insecurely correlated with all of the other primary goods; thus Jews in Europe in many cases did well enough on income and wealth, but very poorly on the social bases of self-respect. Later Rawls recognizes this problem, saying that "the initial definition of expectations solely by reference to such things as liberty and wealth is provisional; it is necessary to include other kinds of primary goods and these raise deeper questions" (396–7). We are never told, however, how to solve the problem.

far. It is highly attentive to concerns about pluralism and paternalism, and yet at the same time it takes a stand about the importance of basic liberties and opportunities for all citizens, and about the importance of the material basis of these central areas of choice. In all these respects, Rawls's model seems to provide an excellent basis for further thought about quality of life in the international arena.

Rawls himself pulls back at this point, preferring to regard the political conception of the person, together with the picture of primary goods, as grounding a consensus only within a particular Western tradition of political philosophy.[62] In reality, however, there seems no reason to think that any of the primary goods is particularly Western, nor that the power of forming and revising a plan of life expresses a distinctively Western sense of what is important. The idea of being able to plan and to execute a plan arises without any philosophical backing, out of the struggle of human beings to live in a hostile environment. Certainly these ideas have indigenous roots in the Indian women's movement, where no concepts are more centrally stressed than those of reflection, choice, planning, and control, and where it is perfectly clear that these activities have a material basis in property rights, land rights, access to employment, and so forth. Vasanti's struggle to be in a position to support herself and carry out her plans without being dependent on her brothers is just one example of a general phenomenon. The SEWA movement as a whole is built around the idea of the dignity and independence of the individual, her control over her own material and social environment. As Ela Bhatt says, women don't just want a piece of the pie; they want to choose its flavor themselves and to know how to make it themselves.

Far from being a Western import, this idea, insofar as it is inspired by anything outside women's daily situation, has Gandhian roots. It translates the Gandhian idea of India's self-sufficiency in the colonial struggle against Britain onto the plane of the family and the village, where women, too, struggle to be free from a quasi-colonial oppression.[63] John Stuart Mill emphasized that struggling against the subjec-

---

62 See Rawls, PL, 4–11, and "The Law of Peoples," in *On Human Rights: The Oxford Amnesty Lectures 1993*, ed. Stephen Shute and Susan Hurley (New York: Basic Books, 1993), 41–72, at 50–59. In the latter work, the equality of women is one value that Rawls is prepared to affirm cross-culturally.

63 Personal communication, Mirai Chatterjee, Renana Jhabvala, and Ela Bhatt, SEWA,

tion of women in the family is isomorphic to, and expressive of the same concerns as, the struggle waged by democracy against feudalism.[64] The women of SEWA (and many other working women in similar movements throughout India) independently make the same connection: far from being colonialist, ideas of individual life-control and life-planning are an expression of the struggle against colonialism. People don't need Western philosophers to tell them that they don't like to be pushed around by the world, or to live in a condition of helplessness.

But Rawls's approach, even though more promising as a basis for international thinking than Rawls himself is willing to suggest, nonetheless has some serious difficulties. By measuring who is better off and who worse off in terms of resources, the Rawlsian model neglects a salient fact of life: that individuals vary greatly in their needs for resources and in their abilities to convert resources into valuable functionings. Some of these differences are straightforwardly physical. Nutritional needs vary with age, occupation, and sex. A pregnant or lactating woman needs more nutrients than a nonpregnant woman. A child needs more protein than an adult. A person whose limbs work well needs few resources to be mobile, whereas a person with paralyzed limbs needs many more resources to achieve the same level of mobility. Many such variations can escape our notice if we live in a prosperous nation that can afford to bring all individuals to a high level of physical attainment; in the developing world we must be highly alert to these variations in need. Again, some of the pertinent variations are social, associated with traditional hierarchies. If we wish to bring all citizens of a nation to a given basic level of educational attainment, we will need to devote more resources to those who encounter obstacles from traditional hierarchy or prejudice: thus women's literacy will prove more expensive than men's literacy in many parts of the world. The resource-based approach doesn't go deep enough to diagnose obstacles that can be present even when resources seem to be adequately spread around, causing individuals to neglect to avail themselves of opportu-

March 1997; see also Rose, *Where Women*, 32. Rose notes that the dependence goes in two directions: "Gandhi himself ascribed the tactics employed in the freedom struggle to the tactics he had observed his wife and mother using at home to resist their own exploitation."

64 *The Subjection of Women* (1869), ed. S. M. Okin (Indianapolis: Hackett, 1988), hereinafter SW, especially 16–18; see my "The Feminist Critique of Liberalism."

nities that they in some sense have (such as free public education, or the vote, or the right to work). If we operate only with an index of resources, we will frequently reinforce inequalities that are highly relevant to well-being. This is an especially grave defect when it is women's quality of life we want to consider; for women who begin from a position of traditional deprivation and powerlessness will frequently require special attention and aid to arrive at a level of capability that the more powerful can more easily attain.

Thus even the Rawlsian approach, in the end, doesn't sufficiently respect the struggle of each and every individual for flourishing. To treat A and B as equally well-off because they command the same amount of resources is, in a crucial way, to neglect A's separate and distinct life, to pretend that A's circumstances are interchangeable with B's, which may not be the case. To do justice to A's struggles, we must see them in their social context, aware of the obstacles that the context offers to the struggle for liberty, opportunity, and material well-being. In his discussions of liberty and opportunity, Rawls shows himself well aware that a theory of justice must be cognizant of the different situations of distinct lives, in order to distribute not only liberty, but also equal worth; not only formal equality of opportunity, but also truly fair equality of opportunity. His emphasis on wealth and income as primary goods central to the task of indexing, however, sells short his own respect for the individual.

To sum up: We want an approach that is respectful of each person's struggle for flourishing, that treats each person as an end and as a source of agency and worth in her own right. Part of this respect will mean not being dictatorial about the good, at least for adults and at least in some core areas of choice, leaving individuals a wide space for important types of choice and meaningful affiliation. But this very respect means taking a stand on the conditions that permit them to follow their own lights free from tyrannies imposed by politics and tradition. This, in turn, requires both generality and particularity: both some overarching benchmarks and detailed knowledge of the variety of circumstances and cultures in which people are striving to do well. The shortcomings of both the utilitarian and the resource-based approaches suggest that we will take a stand in the most appropriate way if we focus not on satisfaction or the mere presence of resources, but on what individuals are actually able to do and to be. General benchmarks based on utility or on resources turn out to be insensitive to contextual variation, to the way circumstances shape preferences and the ability of individuals to convert resources into meaningful human activity. Only a broad concern for functioning and capability can do justice to the complex interrelationships between human striving and its material and social context.

IV. CENTRAL HUMAN CAPABILITIES

The most interesting worries about universals thus lead us to prefer universals of a particular type. I shall now argue that a reasonable answer to all these concerns, capable of giving good guidance to governments and international agencies, is found in a version of the *capabilities approach* – an approach to quality of life assessment pioneered within economics by Amartya Sen,[65] and by now highly influential through the *Human Development Reports* of the United Nations Development Programme (UNDP).[66] My own version of this approach (which began independently of Sen's work through thinking about Aristotle's ideas of human functioning and Marx's use of them)[67] is in several ways different from Sen's, both in its emphasis on the philosophical underpinnings of the approach and in its readiness to take a stand on what the central capabilities are.[68] Sen has focused on the role of capabilities in demarcating the space within which quality of life assessments are made; I use the idea in a more exigent way, as a foundation for basic political principles that should underwrite constitu-

---

65 The initial statement is in Sen, "Equality of What?" in S. McMurrin, ed., *Tanner Lectures on Human Values* 1 (Cambridge: Cambridge University Press, 1980), reprinted in Sen, *Choice, Welfare, and Measurement* (Oxford and Cambridge, MA: Basil Blackwell and MIT Press, 1982), hereinafter CWM; see also his various essays in *Resources, Values, and Development* (Oxford and Cambridge, MA: Basil Blackwell and MIT Press, 1984), hereinafter RVD; *Commodities and Capabilities* (Amsterdam: North-Holland, 1985); *Well-Being, Agency, and Freedom: The Dewey Lectures 1984, The Journal of Philosophy* 82 (1985); "Capability and Well-Being," in QL, 30–53; "Gender Inequality and Theories of Justice," in WCD, 153–98; *Inequality Reexamined* (Oxford and Cambridge, MA: Clarendon Press and Harvard University Press, 1992).

66 *Human Development Reports: 1993, 1994, 1995, 1996, 1997* (New York: United Nations Development Programme).

67 See NFC, HN.

68 For a discussion of differences between our approaches, see David Crocker, "Functioning and Capability: The Foundations of Sen's and Nussbaum's Development Ethic, Part I," *Political Theory* 20 (1992), 584–612, and ". . . Part II," in WCD, 153–98.

tional guarantees. I shall not comment on those differences further here, but simply lay out the approach as I would currently defend it. Like any universal approach, it is only valuable if developed in a relevant way: so we need to worry not just about the structure of the approach, but also about how to flesh out its content in a way that focuses appropriately on women's lives. Otherwise promising approaches have frequently gone wrong by ignoring the problems women actually face. But the capabilities approach directs us to examine real lives in their material and social settings; there is thus reason for hope that it may overcome this difficulty.

The central question asked by the capabilities approach is not, "How satisfied is Vasanti?" or even "How much in the way of resources is she able to command?" It is, instead, "What is Vasanti actually able to do and to be?" Taking a stand for political purposes on a working list of functions that would appear to be of central importance in human life, we ask: Is the person capable of this, or not? We ask not only about the person's satisfaction with what she does, but about what she does, and what she is in a position to do (what her opportunities and liberties are). And we ask not just about the resources that are sitting around, but about how those do or do not go to work, enabling Vasanti to function in a fully human way.

Having discovered some answers to these questions, we now put the approach to work in two closely related ways. First, it is in terms of these capabilities to function in certain core areas that we would measure Vasanti's quality of life, comparing her quality of life to that of others. When we aggregate the data from different lives to produce accounts of regional, class, and national differences in quality of life, it is always in the space of the central capabilities that we make those comparisons, defining the least well-off and the adequately well-off in this way. Second, we then argue that in certain core areas of human functioning a necessary condition of justice for a public political arrangement is that it deliver to citizens a certain basic level of capability. If people are systematically falling below the threshold in any of these core areas, this should be seen as a situation both unjust and tragic, in need of urgent attention – even if in other respects things are going well.

The intuitive idea behind the approach is twofold: first, that certain functions are particularly central in human life, in the sense that their presence or absence is typically understood to be a mark of the presence or absence of human life;[69] and second – this is what Marx found in Aristotle – that there is something that it is to do these functions in a truly human way, not a merely animal way. We judge, frequently enough, that a life has been so impoverished that it is not worthy of the dignity of the human being, that it is a life in which one goes on living, but more or less like an animal, unable to develop and exercise one's human powers. In Marx's example, a starving person doesn't use food in a fully human way – by which I think he means a way infused by practical reasoning and sociability. He or she just grabs at the food in order to survive, and the many social and rational ingredients of human feeding can't make their appearance. Similarly, he argues that the senses of a human being can operate at a merely animal level – if they are not cultivated by appropriate education, by leisure for play and self-expression, by valuable associations with others; and we should add to the list some items that Marx probably would not endorse, such as expressive and associational liberty, and the freedom of worship. The core idea is that of the human being as a dignified free being who shapes his or her own life in cooperation and reciprocity with others, rather than being passively shaped or pushed around by the world in the manner of a "flock" or "herd" animal.[70] A life that is really human is one that is shaped throughout by these human powers of practical reason and sociability.

This idea of human dignity has broad cross-cultural resonance and intuitive power. We can think of it as the idea that lies at the heart of tragic artworks, in whatever culture. Think of a tragic character, assailed by fortune. We react to the spectacle of humanity so assailed in a way very different from the way we react to a storm blowing grains

69 For further development of this idea, see HN. For the way in which the capabilities and functionings are individuated, in accordance with an account of distinct spheres of human experience and choice, see NRV.
70 Compare Amartya Sen, "Freedoms and Needs," *The New Republic*, January 10/17, 1994, p. 38: "The importance of political rights for the understanding of economic needs turns ultimately on seeing human beings as people with rights to exercise, not as parts of a 'stock' or a 'population' that passively exists and must be looked after." An excellent treatment of Marx's thought on this issue, with implications for contemporary debates, is in Daniel Brudney, "Community and Completion," in *Reclaiming the History of Ethics: Essays for John Rawls* (Cambridge: Cambridge University Press, 1997), 388–415, although Brudney defends the Marxian view as the basis for a form of comprehensive, rather than political, liberalism.

of sand in the wind. For we see a human being as having worth as an end, a kind of awe-inspiring something that makes it horrible to see this person beaten down by the currents of chance – and wonderful, at the same time, to witness the way in which chance has not completely eclipsed the humanity of the person.[71] As Aristotle puts it, "the noble shines through." Such responses provide us with strong incentives for protecting that in persons that fills us with awe. We see the person as having activity, goals, and projects – as somehow awe-inspiringly above the mechanical workings of nature, and yet in need of support for the fulfillment of many central projects.[72] This idea has many forms, some religious and some secular. Insofar as we are able to respond to tragic tales from other cultures, we show that this idea of human worth and agency crosses cultural boundaries.

At one extreme, we may judge that the absence of capability for a central function is so acute that the person is not really a human being at all, or any longer – as in the case of certain very severe forms of mental disability, or senile dementia. But I am less interested in that boundary (important though it is for medical ethics) than in a higher threshold, the level at which a person's capability becomes what Marx called "truly human," that is, *worthy* of a human being. Note that this idea contains, thus, a reference to an idea of human worth or dignity. Marx was departing from Kant in some important respects, by stressing (along with Aristotle) that the major powers of a human being need material support and cannot be what they are without it. But he also learned from Kant, and his way of expressing his Aristotelian heritage is distinctively shaped by the Kantian notion of the inviolability and the dignity of the person.

Notice that the approach makes each person a bearer of value, and an end. Marx, like his bourgeois forebears, holds that it is profoundly wrong to subordinate the ends of some individuals to those of others. That is at the core of what exploitation is, to treat a person as a mere object for the use of others. Thus it will be just as repugnant to this

---

71 See Seneca, *Moral Epistle* 41, comparing the dignity of such a person to the awe-inspiring sublimity of nature. This passage very likely influenced Kant's famous conclusion to the *Critique of Practical Reason*.

72 For elaboration of this part of the idea, see my "Victims and Agents," *The Boston Review* 23 (1998), 21–24, and "Political Animals: Luck, Love, and Dignity," *Metaphilosophy* 29 (1998), 273–87.

Marxian approach as to a bourgeois philosophy to foster a good for society considered as an organic whole, where this does not involve the fostering of the good of persons taken one by one. What this approach is after is a society in which persons are treated as each worthy of regard, and in which each has been put in a position to live really humanly. (That is where the idea of a threshold comes in: we say that beneath a certain level of capability, in each area, a person has not been enabled to live in a truly human way.) We may thus rephrase our *principle of each person as end*, articulating it as a *principle of each person's capability*: the capabilities sought are sought for *each and every person*, not, in the first instance, for groups or families or states or other corporate bodies. Such bodies may be extremely important in promoting human capabilities, and in this way they may deservedly gain our support: but it is because of what they do for people that they are so worthy, and the ultimate political goal is always the promotion of the capabilities of *each person*.

I believe that we can arrive at an enumeration of central elements of truly human functioning that can command a broad cross-cultural consensus. (One way of seeing this is to think about the ways in which tragic plots cross cultural boundaries: certain deprivations are understood to be terrible, despite differences in metaphysical understandings of the world.) Although this list of central capabilities is somewhat different in both structure and substance from Rawls's list of primary goods, it is offered in a similar political-liberal spirit: as a list that can be endorsed for political purposes, as the moral basis of central constitutional guarantees, by people who otherwise have very different views of what a complete good life for a human being would be. (In part, as we shall see, this is because the list is a list of capabilities or opportunities for functioning, rather than of actual functions; in part it is because the list protects spaces for people to pursue other functions that they value.)

The list provides the underpinnings of basic political principles that can be embodied in constitutional guarantees. For this purpose, it isolates those human capabilities that can be convincingly argued to be of central importance in any human life, whatever else the person pursues or chooses. The central capabilities are not just instrumental to further pursuits: they are held to have value in themselves, in making the life that includes them fully human. But they are held to have a particularly pervasive and central role in everything else people plan and do. In that sense, too, they play a role analogous to that of primary goods in Rawls's recent (political-liberal) theory: they have a special importance in making any choice of a way of life possible, and so they have a special claim to be supported for political purposes in a pluralistic society.[73]

A list of the central capabilities is not a complete theory of justice. Such a list gives us the basis for determining a decent social minimum in a variety of areas.[74] I argue that the structure of social and political institutions should be chosen, at least in part, with a view to promoting at least a threshold level of these human capabilities. But the provision of a threshold level of capability, exigent though that goal is, may not suffice for justice, as I shall elaborate further later, discussing the relationship between the social minimum and our interest in equality. The determination of such additional requirements of justice awaits another inquiry. Moreover, in order to describe how a threshold level of capability might best be secured, much more needs to be said about the appropriate role of the public sphere vis-à-vis incentives to private actors, and also about how far the public sphere is entitled to control the activities of private actors in the pursuit of the capabilities on the list. We could agree that the space of capabilities is the relevant space in which to make such comparisons, and that a basic social minimum in the area of the central capabilities should be secured to all citizens, while disagreeing about the role to be played by government and public planning in their promotion. Since a general answer to this question requires us to answer economic questions that are not in the province of my inquiry, I shall not give a general answer here, although Chapters 3 and 4 will discuss the proper role of law in some particular areas of capability promotion. Many other questions treated by theories of justice are also left undecided by this account of capability.[75]

---

73 As section VII will show, I also envisage a role for international agencies and international human rights law in implementing these capabilities; but on grounds of accountability, the nation state remains the basic unit.

74 To perform this function in a useful way the list must have a more clearly demarcated account of the threshold level than it does in its present form; I discuss that issue later in this section, and in Chapters 3 and 4.

75 Among these topics are the role of private and public property; the idea of justice between generations; the role of civil disobedience; and – with the exception of some brief remarks in section VII – redistributive justice between nations.

The list represents the result of years of cross-cultural discussion, and comparisons between earlier and later versions will show that the input of other voices has shaped its content in many ways. Thus it already represents what it proposes: a type of *overlapping consensus*[76] on the part of people with otherwise very different views of human life. In Chapter 2 I shall argue that this fact about how the list has evolved helps to justify it in an ancillary way, although the primary weight of justification remains with the intuitive conception of truly human functioning and what that entails. By "overlapping consensus" I mean what John Rawls means: that people may sign on to this conception as the freestanding moral core of a political conception, without accepting any particular metaphysical view of the world, any particular comprehensive ethical or religious view, or even any particular view of the person or of human nature. Indeed, it is to be expected that holders of different views in those areas will even interpret the moral core of the political conception to some extent differently, in keeping with their different starting points.[77] Thus, a Muslim may say, "Women are equal as citizens in the political conception because men and women share a single metaphysical essential nature." Some Jews[78] and Christians could say, by contrast, "Women are equal as citizens despite the fact that they have a different essential nature from that of men." A Catholic Thomist may interpret "practical reason" by thinking about St. Thomas's Aristotelian conception of choice. Others will think of choice in a more informal manner, based on their daily experience of planning and deciding. A Finn may interpret play and recreation in terms of a comprehensive conception of life in which solitary contemplation in the forest plays a large role; a resident of Calcutta is likely to have a different set of comprehensive associations in mind. As I interpret Aristotle, he understood the core of his account of human functioning to be a freestanding moral conception, not one that is deduced from natural teleology or any non-moral source.[79] Whether or not I am correct about Aristotle, however, my own neo-Aristotelian proposal is intended in

---

76 See Rawls, PL, 133–72.
77 See Rawls, PL, 144–5.
78 Not all, however: see my "Judaism and the Love of Reason," in Marya Bower and Ruth Groenhout, eds., *Among Sophia's Daughters: Philosophy, Feminism, and the Demands of Faith*, forthcoming.
79 See HN.

that spirit – and also (clearly unlike Aristotle's) as a partial, not a comprehensive, conception of the good life, a moral conception selected for political purposes only.

Since the intuitive conception of human functioning and capability demands continued reflection and testing against our intuitions, we should view any given version of the list as a proposal put forward in a Socratic fashion, to be tested against the most secure of our intuitions as we attempt to arrive at a type of reflective equilibrium for political purposes. (I shall discuss this issue of political justification further in section VII.)

Some items on the list may seem to us more fixed than others. For example, it would be astonishing if the right to bodily integrity were to be removed from the list; that seems to be a fixed point in our considered judgments of goodness.[80] On the other hand, one might debate what role is played by literacy in human functioning, and what role is played by our relationship to other species and the world of nature. In this sense, the list remains open-ended and humble; it can always be contested and remade. Nor does it deny that the items on the list are to some extent differently constructed by different societies. Indeed, part of the idea of the list is its *multiple realizability*: its members can be more concretely specified in accordance with local beliefs and circumstances. It is thus designed to leave room for a reasonable pluralism in specification. The threshold level of each of the central capabilities will need more precise determination, as citizens work toward a consensus for political purposes. This can be envisaged as taking place within each constitutional tradition, as it evolves through interpretation and deliberation. (Most fundamental constitutional rights are initially described at a high level of generality, but this does not mean that they are impractical or non-justiciable: the tradition of interpretation and precedent provides the relevant specifications.) Finally, in its relatively concrete remarks about matters such as literacy and basic scientific education, the list is intended for the modern world, rather than as timeless.[81]

Here is the current version of the list:[82]

---

80 I borrow the phrasing, of course, from Rawls, TJ, substituting "goodness" for "justice," in keeping with the fact that we are talking about the analogue of "primary goods."

81 Some of the items are more timeless than others, clearly. Literacy is a concrete specifi-

CENTRAL HUMAN FUNCTIONAL CAPABILITIES

1. **Life.** Being able to live to the end of a human life of normal length; not dying prematurely, or before one's life is so reduced as to be not worth living.

2. **Bodily Health.** Being able to have good health, including reproductive health;[83] to be adequately nourished; to have adequate shelter.

3. **Bodily Integrity.** Being able to move freely from place to place; having one's bodily boundaries treated as sovereign, i.e. being able to be secure against assault, including sexual assault, child sexual abuse, and domestic violence; having opportunities for sexual satisfaction and for choice in matters of reproduction.

4. **Senses, Imagination, and Thought.** Being able to use the senses, to imagine, think, and reason – and to do these things in a "truly human" way, a way informed and cultivated by an adequate education, including, but

cation for the modern world of a more general capability that may have been realized without literacy in other times and places. All the large general rubrics appear rather timeless, though I do not claim, or need to claim, that human life exhibits an unchanging essence throughout history.

82 The current version of the list reflects changes made as a result of my discussions with people in India. The primary changes are a greater emphasis on bodily integrity and control over one's environment (including property rights and employment opportunities), and a new emphasis on dignity and non-humiliation. Oddly, these features of human "self-sufficiency" and the dignity of the person are the ones most often criticized by Western feminists as "male" and "Western," one reason for their more muted role in earlier versions of the list. See my "The Feminist Critique of Liberalism."

83 The 1994 International Conference on Population and Development (ICPD) adopted a definition of reproductive health that fits well with the intuitive idea of truly human functioning that guides this list: "Reproductive health is a state of complete physical, mental and social well-being and not merely the absence of disease or infirmity, in all matters relating to the reproductive system and its processes. Reproductive health therefore implies that people are able to have a satisfying and safe sex life and that they have the capability to reproduce and the freedom to decide if, when, and how often to do so." The definition goes on say that it also implies information and access to family planning methods of their choice. A brief summary of the ICPD's recommendations, adopted by the Panel on Reproductive Health of the Committee on Population established by the National Research Council, specifies three requirements of reproductive health: "1. Every sex act should be free of coercion and infection. 2. Every pregnancy should be intended. 3. Every birth should be healthy." See Amy O. Tsui, Judith N. Wasserheit, and John G. Haaga, eds., *Reproductive Health in Developing Countries* (Washington, D.C.: National Academy Press, 1997), 13–14.

by no means limited to, literacy and basic mathematical and scientific training. Being able to use imagination and thought in connection with experiencing and producing self-expressive works and events of one's own choice, religious, literary, musical, and so forth. Being able to use one's mind in ways protected by guarantees of freedom of expression with respect to both political and artistic speech, and freedom of religious exercise. Being able to search for the ultimate meaning of life in one's own way. Being able to have pleasurable experiences, and to avoid non-necessary pain.

5. **Emotions.** Being able to have attachments to things and people outside ourselves; to love those who love and care for us, to grieve at their absence; in general, to love, to grieve, to experience longing, gratitude, and justified anger. Not having one's emotional development blighted by overwhelming fear and anxiety, or by traumatic events of abuse or neglect. (Supporting this capability means supporting forms of human association that can be shown to be crucial in their development.)

6. **Practical Reason.** Being able to form a conception of the good and to engage in critical reflection about the planning of one's life. (This entails protection for the liberty of conscience.)

7. **Affiliation. A.** Being able to live with and toward others, to recognize and show concern for other human beings, to engage in various forms of social interaction; to be able to imagine the situation of another and to have compassion for that situation; to have the capability for both justice and friendship. (Protecting this capability means protecting institutions that constitute and nourish such forms of affiliation, and also protecting the freedom of assembly and political speech.)
B. Having the social bases of self-respect and non-humiliation; being able to be treated as a dignified being whose worth is equal to that of others. This entails, at a minimum, protections against discrimination on the basis of race, sex, sexual orientation, religion, caste, ethnicity, or national origin.[84] In work, being able to work as a human being, exer-

---

84 This provision is based on the Indian Constitution, Article 15, which adds (as I would) that this should not be taken to prevent government from enacting measures to correct the history of discrimination against women and against the scheduled tribes and castes. Nondiscrimination on the basis of sexual orientation is not guaranteed by the Indian Constitution, and in earlier versions of the list I did not include it, judging that there was so little consensus on this item, especially in India, that its inclusion might seem premature – although at the same time I stressed the fact that I believe it to be

cising practical reason and entering into meaningful relationships of mutual recognition with other workers.

8. **Other Species.** Being able to live with concern for and in relation to animals, plants, and the world of nature.[85]

9. **Play.** Being able to laugh, to play, to enjoy recreational activities.

10. **Control over One's Environment. A. Political.** Being able to participate effectively in political choices that govern one's life; having the right of political participation, protections of free speech and association.
    B. Material. Being able to hold property (both land and movable goods), not just formally but in terms of real opportunity; and having property rights on an equal basis with others; having the right to seek employment on an equal basis with others; having the freedom from unwarranted search and seizure.[86]

implied by a right to nondiscrimination on the basis of sex, since I view sexual-orientation discrimination as a means of shoring up binary divisions between the sexes that are implicated in sex discrimination. See the Introduction and Chapter 7 in my *Sex and Social Justice*. This year, however, the controversy over the disruption of the feminist film *Fire* has led to much more discussion of sexual orientation in the Indian media, and to a public recognition by feminists and other liberal thinkers of the important links between these issues and women's full equality. I therefore think it no longer premature to add this item to a cross-cultural list that is expected to command an overlapping consensus. I shall discuss this issue further in Chapter 4.

85 In terms of cross-cultural development, this has been the most controversial item on the list: see Chapter 2 for further discussion. Government can do quite a lot about this capability, through its choices of policy regarding endangered species, the health and life of animals, and the ecology. Norway, for example, places tremendous emphasis on this capability. In Oslo one may build only within five miles of the coast; past that "forest line," the inland mountainous region is kept free of habitation to preserve spaces for people to enjoy solitude in the forest, a central aspect of this capability, as Norwegians specify it.

86 ASD argued that property rights are distinct from, for example, speech rights, in the sense that property is a tool of human functioning and not an end in itself. The current version of the list still insists that more property is not ipso facto better, but it expands the role of property rights, seeing the intimate relationship between property rights and self-definition: see Chapter 2 for further discussion. Most obviously, property rights should not be allocated on a sex-discriminatory basis, as they currently are under some of the systems of personal law in India. But it is also important to think of their absolute value, as supports for other valuable forms of human functioning. Thus all citizens should have some property, real or movable, in their own names. The amount requisite will properly be deliberated by each state in the light of its economic situation. Land is frequently a particularly valuable source of self-definition, bargaining power, and economic sustenance, so one might use the list to justify land reforms that appropriate surplus land from the rich in order to give the poor something to call their own. For example, the reform in West Bengal took wealthy landowners' second homes for this purpose. See also CHR.

The list is, emphatically, a list of *separate components*. We cannot satisfy the need for one of them by giving a larger amount of another one. All are of central importance and all are distinct in quality. The irreducible plurality of the list limits the trade-offs that it will be reasonable to make, and thus limits the applicability of quantitative cost-benefit analysis. One may, of course, always use cost-benefit analysis; but if one does so in connection with this approach, it will be crucial to represent in the weightings the fact that each and every one of a plurality of distinct goods is of central importance, and thus there is a tragic aspect to any choice in which citizens are pushed below the threshold in one of the central areas. That tragic aspect could be represented as simply a huge cost; but it is hard to represent clearly in this way the fact that a *distinctive* good is being slighted. One should not suppose, for example, that the absence of the political liberties would be made up for by tremendous economic growth, although the use of a single measure might easily make one think in this way.[87]

At the same time, the items on the list are related to one another in many complex ways. One of the most effective ways of promoting women's control over their environment, and their effective right of political participation, is to promote women's literacy. Women who can seek employment outside the home have exit options that help them protect their bodily integrity from assaults within it. Reproductive health is related in many complex ways to practical reason and bodily integrity. This gives us still more reason to avoid promoting one at the expense of the others.

Some of the items on the list are, or include, what John Rawls has called "natural goods," goods in whose acquisition luck plays a substantial role. Thus, governments cannot hope to make all citizens healthy, or emotionally balanced, since some of the determinants of those positive states are natural or luck-governed. In these areas, what government can aim to deliver is the *social basis of* these capabilities. The capabilities approach insists that this requires doing a great deal to make up for differences in starting point that are caused by natural endowment or by power, but it is still the social basis of the good, not

---

87 Thus phrases such as "Singapore success story" might have been harder to use had the measure of quality of life in terms of GNP per capita not been dominant in development policy.

the good itself, that society can reliably provide. Take women's emotional health. Government cannot make all women emotionally healthy; but it can do quite a lot to influence emotional health, through suitable policies in areas such as family law, rape law, and public safety. Something similar will be true of all the natural goods. But factors we cannot control may still interfere to keep some people from full capability. When we use capabilities as a comparative measure of quality of life, we must therefore still inquire about the reasons for the differences we observe. Some differences in health among nations or groups are due to factors public policy can control, and others are not. Basic political principles have done their job if they have provided people with the full social basis of these capabilities. (See section V for further discussion of this point.)

Among the capabilities, two, *practical reason* and *affiliation*, stand out as of special importance, since they both organize and suffuse all the others, making their pursuit truly human. To use one's senses in a way not infused by the characteristically human use of thought and planning is to use them in an incompletely human manner.[88] To plan for one's own life without being able to do so in complex forms of discourse, concern, and reciprocity with other human beings is, again, to behave in an incompletely human way.[89] To take just one example, work, to be a truly human mode of functioning, must involve the availability of both practical reason and affiliation. It must involve being able to behave as a thinking being, not just a cog in a machine; and it must be capable of being done with and toward others in a way that involves mutual recognition of humanity.[90] Women's work lacks this feature even more often than does men's work.

When we make practical reason and affiliation central in this way, we are not saying that these are two ends to which all the others can be reduced. We are not saying, for example, that health is a mere means to freedom of choice. But we are saying that a government that makes available only a reduced and animal-like mode of an important item such as healthy living, or sensing, has not done enough. All the items on the list should be available in a form that involves reason and affil-

88 See HN, ASD.
89 See HN on the role of this idea in myths of transformation to and from the human.
90 On Marx's view, see Brudney, cited earlier.

iation. This sets constraints on where we set the threshold, for each of the separate capabilities, and also constraints on which specifications of it we will accept.

The basic intuition from which the capability approach begins, in the political arena, is that certain human abilities exert a moral claim that they should be developed. Once again, this must be understood as *a freestanding moral idea*, not one that relies on a particular metaphysical or teleological view. Not all actual human abilities exert a moral claim, only the ones that have been evaluated as valuable from an ethical viewpoint. (The capacity for cruelty, for example, does not figure on the list.) Thus the argument begins from ethical premises and derives ethical conclusions from these alone, not from any further metaphysical premises.[91] Nonetheless, it seems to me that we can get a consensus of the requisite sort, for political purposes, about the core of our moral argument concerning the moral claim of certain human powers. Human beings are creatures such that, provided with the right educational and material support, they can become fully capable of all these human functions. That is, they are creatures with certain lower-level capabilities (which I call "basic capabilities")[92] to perform the functions in question. When these capabilities are deprived of the nourishment that would transform them into the higher-level capabilities that figure on the list, they are fruitless, cut off, in some way but a shadow of themselves. When a turtle is given a life that affords a merely animal level of functioning, we have no indignation, no sense of waste and tragedy. When a human being is given a life that blights powers of human action and expression, that does give us a sense of waste and tragedy – the tragedy expressed, for example, in Mrinal's statement to her husband, in Tagore's story, when she says, "I am not one to die easily." In her view, a life without dignity and choice, a life in which she can be no more than an appendage of someone else, is a type of death, the death of her humanity. "I have just started living," she ends her letter – and signs it, "This is from Mrinal – who is torn off the shelter of your feet." This sense of tragedy crosses cultural boundaries; it does not depend upon any particular metaphysical view of human nature.

91 See HN, with my argument that this is also Aristotle's view.
92 See NFC, with reference to Aristotle's ways of characterizing levels of *dunamis*.

We begin, then, with a sense of the worth and dignity of basic human powers, thinking of them as claims to a chance for functioning, claims that give rise to correlated social and political duties. And in fact there are three different types of capabilities that play a role in the analysis.[93] First, there are *basic capabilities*: the innate equipment of individuals that is the necessary basis for developing the more advanced capabilities, and a ground of moral concern. These capabilities are sometimes more or less ready to function: the capability for seeing and hearing is usually like this. More often, however, they are very rudimentary, and cannot be directly converted into functioning. A newborn child has, in this sense, the capability for speech and language, the capability for love and gratitude, the capability for practical reason, the capacity for work.

Second, there are *internal capabilities*: that is, developed states of the person herself that are, so far as the person herself is concerned, sufficient conditions for the exercise of the requisite functions. Unlike the basic capabilities, these states are mature conditions of readiness. Sometimes readiness simply takes time and bodily maturity: one becomes capable of sexual functioning by simply growing, without much external intervention, although one does need to be adequately nourished. Almost all human children learn to speak their native language: all they need is to hear it spoken enough during a critical period. More often, however, internal capabilities develop only with support from the surrounding environment, as when one learns to play with others, to love, to exercise political choice. But at a certain point they are there, and the person can use them. A woman who has not suffered genital mutilation has the *internal capability* for sexual pleasure; most adult human beings everywhere have the *internal capability* for religious freedom and the freedom of speech.

But even when people have developed a power (usually with much support from the material and social world), they may be prevented from functioning in accordance with it. Finally, therefore, there are *combined capabilities*,[94] which may be defined as internal capabilities

---

93 See NFC, referring to Aristotle's similar distinctions; and, on the basic capabilities, HC. Sen does not use these three levels explicitly, though in practice many of his statements assume related distinctions.

94 Earlier papers called these "external capabilities" (see NFC), but David Crocker per-

combined with suitable external conditions for the exercise of the function. A woman who is not mutilated but who has been widowed as a child and is forbidden to make another marriage has the internal but not the combined capability for sexual expression (and, in most such cases, for employment, and political participation).[95] Citizens of repressive nondemocratic regimes have the internal but not the combined capability to exercise thought and speech in accordance with their consciences.[96] The list, then, is a list of *combined capabilities*. To realize one of the items on the list for citizens of a nation entails not only promoting appropriate development of their internal powers, but also preparing the environment so that it is favorable for the exercise of practical reason and the other major functions.

The distinction between internal and combined capabilities is not a sharp one, because developing an internal capability usually requires favorable external conditions; indeed, it very often requires practicing the actual function. Nonetheless, the distinction does real work, because even a highly trained capability can be thwarted. We see the distinction most sharply when there is an abrupt change in the material and social environment: a person accustomed to exercising religious freedom and freedom of speech is no longer able to do so. Here we feel convinced that the internal capability is fully present, but the combined capability is not. Where there is lifelong deprivation, the distinction is not so easy to draw: persistent deprivation affects the internal readiness to function. A child raised in an environment without freedom of speech or religion does not develop the same political and religious capabilities as a child who is raised in a nation that protects these liberties. (Chapter 2 will discuss this issue at length.) Even in such a case, however, we can observe many instances in which the distinction is salient. Many women who, driven by material need, are eager to work outside the home, and who have skills that they could use to do

suaded me that this misleadingly suggested a focus on external conditions *rather than* on internal fitness. In reality I mean to suggest the appropriate combination of both "internal" and "external."

95 See Martha A. Chen, *The Lives of Widows in Rural India*, forthcoming; and "A Matter of Survival: Women's Right to Employment in India and Bangladesh," in WCD, 37–57.

96 If repression is sufficiently severe and long-lasting, they may also to some degree lack the internal capability for such expression; see the following discussion.

some work, are prevented from working by familial or religious pressures. By insisting that the capabilities on the list are combined capabilities, I insist on the twofold importance of material and social circumstances, both in training internal capabilities and in letting them express themselves once trained; and I establish that the liberties and opportunities recognized by the list are not to be understood in a purely formal manner. They thus correspond to Rawls's ideas of "the equal worth of liberty" and "truly fair equality of opportunity," rather than to the thinner notions of "formally equal liberty" and "formal equality of opportunity."[97]

A focus on capabilities as social goals is closely related to a *focus on human equality*, in the sense that discrimination on the basis of race, religion, sex, national origin, caste, or ethnicity is taken to be itself a failure of associational capability, a type of indignity or humiliation. And making capabilities the goals entails promoting for all citizens a greater measure of material equality than exists in most societies, since we are unlikely to get all citizens above a minimum threshhold of capability for truly human functioning without some redistributive policies. On the other hand, it is possible for supporters of the general capability goal to differ about the degree of material equality a society focused on capability should seek. Complete egalitarianism,[98] a Rawlsian difference principle, and a weaker focus on a (rather ample) social minimum all would be compatible with the proposal as so far advanced. Where women are concerned, almost all world societies are very far from even providing the basic minimum of truly human functioning, where many or even most women are concerned; I therefore leave the debate about levels of equality for a later stage, when the differences become meaningful in practice.

V. FUNCTIONING AND CAPABILITY

I have spoken both of functioning and of capability. How are they related? Becoming clear about this is crucial to defining the relation of

97 See Rawls, TJ, 204–5, 72–75.
98 Notice, however, that capability equality would not necessarily entail equality of resources: that all depends on how resources affect capabilities once we get well above the threshold. Aristotle thought that we reach a point of negative returns: after a certain "limit," wealth becomes counterproductive, a distraction from the things that matter.

the "capabilities approach" both to Rawlsian liberalism and to our concerns about paternalism and pluralism. For if we were to take functioning itself as the goal of public policy, pushing citizens into functioning in a single determinate manner, the liberal pluralist would rightly judge that we were precluding many choices that citizens may make in accordance with their own conceptions of the good, and perhaps violating their rights. A deeply religious person may prefer not to be well nourished, but to engage in strenuous fasting. Whether for religious or for other reasons, a person may prefer a celibate life to one containing sexual expression. A person may prefer to work with an intense dedication that precludes recreation and play. Am I declaring, by my very use of the list, that such lives are not worthy of the dignity of the human being? And am I instructing government to nudge or push people into functioning of the requisite sort, no matter what they prefer?

It is important that the answer to this question is no. Where adult citizens are concerned, *capability, not functioning, is the appropriate political goal*. This is so because of the very great importance the approach attaches to practical reason, as a good that both suffuses all the other functions, making them human rather than animal,[99] and figures itself as a central function on the list. It is perfectly true that functionings, not simply capabilities, are what render a life fully human, in the sense that if there were no functioning of any kind in a life, we could hardly applaud it, no matter what opportunities it contained. Nonetheless, for political purposes it is appropriate that we shoot for capabilities, and those alone. Citizens must be left free to determine their own course after that. The person with plenty of food may always choose to fast, but there is a great difference between fasting and starving, and it is this difference that I wish to capture. Again, the person who has normal opportunities for sexual satisfaction can always choose a life of celibacy, and my approach says nothing against this. What it does speak against (for example) is the practice of female genital mutilation, which deprives individuals of the opportunity to choose sexual functioning (and indeed, of the opportunity to choose celibacy).[100] A person who has opportunities for play can always choose a workaholic life;

99 See HN and its discussion of Marx.
100 See my "Double Moral Standards?" (a reply to Yael Tamir's "Hands Off Clitoridectomy"), *The Boston Review*, Oct.-Nov. 1996, and in expanded form in *Sex and Social Justice*, Chapter 4; and "Religion and Women's Human Rights."

again, there is a great difference between that chosen life and a life constrained by insufficient maximum-hour protections or the "double day" that makes women unable to play in many parts of the world. Recall that I am not saying that public policy should rest content with *internal capabilities*, while remaining indifferent to the struggles of individuals who have to try to exercise these in a hostile environment. In that sense, my approach is highly attentive to the goal of functioning, and instructs governments to keep it always in view. On the other hand, I am not pushing individuals into the function: once the stage is fully set, the choice is up to them.

The reason for proceeding in this way is, quite simply, the respect we have for people and their choices. Even when we feel confident that we know what a flourishing life is, and that a particular function plays an important role in it, we do not respect people when we dragoon them into this functioning. We set the stage and, as fellow citizens, present whatever arguments we have in favor of a given choice; then the choice is up to them.

A subsidiary argument can also be made, suggested by my remark about celibacy. If people do not have choices, and do what they do because of requirements, their actions may no longer have the same worth, and may in effect be different functions. This point, frequently made by supporters of religious toleration against coerced uniformity, applies as well to other capabilities. Play is not play if it is enforced, love is not love if it is commanded. This suggests a reason why even someone who is confident and dogmatic about a particular conception of the good should prefer capabilities and not functioning as the political goal: functioning of the type this person wants will not arrive at all, if it is made the direct political goal in a way that does not allow latitude for choice. This is a supporting argument; the primary argument is the argument from respect for persons. But it does work to persuade a perfectionist opponent that choice is something worth respecting.

The capabilities approach, as I have articulated it, is very close to Rawls's approach using the notion of primary goods. We can see the list of capabilities as like a long list of opportunities for functioning, such that it is always rational to want them whatever else one wants. If one ends up having a plan of life that does not make use of all of them, one has hardly been harmed by having the chance to choose a life that does. The primary differences between this capabilities list and Rawls's list of primary goods are its length and definiteness; its refusal to make thing-like items, like income and wealth, goals in their own right; and in particular, as I have said, its determination to place on the list the social basis of several goods that Rawls has called "natural goods," such as "health and vigor, intelligence and imagination."[101] Since Rawls has been willing to put the social basis of self-respect on his list, it is not at all clear why he has not made the same move with imagination and health.[102] Rawls's evident concern is that no society can guarantee health to its individuals – in that sense, saying that the goal is full external capability may appear unreasonably idealistic. Some of the capabilities (e.g., some of the political liberties) can be fully guaranteed by society, but many others involve an element of chance and cannot be so guaranteed. My response to this is that, with these items as with self-respect, society can hope to guarantee the *social basis* of these natural goods, and that putting them on the list as a set of political *goals* should therefore be useful as a benchmark for aspiration and comparison. Even though individuals with adequate health support often fall ill, it still makes sense to compare societies by asking about actual health capabilities, since we assume that the comparison will reflect the different inputs of human planning, the different degrees to which the *social basis* of these capabilities has in fact been guaranteed to individuals. Such comparisons can be adjusted to take account of more and less favorable natural situations. (Sometimes it is easier to get information on health achievements than on health capabilities; to some extent we must work with the information we have, while not forgetting the importance of the distinction.) The social minimum, however, requires only the social basis of these natural goods, not the goods themselves.

If we aim to produce adults who have all the capabilities on the list, this will frequently mean requiring certain types of functioning in chil-

101 TJ, 62.
102 Rawls comments that "although their possession is influenced by the basic structure, they are not so directly under its control" (62). This is of course true if we are thinking of health: but if we think of the social basis of health, it is not true. It seems to me that the case for putting these items on the political list is just as strong as the case for the social basis of self-respect. In "The Priority of Right," Rawls suggests putting health on the list.

dren, since, as I have argued, exercising a function in childhood is frequently necessary to produce a mature adult capability. Thus it seems perfectly legitimate to require primary and secondary education, given the role this plays in all the later choices of an adult life. Similarly, it seems legitimate to insist on the health, emotional well-being, bodily integrity, and dignity of children in a way that does not take their choices into account; some of this insisting will be done by parents, but the state has a legitimate role in preventing abuse and neglect. Again: functioning in childhood is necessary for capability in adulthood. The state's interest in adult capabilities gives it a very strong interest in any treatment of children that has a long-term impact on these capabilities; in Chapters 3 and 4 I shall grapple with some of the difficult issues this raises when parental and religious claims conflict with these legitimate governmental interests. Similarly, we will often be justified in restricting the scope of choice for adults who do not have full mental and moral powers, promoting actual functioning (for example, in the areas of health, shelter, bodily integrity) rather than simply capability.

Sometimes the state's role in producing adults who have all the capabilities on the list is understood in a narrow way that focuses on literacy and other basic skills that are important for technical and economic development, and perhaps also on political skills understood in a narrow sense. My argument emphatically opposes such a narrow focus. In order to be doing what they should for their citizens, states must be concerned with all the capabilities, even when these seem not so useful for economic growth, or even for political functioning. A particularly interesting case is the capability to play. Now of course it is fairly obvious that it is not desirable to give adults lives in which there is no chance at all for leisured play and self-expression. But we tend to assume that people will play if given the chance, and we therefore tend to neglect developing the capability to play as a part of a child's preparation for adult functioning. We may suppose that children naturally play and express themselves imaginatively in play. This, however, is not precisely true. In many cultures, little girls never get encouragement to play, and in consequence they really don't know how to play. Kept inside for fear of either danger or impurity, made to do housework, these girls become like old women before they are even young women. Little boys are encouraged to be physically and mentally adventurous; they run around and explore their environment with games and schemes. This kind of human development is simply not available to many girls. In many good educational projects that work with such girls, therefore, a great emphasis is placed on games and play, which are seen as at least as important to human development as literacy and skills.[103] Now one cannot exactly command a little girl to play: in this sense, capability and not functioning is the appropriate goal even for children. But one may require that a lot of time be spent in play activities, and one may require a lot of story-telling and art in the curriculum, precisely in order to promote this capability by requiring functioning that nourishes it.

Even where adults are concerned, we may feel that some of the capabilities are so important, so crucial to the development or maintenance of all the others, that we are sometimes justified in promoting functioning rather than simply capability, within limits set by an appropriate concern for liberty. Thus most modern nations treat health and safety as things not to be left altogether to people's choices: building codes, regulation of food, medicine, and environmental contaminants, all these restrict liberty in a sense. They are understood to be justified because of the difficulty of making informed choices in all these areas, and the burden of inquiry such choices would impose on citizens, as well as by the thought that health and safety are simply too basic to be left entirely to people's choices – although the inhabitant of a safe building still has many opportunities for unsafe behavior. We may also feel that health is a human good that has value in itself, independent of choice, and that it is not unreasonable for government to take a stand on its importance in a way that to some extent (though not totally) bypasses choice.

Dignity is another area that is difficult to ponder. Surely we do not want altogether to close off voluntary choices citizens may make to abase themselves or to choose relationships involving humiliation in their personal lives, however unfortunate we may think those choices; in that sense capability remains the appropriate political goal. But it seems important for government to focus on policies that will actually treat people with dignity as citizens and express actual respect for them, rather than policies (whatever those would be) that would extend to

103 Personal communication, Sarda Jain, and observation of a project of this sort in rural Rajasthan.

citizens a mere option to be treated with dignity (for example, by purchasing that right at a low cost), but allow them also the option to be treated with humiliation (say, by refusing to purchase the right). In general, the more crucial a function is to attaining and maintaining other capabilities, the more entitled we may be to promote actual functioning in some cases, within limits set by an appropriate respect for citizens' choices.

I have said that practical reason and affiliation are central to the entire project: they suffuse all the other capabilities, making them fully human. So here too we may feel uneasy when adult citizens want to function in a way that ignores these very prominent capabilities, even though we are convinced they still have them. It is very difficult to imagine a life that really contained no affiliative functioning of any kind. Surely a religious hermit's life is not such a life, because there are many different ways of caring for others, and one reasonable one is to pray for them, think about their salvation, and so on. A life that really manifested no concern at all for others would be a frightening life, and it is hard to imagine that the person living that life really enjoyed the full-blown capability to relate to others. We can certainly say that we would be justified in requiring of such citizens – as of all citizens – some forms of functioning that manifest care for others, such as paying one's taxes and obeying the law.

Where practical reason is concerned, we can more easily imagine the absence of the relevant function: an adult, having learned to think about the planning of a life, decides that he or she simply doesn't want to do that any longer, and joins some authoritarian society (whether a religious cult or the military) that will from now on do her thinking for her.[104] Now of course such a person still functions in accordance with practical reason in small ways, deciding how to brush her teeth and how much to eat at the table. But most of the major choices of life are taken out of her hands. Making capability the goal here for political purposes seems reasonable enough, so long as we are convinced that the capabilities of people as citizens have not themselves been sacrificed. Thus, we want soldiers who will not *simply* obey, when an order

---

104 A former graduate student of mine had left a very rule-bound religious order because he was losing faith. Finding that graduate study in philosophy had too little authority and imposed discipline about it, he joined the Marines and now has a high-level job.

is given, but who will actually be able to think about whether the command is a just command. We want them to obey a lot of the time, but not all of the time.[105] U.S. military academies have instituted courses in ethical reasoning for precisely this reason.[106] Even when a person retreats from political life, we want them to be able to use practical reason as citizens, should the need arise. In short: we may sometimes have reasons to protect capability by requiring a limited degree of functioning, at least when a person is exercising a responsible social function.

In another group of cases, we may suspect that the absence of a function is really a sign that the capability itself has been surrendered. Emotional health is an area in which we can usually make such inferences from absence of functioning to absence of capability: if a person always shows suspicion and fear of other people, we usually infer damage to the capacity for love, rather than saying that this person, though able to love, has made a choice not to. In other areas as well this question often needs to be raised. If certain classes of people seem to be able to vote, and persistently don't do so, we should ask whether there are subtle obstacles, material or social, preventing them from performing this civic role. If we judge that persistent inequalities or hierarchies may have created emotional barriers to full participation, we may be justified in using special incentives to encourage functioning, as when jobs are created particularly for women or minorities. Even compulsory voting would not be ruled out, if we were convinced that requiring functioning is the only way to ensure the presence of a capability. Certainly we don't want to require voting without a very good capability reason; and religious exemptions should certainly be granted.

What should we say when adults, apparently without coercion, want to sign away a major capability in a permanent way? Frequently, though certainly not always, we will judge that interference is justified to protect the capability. Even those who favor legalizing suicide and

---

105 On the role of ordinary soldiers in the Holocaust, see Christopher Browning, *Ordinary Men* (New York: HarperCollins, 1992).
106 Personal communications, instructors at the U.S. Military Academy at West Point (1992) and the U.S. Naval Academy at Annapolis (1998). The Annapolis ethics program is a recent creation, and is being instituted under the direction of philosopher Nancy Sherman. The reasons for its creation included the Tailhook sexual harassment scandal and a widespread cheating scandal.

even assisted suicide believe that these choices must be hedged round with legal procedures to prevent hasty decisions; and few support flatly permitting suicide for all unhappy or depressed people. Similarly with practical reason: we don't allow contracts for voluntary enslavement, even if we think the person to be of sound mind. In Chapter 4 I shall argue that marriages in which capabilities to exit, to work, and so on, are permanently surrendered by contract should not be permitted, although of course partners may always choose not to exercise those capabilities. Laws against drug use typically reflect a judgment that drugs impair capabilities in a long-term and frequently irreversible way. Seat-belt and helmet laws, more controversial, again reflect a widespread view that it is appropriate to protect people's long-term capabilities against the consequences of momentary carelessness. Similarly, risky medical procedures usually require higher standards of choice and due consideration than we require in daily life. Sales of necessary bodily organs are illegal; though there is more controversy about kidneys and other not strictly vital organs, sale of these is currently illegal in most nations. Again, it seems plausible for governments to ban female genital mutilation, even when practiced by adults without coercion: for, in addition to long-term health risks, the practice involves the permanent removal of the capability for most sexual pleasure, although individuals should of course be free to choose not to have sexual pleasure if they prefer not to. Finally, it seems right that capabilities in the area of nature and endangered species be given special protection against permanent loss, even when that permanent loss is favored by a democratic majority.[107]

The issue of permanent capability-surrender arises in an especially difficult form in the area of reproduction, where state concerns about overpopulation frequently lead to policies that actively promote such surrenders as an inexpensive and effective form of contraception. Vasanti's case shows that choices to surrender reproductive capability permanently are often made too lightly, after too little consultation with the affected parties. The state government offered incentives for vasectomies and apparently required only the husband to consent, although

107 These issues obviously also raise the difficult issue of trusteeship for the capabilities of future generations. I do not address that issue here. Other aspects of the environmental issue will be discussed in Chapter 2.

his choice made Vasanti infertile also. Governments may permit such choices, as most do, but it seems questionable to encourage them when we are dealing with central human capabilities. Other strategies for population control should be preferred. Increasing female literacy is the single most effective way to lower birth rates; and it enhances, rather than extinguishing, capabilities.[108]

Other more short-term or partial ways of signing away capabilities may also be controversial, especially in the areas of health and bodily integrity. Thus the victim's consent is not a defense against many types of bodily abuse. Certain extremely bloody sports ("ultimate fighting,"[109] boxing without gloves) are illegal in most places. We don't permit people to buy tainted products or dangerous medicines, even with full knowledge. In other areas (for example, alcohol and tobacco use) governments offer disincentives to health damage, rather than preventing choice outright. All these issues are controversial because they do raise legitimate concerns about paternalism. My own view is that health and bodily integrity are so important in relation to all the other capabilities that they are legitimate areas of interference with choice up to a point, although there will rightly be disagreement about where that point is in each area. Much of this debate does not fall within the scope of basic political principles, and should be left to the democratic processes of each nation.

As with Rawls's list of primary goods, so with the central capabilities: they are not meant to be an exhaustive account of what is worthwhile in life. Some uses of an Aristotelian notion of functioning in political thought, deriving from a particular interpretation of natural-law Thomism, do have that tendency: individuals are viewed as leading substandard lives insofar as they neglect one of the items on the Aristotelian list, or devote themselves to something that is not on the list.[110]

---

108 See Amartya Sen, "Fertility and Coercion," *The University of Chicago Law Review* 63 (1996), 1035–62.

109 This is a kind of rule-free fighting, where blows to any part of the body are tolerated. It is legal in several states in the U.S. but illegal in most.

110 See John Finnis, *Natural Law and Natural Rights* (Oxford: Clarendon, 1980); Robert P. George, *Making Men Moral: Civil Liberties and Public Morality* (Oxford: Clarendon Press, 1992). A life devoted to pleasure (not on Finnis's list) would in that sense be a substandard life, even if it had capabilities for all the functions on his list. Neglecting items on the list is more complicated, because Finnis acknowledges that life is too short to pursue everything; so he allows that a life may be perfectly valuable even when it neglects one or more of the items, *provided that* the person acknowl-

In my own approach, by contrast, the use of the list is facilitative rather than tyrannical: if individuals neglect an item on the list, this is just fine from the point of view of the political purposes of the list, so long as they don't impede others who wish to pursue it. And if they pursue an item not on the list, that is to be expected, and exactly what the list is meant to make possible. It is in this sense that the list is, emphatically, a partial and not a comprehensive conception of the good.

VI. CAPABILITIES AND HUMAN RIGHTS

Earlier versions of the list appeared to diverge from the approach of Rawlsian liberalism by not giving as prominent a place to the traditional political rights and liberties – although the need to incorporate them has been stressed from the start.[111] This version of the list corrects that defect of emphasis. The political liberties have a central importance in making well-being human. A society that aims at well-being while overriding these has delivered to its members an incompletely human level of satisfaction.[112] As Amartya Sen has recently written, "Political rights are important not only for the fulfillment of needs, they are crucial also for the formulation of needs. And this idea relates, in the end, to the respect that we owe each other as fellow human beings."[113] There are many reasons to think that political liberties have an instrumental role in preventing material disaster (in particular, famine)[114] and in promoting economic well-being. But their role is not merely instrumental: they are valuable in their own right.

edges the objective goodness of that item: "It is one thing to have little capacity and even no 'taste' for scholarship, or friendship, or physical heroism, or sanctity; it is quite another thing, and stupid or arbitrary, to think or speak or act as if these were not real forms of good." My conception requires only that citizens support the goodness of the relevant *capabilities*, and this *for political purposes only*. They are perfectly at liberty to say or think what they like about the goodness of the relevant functions, and also at liberty to differ about the metaphysical grounding of the capabilities. And of course, given the protection of the freedom of speech, they are perfectly free to challenge the philosophical basis of the constitutional principles by speaking against the capabilities list.

111 See ASD.
112 See HN.
113 Sen, "Freedoms and Needs," *The New Republic*, January 10/17, 1994, 31–38, at 38. Compare Rawls, PL, 187–8, which connects freedom and need in a related way.
114 Sen, *Poverty and Famines: An Essay on Entitlement and Deprivation* (Oxford: Clarendon Press, 1981). Sen argues that a free press and open political debate are of crucial importance in preventing food shortage from giving rise to famine.

Thus capabilities as I conceive them have a very close relationship to human rights, as understood in contemporary international discussions. In effect they cover the terrain covered by both the so-called first-generation rights (political and civil liberties) and the so-called second-generation rights (economic and social rights). And they play a similar role, providing the philosophical underpinning for basic constitutional principles. Because the language of rights is well established, the defender of capabilities needs to show what is added by this new language.[115]

The idea of human rights is by no means a crystal-clear idea. Rights have been understood in many different ways, and difficult theoretical questions are frequently obscured by the use of rights language, which can give the illusion of agreement where there is deep philosophical disagreement. People differ about what the *basis* of a rights claim is: rationality, sentience, and mere life have all had their defenders. They differ, too, about whether rights are prepolitical or artifacts of laws and institutions. (Kant held the latter view, although the dominant human rights tradition has held the former.) They differ about whether rights belong only to individual persons, or also to groups. They differ about whether rights are to be regarded as side-constraints on goal-promoting action, or instead as one part of the social goal that is being promoted. They differ, again, about the relationship between rights and duties: if A has a right to S, does this mean that there is always someone who has a duty to provide S, and how shall we decide who that someone is? They differ, finally, about what rights are to be understood as rights *to*. Are human rights primarily rights to be treated in certain ways? Rights to a certain level of achieved well-being? Rights to resources with which one may pursue one's life plan? Rights to certain opportunities and capacities with which one may make choices about one's life plan?

The account of central capabilities has the advantage, it seems to me, of taking clear positions on these disputed issues, while stating clearly what the motivating concerns are and what the goal is. Bernard Williams put this point eloquently, commenting on Sen's 1987 Tanner Lectures:

I am not very happy myself with taking rights as the starting point. The notion of a basic human right seems to me obscure enough, and I would rather come at it from the perspective of basic human capabilities. I would

115 The material of this section is further developed in CHR.

prefer capabilities to do the work, and if we are going to have a language or rhetoric of rights, to have it delivered from them, rather than the other way round.[116]

As Williams says, however, the relationship between the two concepts needs further scrutiny, given the dominance of rights language in the international development world.

In some areas, I would argue that the best way of thinking about rights is to see them as *combined capabilities*. The right to political participation, the right to religious free exercise, the right of free speech – these and others are all best thought of as capacities to function. In other words, to secure rights to citizens in these areas is to put them in a position of combined capability to function in that area. (Of course there is another sense of "right" that is more like my "basic capabilities": people have a right (a justified claim) to religious freedom just by virtue of being human, even if the state they live in has not guaranteed them this freedom.) By defining rights in terms of combined capabilities, we make it clear that a people in country C don't really have the right to political participation just because such language exists on paper: they really have this right only if there are effective measures to make people truly capable of political exercise. Women in many nations have a nominal right of political participation without having this right in the sense of capability: for example, they may be threatened with violence should they leave the home. In short, thinking in terms of capability gives us a benchmark as we think about what it is to secure a right to someone.

There is another set of rights, largely those in the area of property and economic advantage, that seem analytically different in their relationship to capabilities. Take, for example, the right to shelter and housing. This kind of right can be analyzed in a number of distinct ways: in terms of resources, or utility (satisfaction), or capabilities. (Once again, we must distinguish the claim that "A has a right to shelter" – which frequently refers to A's moral claim by virtue of being human, possessing what I call *basic capabilities* – from the statement that "Country C gives its citizens the right to shelter." It is the second sentence whose analysis I am discussing here.) Here again it seems

116 Bernard Williams, "The Standard of Living: Interests and Capabilities," in *The Standard of Living*, ed. G. Hawthorne (Cambridge: Cambridge University Press, 1987), 100.

valuable to understand these rights in terms of capabilities. If we think of the right to shelter as a right to a certain amount of resources, then we get into the very problem I discussed in section III: giving resources to people does not always bring differently situated people up to the same level of capability to function. The utility-based analysis also encounters a problem: traditionally deprived people may be satisfied with a very low living standard, believing that this is all they have any hope of getting. A capabilities analysis, by contrast, looks at how people are actually enabled to live. Analyzing economic and material rights in terms of capabilities thus enables us to set forth clearly a rationale we have for spending unequal amounts of money on the disadvantaged, or creating special programs to assist their transition to full capability.

The language of capabilities has one further advantage over the language of rights: it is not strongly linked to one particular cultural and historical tradition, as the language of rights is believed to be. This belief is not very accurate: although the term "rights" is associated with the European Enlightenment, its component ideas have deep roots in many traditions.[117] Where India is concerned, even apart from the recent validation of rights language in Indian legal and constitutional traditions, the salient component ideas have deep roots in much earlier areas of Indian thought – in ideas of religious toleration developed since the edicts of Ashoka in the third century B.C., in the thought about Hindu–Muslim relations in the Moghul Empire; and, of course, in many progressive and humanist thinkers of the nineteenth and twentieth centuries, who certainly cannot be described as simply Westernizers with no respect for their own traditions.[118] Tagore portrays the conception of freedom used by the young wife in his story as having Moghul origins, in the quest of Meerabai for joyful self-expression. Her idea of herself as "a free human mind" is represented as one that she derives, not from any external source, but from a combination of experience and history.

So "rights" are not exclusively Western, in the sense that matters

---

117 On China, see Tu Wei-ming, "A Confucian Perspective of Human Rights," and Joshua Cohen, "Comments on Tu Wei-ming," forthcoming. On both India and China, see Sen, "Human Rights and Asian Values," *The New Republic*, July 14/21, 1997, 33–41.

118 See Sen, "Human Rights and Asian Values." On Tagore, see Sen, *New York Review of Books*, June 1997; K. Bardhan, Introduction to *Of Women, Outcastes*. For the language of rights in the Indian independence struggle, see Nehru, *Autobiography*, 612.

most; they can be endorsed from a variety of perspectives. Nonetheless, the language of capabilities enables us to bypass this troublesome debate. When we speak simply of what people are actually able to do and to be, we do not even give the appearance of privileging a Western idea. Ideas of activity and ability are everywhere, and there is no culture in which people do not ask themselves what they are able to do, what opportunities they have for functioning.

If we have the language of capabilities, do we also need the language of rights? The language of rights still plays, I believe, four important roles in public discourse, despite its unsatisfactory features. When used in the first way, as in the sentence "A has a right to have the basic political liberties secured to her by her government," it reminds us that people have justified and urgent claims to certain types of treatment, no matter what the world around them has done about that. I have suggested that this role of rights language lies very close to the ethical role of what I have called "basic capabilities," in the sense that the *justification for* saying that people have such natural rights usually proceeds by pointing to some capability-like feature of persons (rationality, language) that they actually have on at least a rudimentary level. And I actually think that without such a justification, the appeal to rights is quite mysterious. On the other hand, there is no doubt that one might recognize the basic capabilities of people and yet still deny that this entails that they have rights in the sense of justified claims to certain types of treatment. We know that this inference has not been made through a great deal of the world's history. So appealing to rights communicates more than does the bare appeal to basic capabilities, without any further ethical argument of the sort I have supplied. Rights language indicates that we do have such an argument and that we draw strong normative conclusions from the fact of the basic capabilities.

Even at the second level, when we are talking about rights guaranteed by the state, the language of rights places great emphasis on the importance and the basic role of these spheres of ability. To say, "Here's a list of things that people ought to be able to do and to be" has only a vague normative resonance. To say, "Here is a list of fundamental rights" is more rhetorically direct. It tells people right away that we are dealing with an especially urgent set of functions, backed up by a sense of the justified claim that all humans have to such things, by virtue of being human.

Third, rights language has value because of the emphasis it places on people's choice and autonomy. The language of capabilities, as I have said, was designed to leave room for choice, and to communicate the idea that there is a big difference between pushing people into functioning in ways you consider valuable and leaving the choice up to them. But there are approaches using an Aristotelian language of functioning and capability that do not emphasize liberty in the way that my approach does: Marxist Aristotelianism and some forms of Catholic Thomist Aristotelianism are illiberal in this sense. If we have the language of rights in play as well, I think it helps us to lay extra emphasis on the important fact that the appropriate political goal is the ability of people to choose to function in certain ways, not simply their actual functionings.

Finally, in the areas where we disagree about the proper analysis of rights talk – where the claims of utility, resources, and capabilities are still being worked out – the language of rights preserves a sense of the terrain of agreement, while we continue to deliberate about the proper type of analysis at the more specific level.

VII. JUSTIFICATION AND IMPLEMENTATION: DEMOCRATIC POLITICS

The account of the central capabilities is based on an intuitively powerful idea of truly human functioning that has roots in many different traditions and is independent of any particular metaphysical or religious view. We must now, however, say more about the task of political justification, and its relationship to political implementation.

In general, the account of political justification that I favor lies close to the Rawlsian account of argument proceeding toward reflective equilibrium: we lay out the arguments for a given theoretical position, holding it up against the "fixed points" in our moral intuitions; we see how those intuitions both test and are tested by the conceptions we examine.[119] For example, among the provisionally fixed points might be the judgment that rape and domestic violence are damaging to human dignity. We look to see how the various conceptions we examine correspond to that intuition. We may prefer the capabilities view to the

119 See Rawls, TJ, 20–22, 46–53; PL, 28, 45, 381 n.16.

utilitarian view, for example, when we notice that satisfactions are malleable and people can learn to acquiesce in an undignified situation (see Chapter 2). At other times, our concrete judgments may give way when we discover that the conception we favor on other grounds calls them into question. For example, if we had tended to think private property not very important for political justice, thinking about the role of personal property in the capabilities approach, and the way that approach connects property to other areas of human choice and liberty, might make us reevaluate that initial judgment. We hope, over time, to achieve consistency and fit in our judgments taken as a whole, modifying particular judgments when this seems required by a theoretical conception that seems in other respects powerful, but modifying or rejecting the theoretical conception when that has failed to fit the most secure of our moral intuitions. We follow this procedure in many ways, but, with Rawls, I imagine that we are following it in a specifically political domain, seeking a conception by which people of differing comprehensive views can agree to live together in a political community. This entails that we take into account not only our own judgments and the theoretical conceptions, but also the judgments of our fellow citizens. [120]

My argument in this chapter is envisaged as a first step in the process of reaching toward such a reflective equilibrium. Before that process would be complete (if it ever would be), we would also have to lay out other competing conceptions, compare them in detail to this one, and see on what grounds ours might emerge as more worthy of choice. And we would have to consider the judgments of our fellow citizens, as well as our own. Chapter 2 represents a further stage in this process, comparing the capabilities view in some detail to various forms of subjective welfarism that might be used as the basis for fundamental political principles.

If this process were ever complete, that very fact would give us the confidence to move ahead, boldly building the conception so affirmed into the foundations of both national societies of many sorts and international documents that specify what nations should hold themselves to. Even then, however, we would still need to think about issues of

---

120 See Rawls, PL, 384 n.16: "This equilibrium is fully intersubjective: that is, each citizen has taken into account the reasoning and arguments of every other citizen."

appropriate procedure, and about how to effect a transition from the current status quo in a nation to the capabilities conception. We would be helped by the fact that we would have the actual agreement of all citizens; but we would still need to devise transitional procedures that are appropriately respectful of their choices. What do we do about implementation when the process of political justification remains, as it always very likely will remain, incomplete – when we have a promising conception that has survived many tests and has the backing of many people, but regarding which no wide reflective equilibrium in the full Rawlsian sense has as yet been found? Even though the political conception itself makes a great deal of room for pluralism with regard to comprehensive conceptions of the good, another issue of pluralism arises at this point: how do we proceed when other *political* conceptions still have strong backing? In short: what do I really want to *do* with this idea, given that, as seems likely, not everyone is yet in agreement about it?

Here we must say that the good idea is just that, a good idea. It can be used by international agencies and nongovernmental organizations to pursue programs within nations that have not yet embraced it. It can become the basis for international treaties and other documents that may be adopted by nations and incorporated in that way into national, as well as international, law. But in all implementation, a fundamental role remains for the nation state. The government of India is not a perfect government, to say the least. It has many faults; indeed, there are few faults of democratic government that it does not have. It is corrupt, inefficient, economically disastrous, weak in the defense of minority rights and minority dignity, fond of macho posturing, inattentive to the educational needs of children, ineffective in its discussions of sex equality.[121] Among the regional governments, some (e.g., Kerala) are far better than this description indicates, but some (e.g., Bihar, Andhra Pradesh) are worse, being both corrupt and prone to violence

---

121 For just one example of the last point, consider recent parliamentary debates about the Rajasthan Jagdish Chandra Bose Hostel rape case, in which a 27-year-old woman was gang-raped while a group of men laughed and cheered. Many legislators, especially those from Rajasthan, have attacked the woman's moral character and have defended police failures to apprehend the accused in a timely way and to perform necessary medical tests on the victim: see "Another traumatized victim in rape-prone Rajasthan," *India Abroad*, July 10, 1998, p. 31.

against political enemies. Nonetheless, these governments have one thing in their favor: they are elected. They are accountable to the people of India in a way that international agencies and even extremely fine NGOs simply are not. It would be inconsistent if a defender of the capabilities approach, with its strong role for democratic politics and political liberty, were to seek an implementation strategy that bypassed the deliberations of a democratically elected parliament. Thus at this point the approach is recommended as a good idea to politicians in India or any other nation who want to make it the basis of national or local policy.

Mere recommendation is not the end of the political story. It seems appropriate for nations that have adopted something like this account of human capabilities as the basis for a constitution, in the belief that it can command an international overlapping consensus, to commend this norm strongly to other nations. Where particularly egregious violations of human dignity and personhood are at issue, it seems appropriate for nations to use economic and other strategies to secure compliance. (This has too rarely happened in response to violations of women's dignity: racial and religious issues seem more capable of mobilizing the international community.) Where the government in question is not democratically elected, or where (as previously in South Africa) a nominal democracy fails to represent large segments of the nation's people, such pressures are even more appropriate, and may be used more confidently. Nonetheless, in a case such as India's, if the Constitution is going to change, it will ultimately have to be because the people of India choose such a change. Capabilities theory would be a prescription for tyranny if it bypassed the nation.

In the long run, it is highly desirable that the community of nations should reach a transnational overlapping consensus on the capabilities list, as a set of goals for cooperative international action and a set of commitments that each nation holds itself to for its own people. Such a consensus already exists about some items on the list, and we may hope to build from these to the others.[122] The effective pursuit of many of the items on the list for many nations requires international cooperation; it will also require some transfers of wealth from richer nations

---

122 Here I am in agreement with Thomas Pogge, *Realizing Rawls* (Ithaca, NY: Cornell University Press, 1989).

to poorer nations. I have said nothing here about the justification for such transfers or the mechanisms governing them, but such further arguments will prove important as we strive to make a threshold level of capability available to all the world's people. Especially in an era of rapid economic globalization, the capabilities approach is urgently needed to give moral substance and moral constraints to processes that are occurring all around us without sufficient moral reflection. It may be hoped that the capabilities list will steer the process of globalization, giving it a rich set of human goals and a vivid sense of human waste and tragedy, when choices are pondered that would otherwise be made with only narrow economic considerations in view. Nonetheless, even a highly moralized globalism needs nation states at its core, because transnational structures (at least all the ones we know about so far) are insufficiently accountable to citizens and insufficiently representative of them. Thus the primary role for the capabilities account remains that of providing political principles that can underlie national constitutions; and this means that practical implementation must remain to a large extent the job of citizens in each nation.

My reply to the legitimate worries about universalism thus has five parts. First, *multiple realizability*: each of the capabilities may be concretely realized in a variety of different ways, in accordance with individual tastes, local circumstances, and traditions. Second, *capability as goal*: the basic political principles focus on promoting capabilities, not actual functioning, in order to leave to citizens the choice whether to pursue the relevant function or not to pursue it. Third, *liberties and practical reason*: the content of the capabilities list gives a central role to citizens' powers of choice and to traditional political and civil liberties. Fourth, *political liberalism*: the approach is intended as the moral core of a specifically political conception, and the object of a political overlapping consensus among people who have otherwise very different comprehensive views of the good. Fifth, *constraints on implementation*: the approach is designed to offer the philosophical grounding for constitutional principles, but the implementation of such principles must be left, for the most part, to the internal politics of the nation in question, although international agencies and other governments are justified in using persuasion – and in especially grave cases economic or political sanctions – to promote such developments.

VIII. CAPABILITIES IN WOMEN'S LIVES: A ROLE FOR PUBLIC ACTION

I have argued that legitimate concerns for diversity, pluralism, and personal freedom are not incompatible with the recognition of universal norms; indeed, universal norms are actually required if we are to protect diversity, pluralism, and freedom, treating each human being as an agent and an end. The best way to hold all these concerns together, I have argued, is to formulate the universal norms as a set of capabilities for fully human functioning, emphasizing the fact that capabilities protect, and do not close off, spheres of human freedom.

Let us now return to Vasanti and Jayamma. The script of Vasanti's life has been largely written by men on whom she has been dependent: her father, her husband, the brothers who helped her out when her marriage collapsed. This dependency put her at risk with respect to life and health, denied her the education that would have developed her powers of thought, and prevented her from thinking of herself as a person with a plan of life to shape and choices to make. In the marriage itself she fared worst of all, losing her bodily integrity to domestic violence, her emotional equanimity to fear, and being cut off from meaningful forms of affiliation, familial, friendly, and civic. For these reasons, she did not really have the conception of herself as a free and dignified being whose worth is equal to that of others. We should note that mundane matters of property, employment, and credit play a large role here: the fact that she held no property in her own name, had no literacy and no employment-related skills, and no access to credit except from male relatives, all this cemented her dependent status and kept her in an abusive relationship far longer than would otherwise have been her wish. We see here how closely all the capabilities are linked to one another, how the absence of one, bad in itself, also erodes others. Vasanti also had some good luck: she appears not to have had to put up with abusive in-laws – at least this was no part of the story she chose to tell – and she had brothers who were more than usually solicitous of her well-being, even to the point of getting her a divorce lawyer. Thus she could and did leave the marriage without having to turn to any physically dangerous or degrading occupation. But this good luck created new forms of dependency; Vasanti thus remained highly vulnerable, and lacking in confidence.

The SEWA loan changed this picture. Vasanti now had not only an income, but also independent control over her livelihood. Even when she still owed a lot of money, it was better to owe it to SEWA than to her brothers: being part of a mutually supportive community of women was crucially different, with respect to both practical reason and affiliation, from being a poor relation getting a handout. Her sense of her dignity increased as she paid off the loan and began saving. By the time I saw her, she had achieved considerable self-confidence and sense of worth; and her affiliations with other women, in both groups and personal friendships, had become a new source of both pleasure and pride to her. Her level of participation in political life had also gone way up, as she joined in Kokila's project to prod the police to investigate more cases of domestic violence. Interestingly, she now felt that she had the capacity to be a good person by giving to others, something that the narrow focus on survival had not permitted her to do.

Reflecting on Vasanti's situation, we notice how little the public sector did for her, and how lucky she was that one of the best women's NGOs in the world was right in her backyard. Government failed to ensure her an education; it failed to prosecute her husband for abuse, or to offer her shelter from that abuse;[123] it failed to secure her equal property rights in her own family; it failed to offer her access to credit; and, finally, it failed to handle her divorce case in an expeditious manner. Indeed, the only strong role government played in Vasanti's life was strongly negative, offering cash payment for her husband's vasectomy, something that made her vulnerable position still more vulnerable.

Jayamma's situation provides an interesting contrast. On the one hand, she had a much worse start in life than Vasanti, and has done worse throughout her life on some of the measures of capability. She has had to worry constantly about hunger, and she has at times suffered from malnutrition; she has engaged in extremely dangerous and taxing physical labor. She has had no supportive male relatives, and, though she has had children as Vasanti has not, they have been more of a liability than an asset. She has no savings, and has never even applied for a loan; her property rights to the land on which she squats are unclearly established. She has suffered from discrimination in em-

123 The number of women's shelters in India is extremely low, indeed close to zero.

ployment, with no chance of rectification. And she has had to do what countless women in developing countries routinely do, but Vasanti did not, that is, to shoulder all the burden of raising and caring for children, and running a household with children, while working a full day at a demanding job.

On the other hand, Jayamma has in some ways done better than Vasanti. Her health has been good, no doubt on account of her impressive physical strength and fitness, and she has never suffered physical abuse from her husband, who seems to have been a lot weaker than she was. She doesn't seem to be intimidated by anyone, and she has a consciousness of political issues that Vasanti has developed only recently. Unlike Vasanti, she has never been encouraged to be timid and submissive, and she certainly isn't; and this has meant that through the years she has fought quite effectively to keep her family together and to improve its standing. Nonetheless, despite all her courage, her husband's selfish habits and lack of ambition and her children's uneven lives have left her with nothing to fall back on as old age nears. Her consciousness of lack of equality with others is strong, though based at least as much on class as on sex; and her pride is uneasily combined with the conviction that she cannot expect from life the things that other more privileged people will easily get.

If we look at the role played by government in Jayamma's life, an interesting contrast also appears, for it has been far more positive. First of all, these squatters on government land now have been given property rights in the land, although they will need to go to court to establish their claim clearly. Second, the services provided by government are invaluable aids in Jayamma's taxing day. Water now comes into the squat itself, and a government program built her an indoor toilet (although she eventually gave that up to give her son one part of the house to live in with his wife). Government medical services are close at hand, good, and available free of charge. They even offer a choice between Western and Ayurvedic medicine. The one time Jayamma was seriously sick with the flu, she didn't like the service at the government hospital, both because she had to wait and because the doctor was brusque with her, but that did not matter, since she got treatment she did like at the Ayurvedic clinic. Even though she did not take advantage of educational opportunities for her own children, her grandchildren have profited from the government's aggressiveness against traditions of noneducation. Following a national government policy, the pension office has denied her claim, she believes wrongly; and government has certainly failed to eradicate sex discrimination in wages and promotion at her place of employment. Nor has anything been done to eliminate corruption in the medical sector so that her granddaughter can get a job without paying a bribe. (This points to a big general problem in Kerala today, that of providing jobs commensurate with people's educational qualifications.) But there are at least some significant respects in which the government of Kerala can be given good marks for promoting human capabilities – a conclusion by now well established in the development literature.[124]

The capabilities framework, when used to evaluate these lives, does not appear to be an alien importation: it seems to square pretty well with the things these women are already thinking about, or start thinking about at some time in their lives, and want when they think about them. Insofar as it entails criticism of traditional culture, these women are already full of criticism; indeed, any framework that did not suggest criticism would not be adequate to capture what they want and aim for, and would hardly be an accurate description of the culture in which they live. In particular, the ideas of practical reason, control over environment, and non-humiliation (including sexual non-humiliation) seem especially salient in their thought, alongside more obvious considerations of nutrition, health, and freedom from violence.

In some ways the list goes beyond what the two women are currently thinking. For example, it is possible that Jayamma does not formulate issues of nondiscrimination and fundamental liberties to herself in just the way the list does, though we should hardly rule that out, given her explicit awareness of issues of class. And neither of the women seems to value education in quite the way the list does, although Jayamma is beginning to see changes in her own family that may alter her perception. But that does not mean that the list is a bad way of capturing, for normative political purposes, what is lacking in their situations, and what stands between them and the general goals of independence, dignity, and mastery for which they are both intensely striving. The reason

124 See Drèze and Sen, *India*, and Ramachandran in Drèze and Sen, eds.

they do not yet push for education is that their environment is not yet one in which education will open new routes to these more general goals.

Vasanti and Jayamma, like many women in India and in the rest of the world, have lacked support for many of the most central human functions, and that lack of support is at least to some extent caused by their being women. But women, unlike rocks and trees and horses, have the potential to become capable of these human functions, given sufficient nutrition, education, and other support. That is why their unequal failure in capability is a problem of justice. It is up to all human beings to solve this problem. I claim that a universal conception of human capability gives us excellent guidance as we pursue this difficult task.

ADAPTIVE PREFERENCES AND WOMEN'S OPTIONS

The doctor was rightly upset about [the unsanitary conditions in the women's quarters]; but he was wrong in one respect. He thought that it was a source of constant pain for us. Quite the contrary . . . To those with low self-regard, neglect does not seem unjust, and so it does not cause them pain. That is why women feel ashamed to be upset about the injustice they encounter. If a woman must accept so much injustice in the life ordered for her, then it is perhaps less painful for her to be kept in total neglect; otherwise, she is bound to suffer, and suffer pointlessly, the pain of injustice, if she cannot change the rules governing her life. Whatever the condition that you kept us in, it rarely occurred to me that there was pain and deprivation in it.

Rabindranath Tagore, "Letter from a Wife"[1]

When we make videos, and women like us watch them, we get confidence to try and make changes. When we see women like us who have done something brave and new, then we get the confidence that we can learn something new too. When poor women see other poor women as health workers on the video, they say, "I can also learn about health and help solve these problems in my neighborhood." When other self-employed women see me, a vegetable vendor, making these films, they also have the confidence that they can do things which at first seem impossible.

Lila Datania, SEWA, Ahmedabad, 1992[2]

1 In Bardhan, *Of Women, Outcastes*, 99.
2 Quoted in Rose, *Where Women Are Leaders*, 158.

I. PREFERENCE AND THE GOOD: TWO UNSATISFACTORY EXTREMES

Any defense of universal norms involves drawing distinctions among the many things people actually desire. If it is to have any content at all, it will say that some objects of desire are more central than others for political purposes, more necessary to a human being's quality of life. A wise approach will go even further, holding that some existing preferences are actually bad bases for social policy. The list advanced in Chapter 1 contains many functions that many people over the ages have preferred not to grant to women, either not at all, or not on a basis of equality. To insist on their centrality is thus to go against preferences that have considerable depth and breadth in traditions of male power. Moreover, the list contains many items that women over the ages haven't wanted for themselves, and some that even today many women don't pursue – so in putting the list at the center of a normative political project aimed at providing the philosophical under-pinning for basic political principles, we are going against not just other people's preferences *about* women, but, more controversially, against many preferences (or so it seems) *of* women about themselves and their lives. To some extent, the list avoids these problems of paternalism by insisting that the political goal is capability, not actual functioning, and by dwelling on the central importance of choice as a good. But the notion of choice and practical reason used in the list is a normative notion, emphasizing the critical activity of reason in a way that does not reflect the actual use of reason in many lives.

Think, once again, of Vasanti and Jayamma. Vasanti stayed for years in an abusive marriage. Eventually she did leave, and by now she has very firm views about the importance of her bodily integrity: indeed, she and Kokila spend a lot of their time helping other battered women report their cases to the police and goading the police to do something about the problem. But there was a time when Vasanti did not think this way – especially before her husband's vasectomy, when she thought she might still have children. Like many women, she seems to have thought that abuse was painful and bad, but still a part of women's lot in life, just something women have to put up with as part of being women dependent on men, and entailed by having left her own family to move into a husband's home. The idea that it was a violation of rights, of law, of justice, and that *she herself* has rights that are being violated by her husband's conduct – these ideas she didn't have at that time, and many many women all over the world don't have them now. My universalist approach seems to entail that there is something wrong with the preference (if that's what we should call it) to put up with abuse, that it just shouldn't have the same role in social policy as the preference to protect and defend one's bodily integrity. It also entails that there is something wrong with not seeing oneself in a certain way, as a bearer of rights and a citizen whose dignity and worth are equal to that of others.

Or consider Jayamma, a great defender of her bodily integrity, but very acquiescent in a discriminatory wage structure and a discriminatory system of family income sharing. When women were paid less for heavier work at the brick kiln and denied chances for promotion, Jayamma didn't complain or protest. She knew that this was how things were and would be. Like Tagore's character in my epigraph, she didn't even waste mental energy getting upset, since these things couldn't be changed. Again, when her husband took his earnings and spent them on himself in somewhat unthrifty ways, leaving Jayamma to support the children financially through her labor, as well as doing all of the housework, this didn't strike her as wrong or bad, it was just the way things were, and she didn't waste time yearning for another way. Unlike Vasanti, Jayamma seemed to lack not only the concept of herself as a person with rights that could be violated, but also the sense that what was happening to her was a wrong.

Finally, let me introduce one new example, to show the way entrenched preferences can clash with universal norms even at the level of basic nutrition and health. In the desert area outside Mahabubnagar, Andhra Pradesh, I talked with women who were severely malnourished, and whose village had no reliable clean water supply. Before the arrival of a government consciousness-raising program, these women apparently had no feeling of anger or protest about their physical situation. They knew no other way. They did not consider their conditions unhealthful or unsanitary, and they did not consider themselves to be malnourished. Now their level of discontent has gone way up: they protest to the local government, asking for clean water, for electricity, for a health visitor. They protect their food supplies from flies, they wash their bodies more often. Asked what was the biggest change that the government program had brought to their lives, they immediately said, as if in chorus, "We are cleaner now." The consciousness-raising program has clearly challenged entrenched preferences and satisfactions, taking a normative approach based on an idea of good human functioning.

The normative approach based on human functioning and capability developed in Chapter 1 rejected utilitarian preference-based approaches as a basis for fundamental political principles precisely because they were unable to conduct a critical scrutiny of preference and desire that would reveal the many ways in which habit, fear, low expectations, and unjust background conditions deform people's choices and even their wishes for their own lives. So it is no surprise that the capabilities view ends up conducting just such a critique. But we must now confront head on, and more extensively, the intellectual problem this undertaking raises. For feminists who challenge entrenched satisfactions are frequently charged with being totalitarian and antidemocratic for just this way of proceeding. Who are they to tell real women what is good for them, or to march into an area shaped by tradition and custom with universal standards of what one should demand and what one should desire? Aren't they just brainwashing women, who already had their own ideas of what was right and proper?[3]

It is easy to make a rhetorical connection between the feminist critique of desire and discredited totalitarian ideologies – in part because Marx was among the most interesting and influential developers of a view of "false consciousness," and because feminist strategies of consciousness raising, in the developing world as in the West, frequently show the influence of Marx's account. And yet, the idea that some preferences are deformed by ignorance, malice, injustice, and blind habit has deep roots in the liberal tradition of political philosophy as well: in Adam Smith's ideas about greed and anger, in Mill's ideas about the sexes, in Kant's ideas about the many ways in which people get accustomed to treating one another as means rather than ends, in John Rawls's ideas about the ways in which unjust background conditions shape desire and choice. More recently, the idea of preference

---

3 See Christina Hoff Sommers, *Who Stole Feminism?* (New York: Simon and Schuster, 1994), discussed in Chapter 5 of my *Sex and Social Justice*, and in Chapter 6 of my *Cultivating Humanity: A Classical Defense of Reform in Higher Education* (Cambridge, MA: Harvard University Press, 1997).

deformation has become central in mainstream economic and political thought, in the writings of people as otherwise diverse as Amartya Sen, Jon Elster, and Gary Becker.[4]

One of the things this liberal tradition has emphasized is that people's preference for basic liberties can itself be manipulated by tradition and intimidation; thus a position that refuses to criticize entrenched desire, while sounding democratic on its face, may actually serve democratic institutions less well than one that takes a strong normative stand about such matters, to some extent independently of people's existing desires. (As we shall see, even some committed utilitarians have diverged from utilitarianism for this reason.) So the question of preference deformation should be approached without an initial presumption that there is a problematic tension between a normative sorting of preferences and liberal-democratic values.

There are many questions that might be asked about the role of preferences in personal and political life. The question to be confronted in this chapter concerns the role of existing preferences in grounding political judgments as we formulate political principles that can be used as the basis of constitutional guarantees. Our question is: under what conditions are preferences a good guide to such fundamental issues of social choice, and under what conditions might we be justified in departing from or criticizing some of them in the name of important norms such as justice and human capability? How should such a justification go?

In confronting preference-based views of social choice, we are pursuing a further part of the project of political justification mapped out in Chapter 1. Having made a case for the capabilities approach in intuitive terms by laying out its positive aspects and showing how it can solve certain pressing political problems, we now turn to a detailed confrontation with a major rival conception, the type of welfarism currently dominant in neoclassical economics. By looking at what motivates that view and showing, as I think we can, that the capabilities view responds to those concerns while offering a better treatment of issues that pose problems for welfarism, we advance further toward the goal of a full justification of the capabilities approach.

The capabilities approach, as stated in Chapter 1, has two related

---

4 The work of all these people will be discussed in detail in section IV.

uses. My central project is to work out the grouding for basic political principles to which all nations should be held by their citizens; but an ancillary and related project is to map out the space within which comparisons of quality of life across nations can most revealingly be made. These two parts of the argument are to some extent independent. One might hold that the preference-based view is perfectly all right as a basis for quality of life comparisons, while doubting that it could be an adequate basis for the selection of basic political principles – if, for example, one held that what we want from quality of life measurement is something relatively unambitious, simply an index of how people see their situations. This would, I think, be an implausible position to hold, once one confronts the specific defects of preference-based views: the reasons for thinking them bad bases for political principles are also reasons why they do not do a good job of quality of life measurement. And surely it would be far less plausible to hold that preferences are a bad basis for quality of life measurement, but a good basis for the selection of basic political principles: for if preferences cannot even tell us how people are really doing, then it seems hard to see how they could ground a normative account of constitutional principles. However, throughout this chapter I will focus on the bases for social choice, in the area of fundamental principles, commenting occasionally on how the evolving argument bears on the issue of quality of life measurement.

A further complication now emerges. Economists and others who defend preference-based views rarely make a clear distinction between their use in social choice generally and their use in selecting basic principles that can be embodied in constitutional guarantees. Instead, they tend to make general pronouncements about social choice. Insofar as they do so, I shall simply assume that they make no exception for the special situation in which one is selecting basic political principles, and my critique will be focused on this special situation, rather than other situations in which appeals to preference might well play a valuable role. I think this is perfectly fair, because I do think that my opponents intend their position as a perfectly general account of social choice.

In the debate about how preferences should figure in social choice, we can identify two extreme positions, between which I shall situate my own. The first position can be called *subjective welfarism*.[5] This

---

5 See Cass R. Sunstein, *The Partial Constitution* (Cambridge, MA: Harvard University Press, 1993), Chapter 5, 162–66.

position holds that all existing preferences are on a par for political purposes, and that social choice should be based on some sort of aggregation of all of them. (In what follows I shall abstract from the problems I have already raised in Chapter 1 about the notion of aggregation and the plurality of goods; I shall assume that the welfarist concedes that there is a plurality of relevant metrics along which preferences will be aggregated.)[6]

The second position can be called *platonism*.[7] According to this view, the fact that people desire or prefer something is basically not relevant, given our knowledge of how unreliable desires and preferences are as a guide to what is really just and good. Actual desire and choice play no role at all in justifying something as good. What we need to do is to provide an argument for the objective value of the relevant state of affairs that is independent of the fact that people desire or prefer it; once we have such an argument, we are justified in making even radical departures from people's actual wants.

Both positions are motivated by genuinely important concerns. Welfarism springs from respect for people and their actual choices, from a reluctance to impose something alien upon them, or even to treat the desires of different people unequally. In effect, it starts from respect for persons, interpreting that as equivalent to respect for preferences. Platonism springs from an urgent concern for justice and human value, and from the recognition that in the real world these values are frequently subordinated to power, greed, and selfish indulgence. But both contain obvious problems. Embraced as a normative position, subjective welfarism makes it impossible to conduct a radical critique of unjust institutions; it forces us to say, for example, that because Jayamma has accepted an unjust wage structure as the way things must be, that's the way they should remain; that because the women in Andhra Pradesh don't agitate for medical care and clean water, they don't need those things; that so long as Vasanti puts up with an abusive marriage, that's just her lot. This limitation is especially grave when we are in the process of selecting basic political principles that can be embodied in

6 For one picture of such a utilitarian view, see Amartya Sen, "Plural Utility," *Proceedings of the Aristotelian Society* 81 (1980/81), 193–215.
7 This may or may not be a position held by Plato, who does seem to have given experienced choice a role in his account of value, though it is difficult to say what that role is. (If it is only a heuristic role, and not a justificatory role, then Plato may still be a platonist in my sense.)

constitutional guarantees. Platonism, on the other hand, seems too disdainful of the wisdom embodied in people's actual experience: it seems to care too little about what Jayamma and Vasanti think about changes in their lives, and about the relevance to political choice of the fact that the women in Andhra Pradesh are happy with the improvements made by the government program and wouldn't choose to return to the way they lived before. Any viable modern position, it seems, must try to preserve the important values contained in each of these two extremes, while avoiding their defects.

Probably no modern thinker about social welfare is a thoroughgoing platonist. Certainly no feminist is; feminists, insofar as they endorse a radical critique of desire and choice, typically buttress it with appeals to ideas of what women really want, what will make them truly happy or satisfy their deepest desires. And although there used to be some real subjective welfarists in utilitarian economic thought,[8] nowadays one rarely finds an unqualified version of that position either. In searching for an appropriate "mean" between these extremes, it will be useful to look, first, at why utilitarian economists have rejected pure subjective welfarism, and how they have tried to refurbish the welfarist view. Here I shall focus on arguments of John Harsanyi, Richard Brandt, and Gary Becker, all of whose attempts to say something sensible within the welfarist framework end up revealing just how hard it is to do that. Next, I shall look at some reasons we might have for concluding that the problem of preference-deformation requires us to depart altogether from the utilitarian framework; here I draw on arguments by Richard Posner, Amartya Sen, Jean Hampton, Jon Elster, Cass Sunstein, and Thomas Scanlon. Finally, I shall show how my own view of the central capabilities addresses these issues, arguing that at the level of the central capabilities there is considerable convergence between a "substantive good" approach to social goods and an "informed desire" approach.[9] The list was derived in Chapter 1 using an independent

---

8 For example, Milton Friedman, "The Methodology of Positive Economics," in Daniel M. Hausman, ed., *The Philosophy of Economics* (Cambridge: Cambridge University Press, 1984), 210–24; more recently, one sees such a view in Robert Bork, *The Tempting of America: The Political Seduction of the Law* (New York: 1990), 251–9. Sommers in *Who Stole Feminism?* also seems to hold some such view.

9 For these terms, see Thomas Scanlon, "Value, Desire, and Quality of Life," in QL, 201–207. Scanlon actually uses the term "substantive list," but also notes that the term is

philosophical argument; but it converges in many respects with what an informed-desire approach could be expected to deliver, and this is important. I shall argue that desire continues to play both a heuristic role in arriving at the list of the central capabilities and a limited ancillary role in their justification; nonetheless, it is fruitful to begin from a substantive account of central goods rather than to attempt to derive them from a strictly procedural approach. At any rate, any procedural approach that we can accept will be so laden with normative values that it collapses, in effect, into a substantive good approach. I shall illustrate this conclusion by comparing my own approach to the strongest feminist approach of a proceduralist (albeit non-utilitarian) kind, namely that of Jean Hampton in her important article "Feminist Contractarianism."[10] I shall end with a reflection on the obstacles posed by power and fear to the convergence I envisage between desire and justice.

II. PROBLEMS WITH THE CONCEPT OF PREFERENCE

But first, a note on preferences. I have spoken, so far, of both "desires" and "preferences." In the economic literature, there are two distinct conceptions of what a preference is. According to one approach, championed most notably by Paul Samuelson, there is no conceptual distinction between preference and action: a preference is just something that is taken to be "revealed" by the action that in fact is chosen.[11] There are a number of problems with this approach – among other things, it does not give us any resources for speaking about the wishes and in general the deliberative life of a person except insofar as this mental life gets translated into action. This problem the approach shares with

somewhat perilous, in that it suggests we are talking about a laundry list of unrelated items, rather than a coherent view.

10 In *A Mind of One's Own: Feminist Essays on Reason and Objectivity*, ed. Louise M. Antony and Charlotte Witt (Boulder: Westview Press, 1993), 227–56.

11 This approach was strongly linked with behaviorism in psychology. Thus John Hicks (who at first did not endorse the approach, but later embraced it) stated that the approach permitted us to study human beings "only as entities having certain patterns of market behaviour; it makes no claim, no pretence, to be able to see inside their heads": *A Revision of Demand Theory* (Oxford: Clarendon Press, 1956), 6. For other examples of the idea (characteristic of that era) that a purely behaviorist approach is more scientifically respectable than a mentalist approach, see Sen, "Internal Consistency of Choice," *Econometrica* 61 (1993), 495–521.

its cousin, psychological behaviorism; and psychology has long since concluded that behaviorism is an inadequate explanatory theory.[12] But there are even more obvious problems. Construed as actions, preferences do not obey certain very basic axioms of rationality, such as transitivity and consistency.[13] But this observation takes us to a deeper conceptual issue. An action is not like a statement: it does not wear its characterization on its face. Thus before we can even ask whether preferences construed as actions are either consistent or inconsistent, we must interpret them. But in order to interpret them we must allude to something external to the act of choice, something like the underlying objectives or values that are pursued in choice.[14] Such arguments have long been used against psychological behaviorism;[15] they are equally devastating to the claims of revealed-preference theory.

A more promising approach to the idea of a "preference" is that favored by, among others, Gary Becker and Amartya Sen. According to this view, preferences lie behind actual choices and have psychological reality. They are entities that, together with beliefs, go to explain choices. For users of this approach, preferences are rather like desires; indeed, it would appear that desires are one subset of preferences.

But here is where any philosopher is likely to begin scratching her head. For why are we trying to explain such complex human actions with such an impoverished repertory of explanatory entities![16] Western philosophers, ever since Plato and Aristotle, have agreed that the explanation of human action requires quite a few distinct concepts; these include the concepts of belief, desire, perception, appetite, and emotion – *at the very least*. Many philosophers, including some contemporary ones, have felt that Aristotle was basically right and that we need no

12 For one good discussion of the demise of behaviorism in cognitive psychology, see Richard Lazarus, *Emotion and Adaptation* (New York: Oxford University Press, 1991).

13 See Amartya Sen, "Internal Consistency of Choice"; and the earlier "Choice Functions and Revealed Preference," *Review of Economic Studies* 38 (1971), 307–17, reprinted in CWM, and "Behaviour and the Concept of a Preference," *Economica* 40 (August 1973), 241–59, reprinted in CWM, 54–73.

14 Sen, "Internal Consistency."

15 See especially Martin Seligman, *Helplessness* (New York: W. H. Freeman, 1975); and in philosophy Charles Taylor, *The Explanation of Behaviour* (London: Routledge, 1964).

16 See my "Flawed Foundations: The Philosophical Critique of (a Certain Type of) Economics," *University of Chicago Law Review* 64 (1997), 1197–1214.

concepts beyond the ones he introduced.[17] Others have not been so satisfied. The Stoics introduced the further notion of *impulse (hormê)*, in the belief that the Aristotelian categories didn't sufficiently capture the innate tendency of living things to persist in their being; Spinoza converted this concept into his central category of *conatus*. Kant was partial to the notion of *inclination (Neigung)*, feeling, it seems, that it captured features of emotion and desire not adequately emphasized in the medieval/Aristotelian framework. Some contemporary philosophers have argued that the concept of *intention* is both irreducible to belief/ desire/emotion and an essential part of explaining action.[18] And of course others have defended various concepts introduced by psycho-analysis, such as instinct and drive. Finally, moral philosophers, prom-inently including the late Jean Hampton, have insisted on the complex multilayered structure of real mental life: individuals have not just pref-erences, but also preferences about those preferences, and perhaps pref-erences about those as well.[19] They also have commitments that may be in tension with their preferences; such commitments may even reflect their judgment that their preferences are likely to prove unreliable.[20]

One thing that is clearly wrong with subjective welfarism is that it does not capture this complexity. Because it doesn't explore distinctions such as the distinction between an appetite and an emotion, it cannot adequately reveal the ways in which social conditioning shapes the content of what may be called a "preference." (One standard way of making the distinction would be to say that an appetite, such as the appetite for food, is at least to some extent impervious to social condi-tioning, whereas emotions have a rich cognitive and emotional content

---

17 See, for example, G. H. von Wright, *The Varieties of Goodness* (London: Routledge, 1963); Donald Davidson, *Essays on Actions and Events* (Oxford: Clarendon, 1980).

18 See Michael E. Bratman, *Intentions, Plans, and Practical Reason* (Cambridge, MA: Harvard University Press, 1987). See also G. E. M. Anscombe, *Intention* (Ithaca: Cor-nell University Press, second edition 1969).

19 See Harry Frankfurt, "Freedom of the Will and the Concept of a Person," *Journal of Philosophy* 67 (1971), 5–20; G. Dworkin, *The Theory and Practice of Autonomy* (Cambridge: Cambridge University Press, 1988), 14–20; Gary Watson, "Free Agency," *Journal of Philosophy* 72 (1975), 205–20; Jean Hampton, "The Failure of Expected Utility Theory as a Theory of Reason," *Economics and Philosophy* 10 (1994), 195–242.

20 See Sen, "Rational Fools: A Critique of the Behavioural Foundations of Economic Theory," in CWM, 84–108; J. Elster, *Ulysses and the Sirens* (Cambridge: Cambridge University Press, 1979); G. Dworkin, *The Theory and Practice*, 14–15.

that is usually heavily influenced by social conditioning. Whether this is right or not, it is the sort of point that needs to be explored.) Similarly, it does not consider the possibility that desires themselves may have a complex intentional content, and that different types of desires may have different levels and types of intentional content.[21] Finally, by treating individuals as just bags of unscrutinized desires, it ignores the critical and deliberative character of people in real life, who usually do not respect all of their own desires on an equal footing, but apply some kind of ranking and ordering to their own lives. Welfarism thus puts itself in a position from which it is unlikely to be able to fulfill its own central goal, which (as I have characterized it) is to show respect for persons. Treating them as simple infants rather than as reflective adults is not likely to be a good way of showing respect for them.

In what follows, then, we have to grapple with the sad fact that contemporary economics has not yet put itself onto the map of conceptually respectable theories of human action. (Indeed, it has repudiated the rich foundations that the philosophical anthropology of Adam Smith offered it.) Sometimes it seems like an odd exercise, finding subtle errors in economic theories of behavior, when one's inclination is really to say, we can't even assess a theory this crude, let's throw it all out and begin all over again. And this will become relevant when we come to discuss the issue of respect for people and their mental lives. Nonetheless, we will try to get on with the subtle criticisms, choosing those that would be of interest even against a more complex theory.

III. WELFARISM: THE INTERNAL CRITIQUE

Although subjective welfarism is commonly found in brief gestures toward a normative approach in economics, very few utilitarian economists have been willing to be thoroughgoing subjective welfarists, once

21 On this issue, see Warren Quinn, "Rationality and the Human Good," in *Morality and Action* (Cambridge: Cambridge University Press, 1993), 210–27. This point is a very old one; Aristotle thinks of even appetite as taking "the apparent good" for its object, and as at least sometimes responsive to ethical and social training; Hellenistic philosophers, Epicurean and Stoic, debated this issue with much sophistication, holding, for example, that the need for food, and some general desire for food, are innate and ineliminable, but that social training substantially shapes the sorts of foods that people find desirable. Epicureans held the desire for meat to be entirely the product of social teaching.

they consider normative issues head on and extensively. Milton Friedman probably was the real article: he clearly did hold that concerning differences of value "men can ultimately only fight,"[22] and that, in consequence, there was nowhere for normative theory to go beyond subjective welfarism. Another genuine subjective welfarist about public policy, much influenced by economic discussions, is Robert Bork, who holds that the aggregation of subjective preferences is the only rational way to proceed in normative matters, including the determination of basic constitutional principles. He supports this judgment by stating that the evaluator is "adrift on an uncertain sea" with "no principled way to make the necessary distinctions" that would adequately ground a normative judgment.[23] Usually, however, economists have recognized that it is implausible to treat all existing preferences as on a par for normative purposes, and have recommended at least some winnowing or correcting.

The most obvious such correction involves false belief and lack of information. Even Hume, who in general thought that passions and desires could not be coherently deemed "unreasonable," made exceptions for cases in which one mistakenly believes an object to exist that does not exist, or holds false beliefs about appropriate means to further ends.[24] But most utilitarian followers of Hume go somewhat further than he did in the recognition of cognitive error. To take a representative example, Christopher Bliss, while defending subjective welfarism in a very strong form in connection with the measurement of quality of life in developing countries,[25] recognizes the need to correct for inadequate or false information: "The inhabitants of a poor country for example, may not realize how unhealthy they are, and the consequences of that ill health, whereas an expert will know." Another case in which Bliss would admit expert corrections of existing views is the case in which we need a global overview and individuals are unable to provide this. Again, holds Bliss, this correction is acceptable because it

22 Friedman, "The Methodology of Positive Economics," 210.
23 Bork, *The Tempting of America*, 252, 258; see also "Neutral Principles and Some First Amendment Problems," *Indiana Law Journal* 47 (1971), 1, 6 (arguing that a "value-choosing Court" is inconsistent with the democratic process).
24 Hume, *A Treatise of Human Nature*, book 2, part 3, section 3, concluding with the famous judgment, "It is not contrary to reason to prefer the destruction of the whole world to the scratching of my finger."
25 Christopher Bliss, "Lifestyle and the Standard of Living," in QL, 415–36, at 418–19.

involves "imperfect vision" on the part of the individual. We can correct the individual's vision – give her eyeglasses, so to speak – without losing hold of "the fundamental point that man, if not the measure of all things, is at least the measure of the standard of living."[26] Bliss does not discuss the grounding of basic political principles that underlie constitutional guarantees, so it is possible that he would not endorse a preference-based view in that domain; on the other hand, his zealous defense of preferences in all areas that concern quality of life gives no suggestion that he sees any area in which reliance on preferences would prove problematic.

A much more ambitious set of corrections to existing preferences has been proposed by John Harsanyi, still apparently within the general framework of subjective welfarist theory.[27] Harsanyi begins by announcing "the important philosophical principle of *preference autonomy*. By this I mean the principle that, in deciding what is good and what is bad for a given individual, the ultimate criterion can only be his own wants and his own preferences."[28] (Harsanyi does not clearly explain his reasons for holding this principle, but it would appear that, in addition to the usual concerns about democracy, he is also motivated by the thought that we simply cannot make sense of the idea that what A wants is bad for A, except as a claim that, at some deeper level, A really prefers something else.)[29] On the other hand, Harsanyi recognizes that people's preferences are frequently "irrational." He believes that "any sensible ethical theory" must recognize this fact. "It would be absurd to assert that we have the same moral obligation to help other people in satisfying their utterly unreasonable wants as we have to help them in satisfying their very reasonable desires."[30] But what content can we give to this distinction, compatibly with maintaining the welfarist principle? A normative hedonist, he observes, could easily make the relevant distinction: a rational want will be one whose object really does produce pleasure, and an irrational want will be one whose object

26 Bliss, 419.
27 John C. Harsanyi, "Morality and the Theory of Rational Behavior," in *Utilitarianism and Beyond*, ed. Amartya Sen and Bernard Williams (Cambridge: Cambridge University Press, 1982), 39–62.
28 Harsanyi, 55.
29 *Ibid.*
30 *Ibid.*

doesn't really produce pleasure. But if we don't accept that sort of definite normative theory (and Harsanyi has already rejected it, apparently in favor of a theory that derives normativity from preferences themselves), then what are we to say?

We must say, Harsanyi concludes, that people's manifest preferences are frequently at odds with their "true preferences." A person's rational wants are those that are consistent with his true preferences, the irrational are those that are not. The distinction between the manifest and the true is defined as follows:

[A person's] manifest preferences are his actual preferences as manifested by his observed behaviour, including preferences possibly based on erroneous factual beliefs, or on careless rational choice. In contrast, a person's true preferences are the preferences he *would* have if he had all the relevant factual information, always reasoned with the greatest possible care, and were in a state of mind most conducive to rational choice.[31]

Social utility, he then concludes, should be defined in terms of the true, rather than the manifest, preferences of individuals, and the maximization of social utility is the appropriate social goal. Harsanyi puts forward this idea as a perfectly general theory of social choice, especially in the area of fundamental principles: he characterizes his preference-based ethical theory as an alternative to Rawls's theory of justice.[32]

Notice that to come up with something that seems even prima facie satisfactory, Harsanyi has had to add not only the usual corrections to belief and information, but also the strongly normative procedural idea of careful reasoning and the "state of mind most conducive to rational choice." He does not further describe this last ingredient, but when we think of our cases we can easily spot some people who are *not* in a state of mind that seems conducive to rational choice: Vasanti, intimidated by her husband's physical abuse and terrified about her survival prospects should she leave him; Jayamma, habituated to thinking that unequal control over household income is just women's lot; Tagore's character Mrinal in my epigraph, used to thinking of herself as of little worth. Those conditions certainly don't strike us as conducive to rational choice, and this is just the point Tagore's character is making

31 *Ibid.*
32 Harsanyi, pp. 40–41.

when she explains to her husband how she has finally decided to leave him. For her, adequate choice-making required, first of all, throwing off the slumberous state induced by years of contempt and neglect. But if we were to put absence of traditional hierarchy, absence of fear, and a sense of one's own worth and dignity into the rational choice process, we would be moving very far indeed from a standard welfarist approach. I shall suggest later that these additions really do help us construct an informed-desire approach that is of some heuristic value; but it is quite unclear whether Harsanyi means to take us so far from his welfarist starting point.

Again, consider the women of SEWA in my second epigraph, who see videos of women doing daring new things and thereby gain confidence that they can do these things too. Now clearly it is Lila Datania's point that the experience of watching the videos helps these women make adequate choices for the future – not only by giving them new information but by enhancing their sense of their own possibilities and worth. But we wouldn't think of this as progress, or a correction of malformed preferences in the direction of "true" preferences, if the women were taught by the videos to hide away in the house all day, or to believe that they were made for physical abuse. And yet we know well that videos (violent pornographic videos, for example) can teach people such attitudes about themselves and others. It is because we have an implicit theory of value that holds self-respect and economic agency to be important goods that we think the preferences constructed by the videos are good; it's not clear that there would be any purely formal way to make the distinction.

Datania's point is very similar to one made by economist Gary Becker in his 1992 Nobel address, when he observed that women and minorities frequently underinvest in their own human capital, where education and training are concerned, making bad decisions because they have been brought up to believe that they can't do certain things that other people can do.[33] Becker argued that social prejudices of various sorts, especially "the *beliefs* of employers, teachers, and other influential groups that minority members are less productive *can* be self-

33 Gary Becker, "The Economic Way of Looking at Behavior," in *The Essence of Becker*, ed. Ramón Febrero and Pedro S. Schwartz (Stanford, CA: Hoover Institution Press, 1995), 633–58, at 634.

fulfilling," causing the members of the disadvantaged group to "underinvest in education, training, and work skills" – and this under-investment does subsequently make them less productive. In short, disadvantaged groups – among whom Becker includes "blacks, women, religious groups, immigrants, and others" – internalize their second-class status in ways that cause them to make choices that perpetuate that second-class status.[34] In his normative public policy mode, Becker clearly considers these decisions bad for the people, and contrary to what a wise social policy should encourage.[35] But in making this observation Becker has clearly moved quite far from a standard welfarist normative approach, in a way that, once again, implicitly demands a normative theory of justice and human capability. Harsanyi does not appear prepared to take such a radical step.[36] But his own criteria clearly point in the direction of some such further normative account, and he gives us too little information to tell whether he could spell out his last condition in a way compatible with his welfarist principle. Certainly in practical terms the murky exercise of imagining all the relevant counterfactuals would have to be guided by some sort of relatively independent normative theory.

Harsanyi makes one further correction to welfarism that takes him more clearly away from welfarism. This is, that some people's "true" preferences will have to be excluded altogether from the social-utility function. "In particular, we must exclude all clearly antisocial prefer-

---

34 It is not made clear here whether the preferences are deformed or whether the women are led to make choices that are contrary to what they really prefer (since Becker, unlike Paul Samuelson and other advocates of the "revealed-preference" view of choice, makes a conceptual distinction between preference and choice). Probably one should distinguish two levels of generality: at a more general level, the woman's preference for a flourishing life is not distorted, but is frustrated by the counterproductive choice she makes; at a more concrete level, however, her preference for not getting very much education – which may seem to her the best route available to a flourishing life – can be held to be distorted by the false beliefs she holds.

35 See "Why the Third World Should Stress the Three R's" and "Let's Defuse the Population Bomb – with Free Markets," reprinted in Gary S. Becker and Guity Nashat Becker, *The Economics of Life* (New York: McGraw Hill, 1996), 67–8, 287–9. The former defends increased public spending on education and health for the poor in Brazil and other developing countries; the latter echoes the now familiar point that education is a key to holding down population growth.

36 In part this is because he has convinced himself that the only two normative theories on the table are hedonism and the ideal mental states theory of G. E. Moore, and he does not find either of these very plausible: see Harsanyi, 54.

ences, such as sadism, envy, resentment, and malice."[37] Harsanyi's justification for this move is fascinating for the way in which it reveals moral intuitions of a nonwelfarist kind that lie beneath his welfarism. The "fundamental basis" of our moral commitments to others in utilitarianism, he says, is "a general goodwill and human sympathy." Thus "[u]tilitarian ethics makes all of us members of the same moral community." But if this idea of a moral community is what lies behind utilitarianism and gives its normative judgments their appeal, then we must interpret utilitarianism to demand the exclusion of parts of real people's personalities that are hostile to the idea of a moral community: "A person displaying ill will toward others does remain a member of this community, but not with his whole personality. That part of his personality that harbours these hostile antisocial feelings must be excluded from membership, and has no claim for a hearing when it comes to defining our concept of social utility."[38]

Harsanyi began his article by saying that three ethical theories have influenced his own: the ideal-observer theory of Adam Smith, classical utilitarianism, and Kant's categorical imperative.[39] Throughout most of his argument, the utilitarian influence predominates, and we see rather little of Kant and Smith; but at this point they surface. It appears that an idea of quite a Kantian sort lies, for Harsanyi, at the bottom of the utilitarian social choice function – and it is only as regulated by that ideal vision of a community of ends (or perhaps by Smith's conception of a community of ideally judicious and sympathetic agents) that the utility function can prove acceptable as a basis of social policy. Harsanyi does not say enough here for us to ascribe to him a very definite ethical conception. But we may conclude that Harsanyi's real interest in preferences is, at bottom, something like a Kantian interest in respecting persons, their equality and their autonomy, and that he is not really averse to any departure from utilitarianism that preserves these essential Kantian features. In short, his view is only in appearance a

37 Harsanyi, 56, taking issue with J. J. C. Smart's version of normative utilitarian theory.
38 *Ibid.*
39 Harsanyi, 39–40. The debt to the utilitarians is called his "greatest," but Kant and Smith are given considerable emphasis. He says that he has "benefited from" Kant; he also alludes to the contemporary Kantian theory of R. M. Hare – whose influence might well explain Harsanyi's tendency to think of Kantianism and Utilitarianism as allies rather than antagonists.

welfarist view; in reality, considerations without which welfarism wouldn't appeal to him in the least lead him to propose a radical critique of welfarism.

One more outpost on the road away from welfarism should now be considered, since it probably represents the most intelligent and consistent attempt to refurbish the preference-based view of social choice. This is Richard Brandt's view of "cognitive psychotherapy" in *A Theory of the Good and the Right*.[40] Like Harsanyi, Brandt sees his view as an alternative to John Rawls's theory of justice, and thus as a view that tells us how to choose basic political principles, as well as how to make many other personal and social choices.[41]

Brandt, like Harsanyi (or the apparent Harsanyi) is, ultimately, a welfarist. He holds that the ultimate criterion of both personal and social rationality must be found within each person, not by importing any values external to that person's own values. But since Brandt recognizes that errors are frequently deeply implanted in people and cannot always be driven out by a simple disclosure of the relevant facts, he concludes that we can get to the person's true preferences only by a prolonged process of "cognitive psychotherapy." The desires that result from this process are used to define rationality for persons.[42] The basic principles of society are then defined in terms of what a fully rational person would support. Thus the account of cognitive psychotherapy forms the core of Brandt's view of how to choose basic political principles. We may examine it to see whether Brandt has really produced a consistently welfarist account of social choice.

Cognitive psychotherapy is carefully defined as "value-free reflection" that "relies simply upon reflection on available information, without influence by prestige of someone, use of evaluative language, extrinsic reward or punishment, or use of artificially induced feeling-states like relaxation."[43] This process is then used to define rationality in desire: "I shall call a person's desire, aversion, or pleasure 'rational' if

40 Richard B. Brandt, *A Theory of the Good and the Right* (Oxford: Clarendon Press, 1979).
41 See the discussion of Rawls's theory at 234–45.
42 The argument here has two stages: first, therapized desire is used to define the good for persons; then it is used to define what is morally right. The key link between the two arguments is Brandt's assumption that it is appropriate to appraise morality in terms of the utility or good of agents (184).
43 *Ibid.*, 113.

it would survive or be produced by careful 'cognitive psychotherapy' for that person. I shall call a desire 'irrational' if it cannot survive compatibly with clear and repeated judgements about established facts." We notice already that the absence of authority, intimidation, and hierarchy in the method is itself not so clearly value-neutral; it expresses values – independence, liberty, self-driven choice – that Brandt actually thinks very important. These are indeed important values to build into a procedure for the cognitive scrutiny of desire. They are, moreover, highly pertinent to the situation of women in oppressive surroundings: for frequently what women will say in the presence of oppression is very different from what they will say to those they trust, or reveal in their covert actions.[44] What is questionable is that we should think of the resulting method as entirely value-free.

Brandt now identifies four categories of mistake that cognitive psychotherapy would, in his view, remove.[45] First, there is the large category of desires that depend upon false beliefs (and recall that this must not include beliefs about matters of value, which remain unaffected by the cognitive process). Second, there are generalizations from untypical examples; these, too, can ultimately be dislodged by a more extensive confrontation with a wider range of examples. Third,[46] there is the category called "artificial Desire-Arousal in Culture-Transmission." What Brandt means here is that cultures transmit values by example and precept, frequently in ways that could not have been produced by the real experience of what is talked about, without cultural interference. Brandt's two examples are the occupation of garbage collecting, and "marriage to a person of another race, religion, or nationality." Actual experience with these activities, says Brandt, could prove very satisfying, and certainly there's no reason to suppose that they would produce an intrinsic aversion in someone who had had no prior cultural conditioning. Of course, he continues, the social attitudes of others are themselves real facts with which people have to deal. "But in-

---

44 See Agarwal, *A Field of One's Own*, 422–38, discussing evidence of everyday resistance by women in South Asia, and also discussing the Malaysian evidence presented in J. C. Scott, *Weapons of the Weak: Everyday Forms of Peasant Resistance* (New Haven: Yale University Press, 1976).
45 Brandt, 115–26.
46 I have inverted the order of categories two and three, since I find Brandt's original third straightforward and his original second very problematic.

tense concern with the attitudes of other people is itself founded upon error – the false belief that the attitudes of others are crucially important for an adult, especially if the attitudes in question are those of one's own parents only."

In this fascinating paragraph we see Brandt trying to the utmost to squeeze conclusions that please him out of the allegedly value-free method that he recommends. Brandt's love of liberty, his democratic respect for those who do manual labor, and his dislike of superstition all make him see the attitudes of those who shrink from intermarriage and garbage collecting as profoundly irrational. Probably he is right to say that an untutored child would experience no natural disdain for these things, but it is not clear that this is the line he should take, since an untutored child might also lack the basis for many social attitudes Brandt does not want to get rid of, such as an aversion to cruelty, a concern for the well-being of the poor, a love of free speech, a passion for justice. So the value-free science removes too much, if it really removes all attitudes that require evaluative learning in a culture for their transmission. As for the allegedly value-free false belief that the attitudes of others, including one's parents, are unimportant, once again this is so only given a certain scheme of ends and values, and not given others. In short, Brandt's liberal and democratic instincts clash, as did Harsanyi's, with what his argument can actually deliver – despite the fact that he is more hard-headed than Harsanyi in his attempts to do without values.

Brandt's fourth category of mistake is that of "Exaggerated Valences Produced by Early Deprivation."[47] His example is a letter to the Dear Abby newspaper column, in which a woman complains about her husband, who grew up fatherless during the depression and has now become quite wealthy. Nonetheless, he is obsessed with saving for his old age, to a degree that makes his family unhappy: he buys second-hand clothes, eats stale bread, and so on. (Brandt notes that similar behavior can be observed in laboratory rats.)[48] Here, he says, we have a syndrome in which early deprivation and its associated anxieties lead to an exaggerated later development of desire. He claims that such abnor-

47 Brandt, 122–26.
48 *Ibid.*, 123: rats who have been deprived of food respond by massive hoarding when food becomes abundant.

mally strong desires would diminish once their root causes were brought to the surface – both in the case of money and in the case of other goods, such as love or affection, that might be lacking in one's early life.

But of course the unresolved question is, when is a desire for money, or for love, "exaggerated"? Are we supposed to be able to tell that without a theory of value? And what counts as "deprivation" in early life? Again, we need a normative account of proper love, and proper material support, to get started here. By choosing a very bizarre case, Brandt conceals the depth of this problem. But here again, clearly, he is getting to some characteristic Brandtian value conclusions (for example, that people should not be very dependent on the love and approval of others) through an allegedly factual exercise. A useful parallel is in an earlier article on suicide, in which Brandt judges that suicide for love is "irrational," since "[i]f a person is disappointed in love, it is possible to adopt a vigorous plan of action which carries a good chance of acquainting him with someone else he likes at least as well."[49] Well, perhaps – but that's a substantive moral position, masquerading as value-free science.

In short, the welfarist attempt to refurbish the preference- or desire-based view runs into difficulty; it appears unable to deliver all that the welfarist philosopher/economists themselves would like to get. We can get a certain distance by adding information and correcting logical error. But to get all the way to Harsanyi's ideal of a moral community of equals, or to Brandt's ideal of an independent hard-headed unsuperstitious democratic citizenry, or to Becker's ideal of educated free citizens making choices that are untainted by low self-worth, these thinkers have had to inject value judgments into the procedures of revision – contrary to the original intentions of Harsanyi and Brandt, though Becker more circumspectly keeps a distance between his positive and normative projects.

No discussion of the self-criticism of economists would be complete without mentioning the well-known problems for welfarism raised by two results in formal social choice theory: Kenneth Arrow's impossibility result and Amartya Sen's Paradox of the Paretian Liberal.[50] These

49 R. B. Brandt, "The Morality and Rationality of Suicide," in James Rachels, ed., *Moral Problems* (N.Y.: Harper and Row, 1975), 363–87.
50 Kenneth Arrow, *Social Choice and Individual Values* (New York: Wiley, 1951; 2nd ed. 1963); for further discussion of Arrow's paradox and the wide range of impossibil-

results are so widely discussed in the technical literature that little could be added by a brief discussion in this context; and yet to omit them would be to omit an important part of the story of welfarist dissatisfaction with welfarism. Arrow's theorem showed that there is no social welfare function that can satisfy four conditions, each individually plausible, and each rather weak: *Unrestricted Domain* (all possible *n*-tuples of individual preference orderings are included); *Weak Pareto Principle* (for any pair of alternatives, if everyone strictly prefers one of these to the other, that one will be chosen); *Non-Dictatorship* (there is no person whose strict preference over any pair of alternatives is invariably reflected in social strict preference); and *Independence of Irrelevant Alternatives* (put informally, the idea that the ordering is independent of the relationship of the choices under deliberation to other alternatives not available for the purposes of deliberation). This important result, debated and extended in many ways, has certainly not caused social choice theorists to give up hope for a welfarist (preference-driven) theory of social choice. But it does raise questions, certainly. Such a theory commended itself on grounds of simplicity and rationality; but if even these very weak axioms run into impossibility, then it seems that the entire enterprise needs rethinking in some direction. But the Weak Pareto Principle and Non-Dictatorship, in particular, seem to be assumptions so weak and so fundamental to any preference-based normative theory, that it would certainly be difficult to give them up or even to modify them significantly.

Sen's result is, for our purposes, even more striking. For he shows formally what philosophers have frequently observed intuitively: that a preference-based theory has trouble accommodating liberal rights. Sen shows that we get an impossibility result if we combine Arrow's principle of Unrestricted Domain and his weak version of the Pareto principle with a formal representation of the idea that society should protect spaces within which individuals pursue their own preferences. The reason for this is that, obviously enough, people have preferences about

ity results it generated, see Amartya Sen, "Social Choice Theory: A Re-Examination," in Sen, CWM, 158–200 (based on a paper published in *Econometrica* 45 (1977), 58–89); I follow Sen's discussion of the 1963 version of the theorem. For the Paretian Liberal paradox, see Amartya Sen, "The Impossibility of a Paretian Liberal," *Journal of Political Economy* 78 (1970), 152–7, reprinted in Sen, CWM, 285–90; "Liberty, Unanimity and Rights," *Economica* 43 (1976), 271–45, reprinted in CWM, 291–326; and, for Sen's review of the voluminous literature on his paradox, see CWM, Introduction, 25–8.

the activities of others: Sen's Prude does not want his neighbor, Lewd, to gratify his preference to read *Lady Chatterley's Lover*. This insight, of course, is closely related to the group of insights expressed by Harsanyi when he insisted that malicious, sadistic, and other antisocial preferences must be excluded from the social choice function; given the wide influence of Sen's essay, the issues it raises were inescapable by the time Harsanyi wrote. But Sen's result has a special importance for the development of economic thought on this issue, since it generated the impossibility result using the usual materials of welfarist social choice theory, without importing any surprising Kantian notions or any other philosophical norms. In effect, it gave formal substance and respectability to the idea that some of the deepest commitments of welfarism are in internal tension and require thorough rethinking.

We now arrive at the turning in the road, so to speak, where a dedicated welfarist states that welfarism is inadequate as a basis for public policy. Throughout his early work in law and economics, Richard Posner adopted a fairly standard preference-based view, using it for both positive and normative purposes. Frequently he criticized political choices as irrational (in the normative sense) if they failed to maximize utility, defined in terms of preference-satisfaction.[51] But Posner is also a Millean libertarian. And he eventually became convinced that utilitarianism offers insufficient protection for basic liberties. What Brandt and Harsanyi merely hinted at, Posner states openly: preference-based economic thought is "a potential menace to basic liberties" and "could furnish economic justification for every manner of discrimination against despised minorities." These "illiberal implications" cannot be made to disappear "by judicious assignment of rights." These implications, moreover, don't just include jeopardy to basic liberties; they "seem to include condoning torture and gruesome punishments, enforcing contracts of self-enslavement, permitting gladiatorial contests in which the contestants fight to the death, enforcing Shylock's pound-of-flesh bond, and abolishing all walfare programs and other forms of social insurance." The utilitarian may say that we ought to give effi-

---

51 See, for example, *The Economics of Justice* (Cambridge, MA: Harvard University Press, 1981), criticizing Supreme Court privacy jurisprudence in this way: 329–347, calling the leading cases a "topsy-turvy world." Posner has since taken a very different view of the privacy cases and the recognition of a right of privacy: see *Sex and Reason* (Cambridge, MA: Harvard University Press, 1991).

ciency priority over liberty. Posner responds: "Why should we? Our liberal intuitions are as deep as our utilitarian ones, and there is no intellectual procedure that will or should force us to abandon them."[52] Posner's points are hardly new; philosophers and non-utilitarian economists have been saying just this for a long time. But his decisive statement is interesting for the way in which it confronts forthrightly a deep problem that other economic thinkers try to bury.

IV. ADAPTIVE PREFERENCES AND THE REJECTION OF WELFARISM

It is not surprising, when zealous defenders of the welfarist project still find themselves diverging from it, that others, less wedded to the project, should conclude that for normative purposes – and especially for the purposes of choosing basic political principles – the informed-desire approach is inadequate. In recent years there has been an explosion of work attacking the preference-based approach to normative issues of public choice. But it is worth reviewing the different arguments that have been made, in order to see exactly how far they do break with a preference-based view, and in what ways. Since there are so many interesting writers in this area, it will be best to proceed by argument, rather than by thinker.

1. *The Argument from Appropriate Procedure.* The informed-desire approach struck even Harsanyi and Brandt as in need of procedural supplementation: in different ways, they each built into the procedure the idea of a community of equals, unintimidated by power or authority, and unaffected by envy or fear inspired by awareness of their place in a social hierarchy. And this of course has been a tremendous area of normative work, among thinkers who continue to believe that some form of proceduralism will suffice as a basis for social choice. The views of John Rawls and Jürgen Habermas about fair procedures of public choice are both too familiar and too complex for me to get involved in discussing them here, but both clearly do with rigor and detail what Harsanyi didn't fully do, but only mentioned: that is, model

52 All citations from Richard A. Posner, *Overcoming Law* (Cambridge, MA: Harvard University Press, 1995), 23.

a Kantian ideal of moral community, by introducing constraints on information and procedure. To this distinguished list we should add Jean Hampton, whose feminist proceduralism, in the important article "Feminist Contractarianism,"[53] I shall later compare to my own normative proposal. Still other thinkers about the autonomy of preference and desire, for example Gerald Dworkin and Jon Elster,[54] have placed special emphasis on a procedure of critical scrutiny through which one examines the origins of one's desires in order to make certain that they are not merely the result of habit. This idea of practical reason as engaged in the critical scrutiny of tradition and the construction of a plan of life is clearly a normative notion, and none of the thinkers in question believes it to be just a minor adjustment to the utilitarian project.

Thus, especially in the context of fundamental political choices, even those thinkers who prefer a proceduralist derivation of principles to one based from the start on judgments about goals nonetheless design procedures that incorporate substantive ethical values that are incompatible with welfarism. I shall later suggest that there is, and ought to be, a substantial convergence between such morally laden forms of proceduralism and an approach like mine, which begins from a set of fundamental social goals.

2. *The Argument from Adaptation.* Closely linked to these normative criticisms of utilitarianism is a set of arguments that focus on the phenomenon of *adaptation*, in which individuals adjust their desires to the way of life they know. Jon Elster's account of adaptation is rather narrowly focused. For him, a desire counts as adaptive only if it really has a fox-and-grapes structure: having desired the grapes, the fox, seeing that he can't get the grapes, judges that they are sour. Such preferences are to be distinguished from desire-changes based on learning and experience: for the latter are likely to be irreversible, whereas adaptive preferences (for city life when in the city, for country life when in the

---

53 For a related view, see Thomas E. Hill, Jr., "Servility and Self-Respect" and "Self-Respect Reconsidered," in *Autonomy and Self-Respect* (Cambridge: Cambridge University Press, 1991), 4–24.

54 Gerald Dworkin, "The Nature of Autonomy," in Dworkin, *The Theory and Practice of Autonomy*, 3–20; Jon Elster, "Sour Grapes," in Sen and Williams, 219–38, and in the book of the same title. Subsequent page references are to the article.

country) are far from irreversible. Elster also distinguishes his adaptive preferences from preferences that are the result of precommitment (a deliberate narrowing of the feasible set), from preferences based on deliberate character shaping, from preferences based on wishful thinking (which alter the perception of the situation rather than the desire),[55] and finally, from desires induced by the deliberate manipulation of one's psychology by someone else. Adaptive preferences are formed without one's control or awareness, by a causal mechanism that isn't of one's own choosing – and that is why Elster finds them suspect, bad bases for social choice. He contrasts them with "autonomous preferences," which have in some manner been the object of reflection and have been deliberately chosen or at least endorsed by the agent. Elster's contrast between the adaptive and the autonomous has many applications; but one area in which Elster seems interested in putting it to work is the area of choice of basic social or political principles: for his central example is that of the social revolutions that were inspired by the discontent brought on by the industrial revolution.

Elster's somewhat romantic preference for striving and yearning makes him suspicious of any desire that is formed through adjustment to reality. But it is not at all clear that he should in such a sweeping way condemn adaptive preferences. We get used to having the bodies we do have, and even if, as children, we wanted to fly like birds, we simply drop that after a while, and are probably the better for it.[56] Again, someone as a child may want to be the best opera singer in the world (as I did), or the best basketball player – but most people adjust their aspirations to what they can actually achieve. It seems that these changes do involve the fox-and-grapes structure that Elster rules out as incompatible with autonomy: they are adjustments in response to a perception of one's circumstances, rather than the result of deliberate character formation, and they lack the condition of "freedom to do

---

55 Here we should note that Elster appears to be operating with a rather noncognitive notion of desire, in which desire and perception can be so cleanly separated because desire doesn't have much intentional content. If he is wrong about many desires and emotions (and I believe he is), then this distinction becomes much harder to maintain.

56 Contrast, however, Derek Parfit, *Reasons and Persons* (Oxford: Oxford University Press, 1984), 122, who uses the example of flying as a paradigm of rational desire: "This is someting worth desiring; we can rationally envy birds." I need not deny that it might be rational to envy birds in order to make the point I am making here, that it is not necessarily bad to give up such a desire.

otherwise" that Elster introduces as a necessary condition for autonomous wants, to distinguish them from adaptive wants.[57] I am not free to be a leading opera singer, nor is a short adult free to be a leading basketball player. We have failed to reach the grapes, and we have shifted our preferences in keeping with that failure, judging that such lives are not for us. But clearly this is often a good thing, and we probably shouldn't encourage people to persist in unrealistic aspirations.[58]

The cases that Elster actually has in mind are interestingly different: the way in which feudalism made people not aspire to political equality and material well-being, the way the industrial revolution unleashed a storm of class-based discontent that was ultimately very productive politically and economically. But to distinguish this case from my cases of the bird and the basketball player, he needs something he doesn't give us, a substantive theory of justice and central goods. It was fruitful for these people to hold onto their (pro tempore) unrealizable desires because they were desires for central goods, things people as people have a right to have. People's liberty can indeed be measured, not by the sheer number of unrealizable wants they have, but by the extent to which they want what human beings have a right to have. Thus Vasanti, who hated her domestic abuse, seems a little more free than Jayamma, who acquiesced in discrimination and oppression. Both, however, were unfree in one further crucial way: they lacked an understanding of themselves as citizens who have rights that are being violated. That type of adjustment to bad circumstances is indeed deplorable, and we view it as progress when they come to realize they have a right to better treatment, even if that better treatment is not yet forthcoming. But to say this, we need an account of what types of treatment people have a right to expect in central areas of their lives.

---

57 See 228–9: "We can exclude operationally at least one kind of non-autonomous wants, viz. adaptive preferences, by requiring freedom to do otherwise. If I want to do x, and am free to do x, and free not to do x, then my want cannot be shaped by necessity. . . . And so we may conclude that, other things being equal, one's freedom is a function of the number and the importance of the things that one (i) wants to do, (ii) is free to do and (iii) is free not to do."

58 Contrast Elster, 228, holding that a person's degree of autonomy can be measured by the number of things he wants to do but is not at liberty to do, for such unrealizable wants show that his preference-structure "is not in general shaped by adaptive preference formation."

Once again, proceduralism – even of a more complicated sort – seems insufficient without something in the way of a substantive theory.

Such a theory is to some extent provided by the other prominent economist who discusses adaptive preferences, Amartya Sen.[59] Sen focuses on the situation of women and other deprived people; his central case is that of women who do not desire some basic human good because they have been long habituated to its absence or told that it is not for such as them. For example, in 1944, the year after the Great Bengal Famine, the All-India Institute of Hygiene and Public Health did a survey in an area near Calcutta, including in the survey many widows and widowers. Among the widowers, 45.6% ranked their health as either "ill" or "indifferent." Only 2.5% of widows made that judgment, and none at all ranked their health as "indifferent" (as Sen notes, a more subjective category than "ill"). This was in striking contrast to their real situation, since widows tend to be a particularly deprived group with regard to basic health and nutrition. Sen concludes: "Quiet acceptance of deprivation and bad fate affects the scale of dissatisfaction generated, and the utilitarian calculus gives sanctity to that distortion." One can also make a remark in the other direction: privileged people get used to being pampered and cared for, and may feel an unusually high level of discontent when the one that did the pampering isn't around any longer. Sen concludes that this makes utility quite inadequate as a basis of social choice.

Sen's group of cases is, notice, both broader and narrower than Elster's. It is broader, because Sen includes lifelong habituation, and doesn't focus simply on giving up a desire one once had. And this is important where women are concerned, since most of the interesting cases do involve lifelong socialization and absence of information. The group is narrower because the cases on which he dwells all involve a central human capability. Although Sen has never been willing to endorse a substantive theory of the central capabilities, in practice he does so, and therefore doesn't trouble himself about the adaptive preference of someone who gives up his dream of basketball stardom when he

---

59 See, for example, "Gender Inequality and Theories of Justice," in WCD, 259–73; "Rights and Capabilities," in RVD, 307–24; there are many other articles in which Sen has discussed the phenomenon. On the deprivations associated with widowhood in India, see Martha Chen, *Permanent Moving: Widowhood in Rural India* (Delhi and Philadelphia: Oxford University Press and University of Pennsylvania Press, 1999).

finds that he is never going to be taller than five-feet-four (and let us suppose he's not Muggsy Bogues).[60] There is no romantic preference for striving as a good in itself in Sen's view; the appropriateness of desire is tethered, implicitly at any rate, to a sense of the basic goods of life.

Sen's analysis of adaptation corresponds well to what we find in the cases of Jayamma, Vasanti, and the women of Andhra Pradesh. All to some extent undervalue basic human capabilities that they later come to value, because of social habituation and social pressure. Vasanti's adaptation was the shallowest; for she believed all along that the conditions under which she was living in her marriage were bad. She wanted an end to domestic violence, and she wanted more control over the sources of her economic well-being. But she did not yet have the conception of herself as someone who has *been wronged*, who *has a right* not to be abused, and to seek both employment and credit on a basis of equality with men. Over the years she learned those concepts, and now she teaches other women to see themselves as rights-bearers. Jayamma and the women of Andhra Pradesh had preferences that were in some respects more deeply adaptive, with respect to some central human capabilities. Jayamma didn't think it bad that her husband should use his income on luxuries and make her do all the housework; she didn't think the division of labor at the brick kiln bad. The women in Andhra Pradesh, similarly, didn't think that the absence of electricity, teachers, and bus services was a bad thing, that being the only way they had known. So these women had to go through a two-stage process of awareness: coming to see themselves as in a bad situation, and coming to see themselves as citizens who had a right to a better situation. Sen's analysis of adaptation implicitly points to these two stages; but his analysis can usefully be fleshed out by making them explicit.

Finally, the phenomenon of adaptive preferences was discussed in a particularly illuminating and important way, where women's desires are concerned, by John Stuart Mill in *The Subjection of Women*. Of course Mill is here simply following more or less the whole Western philosophical tradition, most of which has stressed the social origin of

---

60 Muggsy Bogues, five feet four inches tall, was an extraordinary player for the Charlotte Hornets professional basketball team, whose jumping, speed, and dexterity made him a key to his team's success.

many baneful passions (such as anger and excessive greed). But he applies it with fascinating effect to the case of women's subordination, using, like Elster, a judicious analogy with feudalism. What he newly does is to bring out the similarity between the adaptive preferences of lords and vassals and the adaptive preferences of men and women. Just as lords get used to being superior and vassals to being inferior, so too with women and men – with one salient difference. This is, that lords maintained their power by physical force. Men often do so, but they also want something more:

Men do not want solely the obedience of women, they want their sentiments. All men, except the most brutish, desire to have, in the woman most nearly connected with them, not a forced slave but a willing one, not a slave merely, but a favourite. They have therefore put everything in practice to enslave their minds. The masters of all other slaves rely, for maintaining obedience, on fear . . . The masters of women wanted more than simple obedience, and they turned the whole force of education to effect their purpose. All women are brought up from the very earliest years in the belief that their ideal of character is the very opposite to that of men; not self-will, and government by self-control, but submission, and yielding to the control of others.[61]

Mill argues, further, that these ideals shape not only moral sentiments, but also sexuality itself: for men come to eroticize submissiveness, and women to believe submissiveness erotically essential. (With Andrea Dworkin, he could have added that they in turn frequently learn to eroticize power and domination.)[62]

How does Mill, a Utilitarian, criticize these adaptive preferences? Clearly, with a normative theory of liberty and equality. He makes some instrumental arguments about the social good that will be done by a more thorough use of women's talents, but the central advantage to which he points is "the advantage of having the most universal and pervading of all human relations regulated by justice instead of injustice."[63]

This is hardly an occasion on which to conduct a probing examination of Mill's Utilitarianism and its connection with his theory of lib-

61 Mill, SW, 15–16.
62 See my "Rage and Reason," *The New Republic*, August 11 and 18, 1997, pp. 36–42, and Chapter 9 in *Sex and Social Justice*.
63 SW, 86.

erty. But we can say at least this, and it is revealing for our purposes. Mill does think it highly relevant that the values he defends are in some sense rooted in human desire – that people who have tried both liberty and its lack will prefer liberty, that justice is a prominent object of human striving. He supports his proposals in *On Liberty* with reference to a quite Aristotelian account of the human powers and their flourishing, referring to "a Greek ideal of self-development," and calling human nature "a tree, which requires to grow and develop itself on all sides."[64] In a manner closely related to my argument in Chapter 1, he speaks of liberty as a development of basic human mental powers, which, like physical powers, are developed only by being used; in a society without liberty, "human capacities are withered and starved."[65] But he also links this Aristotelian notion of self-development to a notion of experienced desire, saying that liberty is good in part because it satisfies certain "permanent interests" of human beings and, further, because it permits individuals to satisfy more of their other interests (given differences of taste that need liberty for their expression). His notion of utility is plural, more like an Aristotelian notion of flourishing than like Bentham's hedonism; he famously insists that pleasures differ in quality as well as quantity, a view that undermines key aspects of Bentham's maximization strategy. But, like Aristotle, Mill regards it as more than a contingent matter that the constituent parts of flourishing are in fact powerfully and deeply desired. This doesn't rescue the welfarist project in its original form – but it does constrain the move to platonism, in an appropriate way. For it would hardly be plausible to say that good nutrition for women in Andhra Pradesh, or Vasanti's bodily integrity, or Jayamma's equality as a laborer, are things to be pursued altogether independently of their relationship to human desire and choice. The welfarist project fails, in its simplest form; but it gets something important right.

3. *The Institutional Argument.* A closely related group of arguments has recently been advanced, in law, political philosophy, and public policy. These arguments show, in various ways, that people's preferences are in many ways constructed by the laws and institutions under

64 John Stuart Mill, *On Liberty* (1859) (Indianapolis: Bobbs Merrill, 1956), 76, 72.
65 *Ibid.*, 71, 75.

which they live. This being the case, we can hardly use preferences as a bedrock in our deliberation about what laws and institutions we wish to construct. John Rawls, for example, emphasizes that "the institutional form of society affects its members and determines in large part the kind of persons they want to be as well as the kind of persons they are."[66]

Legal theorist Cass Sunstein develops this point with a rich range of examples.[67] Welfarist views, he argues, entrench the status quo. But people's preferences are shaped by the sheer fact of existing endowments. Studies of the so-called endowment effect, for example, show that people value the very same item more highly when they have it and the question of parting with it arises than when they do not have it, but have an option to purchase it. In short: "A powerful status quo bias affects reactions to risks and losses. It is for this reason that status quo neutrality is not neutrality at all."[68] But if legal rules are involved in the creation of preferences, then they cannot be justified simply by appealing to those same preferences. Sunstein concludes that democracy needs a normative notion of free preference formation with substantive moral constraints; instead of simply responding to the way preferences already are, the basic constitutional structure must protect the process of free deliberation.[69]

These arguments are really just new instances of the adaptation argument, since they speak of the way in which habituation shapes desire and aspiration. (Sunstein refers to Sen's arguments.) But Sunstein's focus on society's basic institutional and legal/constitutional structure makes his arguments worth considering separately. The point is that here we see a particularly acute problem for welfarists in the area of the present project: precisely what thinkers such as Haranyi and Brandt want to use preferences to construct – the public institutional structure

---

66 John Rawls, PL, 269.

67 Sunstein, *The Partial Constitution*, Chapter 6: "Democracy, Aspirations, Preferences"; also "Preferences and Politics," *Philosophy and Public Affairs* 20 (1991), 3–34, reprinted in revised form in *Free Markets and Social Justice* (New York: Oxford University Press, 1997), 13–31.

68 Sunstein, *Partial Constitution*, 168. Sunstein cites John Dewey as another thinker who made similar criticisms of existing preferences, holding that "social conditions may restrict, distort, and almost prevent the development of individuality"; Dewey calls for "the positive construction of favorable institutions, legal, political, and economic" (Sunstein, *Partial Constitution*, 176, citing "The Future of Liberalism").

69 Sunstein, *Partial Constitution*, 177.

– is what turns out to be a major source of the preferences themselves. Rather than using preferences to model institutions, Sunstein argues, we should use institutions to create free preferences.

4. *The Argument from Intrinsic Worth.* Even if the welfarist can show that people desire liberty and justice, and even if some modification of the welfarist procedure could be devised that reliably generated those goods (without smuggling them somehow into the structure of the procedure itself), it would not be clear that this is the right way to justify our social interest in these goods. In general, the failure of a person to have various basic human capabilities is important in itself, not just because the person minds it or complains about it.[70] As Amartya Sen puts this point, "If a person is unable to get the nourishment he or she needs, or unable to lead a normal life due to some handicap, that failure . . . is itself important, and not made important only because he or she incurs dissatisfaction or disutility from that failure." Another way to put this is to say that even if we could engineer things so that people were reliably adapted to a very low living standard – and, as Mill says, the "masters of women" have in many areas done exactly that – this would not be the end of the issue of what is good or right. These failures themselves have importance, and just the bare fact that human beings are undergoing them should be enough for us.

This argument is the flip side of the adaptation argument. It tells us positively what that argument told us negatively, that we need a normative theory – preferably a theory of human capability that includes accounts of equality and liberty – to provide the normative basis that desire fails reliably to provide us.

Notice, however, that there are a number of ways of making this argument, many stopping well short of outright platonism. The platonist will indeed say that these eternal intrinsic values have the value they do altogether independent of human history, human choice, and human desire. But one might adopt a different account of justification, one that would make at least a qualified reference to choice and desire. Rawls's Socratic account of justification proceeding toward "reflective equilibrium" may be one such account; Aristotle's use of the person of practical wisdom as normative criterion is another; Dewey's pragma-

70 See Sen, "Family and Food: Sex Bias in Poverty," in RVD, 346–65, at 363.

tism offers another;[71] as we have seen, various norm-laden forms of proceduralism also justify with at least a certain sort of qualified reference to desire and choice.

Thus we can accept the argument from intrinsic value without accepting the extreme rejection of desire urged, for example, by Thomas Scanlon in his "Value, Desire, and the Quality of Life," and repeated in his recently published book.[72] Scanlon argues that there are only two reasons that desire is of any interest at all in the process of justifying an account of quality of life. One reason is hedonic: the satisfaction of a desire may bring pleasure, and pleasure is an intrinsic good. The other reason is heuristic: desire steers us in the direction of some intrinsic goods. But in either case, the reference to desire is dispensable: the hedonic reason points back to the intrinsic value of pleasure, which is (on this view) not valuable simply because it is desired; the heuristic reason points to items whose value must be independently arrived at. Given all this, and given that desire is frequently not such a good guide, there is no particular reason to be interested in it in constructing an account of quality of life.

I am not fully persuaded by this argument, for two reasons. First, in his article Scanlon never asks how, in the long run, we are actually going to justify a "substantive list" of values of the sort he prefers, without making at least some sort of reference to desire. He probably is not a thoroughgoing platonist, but in this article he never tells us what he really is, and what the "other grounds" are on which he would rest a judgment of desirability. In the book (and in his earlier "Preference and Urgency"),[73] Scanlon adopts a contractualist procedure of justification; but then he appears to be distinguishing choice strongly from desire, and it seems to me that he does not say enough to justify such a position. Kantian accounts of choice distinguish choice strongly from desire; Aristotelian accounts hold that choice is a deliberative type of desire. The absence of argument on these issues of moral psychology

---

71 See Hilary Putnam, "Pragmatism and Moral Objectivity," in WCD, 199–224. See also H. Putnam, *Pragmatism: An Open Question* (Oxford and Cambridge, MA: Blackwell, 1995), 57–75.

72 See note 9, and Scanlon, *What We Owe to Each Other* (Cambridge, MA: Harvard University Press, 1999), 41–49.

73 Thomas Scanlon, "Preference and Urgency," *The Journal of Philosophy* 72 (1975), 655–69.

leaves Scanlon with only inconclusive arguments for his platonist conclusion.

Second, Scanlon fails to consider a very strong reason we have for giving desire at least some role in our process of justification: the reason of respect I have already endorsed. The fact that human beings desire something does count; it counts because we think that politics, rightly understood, comes from people and what matters to them, not from heavenly norms. I do not think Scanlon disagrees with this; but then I remain puzzled by the dismissive attitude he takes to informed-desire approaches. We may perhaps make progress in understanding Scanlon's view by turning to "Preference and Urgency."[74] In that paper, Scanlon does endorse the reason of respect that I have discussed, but he argues that, so understood, the appeal to desire once again points back to an "objective" substantive good, viz., respect for persons; once again, desire is of no weight in and of itself.[75] Now this all seems very true, and yet I am not sure that it gets us all the way to a platonist conclusion: for we still need to know why respect for persons is appropriately shown by giving their desires some weight. And the answer to that question seems to be that we think of persons in a certain way, namely as creatures of whom it is true that the fact that they reach out for something has itself some importance, some dignity. They are not a passive herd or flock, but active and striving beings. Saying this, we are surely, in the terms of "Preference and Urgency," ascribing an objective value to desire. But I do not think this suffices to support the conclusion of the later article, in which all reference to desire becomes ultimately dispensable, being cashed out either in terms of the intrinsic value of pleasure or in terms of the other substantive goods on the list.

Once again, the puzzles generated by Scanlon's position appear to

74 A problem in putting this article together with the article in QL is that the basic conceptual categories of the two articles are rather different; in the earlier, the operative contrast is between "subjective" and "objective" factors; in the latter, the contrast is instead between informed-desire approaches and "substantive good" approaches.
75 "A high objective value may be attached to providing those conditions which are necessary to allow individuals to develop their own preferences and interests and to make these felt in the determination of social policy . . . What I take to be central to the objectivist position, however, is the idea that . . . it is an objective evaluation of the importance of these interests, and not merely the strength of the subjective preferences they represent, that is relevant."(658)

be created by his implicit adoption of a Kantian view of desire, which distinguishes sharply between desire and choice, desire and reason. Even if one thought of desire as brutish and unintelligent, as just a mindless "push" that moves people toward objects without involving any selectivity or intentionality, such a view would still not entail Scanlon's dismissive position – one might still think we have reason to attend to the pushes that people have in their natures and to give these some weight – but it would at least explain why a basically Kantian moral position would be inclined to bypass desire in favor of something that resides in the moral domain. On the other hand, if one thinks of desire, as I do, in a more Aristotelian way, as a reaching out for "the apparent good," and thus as involving, even at the level of appetite, a high degree of selective intentionality and responsiveness, one will have in that very picture of desire some strong reasons not to bypass it, for it seems to be a part of our humanity worthy of respect and voice.[76] In his recent book, discussing the views of Warren Quinn, Scanlon seems to grant that many desires have an evaluative element; and yet he continues to deny that, even so construed, they provide any independent reason for pursuing the object so evaluated. Once again, he argues, either they provide no reason at all, or the reason points back to pleasure, or some other independent good.[77] Once again, he endorses a strong distinction between desire and choice. Thus he seems to be willing to grant desire a heuristic role, while denying it any independent role in justification.

Scanlon's position is subtle, and its differences from my own are narrow. One way of putting his argument is to say that he thinks about

76 For my own account of emotions, appetites, and desires, see *Upheavals of Thought: A Theory of the Emotions* (Cambridge: Cambridge University Press, forthcoming); really, such a discussion needs the richer moral psychology I mentioned above, and needs to make distinctions among these three notions. For an account of desire I would favor, see Warren Quinn, "Rationality and the Human Good" and "Putting Rationality in Its Place," in Quinn, *Morality and Action* (Cambridge: Cambridge University Press, 1993), 210–55.

77 See also "Putting Desire and Irrationality in Their Places," paper delivered at a memorial conference for Warren Quinn, UCLA, April 15, 1995. In the latter paper, Scanlon agrees with Quinn that subjectivist accounts of desire that leave out the element of "evaluation" internal to desire are "impoverished," and he concludes that the term "desire," as used in many such discussions, is a slippery and ambiguous one; some desires are relatively independent of practical reason and some are not. The "desire satisfaction" model ignores such distinctions at its peril.

desire what I have already argued to be true of the concept of preference: that it is not a single concept but a multiple concept, whose different elements are frequently confused. Once we disentangle them, we are left, on the one hand, with impulses that do not by themselves provide reasons for action; on the other hand, with intelligent choice-like elements of the personality that do contain, and provide the agent with, reasons. I am not unhappy with this way of formulating the issue, but I think that it may possibly obscure a continuity between the intelligence and selectivity of basic appetitive elements in our animal nature and more complex choice-like elements, a continuity that is recognized and made salient by the general Aristotelian concept of desire, of which these types are multiple species. I shall argue that the very fact that human beings characteristically desire play, and intimacy, and control over their environment provides at least some reason for politics to secure these things to people, a reason that is not fully reducible to the other reasons we have for saying that these things are good. (In saying this I differ from Scanlon at least in the emphasis of my argument, and perhaps in substantive matters of moral psychology.) As we shall see, this will give desire a role in political justification that is more than merely heuristic.

V. DESIRE AND JUSTIFICATION

In my own view, the account of the central capabilities provides a necessary focus for political planning, giving not a complete account of the good or of human flourishing, but a political account, specifying certain capacities, liberties, and opportunities that have value in any plan of life that citizens may otherwise choose. Chapter 1 supported this approach with an argument based upon an intuitively powerful idea of truly human functioning, functioning that is worthy of the dignity of the human being. I claimed there that citizens with a wide range of comprehensive conceptions of the good can endorse this list – as a list of capabilities, remember, not a list of actual functions – as a basis for getting on with life, including prominently political life. These basic goods supply a set of political constraints – citizens should be provided with these, whatever else politics also pursues. In this sense, as I argued, there is a very close connection between the account of central capabilities and an account of basic human rights;

indeed, the capabilities account is one way of further fleshing out an account of human rights.[78]

It seems to me that the capabilities account deals well with the problems that plagued the preference-based approach. It does not waste time trying to smuggle a substantive account of central capabilities into a procedure for winnowing desire: it goes directly and forthrightly to the good (and the right),[79] taking an unambiguously clear stand on the need for these items, as an enabling core of whatever else human beings choose. It addresses the problem of adaptive preference, again, by substantive rather than formal devices, as seems necessary. A habituated preference not to have any one of the items on the list (political liberties, literacy, equal political rights, or whatever) will not count in the social choice function, and an equally habituated preference to have such things will count.[80] Finally, the list does justice to the intrinsic value of the items it contains, by not subordinating them to something else, such as preference-satisfaction.

It will be apparent by now that the list is not totalitarian in the usual sense, for the five reasons given at the end of Chapter 1, spelling out the ways in which a respect for pluralism is built into the project. Chapter 1 also rebutted the charge that the list is imperialistic in another way, that it imports a Western account of value that derives from discredited colonialist projects. But we should now return to this question, with our interest in preference deformation in mind. Does the recognition of adaptive preference in a subordinated group constitute a colonialist judgment on them and a depreciation of their own minds and choices? Far from it, history shows. For it was precisely the recognition of adaptive preferences that was one of Jawaharlal Nehru's strongest arguments for condemning the legacy of British rule in India. Very much in the spirit of Mill, he recognized that enslavement ends by making a willing collaborator of the slave:

---

78 See I.vi and CHR.

79 Basic liberties and opportunities, and the dignity and equality of persons, are all included in the account of the basic capabilities.

80 Recall, too, that the list is concerned with *combined capabilities*, not just *internal capabilities* (see Chapter 1): so the related principles will not simply adjust people's inner capacity to pursue certain aims and goals, they will also take thought for the actual options they have. On the importance of this issue, see Joseph Raz, *The Morality of Freedom* (Oxford: Clarendon Press, 1986), 373–5.

For many generations the British treated India as a kind of enormous country-house (after the old English fashion) that they owned. They were the gentry owning the house and occupying the desirable parts of it, while the Indians were consigned to the servants' hall and pantry and kitchen. . . . The fact that the British Government should have imposed this arrangement upon us was not surprising; but what does seem surprising is that we, or most of us, accepted it as the natural and inevitable ordering of our lives and destiny. We developed the mentality of a good country-house servant. Sometimes we were treated to a rare honour – we were given a cup of tea in the drawing-room. The height of our ambition was to become respectable and to be promoted individually to the upper regions. Greater than any victory of arms or diplomacy was this psychological triumph of the British in India. The slave began to think as a slave, as the wise men of old had said.[81]

In these words, written in a British prison, Nehru expressed the view that to recognize the adaptive nature of one's preferences is the beginning of a search for independence – which, of course, he famously expressed in the language of "inalienable rights," liberty, and opportunity.[82] So too for women: recognizing the adaptive character of many preferences is a beginning of the search for true self-definition, and the liberties that protect that search are the true opponents of feudal and colonial tyranny.

But what role is played by desire in the process of justifying the list of the central capabilities? On the general issue of political justification, it is plain that people's intuitions about how to proceed vary greatly: some think we only put things on a sound footing when we devise a procedure that generates the good as an output, and others (including I myself) tend to think that our intuitions about the central capabilities are at least as trustworthy as our intuitions about what constitutes a good procedure.[83] I have said so far that the capabilities view embodies

81 Nehru, *Autobiography*, 417.
82 *Ibid.*, 612: see 1.
83 Jürgen Habermas's recent discussions of human rights make this difference especially plain: he thinks women's rights to be free from various abuses must be justified as necessary preconditions for political participation; my own view is that this is too indirect, unreliable, and puts things in the wrong order. See, for example, "On the Internal Relation between the Rule of Law and Democracy," *European Journal of Philosophy* 3 (1995), 12–20. Habermas grants that this reply is most plausible for traditional civil rights, less so for others; and he recognizes that other rights, too, "have an intrinsic value, or at least they are not reducible to their instrumental value for democratic will-formation" (17). But it is not clear how this insight will ultimately be captured without diverging in a major way from Habermasian proceduralism.

an intuitively powerful idea of truly human functioning that has deep roots in many different traditions. I have used this intuitive idea to justify the list and its political role. But now I must make plain what role or roles I do assign to desire in the procedure for arriving at and justifying the list.

In Chapter 1, section VIII, I defended an account of political justification based on the Rawlsian account of argument proceeding toward reflective equilibrium: we lay out the arguments for a given theoretical position, holding it up against the "fixed points" in our moral intuitions, and seeing how those intuitions both test and are tested by the conceptions we examine, hoping, over time, to achieve consistency and fit in our judgments taken as a whole. My argument in Chapter 1 was envisaged as a first step in the process of reaching toward such a reflective equilibrium. Before that process would be complete (if it ever would be), we would also have to lay out other competing conceptions, compare them in detail with this one, and see on what grounds ours emerged as more choiceworthy. This chapter has taken one step in that further project, by comparing the substantive-good conception with various preference-based conceptions. Now the question should be: what part in this procedure of reaching toward reflective equilibrium is played by desire? I believe that desire plays two roles here: both an epistemic role and an ancillary role in justification.

First, it seems to me very important that people from a wide variety of cultures, coming together in conditions conducive to reflective criticism of tradition, and free from intimidation and hierarchy, should agree that this list is a good one, one that they would choose. Finding such areas of informed agreement is epistemically valuable, in two ways: first, it points us to areas of human expression that we might have neglected or underestimated. Second, it tells us that our intuitions about what would make a political consensus possible are on the right track. The methodology that has been used to modify the list shows this: for I have drawn both on the results of cross-cultural academic discussion and on discussions in women's groups themselves designed to exemplify certain values of equal dignity, non-hierarchy, and non-intimidation. In other words, I have proceeded as if it is important that there should be a substantial convergence between the substantive account and a proceduralist account, where the procedure itself is structured in accordance with certain substantive values. (Notice that the substantive values that structure the procedure are closely related to the central capabilities on the list, in the sense that some of them, at least, seem to be important signs that the resulting judgments are likely to be reliable. When people are respected as equals, and free from intimidation, and able to learn about the world, and secure against desperate want, their judgments about the core of a political conception are likely to be more reliable than judgments formed under the pressure of ignorance and fear and desperate need.) Informed desire plays a large role in finding a good substantive list, for epistemic reasons. What we are trying to find is something that people can live by together, thereby generating political stability among other values. That a conception has a certain relation to informed desire is at least one part of what makes it likely to do the job we want it to do.

But the fact that informed desire plays this epistemic role in discovering that which is likely to promote political stability shows that it also plays a limited and ancillary role in justifying the political conception: for, however attractive the conception looks, if we cannot show that it is likely to remain stable – not just as a modus vivendi but as the object of a consensus – it will be difficult to justify it. It seems right to include stability "for the right reasons" (Rawls's phrase) among the considerations that is important in justifying a political conception. And I argue that we cannot show that our conception is likely to remain stable "for the right reasons" without some reference to informed desire.

Our interest in adaptive preferences gives us another way of approaching this issue of stability. Our examples give us many reasons to suppose that Mill is correct: the preference for the central human capabilities is not merely habitual or adaptive, but has much more the unidirectional structure of preferences formed by learning (as Elster has introduced this distinction). This gives us, again, confidence that we are on the right track in designing a political conception, where stability is concerned. We learn something about the likely stability of a consensus based on central capabilities when we note, as we do, that women who have become literate find literacy valuable and even delightful, that they report satisfaction with their new condition, and that the transition in their lives begun by literacy is not one that they would wish to reverse. The same is evidently true for health and sanitation, for learning to stand up against domestic violence, and for acquiring political liberties and capabilities: people who once learn and experience these capabilities don't want to go back, and one really can't make them go back. The stories of Vasanti, of the women from Andhra Pradesh, of the video watchers in Gujarat, and of Tagore's departing wife – none of these stories could plausibly be told in reverse. Even Jayamma, who hasn't moved very far along the capability measure, has learned to demand things from the health care system and from the government, in ways that, again, appear to be irreversible. The delight and satisfaction that makes people unwilling to go backward is a very important sign that the conception we are developing is likely to be a stable one, and that regimes that thwart central capabilities are likely to prove unstable. Thwarting permanent human interests, as Mill argued, is not a wise political strategy. And this epistemic role for desire is at the same time, once again, an ancillary justificatory role, in the sense that it is important in order to justify our conception to show that it can be expected to have a reasonable degree of stability.

Women do, of course, choose to return to traditional lives in the home from lives of employment outside the home. They also choose to return to veiling from non-veiling. But notice that this is a change in their mode of *functioning*, not in their level of political *capability* as citizens. To argue that the preference for the central capabilities is not unidirectional, we would need to argue that people wish to give up *choices* and *opportunities* in this area, as citizens choosing basic political principles. And this is far more difficult to show. What we would need to show is that women who have experienced the full range of the central capabilities choose, with full information and without intimidation (and so forth), to deny these capabilities, politically, to all women. But usually women who prefer traditional lives, after having led other lives, do not campaign for a political denial of choice to all citizens. In Chapter 3, I will discuss the case of Hamida Khala, a traditional Muslim woman who regretted leaving the practice of veiling, and wished in some respects to return to that life. It is very striking, however, that this same woman vehemently opposed mandatory veiling of all Pakistani women, when a political lobby approached her for help. She felt that the problem with non-veiling was primarily a problem of male conduct, and that men should restrain themselves, rather than depriving other women of choice. Even in the case where experienced women apparently do campaign on behalf of general restrictions, as seemed to be the case in Iran, it is extremely unlikely that these women foresaw and desired the highly repressive regime that ensued. That regime has not been stable, because it thwarts central capabilities. Nor would a regime of mandatory veiling in Pakistan have been at all stable. The Pakistani regime in which Hamida Khala lived, which permits veiling, creates and respects spaces for that choice, and yet grants women the opportunity to be equal citizens if they make the contrary choice; it is stable, and conservative women themselves do not wish to upset it, when they have experienced both ways of life.

But stability is not the only issue we should consider. I have argued that desire is an intelligent part of the human being that deserves respect in itself in any procedure of justification we would design. Thus it seems to me that it is not only on account of stability that we refer to desire, but also because we respect that aspect of the human personality. It is an important part of showing such respect that we do consult people from many cultures about what (under suitably informed conditions) they would wish; and their answers to such questions, again, play an ancillary role in justifying the list. It is important, again, that we take note of the delight women experience when they achieve a greater measure of capability in the central areas of human functioning: for this delight itself helps us to justify our list as one that is respectful of their personalities. Finally, of course, desire plays a role in the fact that the goal is expressed in terms of capabilities and not actual functionings, as we said in Chapter 1. We respect the importance of desire and preference by building into the most basic level of the account the option to pursue the goal or not to pursue it. Desire's role is certainly heuristic; but it would also appear to be partially constitutive of the goodness of the capabilities, for political purposes, in the following sense: if the vast majority of people characteristically and pervasively and over a long period of time did not desire these capabilities, we might still have some arguments for thinking them good for people; but one very important political reason would be lost. Without denying that desire is unreliable and easily distorted, we can give it in this way a partial role in justifying the political conception. This ancillary role for desire is related to a picture of democratic choice: we think it best if democratic choice is reflective and deliberative, but we also think it good that it record what people want, and we think that this good is to at least some extent independent of its other virtues.

Approaches that sharply distinguish choice from desire can say at this point that we give choice a role as a human faculty worthy of respect, but that this does not entail giving a role to desire, a part of our animal makeup that does not, in itself, deserve such respect. Once again, it is important to say that my approach (unlike Scanlon's) does not make this sharp separation. Aristotle defines choice as "desiderative deliberation or deliberative desire." Similarly, I would argue that the emotions, desires, and even appetites of a human being are all humanly significant parts of her personality, deserving of respect as such. The personality is a unity, and practical reason suffuses all of its parts, making them all human rather than animal.

And yet: why, given all the critical things I have said about desire and its propensity to adapt to unjust situations, should I give it any role at all in designing a view of basic justice? Showing that desire has an evaluative element does not remove this question, for people's evaluations themselves are easily manipulated by fashion, deprivation, or power. Given this malleability of desire, the argument from political stability seems suspect: for it seems that any political scheme could justify itself by pointing to desires that it has itself formed. And the argument from respect for persons seems no better, if people's desires simply express the background conditions, just or unjust, in which they live.

If people's desires were really adaptive through and through, this would be a powerful retort – although it would surely leave us wondering what we could appeal to, given that we have said that choice and desire are very intimately linked. I believe, however, that the human personality has a structure that is at least to some extent independent of culture, powerfully though culture shapes it at every stage. As the Greek philosopher Sextus Empiricus wrote, "In the person burdened by hunger and thirst, it is impossible to produce by argument the conviction that he is not so burdened." Desires for food, for mobility, for security, for health, and for the use of reason – these seem to be relatively permanent features of our makeup as humans, which culture can blunt, but cannot altogether remove. It is for this reason that regimes that fail to deliver health, or basic security, or liberty, are unstable. My stability argument relies on this view of the personality, as not thoroughly the creation of power. Of course we still have to recognize that there is a considerable space for social deformation of desire: it is for this reason that we rely, primarily, on an independently justified list of substantive goods. But we give desire the ancillary role I have given it, because we think that it does have a structure that is in at least some ways more robust than social whims and fads. This structure contains things that are problematic and bad, as well as things that are good: aggression as well as the need for food, for example. So we do not read off norms from the facts of human personality, even to the limited extent to which we do rely on desire. We still have to evaluate what we find, and ask whether it is worth including. This, again, is a strong reason to avoid trusting desire too much. But it is compatible with trusting it a little bit, as a guide to what politics should give people.

I can illustrate my views about justification by focusing on two capabilities that have been causes of some controversy and modification in the list. The first is the capability to hold property on a basis of equality with men. Property rights were little stressed in earlier versions of the list. I held that property was merely an instrument of human functioning, and I included it under a general capability to lead one's own life, without giving it a very prominent role. To some extent my judgment was influenced by the fact that when one teaches in a modern American law school one hears constant reference to the central importance of property rights in connection with a libertarian attack on the redistribution of wealth and income. So I came to associate the appeal to property rights with that position, one that is indifferent to the interest of poor people in having some property in their own names. (Land reforms have been a major source of social amelioration in India in the post-independence period.) But my experience in India showed me that women attach intense importance to the right to hold property – demanding, at the very least, equal inheritance and property rights with men, but also attaching considerable importance to the possibility that they will be able to acquire some land in their own names. Listening to these voices (in a context shaped by the marks of a norm-infused proceduralism), I came to the conclusion that my own thinking had simply been muddled in this area; the evidence of desire led me to see something that I had refused to see before. Property rights play an important role in self-definition, in bargaining, and in developing a sense of self, as I shall argue in Chapter 4. So they now play a much more prominent role than they did in earlier versions of the list. Seeing their importance in this way does not, of course, entail a return to the libertarian position that I had begun by rejecting; for if they are important sources of capability for all citizens, this may in some cases underwrite land reforms such as the one carried out in West Bengal, under which wealthy citizens lost their second homes, and a general attempt was made to restrict luxury in order to give poor citizens property in their own names. Similarly, the government of Kerala has given citizens private rights in what was once government land, recognizing the importance to the poor of this sphere of self-definition. My current list strongly underwrites these measures, and above all it insists that whatever the scheme of property rights is, women should have the same capabilities in this area as men. To achieve this situation, reforms focused affirmatively on women's land rights may frequently be necessary. Desire here plays a heuristic and evidentiary role; and it also plays an ancillary justificatory role, convincing us that we are likely to be on the right track.

Now I turn to the capability that has in many ways been the most controversial of the items on the list, showing how the question of justification looks at this point. This is the ability to live in a fruitful relationship with animals and the world of nature. This was not on the initial list that I drafted, and was added at the insistence of Scandinavian participants in the project, who said that this was something without which, for them, no life could be truly human. As we reflected, it became clear that many of us also held such a view, though we hadn't theorized it as elaborately as had our Scandinavian participants. There were participants from South Asia who never thought this very important, who actively disliked animals, and who thought it a kind of romantic Green Party flourish to put this on the list when people were suffering. On the other side, as time went on, there were people who questioned the anthropocentricity of the entire list, judging that we had no reason to give the human capabilities priority over other capabilities, and objecting to the idea that other species would be brought in only on account of their relationship to the human.

It seems to me that this whole question is quite unresolved at this point, and we have not yet achieved a political consensus – precisely because there is not yet the kind of convergence between informed desire and the substantive account that we generally get elsewhere. Political stability may or may not be threatened within individual nations: for some nations obviously do have a political consensus on these issues. But we cannot confidently propose this item as part of a completely international political consensus at the present time. These preferences appear to be things about which people in the best of circumstances differ, though we can at least get agreement about the instrumental importance of environmental factors. And they are much more Elster-like than the other preferences on our list: that is, it would appear that people who learn to get used to nature can also get used to a life without much access to nature, and vice versa. Learning doesn't play the unidirectional role it plays in other cases. I conclude that all this should quite properly lessen our confidence in the place of this item on the list, although I personally remain strongly of the belief that it does have a role. Insofar as it remains on the list, we can at least take comfort from the fact that we respect the preferences of those who don't care about animals and plants by making a capability the goal, not the actual function. (This doesn't mean that we don't also want a separate account of our duty to avoid causing pain and damage to animals; the capability account is not intended to provide a complete moral theory.)

In other words, as we should expect, there is and should be a good measure of convergence between an intelligently normative proceduralism and a substantive good theory of a non-Platonist kind, sensitive to people's actual beliefs and values.[84] To see this yet again, let me now turn to the strongest proceduralist account that explicitly addresses the particular problems faced by women, Jean Hampton's "Feminist Contractarianism." Hampton first considers the Hobbesian approach to the social contract. She finds this defective, considered as a view feminists might use, because it does not contain the idea that each person deserves respect simply because he or she is a person. It makes respect contingent on "emotional sentiment," and fails to regard persons as having intrinsic value. This failure, of course, is an especially grave failure for feminism, since women have all too frequently been valued in this contingent way, because someone happens to care for them rather than because they have dignity as persons.

Hampton therefore turns to the defense of a version of contract theory based in Kant. At this point it might be thought that she is no

---

84 On this convergence, see James Griffin, *Well-Being: Its Meaning, Measurement and Moral Importance* (Oxford: Clarendon, 1986), 33.

longer pursuing the informed-desire approach at all, given Kant's account of the way in which desire is related to choice, which does appear to split the personality into two parts. But Hampton herself would appear to hold a more Aristotelian account of desire and emotion; indeed, she has criticized economics for failing to give its notions of desire sufficient complexity and cognitive content.[85] Hampton does not comment on this issue in "Feminist Contractarianism," but there is no reason to think that her proceduralism altogether repudiates desire.

Hampton now proposes a procedural approach with Kantian features, designed in particular for the assessment of intimate personal relationships – precisely an area where feminists often feel a contract approach has no place. In developing an appropriate test, designed to weed out cases in which persons are used and exploited through their propensity to give love and care, Hampton introduces a series of substantive conceptions: first, a Kantian *conception of human worth* that prominently includes the ideas of *equal worth* and *nonaggregation* (that is, we aren't to aggregate the good across persons, but to consider the separate good of each, thinking of each as an end); and second, a conception of *a person's legitimate interests*, which Hampton doesn't spell out further in her article.

In my view, this is a promising procedural approach, and one that, as she argues, makes progress beyond other related contractarian approaches. But notice, first, how much like a substantive-good approach it really is. The ideas of equal worth, dignity, and nonaggregation are all elements on the capabilities list itself, through its emphasis on non-discrimination, on practical reason, on dignity and non-humiliation. And the concept of *legitimate interests*, if it is to have any bite at all, would ultimately have to be fleshed out much more, in a way that would, I suppose, bring in a lot more of the items on the list.

To the extent that the approach is *not* like a substantive-good approach, I think it is often too vague to offer good guidance. We have a hard time talking about justice in the family until we know whether the right to seek employment is a basic good, whether political liberties and the opportunity to participate in politics are basic goods, whether the capability for sexual expression is a basic good, and so on. The list

85 Hampton, "The Failure of Expected-Utility Theory."

gives us somewhere to go in saying whether the treatment of women is or is not exploitative. I don't think the thin procedural approach gives us enough without this.

On the other hand, we would not conclude that the right to seek employment, property rights, and other items on the list were central human goods unless we heard women saying so, when questioned in a procedure that has Hamptonian features. In that sense, once again, proceduralism of a suitably norm-laden sort proves an essential complement to the substantive-good approach. Through a dialogue between the two, we gain confidence that we are on the right track.

One final issue remains to be considered. In Chapter 1, I argued that the appropriate political goal is capability and not functioning. This means that we leave a great deal of room for citizens to pursue their own desires, whatever they are, and however they are formed. I said that the reason for this way of conceiving of the goal is a reason of respect: if we dragoon people into a total mode of functioning, we are not fully respectful of them. In this chapter, by contrast, I have argued that in justifying the political conception we consult not all actual desires, but only some of them, desires formed under appropriate conditions; and even then we do not let desire have the last word. Am I not in danger of just the kind of paternalism I set out to avoid in Chapter 1?

It appears to me that the answer to this question is no. As I argued in Chapter 1, paternalism is all about respect for choice; opposition to it therefore entails that we protect certain opportunities for choice (religious liberty, the liberty of speech, and the rest), plus their material conditions, in a way that puts these opportunities beyond the whim of majoritarian politics. To say this is perfectly consistent with saying that these spheres are there to be used by people as they please, even if their actual desires are corrupt and mistaken. But to consult all actual desires, including the corrupt and mistaken, when we justify the list of basic entitlements and opportunities itself would put the political conception, and the liberties of citizens, on much too fragile a foundation. Just as it is consistent to say both that we will not impose a single religion on citizens even if we believe it to be correct, and also that we will impose on all citizens a duty to respect citizens' liberty of conscience, thus protecting spheres of choice within which various different conceptions can be pursued, so too it is consistent to use a substantive approach (combined with a substantively infused informed-desire approach) when justifying the list of central capabilities that forms the basis of the political conception, and also to say that within the conception we are protecting and promoting spheres of choice in a way that shows respect for people's desires, even their mistaken desires, so long as these involve no harm to others.

Of course it is also true that securing to people the capabilities on the list will promote conditions in which people will be likely to develop more adequately informed desires: it is in this sense that there is a strong convergence between the substantive list of capabilities and the norms that shape a sensible informed-desire approach. By promoting education, equal respect, the integrity of the person, and so forth, we are also indirectly shaping desires, and desires formed under these conditions are likely to be more adequately informed than those formed under conditions of isolation, illiteracy, hierarchy, and fear. But people living under a just regime will still on occasion be ignorant or hasty; they may also be intimidated or envious. The political conception makes room for these inadequate desires and respects them, and choices motivated by them, by protecting spheres of choice and aiming at capability rather than functioning. In these ways, it aims to avoid the charge of paternalism, and to respect persons even when they are not wise.

VI. POLITICAL STABILITY AND THE DEPTH OF HABIT

By focusing on the stories of women in self-help groups of various types, we have given an optimistic slant to the issue of preference-deformation. In case after case, we see women quickly dropping habituated preferences and adjusting their aspirations in accordance with a new sense of their dignity and equality. When we see that in just a few weeks women learn to want employment rights, property rights, clean water, and many of the other items on the list; when we hear Vasanti talk about the change in her life made possible by the SEWA loan; when we see how Jayamma's sense of what the world owes her has been energized by government programs; when we see how the women in Andhra Pradesh start fighting for their rights even before they get into a decent state of health – it is easy to think that achieving a political consensus about the central capabilities is an easy matter. All we have to do is to give people a taste of them, and they refuse to return to any other way.

But our political optimism about the stability of an overlapping consensus should be tempered by the fact that, so far, we have been looking at only half the story. We have looked at what women want, or come to want, for themselves. But we haven't asked about the adaptive preferences of men, and how easy or difficult it may be to achieve the same happy convergence between an informed proceduralism and a theory of substantive goods when we consider what they are willing to grant to women. What Mill wrote in 1869 still appears to be all too true of many people: "the generality of the male sex cannot yet tolerate the idea of living with an equal."[86] Obviously Harsanyi is right: if we decide that people are indeed motivated by malice or sadism, then we should not allow those preferences to count in the social choice function. It is also clear that any proceduralism we would accept – Hampton's, for example – builds in, on the ground floor, the value of each person as an end, and that this should be understood to be incompatible with systematic subordination of one person's ends to those of another. And yet, we have hardly begun to take the measure of the full weight of habit, family and community pressures, and the sheer fear of change, when we think about how men who are not basically evil or sadistic frequently resist such changes, while believing that they do treat women as ends.

I therefore want to conclude this chapter with one such story of failed proceduralism, Rabindranath Tagore's short story "Haimanti," written in 1913.[87] The story is told in the first person by the young bridegroom – and what is striking throughout is the thoroughly informed lucidity with which he chronicles his own moral cowardice. His parents contract for him a marriage with a girl somewhat older than the usual age, who therefore has had more time than usual to form her character in her own natal home – in this case, under the supportive tutelage of a progressive father who respects her intelligence, fosters her education, and treats her as an independent being of worth in her own right. After the wedding, he asks his new son-in-law to see her

86 Mill, SW, 53. He prefaces this statement by saying, "I believe that their disabilities elsewhere are only clung to in order to maintain their subordination in domestic life."
87 Translated in Bardhan, Of Women, Outcastes, 84–96.

that way too – and indeed he does. He discovers, in fact, that the way to win her love is to respect her mind:

I was worried that I did not know how to win the mind of an educated, grown-up girl. But soon I found out that there was no conflict between the road to the bookstore and the road to her heart. I do not know exactly when the pure white of her mind gradually started changing to colors, when her body and her mind turned toward me with eagerness.

But now comes the less beautiful part of the story – as the narrator says himself. (The story is tragic in large part for the way in which the hero sees so clearly what is bad in his behavior, and yet is unable to stop it.) After a while, his family learns that Haimanti's father is not nearly as wealthy as they had previously believed – and, no longer regarding the bride as a potential source of further income (over and above the dowry already given), they begin to mistreat her emotionally, belittling her, requiring her to tell useless lies in ways that deform her integrity, and attacking her beloved father to her face and forbidding her to defend him. The groom, seeing that her unhappiness is leading to a decline in her health, summons Haimanti's father, who gets a good doctor; the doctor says she will become very ill if she does not take a break from the family. But the groom's father refuses to let her go, once again insulting her father.

At this point, the groom could easily have taken her away himself. He loves her. He sees her worth. He sees that it is the only way of saving her mental and physical health. But because his father yells at him, he doesn't do it.

Some of my friends asked me later why I did not do what I had said I would do. All I had to do was just leave with my wife. Why did I not take such an obvious simple step? Why indeed! If I am not to sacrifice my true feelings for what people regard as proper, if I am not to sacrifice my dearest one for the extended family, then what about the ages of social indoctrination running in my blood? What is it there for?

Don't you know that on the day the people of Ayodhya demanded the banishment of Sita, I was among them? Those who sang the glory of that sacrifice, generation after countless generations, I was one of them too. All those authors of articles published in monthly magazines, acclaiming the virtue of abandoning a beloved wife to please the people, I had read them. Had I ever thought that one day I would be writing my own story of the banishment of Sita, writing it with the blood of my heart's arteries?

He does nothing. Soon Haimanti dies. Now his mother is looking for a more suitable girl for him. He has resisted, but he knows that soon he will give in.

Here we have what looks like a clear contrast between a person's true preferences, elicited through a procedure that bears many of the marks of Hamptonian proceduralism, and the preferences that actually guide his actions, and that are in some sense also quite truly his and him. He says that the true preferences are those that express respect and love, whereas the false are those dictated by habit. But then, immediately after that, he says, more plausibly, that he *is* those habits, as well as his love, and that his character is expressed even more truly by his cowardly act than by his weaker impulses of love. The preferences that ratify his nonaction seem to be adaptive preferences in Elster's sense: they tell him that something that is not psychologically available to him is not really a good, and that the cowardly course is in some sense best. But the romantic Elster view, according to which the adaptive preferences are false and beneath them lie true authentic preferences, is not a true account of the way many people are. Their personalities have a definite structure, to the extent that they want food, and shelter, and stability, and perhaps even liberty, for themselves. But with respect to their relations with at least some others, it would appear that they just *are* their adaptive habits, and that there is no autonomous person beneath the weight of those habits.

And this means that it is no longer clear that the procedure that considers Haimanti as an end in her own right, and considers her interests to be on a par with his own, really does deliver to him the conclusion that we, with Tagore, support: that he should fight tradition and help her depart. The narrator's initial formulation is not his final insight, which is that when we consider each person with equal respect, we get, simply, the conclusion that all are equally under the weight of the past, and all equally in thrall to duties of non-autonomy. The problem isn't that the husband reaches the right conclusion but somehow fails to act. He actually veers round to the wrong conclusion, though in a way that seems to conform to procedural norms of equal treatment. He treats her, ultimately, and indeed respects her, exactly as he treats and respects himself, namely as a pawn of forces too big to be resisted. (Those forces, conveniently enough, protect his capabilities even while they demote hers: so the structure of desire in his personality provides no keen incentive to discontent.) It seems difficult to show that this is not what proceduralism would deliver in this case, without designing the procedure in such a way as to build into it all the relevant substantive goods: autonomous practical reason, non-humiliation, the right to travel, the right to seek employment, equal property rights, and all the rest. Autonomy has to be constructed by laws and institutions, and some people, even privileged people, don't have it. They let tradition become the self – especially when tradition conveniently serves their own interests and demotes the interests of others.

The problem of adaptive selves does not threaten the justification of the capability list in general, since for that purpose the most relevant preferences are those of Haimanti herself, and those clearly support the capabilities list. But it does bear on the issue of stability, and I have argued that stability is at least one part of the question of justification. In relation to stability, the problem of adaptive selves suggests that in the first generation we cannot expect the same convergence between an informed-desire account and a substantive-good account that we might expect over several generations. Powerful people simply will not yield power happily, and in the first generation moral education cannot possibly alter deeply enough people's perceptions of the equality of citizens. If they accept the capabilities list as a goal for all, they will not all do so with real endorsement, but merely as a modus vivendi. I believe that this does not threaten the justification of the overlapping consensus, since stability must be considered as a long-term issue, and stability would only be threatened if we found that over several generations men could not be brought up to endorse a political conception that treats women as equal citizens. I believe experience in this century (for example in the Nordic countries) shows that this is false. But the problem does show us that in the short term we need to choose between relying on an informed-desire approach and relying on a substantive-good approach to guide us. Although we expect a long-term consensus between informed desire and the substantive good, the Haimanti problem shows us, I would argue, that in the short term we should prefer, as our political guide, an account that takes its stand squarely, endorsing a list of human capabilities that are indispensable for any citizen.

Elster's proceduralism clearly doesn't get to the root of the husband's problem: for he consciously evaluates the forces that bear upon him, and prefers to take his stand with habit and tradition. Maybe a proceduralism as norm-laden as Hampton's could show that his behavior is exploitative – if she fleshed out the concept of the person's interests in a sufficiently robust way. But what the story shows is the depth at which cowardice, habit, and not wanting to be the author of one's own actions infect human desire and choice. If love can't change that, as the story tragically shows, it's not clear that any formal deliberative procedure devised by economists can deliver the goods. So we are better off if we don't trust to these unreliable forces very much. While not dismissing desire, as I have said, while keeping it around as a witness and respecting it as an intelligent part of the human personality – we had better take our stand squarely in the camp of the substantive good.

3

THE ROLE OF RELIGION

What is left of the Law of the kings? From of old, we have heard, they do *not* bring law-minded women into their hall. This ancient eternal law is lost among the Kauravas ... For this foul man, disgrace of the Kauravas, is molesting me, and I cannot bear it any longer.

> Queen Draupadī, as the men of Duryodhana's entourage attempt to undress and molest her, in *The Mahābhārata*,[1]

Although all religions were initially founded with the aim of purifying men and women and helping them to lead ethical lives through prayer, it was found in some instances that blind traditions, customs and superstition often resulted in – not the cathartic effects of religion – but the spread of communalism, fanaticism, fundamentalism and discrimination.

> Heera Nawaz, law student, Bangalore College of Law, 1993[2]

---

1 *The Mahābhārata*, II.62, trans. J. A. B. van Buitenen, vol. 2 (Chicago: University of Chicago Press, 1975), 148. Draupadī is wagered, along with many material objects, by her dice-obsessed husband Yudhiṣṭira, and one of the unresolved questions of the episode is whether he had any right so to wager her. (The dice game was reluctantly authorized by King Dhṛtarāṣṭra at the request of his son Duryodhana.) Vidura, a wise uncle of both contending groups, argues that Yudhiṣṭira was no longer of sound mind when he made the wager. The aged Bhīṣma, uncle of Pāṇḍu and Dhṛtarāṣṭra (thus great-uncle to the contending groups), maintains that wives belong to their husbands (60); nonetheless, a person without property cannot wager another person's property, and Yudhisthira has already lost all his property, while Draupadī belongs to all five Pāṇḍava brothers. So he says there is no clear legal solution. Draupadī, unsurprisingly, is not satisfied by this reply, and Bhīma, her second-oldest husband, protests vigorously, noting that even prostitutes are not used as commodities in gambling (61). He takes the view that Yudhiṣṭira had no right at all to wager Draupadī, not because of his own property interest in her, but because of sympathy for the plight of Draupadī herself. He threatens to assault his brother, until Arjuna restrains him. Nowhere, however, is the view that a wife is property explicitly repudiated.

2 From Nawaz, "Towards Uniformity" (a defense of a uniform civil code) in Indira Jais-

I. RELIGIOUS LIBERTY AND SEX EQUALITY: A DILEMMA

Modern liberal democracies typically hold that religious liberty is an extremely important value, and that its protection is among the most important functions of government. These democracies also typically defend as central a wide range of other human interests, liberties, and opportunities. Among these are the freedom of movement, the right to seek employment outside the home, the right to assemble, the right to bodily integrity, the right to education, and the right to hold and to inherit property. Sometimes, however, the religions do not support these other liberties. Sometimes, indeed, they deny such liberties to classes of people in accordance with a morally irrelevant characteristic, such as race or caste or sex. Such denials may not mean much in nations where the religions do not wield much legal power. But in nations such as India, where religions run large parts of the legal system, they are fundamental determinants of many lives.

In this way, a dilemma is created for the liberal state. On the one hand, to interfere with the freedom of religious expression is to strike a blow against citizens in an area of intimate self-definition and basic liberty. Not to interfere, however, permits other abridgments of self-definition and liberty. It is not surprising that modern democracies should find themselves torn in this area – particularly a democracy like India, which has committed itself to the equality of the sexes and non-discrimination on the basis of sex in the list of Fundamental Rights enumerated in its Constitution – alongside commitments to religious liberty and nondiscrimination on the basis of religion.[3]

---

ing, ed., *Justice for Women: Personal Laws, Women's Rights and Law Reform* (Mapusa, Goa: The Other India Press, 1996).

3 Article 14 guarantees the equal protection of the laws to all persons; Article 15 prohibits discrimination on the grounds of religion, race, caste, sex, or place of birth; Article 16 guarantees all citizens equality in matters relating to employment, and prohibits employment discrimination on the basis of religion, race, caste, sex, descent, place of birth, and residence; Article 17 abolishes untouchability: "its practice in any form is forbidden." Article 19 guarantees all citizens rights of free speech and expression, assembly, association, free movement, choice of residence, choice of occupation; Article 21 (the basis for privacy jurisprudence in cases involving marital rape and restitution of conjugal rights) says that "no citizen shall be deprived of his life or personal liberty" without due process of law; Article 25 states that all citizens are "equally entitled to freedom of conscience

Consider these three cases, all involving conflicts between claims of religious free exercise and women's claims to other important rights under the Indian Constitution:

1. In 1983, Mary Roy, a Syrian Christian woman, daughter of wealthy parents, went to court to challenge the Travancore Christian Act, under which daughters inherit only one-fourth the share of sons, subject to a maximum of Rs. 5,000. The Indian Supreme Court declared that the relevant law superseding the Travancore Christian Act was the Indian Succession Act of 1925, which gives equal rights to daughters and sons.[4] (By ruling in this narrowly technical way, the Court avoided confronting the question whether the act violates constitutional guarantees of sex equality.) The Court also declared the change retroactive to 1951, thus bringing the property of many Christian males into dispute. Protest greeted the judgment. A Christian MP from Kerala (representing a district including many wealthy Christian landlords) introduced a Private Member's Bill in Congress seeking to block the retroactive effect of the law. Meanwhile, the Christian churches of Kerala vociferously protested the Court's interference with the free exercise of religion. It was argued that the judgment would "open up a floodgate of litigation and destroy the traditional harmony and goodwill that exists in Chris-

and the right freely to profess, practice and propagate religion," although there is an explicit qualification stating that this does not prevent government from abolishing the caste system and "throwing open . . . Hindu religious institutions of a public nature to all classes and sections of Hindus"; Article 26 gives religious denominations the right to manage their own affairs and to acquire property, "subject to public order, morality, and health"; Article 28 guarantees freedom to attend religious schools, states that no religious instruction shall be provided in institutions wholly funded by the state, and also states that where a school is aided by state funds students may not be compelled to perform religious observances. Finally, Article 13 renders invalid all "laws in force" that conflict with any of these Fundamental Rights and forbids the state to make any new laws that take away or abridge a Fundamental Right. (A subsequent judicial decision, however, declared that "laws in force does not include the religious systems of personal law": see *State of Bombay v. Narasu Appa Mali*, 1952.) For related constitutional discussion, see my "Religion and Women's Human Rights," in *Religion and Contemporary Liberalism*, ed. Paul Weithman (Notre Dame: University of Notre Dame Press, 1997), 93–137, and, in a revised form, my *Sex and Social Justice* (New York: Oxford University Press, 1999).

4 *Mrs. Mary Roy v. State of Kerala and Others*, AIR 1986 SC 1011. (Mary Roy is the mother of Booker Prize–winning novelist Arundhati Roy.) For discussion of this case, see Bina Agarwal, *A Field of One's Own: Gender and Land Rights in South Asia* (Cambridge: Cambridge University Press, 1994), 224–6, and Archana Parashar, *Women and Family Law Reform in India: Uniform Civil Code and Gender Equality* (Delhi: Sage, 1992), 190–2. For a general description of the system of personal laws, see the following discussion.

tian families."[5] The Synod of Christian Churches took an official position against the ruling and actively mobilized protests against it.[6] Priests belonging to the Roman Catholic, Jacobite, Church of South India, and Kananya Christian Churches all criticized the judgment from the pulpit. One reason for the strength of opposition may be that a portion of the traditional daughter's inheritance automatically went to the church; this would not be the case under the Indian Succession Act.[7]

2. In 1947, at the time of Independence, the Hindu Law Committee submitted a list of recommendations to reform the system of Hindu personal law. These were presented to Parliament in the form of the Hindu Code Bill. Backed by Nehru's law minister, B. R. Ambedkar, the bill proposed to grant women a right to divorce, remove the option of polygamous marriage for men, abolish child marriage for young women, and grant women more nearly equal property rights.[8] A storm of protest from Hindu MPs (led by conservative Pandits or Hindu religious authorities) greeted the proposed legislation. Debate focused on the new laws' alleged violations of the free exercise of religion, as guaranteed in the new Constitution. Pandit Mukul Behrilal Bhargava held that equal property rights for women represented a forcible intrusion of Muslim ideas into the Hindu tradition. (Muslim women in India had had somewhat more equal inheritance rights since 1937, when the Shariat was substituted for customary law.)[9] Others objected to the fact that monogamy would be required for Hindus but not for Muslims. Still others objected to the whole idea of state-initiated reform of the Hindu code: "Hindu law is intimately connected with Hindu religion and no Hindu can tolerate a non-Hindu being an authority on Hindu law." Traditional Hindu

5 P. J. Kurien, author of the Private Member's Bill, in a public statement.
6 See *Indian Express*, June 20, 1986.
7 See E. D. Devadasan, *Christian Law in India* (Delhi: DSI Publications, 1974).
8 For discussion of the debates, with many references, see Shahida Lateef, "Defining Women through Legislation," in Zoya Hasan, ed., *Forging Identities: Gender, Communities, and the State in India* (Boulder: Westview, 1994), 38–58. This issue had already been dealt with in the Child Marriage Restraint Act of 1929, the first occasion on which the Indian women's movement achieved a big legislative success. It was now included in a more comprehensive package of reforms for the new republic.
9 The year 1937 saw passage of the Shariat Act, which stopped the custom of leaving all property to male heirs and returned the Muslim community from customary law to the prescriptions of the Shariat (where, however, women do not have fully equal shares). The bill was supported by Jinnah on grounds of sex equality: he stated that "the economic position of woman is the foundation of her being recognized as the equal of man and shar[ing] the life of man to the fullest extent." Nonetheless, the bill explicitly exempted agricultural land; thus many inequalities remained unaddressed. See Parashar, 145–50; Agarwal, *A Field of One's Own*, 98–9, 227–37; Agarwal, "Women and Legal Rights in Agricultural Land," *Economic and Political Weekly*, March 25, 1995.

MPs attacked female MPs for violating Hindu tradition, speaking of "the tyranny of modern women . . . [T]he days of their persecution are gone, it is nowadays men who are being persecuted."

Shortly after the new Constitution took effect, in the summer of 1951, a tumultuous session of Parliament formally debated the bill; conservative Pandit Govind Malviya spoke for two hours against the bill, which he called "wrong in principle, atrocious in detail and uncalled for in expediency." Despite Ambedkar's passionate support, the bill seemed bound for defeat, and even Nehru withdrew his support for the time being. In consequence, Dr. Ambedkar resigned his ministerial position, saying: "To leave untouched the inequality between class and class, between sex and sex, and to go on passing legislation relating to economic problems is to make a farce of our Constitution and so build a palace on a dung-heap." The bill lapsed. Its provisions were eventually adopted in 1954, 1955, and 1956.

Fifty years after the initial proposal, these provisions continue to arouse controversy. The new laws are weakly enforced. Child marriage, for example, remains common in some regions, and is vigorously defended in both religious and cultural terms.[10] With the rise of Hindu fundamentalism, charges of violation of free exercise and discrimination in favor of Muslims are increasing, especially over the issue of polygamy. Substantial numbers of Hindu men continue to make bigamous marriages; others have converted to Islam in order to escape the polygamy prohibition.[11] To make things more complex still, Hindu courts have recently adopted an extremely stringent definition of a valid marriage, with the result that a large number of existing Hindu marriages, if challenged in court, would not withstand scrutiny, and the male would be acquitted of charges of bigamy attendant on a second marriage. [12]

10 See "Children Are Still Married off in Indian State," Agence-France Press, May 26, 1997, describing mass ceremonies in Rajasthan involving girls as young as seven, and supported by overwhelming community sentiment. Also John F. Burns, "Though Illegal, Child Marriage Is Popular in Part of India," New York Times, May 1998, pp. A1, 8. Police say that if nobody makes a complaint they cannot arrest anyone. Child marriage does not necessarily imply sexual consummation, which is usually delayed until after puberty. Nonetheless, the child bride leaves her natal home and is transferred to the power of the husband's home; usually her schooling ends at this point.
11 See Indira Jaising, "Towards an Egalitarian Civil Code," in Jaising, ed., Justice, 24, describing a conversion and remarriage in Bombay high society; six months later, however, the Supreme Court declared the new marriage invalid and stated that the husband was liable to be prosecuted for bigamy.
12 The requirement is now that all steps of the traditional Brahminic religious ceremony must have been performed. Many couples omit one or more steps – in some cases in order to indicate opposition to women's subordination. Others use distinct regional forms, or simply marry before a registrar; in all these cases marriages have been de-

3. In Madhya Pradesh in 1978, an elderly Muslim woman named Shah Bano was thrown out of her home by her husband, a prosperous lawyer, after forty-four years of marriage. (The occasion seems to have been a quarrel over inheritance between the children of Shah Bano and the children of the husband's other wife.) As required by Islamic personal law, he returned to her the *mehr*, or marriage settlement, that she had originally brought into the marriage – Rs. 3,000 (less than $100 by today's exchange rates). Like many Muslim women facing divorce without sufficient maintenance, she sued for regular maintenance payments under Section 125 of the uniform Criminal Procedure Code, which forbids a man "of adequate means" to permit various close relatives, including (by special amendment in 1973) an ex-wife,[13] to remain in a state of "destitution and vagrancy." This remedy had long been recognized as a solution to the inadequate maintenance granted by Islamic personal law, and many women had won similar cases. What was different about Shah Bano's case was that the Chief Justice of the Supreme Court of India, awarding her maintenance of Rs. 180 per month, remarked in his lengthy opinion[14] that the Islamic system was very unfair to

clared invalid. See discussion of cases in Saumya, "Bigamous Marriages by Hindu Men: Myths and Realities," in Jaising, *Justice*, 27–33. Sometimes the first marriage is shown to be invalid, sometimes the second. The risk of invalidation deters prosecution by first wives, and also makes the task of gathering the requisite evidence of bigamy far more difficult.

13 The recognition of ex-wives as included relations under Section 125 was itself controversial in 1973. When the amendment was discussed in the Lok Sabha, members of the Muslim League objected, claiming violations of free exercise. Initially the government denied that there was any religious issue: the purpose of the amendment was simply humanitarian. Later, however, the government changed its stand, adding yet a further amendment to exclude divorced Muslim women from the purview of the new amendment. Nonetheless, Muslim women continued to bring petitions to the courts, and the Supreme Court explicitly pronounced, in two prominent judgments, that they were entitled to do so: the purpose of the law was to help destitute women, and the text had to be interpreted in accordance with this social purpose. See *Bai Tahira v. Ali Hussain*, 1979 (2) Supreme Court Reporter, 75, and AIR 1980 Supreme Court 1930. Thus the conflict between the Supreme Court and the Muslim leadership was of long standing.

14 The opinion opens as follows:

"This appeal does not involve any questions of constitutional importance but, that is not to say that it does not involve any question of importance. Some questions which arise under the ordinary civil and criminal law are of a far-reaching significance to large segments of society which have been traditionally subjected to unjust treatment. Women are one such segment. *Na stree swatantramarhati* said Manu, the Law-Giver: The woman does not deserve independence. And, it is alleged that the 'fatal point in Islam is the degradation of woman.' [Footnote reference is made to a British commentary on the Quran by Edward Lane.] To the Prophet is ascribed the statement, hope-

women, and that it was high time that the nation should indeed secure a Uniform Civil Code, as the Constitution had long ago directed it to do. The Chief Justice wrote, "Undoubtedly, the Muslim husband enjoys the privilege of being able to discard his wife whenever he chooses to do so, for reason good, bad, or indifferent. Indeed, for no reason at all." Although of Hindu origin, the Chief Justice also undertook to interpret various Islamic sacred texts and to argue that there was no textual barrier in Islam to providing a much more adequate maintenance for women.

A storm of public protest greeted the opinion. Although some liberal Muslims backed Chief Justice Chandrachud, he had made their task difficult by his zealous incursion into the interpretation of sacred Islamic texts. The Islamic clergy and the Muslim Personal Law Board organized widespread protest against the ruling, claiming that it violated their free exercise of religion. In response to the widespread outcry, the government of Rajiv Gandhi introduced the Muslim Women's (Protection after Divorce) Act of 1986, which deprived all and only Muslim women of the right of maintenance guaranteed under the Criminal Procedure Code. Women's groups tried to get this law declared unconstitutional on grounds of both religious discrimination and sex equality, but the Supreme Court (in rapid retreat from charges of religious intolerance and excessive activism) refused to hear their claim. Hindu activists, meanwhile, complained that the 1986 law discriminates against Hindus, giving Muslim men "special privileges."[15]

fully wrongly, that 'Woman was made from a crooked rib, and if you try to bend it straight, it will break; therefore treat your wives kindly.'

"This appeal, arising out of an application filed by a divorced Muslim woman for maintenance under section 125 of the Code of Criminal Procedure, raises a straightforward issue which is of common interest not only to Muslim women, not only to women generally, but, to all those who, aspiring to create an equal society of men and women, lure themselves into the belief that mankind has achieved a remarkable degree of progress in that direction."

From these words alone, one can get a sense of the strange combination of progressive courage and political obtuseness (referring to a *British* critic of Islam!) that characterize the opinion throughout.

15 *Mohammed Ahmed Khan v. Shah Bano Begum & Others* SCR (1985). This famous case has been discussed in many places. The central documents are assembled in Asghar Ali Engineer, ed., *The Shah Bano Controversy* (Delhi: Ajanta Publishers, 1987). See also Veena Das, *Critical Events* (Delhi: Oxford University Press, 1992), Chapter 4; Kavita R. Khory, "The Shah Bano Case: Some Political Implications," in Robert Baird, ed., *Religion and Law in Independent India* (Delhi: Manohar, 1993),121–37; Amartya Sen, "Secularism and Its Discontents," in *Unravelling the Nation*, ed. Kaushik Basu and Sanjay Subrahmanyam, 1995; Parashar, 173–89 (an unusually comprehensive account of different attitudes within the Islamic community); Zoya Hasan, "Minority Identity, State Policy and the Political Process," in Hasan, ed., *Forging*, 59–73; Danial

Here are three examples of our dilemma, no different in kind from dilemmas that arise in the U.S. and Europe, but different in degree, since the religions in India control so much of the legal system. On one side is the claim of religious free exercise; on the other, women's claims to various fundamental rights. In the first case, women won a clear victory – interestingly, in a case involving a small and politically powerless religion. In the second case, women made some strides, but the provisions are weakly enforced, and the current climate of Hindu fundamentalism and conservatism makes the future very unclear. In the third case, women suffered a particularly painful and prominent defeat. Free exercise and sex equality appear, at least sometimes, to be on a collision course.

II. SECULAR HUMANISTS AND TRADITIONALISTS

Feminists have taken a range of positions on this dilemma. Here are two extremes, both prominent in the international debate. The first position, which I shall call the position of *secular humanist feminism*, treats the dilemma as, basically, a non-dilemma.[16] The values of

Latifi, "After Shah Bano," in Jaising, ed., *Justice*, 213–15, and "Women, Family Law, and Social Changes," 216–22 (criticizing Muslims who opposed the Supreme Court decision). On general issues about the Indian legal system and its history, see also John H. Mansfield, "The Personal Laws or a Uniform Civil Code?" in Baird, ed., *Religion and Law*; Tahir Mahmood, *Muslim Personal Law, Role of the State in the Indian Subcontinent* (Nagpur, second edition 1983).

16 Secular humanist feminism is a very common position among feminists; in American philosophy, it is perhaps the most common position. But today's secular philosophers rarely follow the example of Bertrand Russell, attacking religion explicitly. Instead, they tend to ignore it, and thus secular humanists in philosophy rarely write about religion. Many major works of feminist political philosophy include no discussion of religion at all: to cite just two examples, Alison Jaggar's *Feminist Politics and Human Nature* (Totowa, N.J.: Rowman and Littlefield, 1988) and Catharine MacKinnon's *Toward a Feminist Theory of the State* (Cambridge, MA: Harvard University Press, 1989). The two best recent anthologies of feminist social-political thought devote no space to religion, although they discuss many topics only contingently linked to feminism, such as environmentalism and vegetarianism: Alison Jaggar's *Living With Contradictions: Controversies in Feminist Social Ethics* (Boulder: Westview, 1994) and Diana Meyer's *Feminist Social Thought: A Reader* (New York: Routledge, 1997). In law, feminists more frequently take on religion, because it is a part of their material: thus one striking representative of the secular humanist position I have in mind here is Mary Becker's fine article "The Politics of Women's Wrongs and the Bill of 'Rights': A Bicentennial Perspective," *The University of Chicago Law Review* 59 (1992), 453–517.

women's equality and dignity, and of the basic human rights and capabilities more generally, so outweigh any religious claim that any conflict between them should not be seen as a serious conflict, except in practical political terms. Indeed, the secular feminist tends to view religion itself as irredeemably patriarchal, and a powerful ally of women's oppression throughout the ages. She is not unhappy to muzzle it, and does not see it as doing a whole lot of good in anyone's life.[17]

Many secular humanist feminists are Marxists; if they follow Marx on religion, they are bound to take a negative view of religion's social role, and are unlikely even to give the free exercise of religion a high degree of respect. But some liberal feminists also take a secular humanist line. These feminists – usually comprehensive rather than political liberals – will be committed to preserving the liberty of conscience, but

I shall use this article as my central example of the position criticized, in part because I admire it. It is not a perfect example, because the article ends by proposing less radical change in current policies than its argument would suggest – largely, but not wholly, for practical political reasons.

A perspective closely related to Becker's is developed by Susan Okin in "Is Multiculturalism Bad for Women?", first published in *The Boston Review*, October/November 1997, 25–28, and now in *Is Multiculturalism Bad for Women?*, ed. J. Cohen, M. Howard, and M. Nussbaum (Princeton: Princeton University Press, 1999), 7-26: see my response in the same volume, "A Plea for Difficulty," 105–14. Okin's position is more nuanced than Becker's; insofar as she focuses on cases of genuinely egregious violation of woman's capabilities, our practical conclusions are not very dissimilar.

17 Becker does note that "all people need sources of authority outside government" (486), and considers this a reason not to muzzle religion too much. But all her other general statements about religion are strongly negative: "religion perpetuates and reinforces women's subordination, and religious freedom impedes reform" (459); "[r]eligions . . . contribute to women's subordinate status, not only within religious communities' hierarchies, but also in the broader culture" (460); "[a]ll mainstream religious traditions in the United States replace the wonder of women's reproductive power with stories of creation by a male god" (461); "[r]eligion encourages women to live with the status quo rather than destabilizing it by insisting on equality." Okin has a more subtle position, contrasting "progressive, reformed versions" of various major religions with their "more orthodox or fundamentalist versions," but even this begs many questions. Reform Jews typically understand the core of Judaism as a set of timeless moral ideas that are imperfectly captured in biblical and legal texts: thus they do not concede that their version is less "orthodox" than that of the people who call themselves "orthodox," and they understand the term "reform" to mean not that they advocate a religion "reformed" from the original Judaism, but rather that they advocate a reform of defective historical practices in the direction of a full realization of Judaism. Nor, of course, do Roman Catholics and mainstream Protestants concede that "fundamentalist" versions are more original or authentic or that their own positions are "reformed" from an original authentic position.

only within limits firmly set by a secular moral understanding of basic human rights and capabilities: religion, as Kant would have it, "within the limits of reason alone." This is in effect the position of J. S. Mill in *On Liberty*, where he excoriates Calvinism as an "insidious . . . theory of life" that creates a "pinched and hidebound type of human character." Mill holds that it is perfectly proper for public policy to be based on the view that by teaching obedience as a good, Calvinism undermines "the desirable condition of human nature." He thus advocates liberalism as a comprehensive doctrine of life, rather than (in political-liberal fashion) as simply the basis for core political principles.[18] Some secular humanists in this comprehensive liberal tradition manifest, like Marxists, a general hostility to religion; Bertrand Russell is just one obvious example of a widely held view among liberal intellectuals. Others are not hostile to religion as such, but simply insist that it fall in line with a rational secular understanding of value; Joseph Raz and Susan Okin would seem to be in this group.

The second approach, which I shall call that of *traditionalist feminism*, also sees the dilemma as basically a non-dilemma. The understandings of each community, both religious and traditional, are our best, perhaps our only, guides in charting women's course for the future. All moral claims not rooted in a particular community's understanding of the good are suspect from the start; but those that challenge the roots of traditional religious practices are more than usually suspect, since they threaten sources of value that have over the ages been enormously important to women and men, forming the very core of their search for the meaning of existence.[19] Although such a position will frequently converge with mere traditionalism and antifeminism, I think it can be a genuine type of feminism, in the sense that its proponents are committed to defining feminism in terms of what has deep

18 The comprehensive liberalism of Joseph Raz in *The Morality of Freedom* (Oxford: Clarendon Press, 1986) appears to have similar consequences: religious liberty within limits set by a shared comprehensive public view of autonomy. Unlike Mill, Raz discusses religion only briefly (251–2), and only to advocate religious liberty. Okin discusses her views on this question in *Is Multiculturalism Bad for Women?*, 129–30.

19 Examples of this position include Stephen A. and Frédérique Marglin, eds., *Dominating Knowledge: Development, Culture, and Resistance* (Oxford: Clarendon Press, 1988), esp. essays by the Marglins and A. Nandy; in the American context, Christina Sommers, *Who Stole Feminism?* (New York: Simon and Schuster, 1994); Elizabeth Fox-Genovese, *"Feminism Is Not the Story of My Life"* (New York: Doubleday, 1996).

importance to real women, and in sheltering those deep values from the assault of other feminists.

Some traditionalist feminists are cultural relativists, who hold that as a matter of theory it is impossible to justify any cross-cultural moral norms. (I criticized this view in Chapter 1.) Some, on the other hand, are worried more about normative moral substance than about justification: they simply think local sources of value are more likely to be good for people than are international human rights norms, more in tune with and beneficial to the real lives people lead. In Indian terms, traditionalist feminists typically make common cause with other "nativist" defenders of tradition, opponents of secularization and modernization, who hold that the essence of Indian national identity resides in Hindu traditions,[20] and that traditional female roles lie at the core of a Hindu identity. (Analogous claims are made on the Muslim side.) Nativists often support their attack on human rights norms by holding that Indian values are radically different from Western values. I have extensively criticized this position in Chapters 1 and 2.

Secular humanism is deeply appealing to feminists, since there is no doubt that the world's major religions, in their actual historical form, have been unjust to women both theoretically and practically. In contemporary politics, religious groups have frequently had a pernicious influence on women's lives, as our three cases from India suggest. It is indeed very tempting to say, fine, let religion exist, but let it clean up its act like anything else, bringing its own norms and conduct into line with a basic set of international moral standards, without receiving any special protections from the state.[21] When religion is clearly doing

---

20 Such as the Marglins and Ashis Nandy. This group is known for its nostalgic treatment of child temple prostitution: see F. Marglin, *Wives of the God-King: The Rituals of the Devadasis of Puri* (Delhi: Oxford University Press, 1985), and for ambiguous statements about the positive value of *sati*, see Ashis Nandy, article on the Roop Kanwar *sati* in *Mainstream*, February 1988, reprinted in M.R. Anand, ed., *Sati* (Delhi: B.R. Publishing Corporation, 1989). For a different view of *devadasis*, see Gail Omvedt, "*Devadasi* Custom and the Fight Against It," *Manushi* 4 (Nov.–Dec. 1983), 16–19. For critique of Nandy's position on *sati*, see Sanjukta Gupta and Richard Gombrich, "Another View of Widow-Burning and Womanliness in Indian Public Culture," *Journal of Commonwealth and Comparative Politics* 22 (1984), 262–74, and Imrana Qadeer and Zoya Hasan, "Deadly Politics of the State and Its Apologists," *Economic and Political Weekly* 22 (1987), 1946–49. For further discussion of laws forbidding the glorification of *sati*, see my "Religion and Women's Human Rights" (note 3).
21 This is in essence the position of Judith C. Miles, "Beyond *Bob Jones:* Toward the Elimination of Governmental Subsidy of Discrimination by Religious Institutions,"

wrong, this position seems sensible. This was, it seems, the position of Chief Justice Chandrachud in the Shah Bano case, when he called for an end to state protection for religious courts.[22]

There are deep pragmatic difficulties with secular humanism, as the Shah Bano case shows us. It is rash and usually counterproductive to approach religious people with a set of apparently external moral demands, telling them that these norms are better than the norms of their religion. In the Indian situation it was bad enough when the demands were made by Hindus to Hindus; but when similar demands were made by Hindus to Muslims, they were read, to some extent correctly, as both insulting and threatening, showing a lack of respect for the autonomy of a minority cultural and religious tradition. Today, such demands are all the more clearly threatening, since the call for reform of Muslim personal law has been taken up as a rallying cry by Hindu nationalist forces, eager to portray Hinduism as enlightened toward women, and Islam as backward and oppressive. Although the goal of a uniform code continues to be backed by many feminist and otherwise progressive thinkers, in practice it is so prominent a part of the goals of Hindu fundamentalism that it is difficult to dissociate it from the idea of Hindu supremacy and a relegation of Muslim citizens to second-class status.

A related pragmatic error of the secular humanist is to fail to pursue alliances with feminist forces within each religious tradition. Religious traditions have indeed been powerful sources of oppression for women; but they have also been powerful sources of protection for human rights, of commitment to justice, and of energy for social change. For example, they have been primary sources of U.S. abolitionism and of the more recent civil rights movement, and in India they have been primary sources of the Gandhian anticolonialism and of the contemporary Gandhian SEWA movement.[23] Muslim feminists like Heera Na-

---

Harvard Women's Law Journal 8 (1985), 31–58. Miles, on sex-equality grounds, favors ending all tax benefits and other related benefits (postage, etc.) to religious institutions, not only to those that have discriminatory practices. Becker sympathizes with this approach, but in the end does not favor it: she would ban tax exemptions and postal subsidies only for those religions that close leadership positions to women.

22 The Chief Justice was not a total secular humanist, however: although he advocated getting rid of religious courts of law, he did not advocate abolishing special constitutional protections for religion.

23 See, for example, Kalima Rose, *Where Women are Leaders*, 83–4, where the story of Draupadi's prayer to Krishna is used to illustrate an episode in Ela Bhatt's life. Bhatt told me in conversation that at the death of her father, a prominent Brahmin judge,

waz find ideas of justice in their religion important sources of empowerment. By announcing that she wants nothing to do with religion, or even (in the milder cases) by announcing that religion will be respected only insofar as it lives up to a comprehensive liberal view of life, the secular humanist dooms herself to a lonely and less-than-promising struggle, and insults many people who would otherwise be her allies. In the Indian context especially, secularist grassroots politics has had a hard time capturing people's imaginations. By ceding religion's moral authority and all its energy of symbol and metaphor to the side of patriarchy, or even (in the milder cases) by insisting that religions be feminist or liberal in all respects, the secularist further compromises her own political goals. Finally, she abandons the terrain of argument on which she is strongest, namely sex equality, and wades into contentious metaphysical issues. Why do this, when she doesn't need to?

But the difficulties with secular humanism are not merely pragmatic and political. Three arguments cast doubt upon it at a deeper level. First is an argument from the *intrinsic value of religious capabilities*. The liberty of religious belief, membership, and activity is among the central human capabilities. Because the religious capabilities have multiple aspects, I have included them among the capabilities of the senses, imagination, and thought, and also in the category of affiliation. This strategy reflects my view that religion is one extremely important way of pursuing these general capability goals, but not the only one that deserves protection.[24] I do insist, however, that it is among the specifications of these general capability goals that it is most important to protect for political purposes. To be able to search for an understanding of the ultimate meaning of life in one's own way is among the most important aspects of a life that is truly human. One of the ways in which this has most frequently been done historically is through religious belief and practice; to burden these practices is thus to inhibit many people's search for the ultimate good. Religion has also been intimately and fruitfully bound up with other human capabilities, such as the capabilities of artistic, ethical, and intellectual expression. It has been a central locus of the moral education of the young, both in the family and in the larger community. Finally, it has typically been a

___

her family (in a step unusual for her caste) granted her wish to perform the religious death ceremonies, which are traditionally assigned to a male.

24 I comment on the difficulties this presents for the defense of my balancing test later, in section IV.

central vehicle of cultural continuity, hence an invaluable support for other forms of human affiliation and interaction. To strike at religion is thus to risk eviscerating people's moral, cultural, and artistic, as well as spiritual, lives. Even if substitute forms of expression and activity are available in and through the secular state, a state that deprives citizens of the option to pursue religion has done them a grave wrong in these important areas.

For political purposes, the capabilities approach aims at religious capability or opportunity, rather than religious functioning, in order to leave to citizens the choice whether to pursue the pertinent human functions at all, and whether to pursue them through religion or through secular activity. For political purposes, then, the liberal state, as I envisage it, takes the position that citizens may reasonably pursue both religious and nonreligious conceptions of the good – or no definite conception. But the very fact that we insist that religious forms of these capabilities are among the specifications that must be defended for all citizens involves the recognition that religious functioning has had in many cases high intrinsic value: religious conceptions of value are among the reasonable ones that we are determined to make room for, as expressions of human powers.

Because religion is so important to people, such a major source of identity, there is also a strong argument from *respect for persons* that supplements these considerations of intrinsic value. When we tell people that they cannot define the ultimate meaning of life in their own way – even if we are sure we are right, and that their way is not a very good way – we do not show full respect for them as persons. In that sense, the secular humanist view is at bottom quite illiberal. It is precisely this consideration that led me to prefer *political liberalism* to *comprehensive liberalism* in Chapter 1; the secular humanist view is a form of comprehensive liberalism. Obviously no state can allow its citizens to search for the ultimate meaning of life in any way they wish, especially when that way involves harm to others. But secular humanism frequently errs in the opposite direction, taking a dismissive and disrespectful stance toward religion even when no question of harm has arisen. Even if such a position were correct, even if a certain group of religious beliefs (or even all beliefs) were nothing more than retrograde superstition, we would not be respecting the autonomy of our fellow citizens if we did not allow them these avenues of inquiry and self-determination. As Roman Catholic thinker Jacques Maritain expressed the point:

There is real and genuine tolerance only when a man is firmly and absolutely convinced of a truth, or of what he holds to be a truth, and when he at the same time recognizes the right of those who deny this truth to exist, and to contradict him, and to speak their own mind, not because they are free from truth but because they seek truth in their own way, and because he respects in them human nature and human dignity and those very resources and living springs of the intellect and of conscience which make them potentially capable of attaining the truth he loves, if someday they happen to see it.[25]

Frequently I sense that my fellow feminists do not sufficiently respect the "springs of conscience" in religious women (and men), when they treat religion dismissively, as a mere "opiate of the masses."

Finally, there is an argument from the *internal diversity of the religions*. Secular humanists who marginalize religion tend to treat religion as an enemy of women's progress. In so doing, they make a most unfortunate concession to their traditionalist opponents: they agree in defining religion as equivalent to certain reactionary, often highly patriarchal, voices.[26] This, as I have already said, is a pragmatic error: the humanist feminist thus alienates people who could become some of her

25 Maritain, "Truth and Human Fellowship," in *On the Uses of Philosophy: Three Essays* (Princeton: Princeton University Press, 1961), 24.

26 Becker states that "Jewish marriage and divorce law do not treat women and men as equals" (464) and that "for purposes of the minyan . . . , [a woman] does not count at all" (464) – ignoring the fact that both of these features have been challenged since the early nineteenth century, and a vast majority of American congregations have rejected such practices. Similarly, Becker ascribes to Judaism as a whole the prayer in which a man thanks God that he was not born a woman (464): this again was rejected by many early in the nineteenth century, and is relatively rare by now. Again, she claims that "the Jewish faith relegates women to serving others," rather than recognizing them as creatures with important spiritual lives" (464) – inaccurate concerning a tradition three out of whose four major branches in the U.S. treat women as full equals in all liturgical and political as well as spiritual matters; the fourth (Orthodox) certainly would also reject this characterization, holding that women have very important spiritual lives, only in a different style from that of males. (Becker's presentation is sometimes hard to follow because she alternates between claims about what "Orthodox" women do and claims about "Judaism" and "the Jewish faith," making no distinction.) Similarly one-sided is Becker's claim that "the Christian valuation of suffering encourages women to accept abuse" (465), and that the Christian view of women's sexuality is consistently negative (466–7). Okin stresses internal diversity, though she understands the more egalitarian versions of Judaism to be "reformed" versions of the tradition rather than its authentic form, a highly controversial (and to my mind mistaken) claim.

most influential allies, by indicating that she considers their whole enterprise of effecting change (or a return to better earlier norms) within their religious traditions a silly waste of time. Sometimes she even reveals ignorance of the very existence of such contesting voices.[27] But her error is also a theoretical error about what a religious tradition is. In Chapter 1, I criticized the error of treating cultures as homogeneous, neglecting internal diversity and conflict. The same point can be made at least as emphatically about religious traditions. No religious tradition consists simply of authority and sheeplike subservience. All contain argument, diversity of beliefs and practices, and a plurality of voices – including the voices of women, which have not always been clearly heard. All, further, are dynamic: because they involve a committed search for ultimate meaning, they shift in at least some ways in response to participants' changing views of meaning; and because they are forms of communal organization, they shift in response to their members' judgments about the sort of community in which they want to live.[28] What counts as Jewish, or Muslim, or Christian is not in any simple way read off from the past: although traditions vary in the degree and nature of their dynamism, they are defined at least in some ways by where their members want to go.

Thus any account of Judaism that fails to include the fact that Reform and Reconstructionist congregations address God as "you" rather than "he," and acknowledge the (four) mothers alongside the (three) fathers, is a false account of what the Jewish tradition is.[29] By this argument, secular-humanist feminists are giving a false account of Judaism when they call it inherently patriarchal; equally false is the ac-

---

27 See the remarks on Becker in the previous note. Okin is generally less polemical, but she simply asserts that God in Christian, Jewish, and Islamic traditions is male; again, this claim would be rejected by large numbers of believers in all these traditions (and not only the most evidently liberal), who would insist that a transcendent being is correctly understood to be entirely beyond gender, and that mythic personifications of God as male are not at the core of the religious conception.

28 This is true even of small communities relatively separate from mainstream culture, which have often been portrayed, nostalgically, as zones of homgeneity and harmony. For a fascinating account of internal diversity and conflict in one such religious tradition, see Fred Kniss, *Disquiet in the Land: Cultural Conflict in American Mennonite Communities* (New Brunswick: Rutgers University Press, 1997).

29 See my "Judaism and the Love of Reason," forthcoming in Marya Bower and Ruth Groenhout, eds., *Among Sophia's Daughters: Reflections on Philosophy, Feminism, and Faith* (Indiana University Press).

count given by political forces in Israel that would refuse recognition to non-Orthodox branches of Judaism.[30] Any account of the Roman Catholic tradition that treats it as in principle anti-Semitic neglects a recent evolution in doctrine prompted by statements and actions of the current Pope. Jews may have good historical reasons for doubting whether the leopard can change its spots, but they also should not be deaf to what is going on. A similar evolution may eventually take place with regard to women's role in the priesthood; many Catholics support such a change. Such changes, of course, have already been made in most major Protestant denominations.[31] Any account of the Hindu tra-

30 One might reply that Orthodox Jews really do not accept the non-Orthodox as Jews, so in calling their view false I am simply taking one side in this debate. Here I can make two replies. First, it is simply dishonest to refuse to recognize the historical reality of the evolution of Judaism *in some way*, whether by treating the other branches as separate religions, analogous to Christianity, or by recognizing them as Jews. What is objectionable about the Israeli situation is that neither course has been taken, and thus Christians have far more rights than Reform and Conservative Jews. Second, it simply is not true that Orthodox Jews do not and cannot recognize Reform and Conservative Jews as Jews. Very few Orthodox Jews, or even Orthodox rabbis, make such a judgment. I was converted by an Orthodox rabbi, who knew that my practice would not be Orthodox. He gave me some reasons why I should consider Orthodox practice, but he also listened respectfully to my reasons against it; in the end, we agreed to share a core group of commitments, while differing about others. He performed the conversion ceremony, and he maintained vigorously to my fiancé's grandmother that this conversion did in fact make me a Jew. This is a common position. Respect for the Jewishness of other Jews is perfectly compatible with a personal commitment to the idea that Orthodoxy is the only fully correct way of being a Jew: indeed, a common U.S. position resembles the sort of political consensus that members of different comprehensive views are imagined as forming within Rawlsian political liberalism. Thus, for example, the director of the University of Chicago Hillel, David Rosenberg, is an Orthodox rabbi; qua rabbi, he believes that his type of Jewish practice is best; nonetheless, as he has prominently stated, qua director of Hillel, he is committed to recognizing, respecting, and working with Jewish individuals and groups of all types *as Jews*, including the gay and lesbian Jewish students and many others. He has made a point of this political stance, which clearly involves more than a mere modus vivendi. For valuable discussions of feminism in the Jewish tradition, see Judith Plaskow, *Standing Again at Sinai: Judaism from a Feminist Perspective* (San Francisco: Harper San Francisco, 1990); Rachel Adler, *Engendering Judaism: An Inclusive Theology and Ethics* (Philadelphia and Jerusalem: The Jewish Publication Society, 1998).

31 For one clear, balanced, and well-argued treatment of Christian feminism, see Lisa Cahill, *Sex, Gender, and Christian Ethics* (Cambridge: Cambridge University Press, 1996).
   An excellent illustration of the point about dynamism can be found in the recent election of Frank Tracy Griswold, bishop of Chicago, to the office of presiding bishop of the Episcopal Church of the United States of America. Griswold (who was a strong defender of women's role in the church long before it was fashionable, when he was a

dition that holds that Rama is the one central divinity, or that Hinduism is in principle inseparable from the tradition of misogyny exemplified by the *Laws of Manu*, is again a false account, one that neglects the tremendous regional, temporal, and ideological diversity that has always obtained within Hinduism – including the deep religious commitments of campaigners for sex equality such as Rammohun Roy in the eighteenth century, Rabindranath Tagore in the early twentieth century, and Ela Bhatt of our own generation, all of whom have understood themselves to be representing an authentic Hinduism, freed from historical and cultural distortions.[32] Any account of Islam that holds it to be essentially and irredeemably misogynistic once again confuses fundamentalist voices (which frequently purvey their own highly synthetic accounts of tradition) with the whole of the tradition, and displays considerable ignorance about the texts (for example, about the fact that equal inheritance for women was secured by a return to the Quran from less authoritative interpretations, and that both Quran and Hadith regard men and women as sharing a single essential nature).[33]

young assistant minister at the Church of the Redeemer in Bryn Mawr, which I attended as a girl) campaigned for office on a long record of support for women in the priesthood, as well as a more cautiously expressed support for the ordination of openly gay priests. His opponent, an African-American, took more conservative stands on both issues. Griswold won: the voting body decided that this was where they wanted the church to go. His opponents currently speak of him as a "heretic" – see "The Bishop Moves Up a Rank," *Chicago Tribune*, December 30, 1997, section 5, pp. 1, 10; but history will likely judge that theirs are the outlier views (as is currently the case with Roman Catholics who refuse the vernacular Mass and other changes introduced by Vatican II).

32 Here the historical falsity is even more patent, since Hinduism has no conception of heresy, and has always been a loosely organized set of practices exhibiting much regional variation. This was also true of the Hindu legal system – until the British decided to systematize it for the nation as a whole! Contemporary Hindu fundamentalism is a recent social construct that no more represents Hinduism as a whole than the views of Pat Robertson represent Christianity as a whole.

33 A valuable general exposition of Islamic positions on interpretation and change (criticizing Okin's treatment of Islam) is in Azizah Y. al-Hibri, "Is Western Patriarchal Feminism Bad for Third World/Minority Women?" in *Is Multiculturalism Bad for Women?*, 41–6. For the role of ideas of equal nature in the Muslim women's movement, see Barbara Metcalf, "Reading and Writing about Muslim Women in British India," in Hasan, ed., *Forging*, 1–21. On the construction of "synthetic traditions" that represent themselves as having great antiquity but do not accurately represent a tradition in all its complexity, see Hannah Papanek, "Afterword: Caging the Lion, a Fable for Our Time," in Rokeya Sakhwat Hossain, *Sultana's Dream*, ed. Roushan Jahan (New York: The Feminist Press at the City University of New York, 1988), 58–85, at 61, discussing the wide range of Muslim practices regarding *purdah*. On the creative

THE ROLE OF RELIGION

Such ignorance is offensive to fellow citizens, and is objectionable for that reason alone – but it is also simply bad to be wrong!

If secular humanism has these practical and theoretical problems, how does traditionalist feminism fare? Interestingly enough, it suffers from very similar problems. In practical terms, as we shall soon see in more detail, it is highly divisive to neglect critical and dissenting voices within a religious tradition, equating it with its most patriarchal elements[34] and failing to acknowledge each tradition's dynamic character. Such ways of thinking about both Islam and Hinduism are implicated in the current bad state of group relations in India; narrow and static representations of tradition by the members of the traditions themselves are at least as much to blame for this as are ignorant representations by outsiders. Similarly, traditionalists about women's role have made the pragmatic political error of dividing where they could fruitfully pursue alliances, since feminists of all stripes share certain common goals in the area of material well-being.

In the theoretical domain too, similar problems can be identified. The traditionalist feminist seems to slight the intrinsic value of women's religious capabilities just as much as does the secular humanist, refusing to acknowledge the many ways people search for religious meanings outside the most patriarchal[35] element of a tradition. The ultraorthodox

role of powerful women in the formation of Shi'ite Islam in India, see Juan R. I. Cole, "Shi'ite Noblewomen and Religious Innovation in Awadh," in Violette Graf, ed., *Lucknow: Memories of a City* (Delhi: Oxford University Press, 1997), 83–90. Cole shows that women were so successful in inscribing women's reproductive role into the idea of religious leadership that male leaders had to adopt a female gender model in order to create new rituals. Here is one example from the 1820s – the son of the creative female religious leader Badshah Begum: "On the day of the birth of the Imams he would behave like a woman in childbed and pretended that he was suffering from the pains of childbirth . . . The selected attendants prepared dishes used by women in childbed and served them to the king."

34 These may, of course, be not at all the same. In quite a few religions, including Judaism, Hinduism, Islam, and Christianity, there is evidence that earlier practices were much less patriarchal than later ones: Draupadi enjoys a status unknown to the laws of Manu, Deborah plays a prophetic role unknown again among Jewish women until recently, and early Christian communities seem to have been more egalitarian than post-Pauline communities. Similarly, many Islamic feminists believe that many, if not most, oppressive patriarchal elements were introduced by the interpretive tradition and have no solid basis in Quran and Hadith.

35 Again, one should not say "oldest" or even "most orthodox" because this begs all kinds of questions about what the tradition really is. The version of Hinduism espoused by the Bharatiya Janata Party (BJP), for example, is quite new. Moreover, many liberal

in Israel slight the intrinsic value of religious capabilities when they deny Conservative and Reform Jews the free exercise of their religion in areas such as marriage, divorce, and conversion; in similar ways, traditionalist Hindu, Islamic, and Christian authorities slight the value of dissident types of functioning in their own traditions, defining their way as the only legitimate way. This error is not only an assault on intrinsic value, it is also very much an assault on one's fellow citizens, who ought to be respected when they search for the good in their own ways, even when one holds, as fundamentalists typically do, that critical ways are erroneous departures from the correct way. Finally, it is evident that these traditionalists are frequently engaged in massive simplifications and rewritings of their own traditions, which distort and deform tradition and history by denying both diversity and dynamism, just as surely as do secularist feminists' misreadings.

The traditionalist view has one further difficulty that does not appear to be present in the secular humanist view. Namely, in at least some of its political forms, it rides roughshod over other human capabilities, giving religion (tendentiously interpreted) broad latitude to determine a woman's quality of life, even when that threatens not only dignity and equality, but also health, the wherewithal to live, and bodily integrity.[36] The secular humanist is at least motivated by an admirable goal: to guarantee to women the full range of rights and capabilities, including both those already on the agenda for men and those

---

religious thinkers deny that the oldest stratum of the religion is the most important or essential.

36 Thus F. Marglin seems little interested in the constraints brought to bear on young girls who enter the *devadasi* way of life, or on the material conditions of their lives. The book focuses on traditions of dance, on symbolism, and on ritual, in quite a nostalgic manner, without asking about issues such as bodily integrity and health. Marglin was led to the study of *devadasis*, she says, by her own training in classical Indian dance; and throughout she tends to regard the life of temple prostitutes as an aesthetic activity, and to assail the critique of this form of prostitution as inspired by Western values. Nonetheless, the practice is strongly opposed by the indigenous women's movements in India: the federal government's Mahila Samakhya program, for example, both documents and supports poor rural women's resistance to the pressure to sell daughters into this life, in part by providing free residential schooling to girls who are thought to be at risk (personal communication, Yedla Padmavathi of the Andhra Pradesh office of Mahila Samakhya); numerous similar programs exist throughout the country. In an extremely poor rural desert area of Andhra Pradesh that I visited in March 1997, illiterate women, asked to draw what they wanted, drew a little girl dressed as a *devadasi*, with a big red X across the picture.

that involve women's freedom from gender-specific abuses. I have argued that in the process, she slights a very important range of concerns related to religious capabilities and respect for persons; but she does so, often, without fully recognizing this fact, and with an eye to promoting women's equal citizenship. I don't think there is anything so positive to be said about the motives lying behind traditionalism, where women are concerned. It is rare to find a serious argument to the effect that a certain type of harm or inequality toward women is required, as such, by the spiritual or moral values inherent in a religious tradition. It was not argued that unequal inheritance rights for Mary Roy were a noble goal, essential to Christian worship; that polygamy and child marriage were of the essence of Hindu spiritual values; or that the failure to pay a monthly maintenance to Shah Bano was a high moment in Islam. Usually, instead, even the overt arguments of traditionalists allude to the value of preserving the power of traditional religious courts of law and traditional religious authorities – a value far more dubious in moral terms than the value of the basic human capabilities. And frequently their arguments have the paradoxical result of allowing women to suffer discrimination in regard to property rights, or maintenance, or whatever, just because they happen to be members of that particular religion – surely a dubious way of showing respect for the moral values inherent in that tradition. At some point we must draw the line and deny that these approaches deserve the title "feminist" at all; that point is surely reached when not even a show is made of defending the traditional norms as supportive of women's interests. Insofar as serious moral argument is made, it is most commonly indirect, alleging that the power of traditional authorities or courts is necessary for the maintenance of other valuable aspects of tradition.[37] But such claims are empirical, and should be tested.

III. TWO ORIENTING PRINCIPLES

Any adequate approach to the dilemma must, then, begin by treating it as a real dilemma, acknowledging the weight of the values on both

37 This is the type of argument that prevailed in *Wisconsin v. Yoder*: see section VII; it was argued that requiring children to attend school until the age of sixteen would damage the free exercise of adult members by undermining the future of the community itself.

sides. I have argued that it must respect the intrinsic value of religious capabilities and of religious women and men as choosers of a way of life (a basic commitment of political liberalism), while at the same time taking just as seriously the importance of the full range of the human capabilities that are sometimes at risk for women in traditional religious cultures. Finally, it must understand and respect the plurality and diversity of voices in each religious tradition, both traditional and critical, both female and male. This entails being skeptical from the start of any account that fails to recognize the complexity both of religion and of women's interests.

Two further principles now orient my approach. The first guiding principle has been with us from the start of this project: it is the *principle of each person as end*, reinterpreted in Chapter 1 as a *principle of each person's capability*. Like all the central capabilities, religious capabilities are capabilities of individual people, not, in the first instance, of groups. It is the person whose freedom of conscience and freedom of religious practice we should most fundamentally consider. Although religious functioning is usually relational and interactive (like political functioning and functioning in the family), and although it often involves shared goals and ends, the capabilities involved are important *for each*, and it is *each person* who should be allowed access to these capabilities. As with politics and the family, so here: an organic good for the group as group is unacceptable if it does not do good for the members taken one by one. Citizens of liberal democracies typically hold that not just some but *all* citizens should enjoy the political rights and liberties. The religious analogue is the idea that *all* (in the sense of *each and every one*)[38] should enjoy the liberty of conscience and religious exercise (and the other human capabilities). Thus, any solution that appears good for a religious group will have to be tested to see whether it does indeed promote the religious capabilities (and other capabilities) of the group's members, taken one by one. To subordinate the capabilities of some to the organic purposes of the whole is to

38 Aristotle already makes the distinction between a corporate sense of "all" and a distributive sense at *Politics* 1261b16–27, saying that in Plato's ideal city it may possibly be true that "all" the city, taken as a whole, will use the terms "mine" and "not mine" in the same way, but not in the sense that "each one of them" will use these terms of the same objects.

violate people with respect to a capability that may lie at the heart of their lives.

I am emphatically not saying that all religious functioning, to be acceptable, must be individualistic, in the sense that the individual regards herself as an independent and self-willed member of the religious group. Such an account of religious functioning and capability would obviously leave out many of the ways in which people search for the good by subordinating themselves to authority or hierarchy, or by aligning themselves with the purposes of a corporate body. What is ruled out by the type of focus on the person for which I have argued is any approach that seeks a good for Hinduism or Judaism, let us say, by denying the liberty of conscience of individual Hindus or Jews. Israel's failure to give legal recognition to Reform and Conservative Judaism, for example, violates this principle: for it says, for the sake of a strong Judaism let us forbid individual Jews to worship in their own way, where marriage, conversion, and divorce are concerned. Whether this is indeed conducive to a strong Judaism may be doubted; but it certainly runs afoul of my principle.[39] So does the failure of the Indian system generally to allow individuals free egress from one religious tradition into another, given the impossibility of extricating ancestral property from the system of personal law into which one is born.

A good way of thinking of the type of focus on the individual person in religious matters that I am proposing is to think of the twin U.S. constitutional principles of non-establishment and free exercise. The motivation behind the establishment clause is to prevent citizens from being violated in conscience and practice by the pressures of a dominant religious group backed by political and legal power; the motivation behind the free exercise clause is to prevent belief and worship from being impeded or burdened by public action. The history of these clauses is notoriously difficult and tortuous. At times they have appeared to be on a collision course with one another; at other times it is difficult to separate the strands of argument that the two clauses suggest. But in the most abstract terms we can say that together they aim at a regime in which each citizen's liberty of conscience is preserved

---

39 Similar was the resistance to legal adoptions in India on the grounds that Islam does not permit adoption: see details in "Religion and Women's Human Rights."

inviolate, despite the pressures that corporate bodies of various types, whether religious or secular, may bring to bear. As we shall see, this tradition has been cognizant of the fact that one way of denying individuals the free exercise of their religion would be to destroy a group or tradition of which that person is a member; so group values do enter into the equation.[40] But they are not considered to be ends in their own right, and certainly they are not permitted to trump the value of the individual person's conscience.

My second orienting principle is one that I shall call *the principle of moral constraint*. Religion is given a high degree of deference and protection in many constitutional conceptions, as it will be in mine. One reason for this deference is surely that religion is extremely important to religious people, as a way of searching for the ultimate good. But another important part of this deference involves the role religions play in transmitting and fostering moral views of the conduct of life. As Heera Nawaz says: the major religions are all, at their heart, concerned with the conduct of life, and all the major traditions can plausibly be seen as attempts to reform or improve the conduct of life. Furthermore, it would not be too bold to add that all the major religions embody an idea of compassion for human suffering, and an idea that it is wrong for innocent people to suffer. All, finally, embody some kind of a notion of justice. This doesn't mean that religions do not concern many other things, such as faith and ritual practice and celebration and pleasure and contemplation; but at least a part of what they are about is moral.

When we give deference to religion in politics, we do not do so simply because of the moral role of the religion; nor need the political liberal assert that this moral role is the central object of the state's interest. To say such things would involve an unacceptably paternalistic stance toward religious traditions and what is central in them. We may and do, however, judge that any cult or so-called religion that diverges too far from the shared moral understanding that is embodied in the core of the political conception does not deserve the honorific name of religion. Thus U.S. law has persistently refused to give religious status to satanist cults and other related groups. Controversies over Scientology have a similar character: insofar as states judge that this organiza-

40 *Wisconsin v. Yoder*, discussed later.

tion is really a shady con game, they refuse to give it the honorific status of religion. Comprehensive ethical or political views do not suffice to constitute a religion under U.S. law; I shall express my own unease about this situation below. But systematic views of the conduct of life that are nontraditional, and in the end rather hard to distinguish from comprehensive ethical views, have been granted religious status in two draft board cases.[41] It has been explicitly stated that belief in a deity is not required: otherwise Buddhism and Taoism would not be protected, as they clearly are. A moral constraint is applied, then, to the definition of what counts as religion when we protect religion.

Furthermore – what interests me here – such a constraint is also applied to state protection of the recognized religions. Even when a group clearly counts as a religion, we sometimes judge that it forfeits its claim to state deference when it goes outside of certain moral understandings, especially those that are protected in the core of the basic constitutional conception. Thus U.S. constitutional law has consistently denied that expressions of racial segregation or hierarchy are legitimate prerogatives of religion as such, when the state gives religion special tax benefits.[42] The Indian Constitution made a similar move when it

41 *U.S. vs. Seeger* and *Thomas v. Review Board*, to be discussed in note 72.
42 In *Bob Jones University v. United States* 461 U.S. 574, 103 S. Ct. 2017 (1983), the Court upheld the Internal Revenue Service's denial of tax-exempt status to a religiously grounded institution that had a racially discriminatory admissions policy. Although not affiliated with any specific denomination, the school's stated purpose is "to conduct an institution of learning . . . , giving special emphasis to the Christian religion and the ethics revealed in the Holy Scriptures." (2922) The primary focus of the institution was on preventing interracial dating. Until 1973, the institution completely refused to admit black students; from 1971 to 1975 it admitted only black students "married within their race," giving a few exceptions to long-term members of the university staff. Since 1975, unmarried black students had been permitted to enroll, but a disciplinary rule forbade interracial dating and marriage, stating that violators would be expelled. The Court argued that the government's fundamental, overriding interest in eradicating racial discrimination in education substantially outweighs whatever burden denial of tax benefits places on petitioners' exercise of their religious beliefs. "Petitioners' asserted interests cannot be accommodated with that compelling governmental interest, and no less restrictive means are available to achieve the governmental interest." The opinion concludes that a racially discriminatory institution is not a "charitable institution" within the meaning of established Internal Revenue standards. The opinion did not deny that the refusal of tax-exempt status imposed a burden on religiously based conduct (so it did not exactly express the principle of the moral core in my sense), but it did hold that the compelling state interest in eradicating racial discrimination justified the burden. McConnell, in "Free Exercise Revisionism and the *Smith* Decision," *University of Chicago Law Review* 57 (1990), 1109–53, argues that this is a case where

offered religion protection similar to that given it under the U.S. Constitution, and yet made untouchability illegal; Hinduism is protected only within moral constraints supplied by the core constitutional understanding of the equal worth of citizens. Laws against *sati* express a similar idea.

In keeping with the idea of political principles developed in Chapter 1, we understand the moral constraints in terms of the list of central capabilities, in the following way. We should refuse to give deference to religion when its practices harm people in the areas covered by the major capabilities. Obviously problematic will be practices involving harm to nonmembers of the religion (e.g., a refusal by Hindus of a certain caste to allow any woman to go outside because their own caste norms forbid that); but practices involving harms to coreligionists will also be problematic, where they significantly infringe a central capability – particularly where there is reason to doubt the voluntariness of the practice.[43] (Such problems are especially grave when there are rea-

government should make an accommodation: if harm is inflicted on non-coreligionists, it is only through the offensive speech of the institution, and this speech is protected by the free speech clause of the First Amendment. The "direct effects" of the prohibition "are purely internal to the religious group." One difficulty in assessing this argument is that there is no determinate "religious group" in question, since the school is non-denominational; a second difficulty is occasioned by the fact that many of the parties affected would be minors, who may not choose to attend Bob Jones and who cannot easily extricate themselves from the situation if they don't like the practices. (Presumably black parents would choose such a school for a variety of economic and geographical reasons, prominently including the fact that they were themselves employees of the institution; their children might have little say in the matter if they wished to continue their education.) McConnell argues that the harm these practices may impose on outsiders, if the tax exemption were to be granted, would be a form of speech protected by the free speech clause of the First Amendment. This is highly dubious. It is not the institution's speech that is in question – obviously there was never any question of making their expressive conduct illegal – it is, rather, the act of the government in giving that institution a favored status. For the federal government to favor a discriminatory institution by granting it a tax exemption would involve the federal government in supporting or at least countenancing racial discrimination.

43 Thus *sati* would always be suspect, even when practiced entirely within a religious tradition, because its voluntariness is generally suspect. Even a fully consensual case could be made illegal on the principles adopted in Chapter 1, because the state has reason to prevent citizens from forfeiting life and (in certain ways) health, except in special circumstances. Similarly problematic would be refusals to permit women to go out to look for work, where women are not choosing modesty as a norm but are being forced into this practice by economic dependence, intimidation, and so forth. For an interesting development of the distinction between harms to coreligionists and harms to others, see McConnell, "Free Exercise Revisionism," at 1145, urging that govern-

sons to suppose that individual members do not have the opportunity to leave the religion should they disapprove of it.) Thus refusals by Hindus to allow Hindu women to go outside to work will also get critical scrutiny, especially when we feel that women are under duress and threat in this matter, and also when we have doubts about their opportunity to define themselves as non-Hindu should they wish to.

Formally and in the core of the political conception, the *principle of moral constraint* says nothing about matters internal to the religion itself. Political liberalism prevents this: the public political conception should take no stand on disputed issues of the good outside the core of the constitutional principles. But the principle of moral constraint has an informal social corollary, which members of the religion may use in discourse with one another, and which may also be used across religious lines in informal social deliberation. One of our greatest problems, in talking about the prerogatives of religious actors and groups, is to decide when there is a legitimate religious issue on the table, and when the issue is, instead, cultural or political. Religions are intertwined in complex ways with politics and culture. Even when a religion is based on a set of authoritative texts, culture and politics enter into the interpretation of texts and the institutionalized form of traditional practice. Jews differ about where to draw the line between what is genuinely religious in the tradition and what is the work of specific contextual and historical shaping. Similar debates arise in Christianity and Islam. In all cases, many interpreters are inclined to regard at least a part of the tradition or even the text as a historical or cultural artifact,

---

mental interests do not extend to protecting the members of a religious community "from the consequences of their religious choices." Thus he defends an exemption to minimum wage/maximum hours laws for a sect that urged members to work without wages for the glory of God (*Alamo Foundation v. Secretary of Labor*, 471 US 290 1985). That this practice involves no harm to nonmembers may surely be questioned: on this, see William P. Marshall, "In Defense of *Smith* and Free Exercise Revisionism," *The University of Chicago Law Review* 58 (1991), 308–28, at 314, arguing that business competitors are unfairly disadvantaged by the foundation's reduced labor costs. But we should also ask some questions about the voluntariness of the practice: are members of the foundation, including its dependent and female members, coerced into working without wages? How free are they to leave? I am inclined to think that the potential for exploitation of the powerless is so great that such an exemption should never be granted. McConnell's other central example of an intrareligious practice that should be accommodated is the *Bob Jones* case, which I discuss later. Once again, I shall disagree with his conclusion.

expressive of human ideas of the good at a particular time, but not binding without translation for our time.[44] Where Hinduism is concerned, the absence of scriptural authority makes it all the more difficult, if not virtually impossible, to identify a necessary religious core distinct from layers of history and culture, all powerfully infused with imperfect people's desire for political power.

When, then, we are thinking of curtailing some activity highly desired by some religious actor or actors speaking in the name of religion, it is useful to determine whether they are *really* speaking religiously, accurately understanding the core of that religion, or just going all out for political power. But it is more than just difficult to discover this; sometimes there may be no determinate answer to be discovered. Judges are not well qualified to judge in such matters, and in general they are rightly deferential to the claims of religious actors about what a legitimate claim of free exercise in their religion is.[45] They properly stick to a strictly limited *political use* of the *principle of moral constraint*. But in more informal social discourse it is sometimes important to take a stand. Do the Christians have a case that Mary Roy's inheritance claim jeopardizes Christian worship, or is this simply a ploy on the part of church leaders to keep tax revenue? Do Nehru's and Ambedkar's opponents have superior insight into the essence of Hinduism, or are they just trying to shore up power for religious courts?

The *social version* of the principle allows us to go further in commenting on these questions. It suggests that when we assess such debates we should be skeptical of any element that seems prima facie cruel or unjust – again, especially in the area of the central capabilities. But now, in addition to saying that we may not give such elements state

---

44 For Islam, see Abdullahi An-Na'im, who distinguishes between two Koranic periods: see his *Toward an Islamic Reformation: Civil Liberties, Human Rights and International Law* (Syracuse: Syracuse University Press, 1990); Azizah Al'Hibri distinguishes between the Koran, which must, she holds, remain uncriticized, and later schools of interpretation. For a valuable discussion of the Koranic sources for *purdah* – where an adjacent verse, rarely mentioned, mandates a symmetrical norm of purity and modesty for men – see Huma Ahmed-Gosh, "Preserving Identity: A Case Study of Palitpur," in Hasan, *Forging*, 169–87; the relevant verses are cited later in note 49.

45 See K. Greenawalt, "Five Questions about Religion Judges Are Afraid to Ask," forthcoming in Nancy Rosenblum, ed., *Law and Religion: Obligations of Citizenship and Demands of Faith* (Princeton: Princeton University Press, 1999), for examples of this, and also examples of when judgments have to be made. See also Michael McConnell, "Free Exercise Revisionism."

deference, we press the question whether that element really is central to the religion. You say that your religion is dedicated to the good, we argue. But this is so patently bad that it seems dubious that it can really be a part of the religion, as we understand its central purposes.

This social principle would strike me as a valuable one even if major religions had not endorsed it. But it clearly has deep roots in Indian religious history, as well as in the West. When the emperor Ashoka (a convert to Buddhism who reigned during the third century B.C.) saw acts of religious intolerance being carried out in the name of religion, he invoked the principle of moral constraint in order to conclude that damage to other religions is simply not a way of expressing or exalting one's own:

... the sects of other people all deserve reverence for one reason or another. By thus acting, a man exalts his own sect, and at the same time does service to the sects of other people. By acting contrariwise, a man hurts his own sect, and does disservice to the sects of other people. For he who does reverence to his own sect while disparaging the sects of others wholly from attachment to his own, with intent to enhance the splendour of his own sect, in reality by such conduct inflicts the severest injury on his own sect.[46]

In other words, no matter what religious actors say about their conduct, we may conclude that they are in error about what religion requires: acts of intolerant harm damage, and do not express or glorify, one's own religion, Hindu or Buddhist. Had he been a state actor in a political-liberal state, Ashoka would have been well advised to speak in a more restrained way, simply saying that when people behave this way they forfeit a claim to state protection. But his informal social use of the stronger social version of the principle is highly effective.

A similar appeal to the principle of moral constraint was made by U.S. President Abraham Lincoln, in his second inaugural address, delivered at the end of the Civil War. Speaking of the fact that both (former) slaveholders and abolitionists think of themselves as Christian and their cause as a Christian cause, he commented:

Both read the same Bible, and pray to the same God; and each invokes His aid against the other. It may seem strange that any men should dare to ask

46 Edict XII.

a just God's assistance in wringing their bread from the sweat of other men's faces; but let us judge not that we be not judged.[47]

Lincoln, like Ashoka, says in effect: whatever they think about the religious character of their acts, if the acts are unjust we must be highly skeptical. The idea that God is just lies behind and constrains more specific ideas of what God does and does not endorse. That God is really a backer of slavery is highly implausible.[48] Again, U.S. courts speak more agnostically, simply saying that segregationists lose a claim to state protection in tax matters; but Lincoln's use of the stronger form of the principle is valuable, when religion is being invoked to back evil. For a Christian leader to say that slavery is anti-Christian does not seem to exceed the boundaries of public reason.

Moral constraint arguments naturally arise in the context of women's livelihood. A young wife in Bangladesh, told by local mullahs that religion forbade her to work in the fields alongside men, said that if Allah really was requiring them to stay hungry, then "Allah has sinned." She meant, of course, to express skepticism about the mullah's interpretation. Her view of her religion was that a just and good God would not permit women to starve simply on the ground that it seems to some men improper for a woman to go out of the house. A just God, presumably, would let her gain her livelihood and ask men to conduct themselves modestly toward her (as the Quran, in any case, explicitly requires).[49] Since Allah, by definition, does not sin, then any statement that implies that he does sin must be false. In general, this is the style of argument feminists in all religions have typically used to bring about

47 Lincoln, in *The Viking Portable Lincoln* (New York: Viking, 1992), 321.

48 "Judge not that we be not judged" is an utterance, I think, of mercy rather than exculpation. Lincoln means not, don't say that this was wrong, but rather, withhold the punitive and vindictive attitude that could all too easily animate people at this time. This reading is borne out by the famous conclusion of the speech ("With malice toward none, with charity toward all"), which renounces malice while remaining firm in the right. Lincoln's point is that "firmness in the right" should not lead us into a vindictive attitude that would impair our ability to join together to "bind up the nation's wounds."

49 Often quoted in defense of the veiling of women is Quran 24.31, "And say to the believing women that they should lower their gaze and guard their modesty; that they should not display their beauty and ornaments except what must ordinarily appear thereof." But immediately preceding is 24.30: "Say to the believing men that they should lower their gaze and guard their modesty; that will make for greater purity for them. And God is well acquainted with all that they do." See Ahmed-Gosh, cited earlier.

change: if we're agreed that God is just and good, and if we can show you that a certain form of conduct is egregiously bad, then it follows that this conduct does not lie at the heart of religion, and must be a form of human error, which can be remedied while leaving religion itself intact. Again, it was a bad idea for the Chief Justice to say something like this; in his judicial role, especially as a Hindu, he should have confined himself to the more restricted political version of the principle. But these women, speaking socially and within their own religion, make a powerful use of its stronger social version.

Such arguments are common in both the Hindu and Muslim traditions in India, where women's issues are concerned. Nineteenth-century Bengali reformers Rammohun Roy and Iswarchandra Vidyasagar, campaigning against *sati*, child marriage, and polygamy, based their campaign on a recalling of Hindu tradition to its moral core. Similar moral arguments about Muslim conceptions of modesty are made by reformers, such as Rokeya Sakhawat Hossain, who challenge the seclusion of women from within religious orthodoxy, by pointing to its morally objectionable consequences as well as its non-necessity for truly moral conduct.[50] The Indian Constitution uses the more restricted political version of the principle, as seems appropriate for basic constitutional matters in a pluralistic democracy. It makes no pronouncements about what Hinduism is or is not, it simply makes untouchability illegal. But moral constraint arguments do valuable work socially, in connection with such constitutional reforms.

To invoke the social version of the principle of moral constraint, we need not deny that a given form of immorality may at one time have been absolutely central to the beliefs and practices of the religion. It would be foolish, for example, to deny that the subordination of women was central in many religions at many times, that the caste system was a core feature of Hinduism, that racial hierarchy was a prominent feature of the Church of Jesus Christ of Latter-day Saints,[51]

50 See Rokeya, *Sultana's Dream and Selections from The Secluded Ones*, ed. Roushan Jahan (New York: Feminist Press of the City University of New York, 1988). Especially in *The Secluded Ones*, Rokehya focuses on the moral harms of *purdah*, pointing to damages to women's health and even lives caused by the extremes to which tradition pushed the norm that they should not be seen by men.

51 The church has a doctrine of "continuing revelation" – God's purposes are revealed to us gradually in the course of history – that was invoked on June 9, 1978, to justify admitting males of African descent to the priesthood.

and so forth. What we are saying is that what makes religion worthy of a special place in human life (and of special political and legal treatment) is something having to do with ideals and aspirations, something that remains alive even when formerly core understandings shift in the light of moral debate, and indeed, something that guides that evolution. In the following section I shall focus on the narrower political use of the principle. But we shall later see that the informal social version of the principle does valuable work in guiding debate in a time of religious upheaval.

IV. CENTRAL CAPABILITIES AS COMPELLING STATE INTERESTS

Let me recapitulate. We have two constraints that limit interference with religion: respect for the intrinsic value of religious capabilities, and respect for religious people as citizens. Next, we have a constraint that pushes the other way, toward at least some scrutiny of religion and religious actors: respect for the other central human capabilities. Next, we have two orienting principles: the principle of each person's capability, and the principle of moral constraint, interpreted in terms of the central capabilities. And finally, we have a fact that both secular humanists and traditionalists generally neglect, the internal diversity and plurality of the religions themselves. I shall now describe the approach that I would favor, arguing that it does not violate the constraints and is a good way to follow the guidance of the orienting principles. I shall then show how it would handle each of the three problem cases.

This proposal is conceived of as a good idea, not necessarily as the best reading of any particular constitutional tradition. It draws on ideas in U.S. law, and it is very easy to adapt to the Indian constitutional tradition, which in most cases draws heavily on U.S. constitutional jurisprudence for precedents involving the interpretation of fundamental rights. But obviously, interpreting a particular constitutional tradition involves asking questions other than whether something is a good idea, questions about precedent, text, history, and institutional competence. I have not attempted that larger task here.

My approach is modelled on the United States Religious Freedom Restoration Act of 1993 (RFRA). This act prohibits any agency, de-

THE ROLE OF RELIGION

partment, or official of the United States, or of any state, from "substantially burden[ing] a person's exercise of religion even if the burden results from a rule of general applicability," unless the government can demonstrate that this burden "(1) is in furtherance of a compelling government interest; and (2) is the least restrictive means of furthering that compelling governmental interest."

We now need some background on the origin and current status of this law, in order to see how it grew out of a concern for the protection of minority religions, a central concern in my own argument. For some years there had been an issue, in First Amendment jurisprudence, about how far laws "of general applicability" might be upheld against a religious group or religious individuals, when those individuals claim that the law imposes a "substantial burden" on their exercise of their religion. For quite a few years, the legal situation was, theoretically at least, more or less as RFRA later reestablished it: the Supreme Court consistently held that laws of general applicability might impose a substantial burden on an individual's free exercise of religion only if the law furthered a compelling state interest, and in the least burdensome manner possible. The governing case was *Sherbert v. Verner* (1963).[52] A South Carolina woman refused to work on Saturday, because her Seventh-Day Adventist beliefs forbade it. After being fired, she was also refused state unemployment benefits on the grounds that she had refused suitable employment. She claimed that the state had violated her religious free exercise; the U.S. Supreme Court agreed. The Court held that to attach to a benefit a condition that required violation of a religious duty did impose a substantial burden on her free exercise of her religion; the problem was compounded, the Court held, by the discriminatory impact of the benefits laws on workers who celebrate the Sabbath on Saturday. Under the regime established by *Sherbert*, other laws of general applicability were also found to violate religious free exercise: notable in this regard is the case of compulsory public education of Amish children in *Wisconsin v. Yoder*, which I shall be discussing later.[53]

52 374 U.S. 398 (1963).
53 Both opponents and critics of the *Smith* decision agree, however, that "in practice the Court sided only rarely with the free exercise claimant, despite some very powerful claims" (McConnell, "Free Exercise Revisionism," 1110), usually finding either that

In 1990, however, the Supreme Court changed course with its decision in *Employment Division v. Smith*.[54] Significantly, this case involved an unpopular minority religion and the threatening topic of legalized drug use.[55] The case concerned native American tribes in the state of Oregon, who claimed that it was essential to their religion to use peyote in a particular ceremony, and thus claimed exemption (not generally, but in this one ceremonial instance) from the drug laws of the state of Oregon.[56] The sincerity of their religious claim was not disputed, nor the centrality of the peyote ceremony to their religion.[57]

the free exercise right was not burdened or that the government interest was compelling (see McConnell, 1110, 1127–8; Marshall, "Free Exercise Revisionism," 310–11). In effect, the test in practice was weaker than the usual understanding of "compelling interest," which would have allowed government to override a religious claim only in unusual circumstances; some type of heightened scrutiny was applied, but the relevant standard was never very clearly articulated. It is also clear that claimants from religions that seem closely related to the culture's predominant religious traditions fared better than claimants from religions that seem bizarre. "Thus," as William Marshall puts it, "Mrs. Sherbert's claim that she is forbidden to work on Saturday is likely to be accepted as legitimate; Mr. Hodges's claim that he must dress like a chicken when going to court is not" (311, citing *State v. Hodges*, 695 SW2d 171 (Tenn. 1985), in which the defendant, held in contempt of court, maintained that dressing like a chicken when in court was "his spiritual attire and his religious belief"). On the weakness of pre-RFRA protections of religion, see also C. Eisgruber and L. Sager, "Why the Religious Freedom Restoration Act Is Unconstitutional," *N.Y.U. Law Review* 69 (1994), 437–52.

54 110 S. Ct. 1595 (1990).

55 This helps to explain the otherwise somewhat surprising political lineup of the Court, as Justice Scalia and other usually religion-sympathetic conservatives supported a striking departure from settled precedent (though not practice, as already discussed) in the direction of narrowing the sphere of religious liberty, while three liberals – Justices Marshall, Brennan, and Blackmun – backed the more traditional religious libertarian course. (Centrist O'Connor agreed with the dissenters to the extent of deploring the sharp theoretical departure from traditional free exercise jurisprudence, though she concurred in the judgment in the particular case.) Scalia's argument is less surprising, however, if one focuses on the issue of institutional competence and the limiting of judicial discretion, which is one of the prominent themes of his jurisprudence.

56 For a detailed description of the litigation, see McConnell, "Free Exercise Revisionism," 1111–1114. The plaintiffs were Native American employees of a drug rehabilitation clinic who applied for unemployment compensation after being fired for ingesting peyote sacramentally during a ceremony of the Native American Church. The Oregon Supreme Court repeatedly held that the illegality of the sacramental use of peyote was irrelevant to the determination of unemployment compensation: if religiously motivated, the conduct could not be treated as work-related "misconduct" under the First Amendment. Thus it was somewhat surprising that the question of the law's constitutionality came before the Supreme Court in the first place.

57 Twenty-three states, moreover, specifically exempt the religious use of peyote from

In a lengthy opinion by Justice Scalia, the court held that the free exercise clause did not protect the plaintiffs, since "[w]e have never held that an individual's religious beliefs excuse him from compliance with an otherwise valid law prohibiting conduct that the State is free to regulate." The Court explicitly rejected the "compelling government interest" requirement, as making the lawmakers' job far too difficult.[58] The dissenters, however, emphasized the danger of disfavoring minority religions,[59] and invoked the Founders' interest in securing "the widest possible toleration of conflicting views." Justice O'Connor, who joined this part of the dissenting opinion, concluded: "The compelling interest test reflects the First Amendment's mandate of preserving religious liberty to the fullest extent possible in a pluralistic society. For the Court to deem this command a 'luxury,' is to denigrate "[t]he very purpose of a Bill of Rights." This is an important moment for my approach, because the need to protect minority religions is my central reason for favoring the ample protection of RFRA to the regime inaugurated by *Smith*.

The decision generated public outrage.[60] RFRA was passed in 1993 by an overwhelming bipartisan majority in both houses, and signed into law by President Clinton.[61] It was declared unconstitutional in June 1997, on grounds relating to the scope of Congress's powers under the Fourteenth Amendment.[62] The principle involved in RFRA con-

---

their drug laws; the federal government not only exempts peyote but licenses its production and importation, and Oregon itself does not enforce its own law.

58 Scalia wrote that such a requirement would produce "a private right to ignore generally applicable laws," thus creating "a constitutional anomaly." The three liberal Justices dissented, arguing that no convincing reason had been given to depart from settled First Amendment jurisprudence. The discussion of precedent in the majority opinion is entirely unconvincing, and has received heavy criticism from all sides. McConnell calls it "troubling, bordering on the shocking" (1120; detailed analysis at 1120–27); Marshall says that the majority's "use of precedent borders on fiction" (309).

59 The majority opinion acknowledges this danger: it speaks of "plac[ing] at a relative disadvantage those religious practices that are not widely engaged in."

60 For documentation, see McConnell, "Institutions and Interpretation: A Critique of *City of Boerne v. Flores,*" *Harvard Law Review* 111 (1997), 153–95, at 159.

61 There has been considerable analysis of the debate preceding the passage of RFRA, as to whether it was genuinely deliberative or merely the jockeying of interest groups; I pass over this question, since it is not relevant to my proposal.

62 *City of Boerne v. Flores,* 117 S. Ct. 2157 (1997). The vote was 6–3, and the majority opinion was written by Justice Kennedy. The case concerned a conflict between a Catholic church that wanted to enlarge its building to allow the entire congregation to celebrate Mass at the same time, and the historic landmark preservation laws, which

tinues to enjoy strong support, including, it would appear, the support of a vast majority of the American people. The unresolved issue is how to translate this support into law, and, in particular, how to resolve the thorny issues of institutional competence raised by the clash between the legislative and judicial branches. Since I believe that each nation must resolve those particular issues on its own, in the light of its own traditions and constitution, I make no suggestion on that aspect of the issue here.

My own RFRA-based proposal has two parts: first, that the principle of RFRA be accepted as the guiding principle in dealing with the religious dilemma. The state and its agents may impose a substantial burden on religion only when it can show a compelling interest. *But*, second, protection of the central capabilities of citizens should always be understood to ground a compelling state interest: this is the way we interpret the principle of moral constraint and give content to the otherwise vague and amorphous notion of "compelling state interest."[63] In legal terms, I have suggested that the central capabilities are like a list of fundamental rights that might be embodied in constitutional guarantees. Many of them are already so embodied in the Indian Constitution, and in other constitutions around the world; others are embodied in human rights instruments that most of the nations under discussion have endorsed; still others are embodied in legal precedents through which Indian constitutional law has incorporated considerations of bodily integrity into its jurisprudence. So my proposal is meant as a set

forbade alterations to the building, whose facade was located in a historic district. (The church's plan was to build out from the back wall, leaving the old Spanish-style structure virtually intact, but the city refused to approve any plan of expansion that would require demolition of any part of the church building, whether inside or outside the historic district.) In August 1997, the church and the city came to an agreement that the church may build a new 850-seat sanctuary behind, and partly hidden by, the original building, most of which will be repaired and preserved at church expense; so the church accomplished its primary objective, though at much greater expense.

63 I do not say that nothing other than the central capabilities can ever provide such a compelling interest; I leave that to be hammered out by each legal tradition as it evolves. In the U.S., an account of these interests was evolving, before the demise of RFRA. See, for example, *Mack v. O'Leary* (80 F. 3d 1175), 1996, offering a generous definition of "substantial burden," but holding that the maintenance of order in federal prisons was a compelling state interest; and *Sasnett v. Sullivan* (91 F. 3d 1018), 1996, holding that restrictions on the wearing of religious jewelry in prisons are not justified by any compelling state interest and are in violation of RFRA.

of moral guidelines that could in many respects be legally implemented under existing law.

On this principle, *Smith* ought to come out the other way. No compelling government interest was established in the case as argued, nor would thinking about the central capabilities help us to make a stronger argument than was in fact made. One might point to the parallel Indian case of the legalization of marijuana use during Holi, the Hindu spring festival: it seems just right to say that there is no compelling government interest in forbidding this festival use, and that forbidding it would impose a substantial burden on Hindu religion. (It is obvious, indeed, that Holi raises a far more serious issue for public order than the Native American ceremony, to put it mildly: for when a majority of the population is getting stoned, that can and has led to rioting and looting. Nonetheless, the Indian government is correct, in my view, to tolerate this exception and to focus on controlling disorder.) Other areas in which this principle would support an exemption would include the wearing of yarmulkes in the military,[64] the wearing of religious jewelry in prisons,[65] and reasonable accommodation of the religious dietary needs of prisoners.[66] On the other hand, a case like *Bob Jones*[67] would come out as it did: the government's interest in eradicating humiliating and stigmatizing racial discrimination would count as a compelling interest, in connection with the account of the central capabilities. Later, after I have discussed my Indian cases of sex discrimination, I shall say more about what latitude a religion might have for engaging in forms of sex discrimination internal to that religion; but *Bob Jones* already gives us one paradigm to employ: the government must not give favorable treatment to practices that humiliate and stigmatize individuals on account of their sex, especially where the voluntariness of the individuals' participation in those practices is

64 Contrast *Goldman v. Weinberger*, 475 US 503 (1986).
65 See note 58.
66 See *Hunafa v. Murphy*, 907 F 2d 67 (7th Cir. 1990), upholding a Muslim prisoner's right to receive food uncontaminated by pork and remanded for fact-finding on government interest; the court noted that the intervening *Smith* decision may be raised on remand and may change the outcome. For discussion of other relevant pre-Smith cases, see McConnell, "Free Exercise Revisionism," 1142 n.143.
67 For discussion of the case and McConnell's argument for an accommodation, see note 42.

far from certain.[68] I have already argued in Chapter 1 that such forms of discrimination are straightforward cases of capability failure, in that they compromise the social bases of dignity and non-humiliation.

I do not at all neglect the difficulty of appropriately specifying the level of each capability, but I think that this difficulty obtains in any constitutional tradition when we are trying to hammer out the best account of basic rights and liberties and say when a substantial burden has been applied to one of them. The best way to fix the boundaries more precisely is an incremental way, relying on cases to enlarge our understanding of what we want to say. As I have already stated, I remain agnostic about the proper role of the legislature and the judiciary in this evolution; the resolution of such institutional questions depends on contextual features about the nature of democratic traditions in each nation.

This two-part approach seems to do well by the guidelines I have set out. It respects religious citizens and the intrinsic value of religious capabilities, by imposing a taxing standard on the state in any case of state action that would substantially burden religious free exercise. It also respects the claims of the other human capabilities, giving them a central place in the account of potential limits on religious freedom. It respects the principle of each person's capability by framing the question as that of when government may legitimately burden citizens' free exercise of their religion; it remains to be seen precisely how interference with religious leaders and the authority of religious courts may be related to such burdens. Finally, it obeys the principle of moral constraint, by saying that when a religion does violate a central human capability (whether religious or nonreligious) we will not give religion the deference that is usually due to it.

The most powerful objection to my approach will come from the side of Justice Scalia and the *Smith* opinion. Scalia's claim is that we

68 See Becker, "Women's Wrongs," 484–86, arguing that a *Bob Jones* approach to religion (denying state benefits) is probably constitutionally compelled (not merely permissible) in the case of race, and might also be viewed as compelled in the case of sex. Becker supports banning tax exemptions and postal subsidies and the award of government contracts to religious organizations that close leadership positions to women. She would not favor altogether ending those subsidies, or requiring state regulation of religion to eliminate sexism. As will be clear later, I support Becker's position where educational institutions are concerned, but not with regard to the assignment of religious functions.

give too much latitude to religion when we allow it to be a ground for the violation of otherwise valid laws of general applicability, even in the absence of a "compelling state interest." A public law that is neutral (that applies similarly to all the religions and to the nonreligious) and that has a rational basis, should be obeyed by all citizens, no matter what their religious convictions. Otherwise, Scalia argues, we will face a flood of claims for exemption to the law, and it will be beyond the capacity of judges to sort these out in a way compatible with public consistency and order. Insofar as Scalia's argument rests purely on an issue of institutional competence (he does not, for example, object to the granting of exemptions by individual state legislatures), I have no general disagreement with it; for I have said that questions of institutional division of labor must be settled by each separate constitutional tradition as it evolves. Insofar as the argument rests on more general concerns about arbitrariness of judgment, and on a general view that laws of general applicability should be exceptionless, I believe that it is insufficiently protective of religion, especially of minority religion. But his argument raises important concerns, which must be faced by any proposal in this area. By offering a clear account of "compelling government interest," my capability-based account of what constitutes a "compelling state interest" goes some way, I think, toward reducing the dangers about which he worries. If, however, we can show that even my very generous account of the role of religion still renders unacceptable many actions taken by the religions in the context of sex equality, we will also have shown, a fortiori, that such actions are unacceptable by the more stringent Scalia test.

We now face an important issue: does the approach require equality in basic capabilities, or only a basic minimum threshold? In other words, does sex discrimination with respect to the basic capabilities trigger a claim of compelling state interest, or only discrimination that pushes women into a situation of destitution or extreme capability failure? Let's try to get at this by looking at things in the other direction. Typically, the state has been held to impose a substantial burden on religion when it treats members of one religious group unequally. The plaintiff in *Sherbert v. Verner* was losing a benefit that the state might not have offered at all; but the holding was that, so long as it does offer such benefits, to condition them on a practice that violates some people's religious freedom is to impose a substantial burden on the free exercise of religion. Forcing her to choose between the exercise of her religion and forfeiting benefits was said to be equivalent to fining someone for Saturday worship – a practice that would be unacceptable no matter how small the fine and no matter how great the individual's ability to pay. The inequality of treatment is itself a violation; to make X jump through hoops that Y is not forced to jump through, on account of X's religion, is ipso facto to burden the exercise of that religion. (It may also involve an establishment clause issue, although that was not the way *Sherbert* was argued.) So too, I think we should say, with the capabilities on the other side. The very singling out of women for differential treatment in a central area of human functioning is itself unacceptable, and gives rise to a compelling state interest in eradicating that discrimination, even if women are not by this means pushed into a basement level of functioning. Here we have the Indian Constitution on our side, since, unlike the U.S. Constitution, it contains an explicit provision of nondiscrimination on the basis of sex, listing this among the fundamental rights of citizens. Moreover, as with race, any discrimination that stigmatizes and humiliates is ipso facto a case of capability failure: so even outside the domain of the other capabilities there will be little scope for permissible discrimination, although I shall argue below that some choices internal to the religion should still be protected.

V. NONRELIGION, ESTABLISHMENT, BALANCING

Finally, my RFRA-based approach faces three very difficult questions. First, should religion be singled out for specially protective treatment, or should the same protections apply to all other expressive or ultimate-truth-pursuing activities? In framing and commenting on my list of the central capabilities, I have already suggested that religion is one of the ways in which people use thought and imagination in pursuit of an understanding of what is most important in life; it is also among the ways in which people pursue community and affiliation. But there are other ways, some involving comprehensive ethical views, some involving less systematic forms of personal search, some involving poetry, music, and the other arts. It seems difficult to distinguish religious belief-systems from the nonreligious beliefs and practices in any principled and systematic way. The features that make religion worthy of deference are frequently found in nonreligious belief-systems and practices. Moreover, even if one were to argue that religion is to be preferred not because of its role in people's search for meaning and community, but because it involves loyalty to a transcendent source of authority,[69] an argument I would not favor, this still would not yield a principled way of dividing what is conventionally called religion from what is conventionally called nonreligion: not all religions are theistic, Buddhism and Taoism being only two examples. One attractive feature of the *Smith* decision, for some of its supporters, is its fairness to nonreligious belief systems.[70] To accommodate religion and to reject a similar accommodation for Thoreau's philosophy[71] seems to many arbitrary and unfair.

U.S. constitutional law has handled this question in a very complex and sometimes quite murky manner, through the twin principles of nonestablishment and free exercise. With respect to free exercise claims, religion is given special deference. But any privileging of religion over nonreligion can potentially trigger an establishment clause issue, and with respect to establishment issues, religion is in some respects more curtailed than nonreligion. Thus a public display honoring Thoreau would present no problem; such a display honoring Moses, or Jesus, would potentially raise an establishment issue. Government endorsement of environmentalism is appropriate; government endorsement of Christianity is not. The two clauses to some extent balance one another; thus, it has recently been argued that any free exercise exemption to laws of general applicability "offends Establishment Clause principles" and "connotes sponsorship and endorsement."[72] If we focus only on the free exercise side, however, we ought to feel uneasy when a

---

69 This is the argument made by McConnell in "Free Exercise Revisionism."

70 See Marshall, "Free Exercise Revisionism"; Marshall does not defend the argument in *Smith*, only the result.

71 *Thomas v. Review Board*, 450 US 707, 713 (1981).

72 Marshall, 320. McConnell, while not accepting that particular argument, also draws attention to the balancing effect of the two clauses, arguing that favoring religion in the context of free exercise is not unfair, since religion is disfavored in the context of establishment: see his "A Response to Professor Marshall," *The University of Chicago Law Review* 58 (1991), 329–32. McConnell has in some areas sought to mitigate the unequal treatment of religion under the establishment clause: see his brief in *Rosenberger v. Rector and Visitors of the University of Virginia*, 115 S. Ct. 2510 (1995).

religious capability is supported and another highly similar human capability is impeded. Since I shall recommend remaining neutral about establishment, this is an especially serious problem for my approach.

We have two distinct issues, a theoretical/moral issue and a practical issue. On the side of theory, there seems little to be said in favor of privileging religion over nonreligious beliefs and practices. A political-liberal political conception based on an idea of human capability should not play favorites among the comprehensive conceptions of the good citizens may reasonably hold; my approach reflects this by making religion one of the permissible ways of pursuing a wide variety of human capabilities, rather than a separate capability all its own, albeit one that is singled out on the list as deserving of protection for all citizens.

On the practical side, however, there are enormous difficulties involved in treating religious and nonreligious conceptions equally. Religion is usually organized and involves some publicly accepted body of doctrine or practice. It is not open to any and every believer to state ad hoc that a given law offends against his religion; however difficult such an inquiry may be, and however problematic an exercise of judicial faculties it may involve, such an inquiry must and frequently does take place. The Court in *Yoder* satisfied itself of the centrality of work in the Amish understanding of community; the Court in *Smith* granted the centrality of the peyote ceremony in Native American religious ceremonies. With nonreligion, such inquiries become absurdly taxing, and frequently they will yield no definite answer. If the belief system is comprehensive and textually based (as, for example, in the Thoreau case), things may not be too bad; but in many other perfectly legitimate cases the task of assessing the claim will be absurdly difficult, beyond the competence of any court or legislative body. If X says that his personal search for the meaning of life requires him to get stoned and listen to Mahler, he may be entirely sincere, and he may well have just as good a case morally as those who use drugs in a religious context; but ascertaining the centrality of this practice to his search for meaning will be virtually impossible, and granting exemptions in this way would quickly make a mockery of the drug laws, of mandatory military service, and many other laws of general applicability.

For some, these difficulties provide a strong reason to prefer *Smith*.

Given that I continue to prefer to give religion a larger measure of deference, because of the pressing danger of disfavoring minority religions and their members, how do I propose to handle such problems? Tentatively, I believe that they can be handled in the following way. First, we confine the explicit area of potential exemptions to religion; but we allow religion to be somewhat broadly defined, including non-theistic belief systems such as the one that won Seeger his draft exemption.[73] It remains essential, however, to determine that the exercise of freedom of conscience is religion-like in having a systematic and non-arbitrary character; thus my Mahler fan, however sincere his practice, would still be excluded.

The disadvantage that would thereby be incurred by the nonreligious can at least to some extent be remedied by adopting strong protections for expressive speech and conduct. Thus, although the Mahler fan will not get an exemption from the drug laws, he can at least count on the protection of his right to listen to the music of his choice, to read the books of his choice, and so forth. By recognizing that the expressive interests involved in artistic and philosophical speech may be very religion-like, involving people's search for meaning and understanding, we give some account of why they should not be peripheral to the concerns of free speech jurisprudence.[74] But these subtleties take us

73 *United States v. Seeger*, 380 US 163 (1965). The Court explicitly distinguished "religious training and belief" from "essentially political, sociological, or philosophical views." The test proposed was "whether a given belief that is sincere and meaningful occupies a place in the life of its possessor parallel to that filled by the orthodox belief in God of one who clearly qualifies for the exemption." In ascertaining that Seeger's beliefs did indeed play such a role, the Court drew attention to Seeger's " 'belief in and devotion to goodness and virtue for their own sakes, and a religious faith in a purely ethical creed.' " Attention was drawn to the systematic nature of his beliefs (and to Seeger's own references to Plato, Aristotle, and Spinoza); to the similarity of his non-theistic ethical creed to aspects of Hinduism, Buddhism, and the Christian theology of Paul Tillich. The Court concluded that if the proposed test is passed by a system of beliefs, it follows that it is not a "merely personal moral code" in the sense already rejected as a legitimate basis for conscientious objection. See also *Thomas v. Review Board*, 450 U.S. 707 (1981): "Courts should not undertake to dissect religious beliefs because the believer admits that he is 'struggling' with his position or because his beliefs are not articulated with the clarity and precision that a more sophisticated person might employ."

74 For a position on "expressive interests" and free speech jurisprudence with which I largely agree, see Joshua Cohen, "Freedom of Expression," *Philosophy and Public Affairs* 22 (1993), 207–63.

rather far from our topic, since all of our Indian cases involve claims made by undisputed religions to exemptions from generally applicable laws involving sex equality.

Our second difficult question is, however, directly pertinent to the case of India. It is the question of religious establishment. I have presented my approach so far in terms of the concept of free exercise alone; I have argued that the central concern in the area of religion is that of religious capabilities, set over against the other capabilities of citizens. But I have also said that in the U.S. case the *combination* of the free exercise clause and the establishment clause offered us a good way of thinking about what it would be to protect religious capabilities: the motivation behind the establishment clause is to prevent citizens from being violated in conscience and practice by the pressures of a dominant religious group with political and legal power behind it; the motivation behind the free exercise clause is to prevent belief and worship from being impeded or burdened by public action. Why, then, have I so far been silent about religious establishment? The answer emerges from the way I have interpreted the function of the establishment clause in the U.S. setting: its function is to protect the capabilities of citizens. In other words, I understand nonestablishment as, at bottom, another way of shoring up free exercise, together with other capabilities of citizens. This approach suggests to me that it should be a contingent contextual question whether that protection is best accomplished through a regime of nonestablishment or through a regime of limited establishment with sufficient safeguards for citizen equality and free exercise. Given the specific history of intolerance toward minority religions, in the U.S. it seems wise for the U.S. to support a strong form of nonestablishment; only this regime, in the social context, guarantees all citizens a genuinely equal religious liberty. In the Scandinavian states, however, it seems plausible that the established Lutheran Churches actually protect religious pluralism more effectively than would a purely secular regime: they have been staunch defenders of religious pluralism in education, for example, and of other measures favorable to minorities. This is absolutely crucial to the case of India, because the existing regime of secularism in India involves a type of limited plural establishment: certain religions are entitled to maintain their own systems of civil law, and others (those too small or too new to have a codified system of personal law) use the secular system. In the next section I shall give this system a highly qualified type of support; given the history of Muslims in India, it seems apparent that any abolition of the system of Islamic law would be a grave threat to religious liberty and a statement that Muslims are not fully equal as citizens, and that even total nonestablishment would be de facto a type of Hindu establishment.

One might argue that any type of establishment puts minorities in a situation of indignity: in the public square a declaration is made that some believers are more privileged than others, even if the rights of others are duly protected. This is a grave point, which should not be dismissed. But I am inclined to think that this argument, too, must be assessed contextually. It is probably true of Britain, given Britain's history of anti-Semitism and xenophobia. But in India it would be disestablishment that would constitute a statement that Muslims were not fully equal citizens, absent a time of mutual respect and civic harmony, which may not come about in the foreseeable future. In the meantime, it seems to me that the totally nonestablished religions in India (Judaism, Buddhism) are not in grave difficulty because of their nonestablished status: in many ways they have an easier time than the others, since they simply go straight to the secular system, avoiding many difficult issues involving conflicts of laws.

In short: if the important issues underlying nonestablishment are really issues about both free exercise and full equality of citizens, it is plausible to suppose that, although nonestablishment is usually the best way of promoting those goals, this may not always be the case.

Finally, a deep methodological issue arises. I have said that the list of capabilities is a list of irreducibly distinct items, each of which is held by the public conception to be essential. We cannot make up for the removal of one by giving citizens more of another. When circumstances beyond the state's control force it to make such trade-offs, it should be acknowledged that a tragic event has occurred. Here, by contrast, I have favored a balancing test involving distinct capabilities, without suggesting that the choice need be tragic. Is this inconsistent with what I said about the list in Chapter 1?

I believe it is not. The cases I have mentioned all involve balancing above the threshold. So too, I believe, do the cases to be described later. Attention to the compelling interests represented by the other capabilities (for example, requiring equal property rights, or mobility, or even compulsory education) does not push the religious capabilities of citizens below the threshold. That is not to say that there could never be such a case – and yet even in *Wisconsin v. Yoder*, it was not maintained that survival of the religion required a totally unacceptable approach to education (for example, no secondary education), which would have triggered an overriding claim of compelling state interest. I recognize in section VIII below that there may be an element of tragedy in some cases using my approach; and yet, usually it is just not correct that protection of the other capabilities involves an unacceptable level of damage to a religious way of life. This is so, in part, because of the dynamic character of religious traditions, which have a way of evolving to meet the challenges of new situations.

Like any balancing test, mine requires a use of judgment in its application to the particular. Notions such as "compelling state interest" and "substantial burden" can certainly be given more definite content than they typically have been under U.S. constitutional law – and I have attempted to make them more definite, through my use of the list of capabilities. Nonetheless, an irreducible element of judgment remains. To those who follow Rawls in wishing to have pure procedural solutions that involve no element of "intuitionism," the approach will therefore perhaps seem defective – even though balancing, here, occurs only at a later stage of political choice, after basic constitutional values are fixed. I can only say that this is indeed an issue worth pondering; but I can reply to the Rawlsian that it appears likely to be unavoidable in any plural list of the elements of the political good. Rawls's own list of primary goods is somewhat thinner than my list of capabilities, but it might still generate conflicts at the legislative stage, just as mine does – where, for example, the freedom of worship might seem to conflict with fully equal equality of opportunity. So I do not think that Rawls's theoretical assault on intuitionism really succeeds in removing this problem; nor does my own approach appear to me to have an unacceptable amount of reliance on intuition – or, as I prefer to say, judgment.

VI. APPLYING THE APPROACH: THE THREE CASES

How does my approach handle the three cases? We must begin by asking how it applies to the whole question of having distinct systems of personal law operated by religions. There is a significant asymmetry between the U.S. and India, since the U.S. has never permitted the religions to take charge of law-making. India, by contrast, since the time of the British Raj, has permitted large areas of civil law to be the province of each of the religions. The areas covered by these systems of "personal law" include family law (marital consent, conjugal rights, divorce, adoption, etc.), property law, and related areas of personal contract (inheritance, above all). By contrast, personal law does not include commercial law or criminal law, since the British early on saw that these were spheres they needed to control and render uniform. Their retention of the personal law systems thus had something of the character of a compromise; but it also reflected a genuine recognition of cultural pluralism.[75]

The systems themselves have a variety of origins. Islamic law had been established in India by the thirteenth century under the Moghul Empire. (The Moghuls left Hindus to be governed by their own customary laws, except in criminal matters.) Under the Raj, Islamic law was modified, notably by the Shariat Act of 1937, which substituted the Shariah for customary laws that prevailed in various regions. By contrast, the whole enterprise of codifying the previously informal and regionally various systems of Hindu law was a British enterprise, and Hindu law bears many marks of the English law (including ecclesiastical law) on the model employed by the British legal thinkers of that era. In 1864 the Parsis won the right to be governed by their own separate system of personal law. Christians came to be governed by a plurality of distinct systems of Christian personal law, which reflect the heterogeneity of national origins of Christians in India. (For example, until recently Catholic Christians in Goa were still governed by the Portuguese Civil Code.) Jews have never had a codified system of personal law; in matters of succession they have been governed by the Indian Succession Act of 1865, and are currently governed by its post-independence successor.[76]

---

75 A comprehensive account of this history, and of later changes in the systems of law, is found in Archana Parashar; see also Barbara D. Metcalf, "Reading and Writing about Muslim Women in British India," in Hasan, ed., 1–21; Kirti Singh, "The Constitution and Muslim Personal Law," in Hasan, 96–107; Maitrayee Mukhopadhyay, "Between Community and State: The Question of Women's Rights and Personal Laws," 108–129; Indira Jaising, ed., *Justice*.

76 India once had a large Jewish population, especially in the princely states of Cochin and Travancore; most of that population has now emigrated to Israel, and one entire

At the time of independence there was some support for a uniform civil code, but the abolition of Muslim personal laws proved too sensitive an issue, given the overriding importance of reassuring Muslims that India was a truly pluralistic nation and not a Hindu nation. The ideal of Indian secularism was always that of state neutrality among the religions, not that of the separation of church and state; therefore it seemed in principle possible to combine a commitment to secularism with the maintenance, for the time being, of the separate systems of religious law. In consequence, the goal of a uniform civil code was included in the Constitution among the unenforceable Directives of State Policy, as something that the state "shall endeavour to secure" in the future – the idea being that when things had calmed down and people were ready for it, this next step would be taken. It never has been taken, and by now it is further away than it was fifty years ago.[77]

The way the system operates is labyrinthine and uneven; it is not easy to get two legal experts even to agree on a description of what the system is.[78] But, to give a reasonable general description: at birth, a child must be classified into some religious group. Usually it is that of both or one of the parents, and usually some religion is chosen, although it is possible not to mention a religion at all. Children who are enrolled as members of some religion are henceforth governed by that system of personal law. Since the passage of the Special Marriage Act in 1954 (itself much opposed by various religious leaders as an infringement of their power), couples may elect secular marriage and secular divorce (although secular laws are quite similar to the reformed Hindu laws). This is usually taken to mean that they will also be governed by secular inheritance law, but in 1975 the relevant law was amended under pressure from Hindu leaders so that two Hindus who elect a

synagogue from Cochin is now displayed at the Israel Museum in Jerusalem. See Orpa Slapak, ed., *The Jews of India* (Jerusalem: Israel Museum Publications, 1995).

77 For a forceful Muslim argument in favor of a uniform code – in the period prior to the Shah Bano case and the rise of Hindu fundamentalism – see Mohammed A. Qureshi, *Marriage and Matrimonial Remedies: A Uniform Civil Code for India* (Delhi: Concept Publishing Company, 1978).

78 The best account of the many contemporary legal systems, with comprehensive detail and many discussions of legal challenges, is in Jaising, ed., *Justice*. The authors are members of the Lawyers Collective, a public interest group affiliated with the Bangalore Law School; Jaising, its director, is a senior advocate of the Supreme Court of India, and has argued some of the important sex equality cases in various parts of the country.

secular marriage will still be governed by the Hindu law of inheritance. Religious conversion typically results in a change of legal system, although there are cases in which Hindus who convert to Islam in order to contract polygamous marriage are still charged with bigamy in Hindu courts, and it remains quite unclear which system finally governs.[79] Conversions to Hinduism are extremely rare – in large part because it would be unclear what the caste of such a convert would be.[80] What makes mobility among systems especially difficult is the arrangement for hereditary property, which typically involves complex family consortia (called the "coparcenary" in the Hindu system), in which individuals have rights, that are not transferable should one individual within the family decide to switch to another system. This discourages conversion, secular marriage and divorce, and the declaration of a secular identity for a newborn child.

What should my two-pronged approach say about this system in general? On the one hand, this brand of secularism is extraordinarily generous to the religious traditions, giving them a type of latitude that is shown them in no European or North American democracy. Given, especially, Muslims' legitimate fears that they would be slighted and unfairly treated in a largely Hindu state – given, indeed, the hostility toward Muslims evident in some Hindu quarters during the constitutional founding – this approach may have been preferable on religious-liberty grounds to the establishment of a uniform civil code. On the other hand, it has large difficulties, which are now evident. First is the sheer practical difficulty of achieving any predictability in a nation governed by so bewilderingly many codes and variants of codes. Second, and more important for my approach, is the likelihood of inequality between the religions (and between religion and nonreligion) in the approach to basic human capabilities. It seems virtually inevitable, in such circumstances, that citizens will end up being unequally treated on the basis of religion in one way or another – getting better inheritance

---

79 See Jaising, *Justice*, 24–6.
80 Converts out of Hinduism lose all caste, something that has large legal relevance, given the affirmative action programs established for "scheduled castes." See Marc Galanter, *Law and Society in Modern India* (Oxford: Oxford University Press, 1989), part 4, for a discussion of legal cases involving converts from Hinduism to Buddhism who still tried to claim these benefits. For a comprehensive account of the affirmative action programs, see Galanter, *Competing Equalities: Law and the Backward Castes in India* (Delhi: Oxford University Press, 1984, paperback edition 1991).

deals or divorce settlements or whatever, on account of being a Hindu or a Muslim – and that the national government will refrain from rectifying the situation for fear of infringing the prerogatives of some religion. So a huge free exercise dilemma is created: an individual incurs a substantial burden by, let us say, being born Hindu rather than Muslim, but the reason the state can't fix this is that the religions say such fixing itself would impose a substantial burden.

Third, the system makes it very difficult to move from one system to another, or to prefer nonreligion to religion. This itself is a huge free exercise problem. One is so wrapped up in religion with respect to one's entire livelihood that one's free exercise is thoroughly compromised, in the sense that liberty of conscience can't by itself settle the question of religious membership. A Muslim wife who doesn't like Islamic divorce law is stuck with it regardless; so too a Hindu child who might wish to inherit under the secular system.

Fourth, and most central for our purposes, other inequalities in basic capabilities, most prominent of which is the inequality between sex and sex, will be much more difficult to rectify in this plural decentralized system. Change of all systems at once is a virtual impossibility. But if one religion changes first, many of its members, as we have already seen, are sure to claim that they are being discriminated against by being made to pay more maintenance, or being denied polygamy, and that other groups are being given "special rights." On the other hand, efforts to do away with those so-called special rights, by bringing the less privileged group into line with equality norms, are seen as sinister attempts to impose (for example) a Hindu standard on Muslims. Interestingly, this has not been the case with the Parsi system, which has amended its inheritance law several times in the direction of gender equality, and since 1991 has had a fully gender-equal law. Regional reforms have also taken place within the Hindu and Muslim systems.[81] But in the current climate of Hindu-Muslim mistrust, full equality across the nation as a whole is unlikely to be achieved by such internal reforms. What frequently emerges instead is a furious race to the bot-

---

81 Kerala abolished joint family property in 1976. Karnataka, Tamil Nadu, Andhra Pradesh and Maharashtra have all amended the Hindu Succession Act to include daughters as "coparceners," in joint family property on a par with sons. In most of South India, the Muslim Shariat Act of 1937 has been amended to include agricultural land in its domain. (I owe these data to Bina Agarwal.)

tom, each group striving to show its power by resisting all change. Such a legal regime makes it difficult to achieve capability equality for women.

On the other hand, nothing in my approach militates against separate systems of personal law, so long as these problems are solved: so long as (a) there are guarantees of sex equality in each, where central capabilities are concerned, and these are enforced; (b) there is adequate provision for individuals who wish to define themselves as nonreligious or to change religions; and (c) there is a continual effort to ensure parity among the religious systems so that individuals do not lose out in basic matters because of the accident of their religious membership. It is surely difficult to solve these problems. But in today's India the most productive approach may well be to keep the separate codes and try one's best to solve them through a vigilant set of legislative and judicial constraints.[82] An alternative, sure to be vigorously resisted, would be to secularize all property law under a uniform code and leave the regulation of family law to the separate systems, with the provisos mentioned. This would go a long way toward easing the burden placed on individuals who wish to leave a religious system, and would also thereby give the religious systems new incentives to retain their members by promoting their interests.

One valuable strategy for solving these problems would be to promote more public dialogue over norms of sex equality within the religious codes. This can probably best be done at present by relying on the international human rights documents that India has ratified, together with a provision in the Indian Constitution that India is bound by the contents of all international treaties it has ratified. In the area of sexual harassment, the Supreme Court has ordered parliament to come up with suitable legislation in conformity with the principles outlined in the Convention on the Elimination of All Forms of Discrimination Against Women (CEDAW).[83] Similarly, the religious legal systems might be invited to submit their plans for reform, showing how they would bring their legal systems into conformity with the Indian Constitution and with international treaty norms. (The capabilities approach

---

82 One plausible reason cited by Muslims for keeping the separate systems is that the secular courts are extremely slow and inefficient: see Danial Latifi, "Women, Family Law and Social Changes," in Jaising, *Justice*, 216–22.
83 See my "The Modesty of Mrs. Bajaj."

itself could be used in this connection.) The tricky issue is who should do the inviting: not the current national government, given its religious bias, and probably not the Supreme Court, given the history of the Shah Bano case. Perhaps concerned NGOs and women's groups, in alliance with political parties that favor pluralism, could succeed in promoting such a dialogue.

Now let us turn to the concrete cases.

The case of Mary Roy is straightforward. The claim that is being made by the Christian Church is simply not a claim about the religious capabilities of individuals. Although judges and other political actors are not well equipped to judge what is central to a religion and what is not, one thing that they can say with confidence is that the ability to take in large amounts of tax revenue, while highly desirable from the point of view of a religious institution, is not itself a religious capability. However difficult it is to say what the core of Christianity is, we ought to be able to agree that the ability of the institutionalized church to enrich itself does not lie within that core. No citizen's Christian worship is being burdened by the drop in church revenue that would be occasioned by the new inheritance structure. Even if the drop meant that some local churches would close their doors, we should say that the church's entitlement to this money in the first place is highly questionable. If the Christian Church were being denied a tax benefit that other churches enjoy, there would indeed be a free exercise issue, as in the U.S. denial of tax-exempt status to a racially discriminatory religious college.[84] But that is not the situation here: Christian inheritance structure was simply being brought into line with the structure that already prevailed in secular law, in Hindu law, and in Islamic law. In fact, the greater burden is the other way around: before the Supreme Court decision, Christian women were being fined, in effect, for being Christian – a situation similar to the one that the U.S. Supreme Court viewed as a paradigm violation of free exercise in *Sherbert v. Verner*, even though in that case the "fine" was imposed by the religion itself on a captive member.

On the other side, the capability of women to control property is among the central capabilities, and as such would supply a compelling

---

84 *Bob Jones v. U.S.*, see above.

state interest even were there a prima facie legitimate claim on the other side. Mary Roy was herself very poor, so in her personal case it was clear that the capability threshold was at issue. Unequal property rights can be shown to be ubiquitous causes of women's general poverty and misery in much of India – certainly before the reforms of Hindu and Muslim personal law, and still in those systems today on account of rigidity in the rules governing control of the "coparcenary" and of jointly owned family land.[85] But I have argued that even in cases where an individual's control of property would in any case be above the threshold, discrimination on the basis of sex with respect to a basic capability is itself a case of capability failure. So it would have been right to declare the inheritance laws unconstitutional in general, not only as applied to women who would otherwise be destitute. It is somewhat unfortunate that the Supreme Court decided the case on a narrowly technical basis, concerning which statute applies to the case, rather than addressing the issue of sex equality head on. Nonetheless, the result for Christian women was a good one.

The reform of Hindu personal law poses far more difficult problems. Hinduism is a diverse set of traditional practices, with no easily identifiable core. But there is no doubt that some of the proposed reforms touched on very central matters: the substantial uprooting of the caste system, the denial of polygamous marriage, the ban on marriage contracts with women still in childhood, women's right to divorce on a basis of equality with men,[86] and the right of women to seek employment outside the home and to participate fully in political life, whether or not they were married and without the permission of any male. (Even property rights for daughters were argued to lie within central religious areas, since it was said that more economic autonomy for women would upset the structure of the Hindu family.) Although it was much stressed, and accurately, that one recognized system of Hindu law already mandated monogamy and gave women divorce rights – so one could say that in some areas the government was simply substituting that system for the more prevalent system[87] – nonetheless

---

85 See Agarwal, *A Field of One's Own*.
86 I see no reason why a religious system, to be acceptable, has to permit divorce, so long as exit from the system is readily available; but if it permits divorce for men, it must do so for women: see the previous discussion.
87 See publication of All India Women's Conference, 1944–5, and discussion in Shahida

it was not surprising that the proposed reforms provoked protest from many Hindu leaders. They protested both the proposed changes per se and the fact that they were imposed on Hindus and not on others.[88]

In at least some of these cases, unlike that of Mary Roy, we should grant that a substantial burden is being imposed by the state on the free exercise of religion. (The abolition of polygamy and caste, along with subsequent laws making dowry giving illegal, are the clearest such cases, since in all of them adults are prevented from performing religious acts they wish to perform. Child marriage is a dubious case of burden, since the child is too young to give meaningful consent, and we should not grant that marrying off a young daughter is a legitimate parental religious prerogative. Divorce rights for women clearly do not impose a substantial burden, since free exercise has never been interpreted to give one person the right to impose his religious will on another.) Moreover, the burden affects the capabilities of individuals, not just of religious institutions and authorities. This burden is all the more invidious because it is imposed selectively and not neutrally, restricting Hindu tradition in a way that other traditions are not restricted. On the other hand, we can see clearly that central human capabilities are at issue on the other side, just as they were in the contemporaneous abolition of caste. Control over property, the right to control the integrity of one's person (at risk in violence associated with dowry), rights to mobility, assembly, and political participation, the right to marital consent and to divorce on an equal basis, all these clearly provide the state with a compelling interest in the proposed reforms. Polygamy seems to do so as well, given its historical connection with unequal control over the integrity of one's person, unequal economic rights, and unequal dignity; but that issue, I think, raises special problems and I shall discuss it separately later. Where the caste system is concerned, fundamental capabilities are once again at issue: equal political rights, rights to the free choice of employment, rights to education and property, and, finally, to equal dignity and self-respect. As *The Hindustan*

Lateef, "Defining Women through Legislation," in Hasan, 49; and Parashar, Chapter 3.

88 A further issue was the extremely broad definition of "Hindu," which included Jains, Buddhists, and Sikhs, without much input from them; these minorities plausibly felt discriminated against by the tough reforms, which did not apply to other minorities such as Muslims, Christians, Parsis, and Jews.

Times commented: "The Hindu Code Bill is the counterpart on the social side of the new Constitution in which is embodied the political ideal of liberty, equality and fraternity."[89]

My approach suggests that in less central matters the state should allow Hindus broad latitude to act in accordance with their traditions. (I have argued, for example, that marijuana use during Holi is one such matter.) But on these matters of fundamental civic dignity and equality, Ambedkar (himself a member of one of the scheduled castes) was correct in saying that the state could not wait for Hinduism to undertake voluntary internal reform: "[W]hatever else Hindu society may adopt it will never give up its social structure – the enslavement of the Shudra and the enslavement of women. It is for this reason that law must come to the rescue in order that society may move on."[90] This decision should not have been, and was not, taken lightly, since it concerned extremely important religious matters. (Ambedkar did not simply adopt a secular humanist stance, for he continued to support ample constitutional protections for religion, which were clearly necessary in the context in order to protect the status of Muslims as equal citizens.) And, although one may understand the political pressures and the legitimate concern for minority rights that led to an uneven implementation of these changes, in principle the reforms should not have been made in a discriminatory fashion. On the other hand, not to make the reforms would have involved the government in other forms of discrimination on the basis of religion: against the lower castes, who would have had unequal rights on account of being Hindu, and against Hindu women, who would have done less well, even at that time, than Parsi and Christian and Muslim women, in at least some of the areas covered by the code. In effect, the reforms upheld the intrinsic value of religious capabilities within limits imposed by the principle of moral constraint – a religious claim should not have the same weight if it involves harms.

Here we should consider the internal diversity of traditions and the social version of the principle of moral constraint. When a step is taken against the core of a tradition in pursuit of a compelling state interest, it is a great help to recall that the tradition itself has contained powerful voices calling for exactly these changes in the name of religion itself,

89 September 22, 1951.
90 *The Statesman*, September 21, 1951.

interpreting the religion in accordance with the contraints of a moral understanding. Thus Mahatma Gandhi defined the essence of Hinduism as "the pursuit of truth by nonviolent means," using this account to launch his famous attack on the caste hierarchy. Other reformers, such as Rammohan Roy and Rabindranath Tagore, also called into question many of the religion's hierarchical practices, including child marriage and the seclusion of women. Like Gandhi, they argued that these practices were not part of the core of Hinduism, but rather expressions of imperfect historical ideas. At the time of reform, it was also pointed out that the very practice of reform and modification was in accordance with traditional precedent, and prominent Hindus were found on both sides of the measures. This internal debate helps show that the burden imposed on the tradition as a result of the state's interest in equality need not be considered a fatal burden; indeed, in some religious quarters it might be considered no burden at all. Thus the social principle helps support the formal political principle.

Subsequent developments in Hindu law have continued to address the religious dilemma in very much the terms my approach recommends. A case in point is the debate over the remedy of "restitution of conjugal rights" in the reformed Hindu Marriage Act of 1955. In retaining this remedy, the new laws failed to protect women's bodily integrity: a woman who had left the marital home could be forcibly returned to it. The remedy originated in British ecclesiastical law (indeed it was abolished in Britain only in 1970), and it had long been a feature of some Hindu systems; but the new codes actually made the remedy more uniformly available. Thus a woman who had suffered from domestic abuse could be forced to return to the scene of her suffering; a woman who no longer wanted to bear a child with the man she lived with could be forced to bear a child. Women could pay a fine to avoid forcible return, but women leaving abusive marriages were not generally in a position to meet that requirement. In 1983, in *T. Sareetha v. T. Venkata Subbaiah*, Judge Choudary of the Andhra Pradesh High Court declared this remedy unconstitutional, on the ground that it violates a women's autonomy interest in controlling the integrity of her body and her childbearing capacities:

A decree for restitution of conjugal rights constitutes the grossest form of violation of an individual's right to privacy. It denies the woman her free choice whether, when and how her body is to become the vehicle for the procreation of another human being. [It] deprives a woman of control over her choice as to when and by whom the various parts of her body should be allowed to be sensed. The woman loses her control over her most intimate decisions.[91]

In a supplementary argument, Judge Choudary pointed out that the law violates the constitution's equality provisions as well. Although formally neutral, given "our social reality," the remedy "works in practice only as an oppression to be operated by the husband for the benefit of the husband against the wife."

As for the religious issue, the judge was careful to point out that the forcible return of a spouse was nowhere mandated in Hindu traditions: the law went beyond tradition by enforcing legally what religion considers to be a moral duty. Indeed, he insisted on the British origin of the remedy. But there was no doubt that his primary concern throughout was the compelling nature of the state's interest in protecting a woman's rights over her body, and that this interest was held to trump the interest of Hindu religion in the maintenance of a (by now) traditional feature of Hindu law. The Supreme Court disagreed, overruling the lower court with the argument that the remedy "serves a social purpose as an aid to the prevention of break-up of marriage." In related decisions, the Court held that a Hindu woman's duty is to live with her husband in the matrimonial home.

Obviously, my approach supports Judge Choudary's constitutional reasoning, which shows that the Indian Constitution contains all the materials necessary to implement this approach. (A similar case in Bangladesh was decided in the same way at the Supreme Court level, so the remedy has now been eliminated from Bangladeshi law.)[92]

The *Shah Bano* case raises difficult issues, since it concerns the rights of a minority religion, the issue that has motivated my approach from the beginning. While it seemed clear that a recognizable version of Hinduism would surely survive the reorganization of Hindu personal law, there were legitimate reasons to fear that Islam in India would

91 AIR (1983) A. P. 356. I discuss Sareetha's case further in *Sex and Social Justice*, Introduction and Chapter 3. Sareetha had become a well-known movie actress after leaving her husband, and the husband's motives were clearly financial. Under the law, a woman is able to avoid forcible return on payment of a fine, so Sareetha was not in physical jeopardy, although she eventually lost her case. Poor women remained vulnerable to the actual restitution.

92 *Nelly Zaman v. Ghiyasuddin*, 34 D. L. R. 221 (1982). See discussion and citation from the opinion in "Religion and Women's Human Rights," which, revised, can be found in *Sex and Social Justice*, Chapter 3.

suffer greatly were the system of Muslim personal law to be gravely curtailed in its power. Chief Justice Chandrachud was probably correct in his argument that the order of maintenance under the Criminal Procedure Code was in no way inconsistent with traditional Islamic law; but the very fact that he undertook to say what constitutes Islamic law was itself alarming, raising the spectre of Hindu domination. He was entitled to invoke the principle of moral constraint, refusing to defer to Islamic law in the matter of basic maintenance; but his attempt to use a strong social moral-constraint argument, declaring what is and is not central to Islam, was incendiary and highly unwise, especially in a case dealing with constitutional fundamentals and matters of basic justice. Typical of the reaction was Z. R. Ansari, a Muslim government minister, who made a speech in Parliament condemning the Court for exceeding its authority by presuming to interpret sacred Islamic scripture: "If you have a *tamboli* (tobacco vendor) doing the work of a *teli* (oil-seller), things are bound to go wrong." The Muslim *ulema* condemned the judgment as an assault on the authority of the Shariat. This clerical reaction (accompanied by widespread street demonstrations) set the scene for an unruly political debate. Moral-constraint arguments were also used by Islamic feminists; and it would have been better to have left to them the role of making such informal social arguments, resting official state policy only on the interpretation of core political principles.

In theoretical terms, there seems little doubt that the issue of maintenance after divorce is a serious issue, affecting central capabilities. This is all the more obvious when we consider the subset of maintenance cases that can be appealed under the Criminal Procedure Code. To win an award of maintenance, the female plaintiff has to show that she would otherwise be without means to support herself, that she has suffered cruelty or neglect that makes it impossible for her to live with her husband, that she did not leave him of her own accord, and that her husband does have adequate means. The refusal to order maintenance in cases like these creates a most dramatic and urgent case of capability failure. Subsequent cases in which maintenance has been denied show the burden that the Muslim Woman's Act has put on Muslim women. Maitrayee Mukhopadhyay's study of West Bengal in the post-1986 period shows women facing grave disadvantages and being forced to depend on relatives for even a meager living. (These women are most often illiterate and untrained for any work; frequently they are of advanced age – Shah Bano was seventy-four when her husband threw her out of the house.) Worse still, the destitution of these women has had the practical effect of crippling their children's education, as children who would otherwise be in school are put to work supporting their mothers.[93]

In addition to the infringement of capabilities, Muslim women can also point to serious problems of free exercise and of discrimination on the basis of religion. The free exercise issue arises from the fact that, although they may not be especially thrilled about their Muslim identity, and may have no interest in being or remaining Muslims, they are classified under the Muslim legal system by the sheer fact of family membership. Once marriage and divorce occur within a particular system, the issue of maintenance must be handled by that system. Shah Bano is thus effectively deprived of her opportunity to define herself as secular, as Hindu, or as whatever else she might like to be.

This leads directly to the issue of discrimination on the basis of religion. Only Muslim women are denied maintenance under the Criminal Procedure Code. As Muslim scholar Zoya Hasan argues, there is "little reason to doubt that the denial of rights to Muslim women, which are available to women of other faiths, is a violation of the constitutional provision that the State shall not discriminate against any citizen on grounds of religion."[94] Muslim women's activist Shahjahan (also known as Apa) put the matter more bluntly in a speech before the House of Parliament on the day the 1986 law was passed:

If by making separate laws for Muslim women, you are trying to say that we are not citizens of this country, then why don't you tell us clearly and unequivocally that we should establish another country – not Hindustan or Pakistan but Auratstan (women's land).

Muslim leaders seem to have been so worried about the impact of the Criminal Procedure Code on the power of Muslim leaders that they simply forgot about the serious religious issues that pointed the other way. In effect, they were indeed treating Muslim women as noncitizens. They violated both the principle of individual capabilities, neglecting

93 See case studies in Mukhopadhyay, in Hasan.
94 Hasan in Hasan, ed., p. 62.

the free exercise and nondiscrimination claims of Muslim women, and also the principle of moral constraint, inflicting harm on a group in order to shore up their own power. As I have mentioned, women's groups have repeatedly challenged the act by petition to the Supreme Court as a violation of constitutional provisions against religious discrimination,[95] although the Supreme Court, having suffered sufficient public abuse in the aftermath of the *Shah Bano* decision, has not responded to any of these petitions.

To summarize: the religious issues themselves do not point in a single direction; indeed, the weightier free exercise claims seem to be on the side of Muslim women. And the capabilities issue is squarely on their side. The result was therefore a very unfortunate one, both for women and for religion.

The case came out this way because the government of Rajiv Gandhi persistently ignored the diversity of the Indian Islamic tradition, listening only to the voices of powerful conservative clerics. Throughout the debate, many Islamic thinkers opposed the retrograde Muslim Women's Bill, among them politicians, intellectuals, and Islamic women's organizations. They made compelling moral-constraint arguments, claiming that compassionate moral concerns central to Islam made more adequate maintenance for destitute women mandatory even in religious terms. Thus they demonstrated very convincingly that there was not really a gap between core constitutional principles and the core of Islamic tradition. But the government totally disregarded their views, according legitimacy to a small group of established patriarchal clerics as the true representatives of the community – even though one Muslim minister resigned from the government in protest against this neglect of Muslim opinion in favor of sex equality. (There are good reasons to believe that Rajiv Gandhi behaved this way because he had struck a deal with leading Islamic conservatives, trading a concession to them on women's maintenance for concessions to Hindus concerning the reopening of the disputed shrine at Ayodhya.)[96] As one of the leading liberal Muslim intellectuals summarizes the matter:

Liberal and progressive opinion within the community was ignored, allowing the ulema to appropriate the task of defining the overarching concerns and

95 For example, see *Susheela Gopalan and Others v. Union of India*, Writ Petition No. 1055 of 1986.
96 See evidence presented in Hasan's essay in Hasan, *Forging*.

interests of Muslims. Admittedly, the objective of the Muslim divines was to defend the Shariat and resist legislation that would, in their perception, lead to a change in divinely ordained laws. But the government should have known better. Interpretations by the ulema were neither final nor irrevocable; there were other trends of thought, other interpretations which the government chose to ignore, partly because the government itself shared the underlying assumption that Muslims are a religious community, that the theologians are its sole spokesmen, and that there exists a clear equation between religious law and community identity.[97]

In effect, the government made the error of my traditionalist opponent at the beginning of this chapter, equating a religious tradition with its most patriarchal and politically entrenched voices. He would have done better to acknowledge the moral-constraint arguments being made within Islam, which supported a change in women's status in the name of religion itself.

This error, though perhaps inspired by serious concern for religious pluralism, has actually left pluralism a great deal worse off, since now Hindu fundamentalists point to the Muslim Women's Bill as a sign that Hinduism is morally superior to Islam. The typical Muslim male, as portrayed in Hindu nationalist discourse, is a polygamous oppressor of women, very likely also a rapist, whereas the Hindu male is represented as both moderate and enlightened, incapable of treating women as mere sex objects. These stereotypes contribute to discrimination against Muslims, including legal discrimination. One magistrate, interviewed under condition of anonymity, stated: "when a Muslim comes to our court we are already biased . . . their 3–4 marriages are repugnant to us." The subdivisional judicial magistrate of the Alipore criminal court stated openly to his (Hindu) female interviewer, expecting approval: "For them marriage is nothing. They get married, have a few children and then they leave their wives. . . . Muslim women are worse off than the household dog."[98] This can hardly be a desirable result for a religion whose basic tenets are in some crucial respects very supportive of sex equality, proclaiming male and female to be equal in nature and

97 Hasan, 68. See also Danial Latifi, "After Shah Bano," in Jaising, ed., *Justice*, 213–15, and "Women, Family Law and Social Changes," 216–22, criticizing the reasoning of conservative Islamic legal scholars.
98 Both interviews by Maitrayee Mukhopadhyay, in "Between Community and State: The Question of Women's Rights and Personal Laws," in Hasan, ed., 108–29. Mukhopadhyay notes that in fact the incidence of polygamy is about the same for Muslim men (5.7%) as for Hindu men (5.8%), although it is not legal for Hindus.

capacity. The actions of the Muslim clerics were thus counterproductive as well as unjust.

In all three of my cases, in different ways, my approach backs laws of general applicability against religious practices. I have said that this would not always be the case; but when would it not be the case, one might ask, with a practice involving the inequality of women? This is a difficult question to answer, since most areas of traditional women's inequality under personal laws do involve central capabilities. But there are areas of religious practice in which the government probably does not have compelling interest in forcing change, at least so long as the freedom of individuals to change their religions is also firmly established. Such areas would prominently include the assignment of religious functions. I have argued elsewhere that public norms of sex equality should not force the Roman Catholic Church to hire female priests, although it probably should force them to hire female janitors on a basis of equality with men.[99] This is so, however, only so long as women are completely free not to be Catholics if they don't want to be – which is not the case in India, given the system as I have described it. Assuming such freedom to be secure, analogous religious practices in all the religions are probably protected by my principle. Orthodox Jews, for example, would be permitted to retain sex-segregated places of worship – although the case for this exemption is surely undercut by government policies that deny equal recognition to non-Orthodox Jews, thus denying women an effective right of choice. Similarly protected would be sex-divided norms of dress and decoration, where these run afoul of some law of general applicability. For example, on this principle the French government would be required to permit girls to attend school in Muslim scarves, even if there is a general sense that the wearing of the scarf is a symbol of sex hierarchy. The schools may and should teach the equality of women and men as citizens, preparing the girls for an independent choice in this matter, and they should back up the girls if they want to take off the scarves. But they should not forbid the practice.

A difficult group of cases involves educational institutions controlled by religious bodies. Racial discrimination cost Bob Jones University its tax-exempt status, but the fact that the president of the University of

99 See "Religion and Women's Human Rights."

Notre Dame is required to be a priest, ergo male, has not cost that university its tax-exempt status. This is a case where, as in *Bob Jones*, the government might appropriately judge that a compelling state interest in sex equality mandates a withdrawal of the exemption. It is characteristic of many modern debates that racial discrimination is taken to be an impermissible expression of religious tradition, while sex discrimination is taken to be just the way things have always been; with regard to a function that is administrative and educational, rather than at the core of worship, we should judge that granting a tax exemption involves the federal government in an unacceptable endorsement of sex inequality. India's universities are mostly public, and thus controlled directly by public norms regarding sex equality; but it has numerous Christian schools, some of which may be appropriate targets of scrutiny under this requirement.

One of the most difficult cases under my principle will be polygamy, typically seen as inextricable from a history of sex discrimination, and yet central to some religious traditions. Should Muslims or Hindus, or Mormons, receive exemptions to laws of general applicability on this account? I believe that no answer can be given to this question in the abstract. There is nothing in polygamy in the abstract that is oppressive to women, especially if the practice is available to both sexes. Women in Kerala, for example, have been able to contract multiple marriages since the eleventh century, and this liberty is a major source of women's high status in that region.[100] What is objectionable about polygamy is that it is often available only to males, and that it is typically connected with a legal and traditional regime under which women have unequal property rights and rights of mobility, association, and self-determination. But it is also the case that the reasons for opposing polygamy have often been very bad reasons, connected with fear and ignorance about a group whose practices are different. Thus, I believe that Mormon polygamy should have been permitted so long as the legal equality of women, and their freedom to leave the community should they wish to, were securely established and protected, and so long as the law extended similar opportunities to women who for some genuine religious reason wished, themselves, to contract polygamous marriages.

In India, the situation today is inseparable from specific aspects of

100 See Introduction.

Hindu-Muslim conflict. Muslim polygamy was first perceived, and to some extent is still perceived, as an enviable liberty, which Hindus struggled to retain for themselves. More recently, it has increasingly been defined by the Hindu right as a practice oppressive of women, hence an opportunity for Hindus to look down on Muslims.[101] I believe that it was right, in practical terms, to eliminate polygamy for Hindus and to retain it for Muslims, despite the inequality involved, given the vulnerability of the Muslim minority at the time of Independence (and given, too, that polygamy is somewhat more central to Muslim than to Hindu practice). Over time, given that polygamy in this context probably cannot be separated from sex hierarchy, it would be good to move toward a general ban – after all, polygamy is practiced by only a small minority of Muslims,[102] is not religiously required, and is nowhere near as religiously central for Muslims as it is for Mormons – but in a climate of respect and support for the Muslim community as a whole. That such a climate does not now exist can hardly be doubted. Polygamy should therefore probably be retained, while an effort is made to promote liberal Muslim viewpoints and to encourage internal reform of the system of personal law.

VII. CHILDREN AND PARENTS

I have focused so far on how my approach will protect the capabilities of adult women as fully equal citizens. But the upbringing of children is equally important and still more complex. In one way, the state has an especially strong interest in protecting the capabilities of children: for they are its future citizens; nor are they voluntary members of the family unit. But in another way, the state should acknowledge at least some limits on its power to intervene in children's lives, given its interest in the maintenance of the family. Parents have an extremely strong interest in bringing up children in their own religions and continuing traditions to which they are attached. The state should acknowledge this interest, and must treat children somewhat differently from adult women – both because their parents have at least some legitimate rights over them and because it is difficult to ascertain the child's own choice,

101 See the earlier discussion for examples.
102 See note 98.

given parental power and the child's economic dependency. Although the larger issue of children's capabilities will be the topic of the next chapter, we need to approach it now in the context of religious education

Numerous conflicts have arisen between parents' religious education of their children and the state's interest in its future citizens. Many of the most interesting cases involve compulsory education and child labor. India has laws mandating compulsory education, usually up to age fourteen, but the nation is in no position to enforce either these laws or laws against child labor at this time (see the Introduction); the constitutional tradition has therefore not yet articulated clear boundaries in this area. I shall therefore turn again to U.S. constitutional law, discussing three cases that provide at least a general idea of what my approach would recommend.

In *Pierce v. Society of Sisters*[103] the Supreme Court invalidated an Oregon law that required parents to send their children to the public school system, and forbade them to elect a religious school. The Court argued that parents have a fundamental liberty interest in directing the education of their children "by selecting reputable teachers and places." The law was held to be an unreasonable interference with that liberty interest: the state cannot "standardize its children by forcing them to accept instruction from public teachers only."[104] The Court was careful to limit the latitude given to parents:

No question is raised concerning the power of the State reasonably to regulate all schools, to inspect, supervise and examine them, their teachers and pupils; to require that all children of proper age attend some school, that teachers shall be of good moral character and patriotic disposition, that certain studies plainly essential to good citizenship must be taught, and that nothing be taught which is manifestly inimical to the public welfare.

Nonetheless, the opinion is a fundamental affirmation of the right of parents to choose religious schooling for their children.

My approach strongly favors this solution, including the reservation

---

103 268 U.S. 510 (1925).

104 The Court's argument is somewhat opaque; it invalidates the law on Fourteenth Amendment due process grounds, rather than on First Amendment free exercise grounds. Nonetheless, its basic principle was invoked in subsequent First Amendment cases.

that the state may require certain studies deemed necessary to citizenship. (I have problems with the idea that the state can require teachers to be "patriotic" and can rule out some areas of study as "inimical to the public welfare," but these are not the issues on which I want to focus here.) The compelling interest the state has in the appropriate education of its future citizens can be satisfied by such appropriate regulation, and does not justify interfering with parents' liberty to the extent represented by the Oregon law. States need to consider carefully what kinds of study are essential to citizenship. It seems to me that Israel has made some grave errors here, by not only certifying, but even funding, ultraorthodox schools that offer no instruction in history or current affairs. John Rawls's suggested requirement that all students be taught the rudiments of civic affairs and of the existing public constitutional order seems a bare minimum, and this teaching would include, in India as in the U.S., the teaching that women, under the public constitutional order, are fully equal citizens with equal rights and responsibilities.[105] This teaching about the public political conception is fully consistent with any religion's continuing to teach, as well, its own comprehensive view. Given that the religion has agreed to sign on to a constitution of a certain type, it will have to figure out how to square this "overlapping consensus" on public political matters of basic justice with the rest of what it teaches.[106] Within these constraints, religious schooling should be a protected (though not, I believe, a publicly funded) option.

Sometimes compulsory education appears to interfere with religious requirements. In these cases, the balancing approach I favor comes into play, as we must ask whether a substantial burden has been imposed on religious free exercise, and whether, if so, the state has a compelling interest in the education in question. In *Wisconsin v. Yoder* [107] members of the Old Order Amish religion sought exemption from Wisconsin's

105 See John Rawls, PL, 199.
106 Thus, for example, a religion may teach that the political conception holds men and women to be equal because they really are in some deeper metaphysical sense equal; or it may teach that, though in some metaphysical sense men and women are ultimately unequal, we agree to count them as equal for certain political purposes. It is not clear whether any of the major religions would actually hold that men and women are "unequal," although many deny women certain privileges and opportunities that they grant to men.
107 406 U.S. 205 (1972).

compulsory schooling law, which would have required them to send their children to public or private school until age sixteen. They declined to send their children after age fourteen, arguing that the continuation of their religious tradition required them to withdraw their children from the secular world at that point, teaching them skills of farming and domestic labor and imparting to them "attitudes favoring manual work and self-reliance." The Supreme Court agreed that the law in question imposed a substantial burden on their free exercise of their religion; they also judged that the state had failed to show a compelling interest in these last two years of education for this particular group of children. The state does indeed, in general, have a "compelling interest" in preparing "citizens to participate effectively and intelligently in our open political system . . . [and] to be self-reliant and self-sufficient participants in society." But the evidence showed, they said, that the Amish are quite effective and self-reliant citizens, and do not "place burdens on society through their educational shortcomings."

This is a truly hard case for my approach; indeed, it shows exactly where the line drawn by my approach falls. On the one hand, the state does have a compelling interest in the capabilities of its future citizens; on the other hand, it is not so clear that these particular two years are the crucial determinant of capability, and to require them clearly does impose a substantial burden on religious free exercise. A further complication is that the case has a serious sex-equality aspect, ignored in the opinions and rarely mentioned in discussions. Male Amish children learn farming and carpentry, skills that are highly marketable in the outside world, while females learn domestic skills that would be less easily marketable should they choose to leave the community. Thus the state's interest in education is connected with an interest in the equality of its citizens, and this might support the view that, after all, the interest is a compelling interest.[108]

In part because the sex-equality aspect of the case remains unexplored, and many controversial empirical issues are involved, this is a truly hard case, where the two parts of my proposal balance one an-

108 For a related argument see Richard Arneson and Ian Shapiro, "Democratic Autonomy and Religious Freedom: A Critique of *Wisconsin v. Yoder*," in Ian Shapiro, *Democracy's Place* (Ithaca: Cornell University Press, 1996), 137–74, arguing that the last two years of required public schooling are crucial in developing abilities of citizenship, especially the ability to question authority.

other in a most difficult way. Surely it indicates a maximum of protectiveness shown toward religion, since it does permit the religion to be exempt from what many believe to be an important part of citizens' capability formation.

Finally, we arrive at the issue of child labor. *Prince v. Massachusetts*[109] involves a Massachusetts child labor law, applied to a nine-year-old girl whose aunt, her guardian, had taken the child with her to distribute Jehovah's Witness pamphlets on the street, as required by that religion. Despite the fact that the child herself plainly wanted to accompany her aunt, and believed that she would be doomed "to everlasting destruction at Armageddon" for failure to do so, the Court held that the state's interest in protecting children's welfare was compelling, trumping both the guardian's and the child's free exercise rights:

To make accommodation between these freedoms and an exercise of state authority always is delicate. . . . On one side is the obviously earnest claim for freedom of conscience and religious practice. With it is allied the parent's claim to authority in her own household and in the rearing of her children . . . Against these sacred private interests, basic in a democracy, stand the interests of society to protect the welfare of children . . . A democratic society rests, for its continuance, upon the healthy, well-rounded growth of young people into full maturity as citizens, with all that implies. It may secure this against impeding restraints and dangers within a broad range of selection. Among evils most appropriate for such action are the crippling effects of child employment, more especially in public places, and the possible harms arising from other activities subject to all the diverse influences of the street.

The state's interest triumphed – although the Court was careful to say that this should not be taken as a warrant for further state intervention into religious upbringing.

I think this is another hard case, but one that was probably wrongly decided. The child was in school; the "labor" in question was neither physically dangerous nor exhausting. Indeed, it is hard to know whether it was "labor" at all, merely on the grounds that people paid five cents for the pamphlets.[110] It seems likely that Jehovah's Witnesses

109 321 U.S. 158 (1944).
110 The Court noted that this question had been resolved against Sarah Prince by the state court's definition of labor, and was no longer in their power to reconsider.

are getting unfair treatment because they are an unpopular religion and because they do their preaching on the street. Like most American children who have a religious upbringing, I spent many hours selling things at church bazaars and fairs, and never encountered the slightest police problem, nor did any child I knew. Could this be because the police don't bother wealthy Episcopalians inside their well-appointed parish halls? And yet, selling cookies at the parish bake sale is far from the core of even Anglican religion, whereas selling the *Watchtower* was very much at the heart of Betty Prince's religion. (Indeed, the police don't even bother children who sell things at their *school* fairs, even though no First Amendment claim prevents them.) It seems to me that the complainants were right to speak of religious discrimination, and that the case, properly understood, does not contain any ills the state has a compelling interest in preventing. However, this case is so far from the Indian situation – where child labor is pervasive, deeply woven into the economy, and ineradicable with existing resources – that it seems almost a mockery of the grave disabilities suffered by Indian children to dwell on cases involving such refined balancing.

To summarize: my balancing test suggests slightly different outcomes for children, since parents have legitimate interests in the religious education of their own children. These interests suggest at least some limitations to the state's interest in education. That interest, however, is on balance and in general a compelling interest, and this gives the state broad power to ensure that all types of schooling prepare children for equal citizenship.

VIII. CAPABILITIES AND LOSS

What is lost, if we follow my approach? Do these proposals involve a tragic aspect? The principle of moral constraint suggests to us that nothing of value is lost when we tell people that they cannot lord it over other people in immoral and harmful ways. By using the central capabilities as our guide, we allow considerable latitude for the preservation of tradition in cases that do not involve grave harms to others. And yet one should nonetheless acknowledge that there are some valuable ways of life that will become difficult to sustain in a climate of choice. Although an emphasis on the capabilities does not in any way preclude the choice to live a traditional hierarchical life, and indeed is intended to protect that opportunity; although we carefully create spaces within which such forms of life may continue and be supported; and although we stress that religion has always been a diverse and changing set of practices, and therefore won't be gravely damaged by being nudged in the direction of support for the capabilities – nonetheless, despite all this, we should acknowledge that at least some price will be paid for the sheer emphasis on choice and capability. There are some ways of life that people find deeply satisfying, and that probably do not involve unacceptable levels of indignity or capability inequality, which are likely to cease to exist in a regime of choice, simply because of social pressure and the availability of alternative choices. Veiling is available in a regime that does not make veiling mandatory, and it seems quite wrong of a regime to impose veiling by force on women who do not choose it. And yet the motivation for such a move can at least be comprehended, when we recognize that women who may wish to remain veiled have an extremely difficult time doing so in a fast-moving capitalist society in which their husbands are likely to be working for multinational corporations, many of whose members view veiling as primitive.

One such story was told to anthropologist Hannah Papanek by an elderly Indian Muslim woman, Hamida Khala.[111] It helps us see where the tragic potential lies in a regime of choice, and also helps us understand how human ingenuity and the dynamic nature of religious practices can surmount tragedy.

Brought up in an educated family in north India, Hamida Khala had a fine education under her father's supervision, and longed to wear the *burqua* as a sign of maturity. At the age of thirteen she was betrothed to a much older widower in the civil service, reputed to be of "modern" views. Hamida consented to the marriage on the condition that if her husband asked her to stop observing purdah she would return to her family. She began living with him at the age of fifteen, and he took her to Calcutta, far away from her family. As a civil servant, he worked with British, Hindu, and Muslim colleagues, and social life was organized around couples who typically attended dinners and tea parties

---

111 Papanek, in "Afterword," in Rokeya Hossain, *Sultana's Dream*, 72–6; Papanek had known Hamida Khala for a long time, and the telling of the story of her life, in the late 1970s, took many days.

together. Her husband began to resent her seclusion, which was cramping his own social life and his professional advancement. Although some colleagues arranged dinner parties at which women sat in a separate room, many refused to do so. And at last one host played a trick.

One night the women were seated at a table with empty seats at every other place. Suddenly a group of men came in and sat in the vacant seats. Hamida recalls this event with tremendous pain:

What I experienced, I just can't tell you. There was darkness all around me. I couldn't see anything. I had tears in my eyes . . . What I ate I don't remember . . . All my attempts, my endeavours to keep my purdah were over. I felt I was without faith, I had sinned. I had gone in front of so many men, all these friends of my husband. They've seen me. My purdah was broken, my purdah that was my faith.

Her husband insisted that he had not been aware of the plan, and apologized profoundly to her. Nonetheless, she recognized that her life would have to change if she were to stay with him. She wrote to her father, asking his advice. He told her that if her marriage might be endangered, she would have to leave purdah, adding that her extreme type of purdah does not represent an ancient Islamic tradition; she could behave with reticence and modesty even after leaving it. After reading sacred texts on her own, she came to the conclusion that there was a way of living as a devout Muslim outside of strict purdah. She worked out her own rules of modest dress and demeanor – long-sleeved blouses, downcast eyes, no makeup or jewelry – and followed them the rest of her life, while going outside and learning how to conduct daily business and social affairs. Her husband supported her and showed respect for her religion.

Hamida reports some good aspects of the change. She developed greater physical agility and strength by walking outside. She learned how to manage accounts, which came in handy when her husband died prematurely of a heart attack. Coming to the conclusion that "the real purdah is modesty," she refused to lend her support to a political campaign to bring back mandatory veiling in Pakistan, when a conservative leader asked her for help. She feels that she has been able to define successfully a Muslim identity that includes the central precepts of her religion – and yet, she acknowledges that there has been a real cost. "It was a big sacrifice for me to leave purdah." If that is so even in this very favorable case, where, because of Hamida's personal strength and her husband's respect, she was able to construct a viable religious alternative, we can easily imagine that other women might experience the sacrifice without discovering a viable alternative. Hard though it is for Western feminists to imagine a life in which physical movement, practical command, and a variety of associative ties are not central, we can see that Hamida's old life contained genuine religious values and did not strike her, even in retrospect, as humiliating or as unacceptably subordinating. She does judge that women should focus more on exercise, and should learn to manage things in case they need to: in these respects she faults the earlier regime. Papanek adds evidence that women in purdah have been and are frequently cheated by middlemen, when they are unable to deal with managers and employers directly.[112] But she appears to think that the old regime was not, as such, unacceptable, and might have accommodated these changes.

This case shows, I believe, that a capability-based approach to religious liberty does involve the potential for tragedy. Nonetheless, it also shows how resourceful deeply religious women and men can be in adapting the religion's moral understanding to a changing reality. It is especially significant that Hamida Khala strongly opposed mandatory purdah. Her final judgment was that she and her husband "learned a lot from each other." Indeed, her response to the conservative leader – which she reported, Papanek says, with great delight – showed that she thinks the problem of modesty can be well solved by women without purdah, if only men will cooperate. "Let a thousand women come out at once, not just a few," she reported herself as saying. "Then you will see how quickly men get used to seeing women and think nothing of it." She had kept her modesty while coming out of purdah, she added to the leader, and that is what really matters.

Through religion, people search for the transcendent. But religious groups and practices are human phenomena. The humanity of religion

112 Papanek, 77, describing Muslim home workers who send their children as intermediaries to deal with the middlemen who sell their products. See also Cornelia Sorabji, *India Calling* (London: Nisbet and Co., 1934) describing her struggle as India's first female lawyer (and the first woman to be allowed to take a law degree at Oxford), helping women in *purdah* who were being cheated by male relatives and were forbidden to see a lawyer, all lawyers being male. The many attempts on Sorabji's life are evidence of the magnitude of the problem.

means that its practices are fallible, and need continual scrutiny in the light of the important human interests that it is the state's business to protect. On the other hand, religion is itself among the important human interests, both in itself and because it represents a central exercise of human choice. For these reasons, any solution to the dilemmas created when religion and sex equality clash must be complex, relying on the ability of judges and other political actors to balance multiple factors with discernment. One thing they should not do, however, is to abandon a commitment to equal justice, in the face of political intimidation.

On November 2, 1985, Shah Bano, in the presence of four male witnesses, signed with her thumbprint an open letter to all Muslims, stating that Islamic leaders had explained to her the commands concerning divorce and maintenance, in the light of Quran and Hadith. Using legal language that she is extremely unlikely to have chosen herself or perhaps even to have understood, she renounces her claim to maintenance and demands that the Indian government withdraw the Supreme Court decision. She further states that "Article 44 of the Indian Constitution, in which there is a directive for enacting a uniform civil code for all, is quite contrary to the Quran and the hadith." She asks that the government renounce the goal of uniformity and resolve that "no interference would be ever attempted in future" with the operation of the Islamic courts. "In the end," she concludes, "I thank Maulana Habib Yar Khan and Haji Abdul Ghaffar Saheb of Indore who showed me the straight path and helped me follow the Truth and thus saved me in this world and in the hereafter."[113]

It is extremely difficult to avoid the conclusion that the faith of a devout and penniless woman is being exploited for political purposes. And, to paraphrase Lincoln, it seems extremely strange that a just God would indeed require a destitute aged woman to renounce her claim to a minimal livelihood. Respecting the freedom of religion does not mean giving a small number of religious leaders limitless license to perpetuate human misery, to inhibit the religious freedom of indi-

113 "Shah Bano's Open Letter to Muslims," published in *Inquilab*, November 3, 1985, and translated into English by A. Karim Shaikh. Reprinted in Engineer, ed., 211–12. Shah Bano died in Indore in 1992, at the age of eighty-nine.

viduals, and to push the law around. It is not an assault on religious freedom, but a deeper defense of its basic principle, to say that in such cases, the law indeed must "come to the rescue" in order that "society should move on."

4

LOVE, CARE, AND DIGNITY

Giribala, at the age of fourteen, then started off to make her home with her husband. Her mother put into a bundle the pots and pans that she would be needing. Watching her doing that, Aulchand remarked, "Put in some rice and lentils too. I've got a job at the house of the *babu*. Must report to work the moment I get back . . ."

Giribala picked up the bundle of rice, lentils, and cooking oil and left her village, walking a few steps behind him. He walked ahead, and from time to time asked her to walk faster, as the afternoon was starting to fade.

Mahasweta Devi, "Giribala," 1982[1]

Accused Md. Jahangir Alam was found after marriage to be a ruthless, cruel and greedy person. Accused petitioner Selema Khatun is mother and accused petitioner Md. Solaiman is younger brother of accused Jahangir Alam. Accused petitioner Thanda Mia is father and accused petitioner Abdul Mannan is maternal uncle of accused Jahangir Alam. Accused petitioner Md. Hashim is a close friend of accused Jahangir Alam. All the accused persons in collusion with each other started torturing complainant Ferdousi Begum both mentally and physically after the marriage with a view to squeeze money (as dowry) from the guardians of complainant Ferdousi Begum. . . . Finally on 30.9.85, accused Jahangir Alam asked his wife Ferdousi Begum to bring 20" Coloured T.V. Set, Radio, Wrist Watch and cash money amounting to Taka 25,000 from her brothers . . . Complainant Ferdousi Begum expressed her inability to go to her brothers with such demand. At this stage all the accused persons . . . became furious and started beating Ferdousi Begum with rod, lathi, etc. At one stage accused Md. Jahangir Alam caught hold of her throat and attempted to murder her by throttling. Accused Jahangir

---

1 Translated from the Bengali by Bardhan, in *Of Women, Outcastes*, 274.

Alam also kicked her several times and caught her hair and pulled her down on the floor, pressed her and dragged her out of the house. Then all the accused persons snatched away her gold ornaments from the body and left her with one cloth in the courtyard where she lost her senses due to inhuman beating and torturing by the accused persons for the whole day. As a result of this beating by all the accused persons she lost hearing capacity of her right ear. Both her legs were so severely injured that she felt difficulty in walking. . . . The spinal cord showed traumatic collapse in X ray and dislocation of bone was also found in the X ray.

> *Salema Khatoon v. State* (F. H. M. Habibur Rahman J.), 1986[2]

In a society in which the menfolk have no mercy, no religion, no sense of justice, no sense of good or bad, in which mere conventionality is considered the chief activity and the supreme religion, let no more women be born.

> Ishwarchandra Vidyasagar (1820–91)

I. A HOME FOR LOVE AND VIOLENCE

Women are givers of love and care. In virtually all cultures women's traditional role involves the rearing of children and care for home, husband, and family. These roles have been associated with some important moral virtues, such as altruistic concern, responsiveness to the needs of others, and a willingness to sacrifice one's own interests for those of others. They have also been associated with some distinctive moral abilities, such as the ability to perceive the particular situations and needs of others and the ability to reason resourcefully about how to meet those needs. These virtues and abilities need to find a place in any viable universalist feminism. Feminists have long criticized male universalist theories for their alleged neglect of these important values, and have frequently argued that universal approaches based on liberal ideas of dignity and equality cannot make sufficient room for them.

---

2 38 D.L.R. (*Dhaka Law Reports*) (1986). Although this case is from Bangladesh, it is typical of the phenomenon of dowry extortion as it commonly occurs in India as well; legal efforts to stem the tide of dowry abuse have been very similar in the two nations. The case has an odd historical parallel – i.e., to the assault by the Thirty Tyrants on the wife of Polemarchus, as described by Lysias in *Against Eratosthenes*. Here too, the woman is dragged out into the courtyard, and Lysias remarks that the extremity of her assailants' greed is shown by the fact that they snatch the gold earrings from her ears.

They have worried that liberal theories of justice would turn havens of love and care into collections of isolated mutually disinterested atomic individuals, each bargaining against the others with a view to personal advancement.

On the other hand, it would be difficult to deny that the family has been a, if not the, major site of the oppression of women. Love and care do exist in families. So too do domestic violence, marital rape, child sexual abuse, undernutrition of girls, unequal health care, unequal educational opportunities, and countless more intangible violations of dignity and equal personhood. For Vasanti, home was a place of drunken physical abuse; and even the genuine support shown her by her brothers struck her as undependable. Jayamma's husband drank and ate up half the family income, forcing Jayamma to do all the housework after her exhausting day at the brickworks. Because of his behavior, moreover, she had no option to educate her children; nor did those children support her in her old age, despite all they owed to her industry and strength.

In many instances, the damage women suffer in the family takes a particular form: the woman is treated not as an end in herself, but as an adjunct or instrument of the needs of others, as a mere reproducer, cook, cleaner, sexual outlet, caretaker, rather than as a source of agency and worth in her own right. The cases in my epigraphs show this tendency clearly. For her husband, Giribala was a domestic servant, rather than a person.[3] Her role was to walk a few paces behind, carrying the lentils. For the family of Jahangir Alam, Ferdousi Begum was little more than a device to extract money from her brothers; her bodily well-being was worth less to them than a twenty-inch color TV set, a radio, a wristwatch, and a small amount of cash.

Family, then, can mean love; it can also mean neglect, abuse, and degradation. Moreover, the family reproduces what it contains. Just as

---

3 The story primarily concerns the later history of the marriage, in which the husband, viewing his daughters, too, as commodities for his use, sells two of them into prostitution. Giribala (who all along has been the family's primary economic agent) leaves him before he can sell the third. "Giribala only regretted that she had not done this before. If she had left earlier, then Beli would not have been lost, then Pori would not have been lost. If only she had had this courage earlier, her two daughters might have been saved. As this thought grew insistent and hammered inside her brain, hot tears flooded her face and blurred her vision. But she did not stop even to wipe her tears. She just kept walking."

it is often a school of virtue, so too (and frequently at the same time) it is a school of sex inequality, nourishing attitudes that not only make new families in the image of the old, but also influence the larger social and political world. (This influence goes in both directions, clearly, since the family and the emotions it contains are shaped by laws and institutions regarding such matters as marital rape, child custody, children's rights, and women's economic opportunities.) It is implausible that people will treat women as ends in themselves and as equals in social and political life if they are brought up, in the family, to see women as things for men's use. As John Stuart Mill long ago observed, when males are brought up to think that being male makes them superior to one half of the human race, this shapes them in the whole of their social behavior, both with women and with other fellow citizens. When a boy thinks himself superior to his mother, when, later in life, he feels a "sublime and sultan-like . . . sense of superiority" to his wife, we cannot expect that this leaves his behavior outside the family unaffected. "It is an exact parallel to the feeling of a hereditary king that he is excellent above others by being born a king, or a noble by being born a noble."[4] And that's probably not so good for democracy.[5]

Since I have endorsed the Aristotelian/Marxian view that fully human functioning requires affiliation and reciprocity with others, I have also endorsed the idea that a variety of forms of affiliation are among the most important of the human capabilities; they also suffuse all the other capabilities. Having made such a strong commitment to affiliation, I now need to confront the questions posed by the presence of the family, and the roles it constructs for women, at the heart of a society that is attempting to promote human capabilities.

I shall argue that the capabilities approach, which treats each individual as an end, is in no sense incompatible with the appropriate valuation of family love and care; indeed, it actually provides the best framework within which both to value care and to give it the necessary critical scrutiny. By thinking of the affiliative needs of each person, as well as each person's needs for the whole range of the human capabilities, we can best ask questions about how the family should be shaped

4 Mill, SW, 87.

5 For an excellent elaboration of this point, with pertinent criticisms of contemporary theorists who romanticize the family, see Susan M. Okin, *Justice, Gender, and the Family* (New York: Basic Books, 1989).

by public policy, and what other affiliative institutions public policy has reason to support. I shall argue that the liberal account of basic capabilities I have been developing provides an even better framework for analysis, here, than standard liberal proceduralist approaches, since it is explicitly committed to a prominent place for love and care as important goals of social planning and as major moral abilities – within a life governed by the critical use of practical reason. At the same time, by not ruling any institution "private" and so off limits for purposes of public scrutiny, the capabilities approach avoids a common defect of at least some liberal theories. Individuals have privacy rights, in the form of associative and decisional liberties. But there is no institution that, as such, has privacy rights that prevent us from asking how law and public policy have already shaped that institution, and how they might better do so. Personal liberty is a central social goal, whether or not it is exercised inside the home; personal dignity and integrity are also central social goals, no matter where the threat to them is located.

II. CAPABILITIES: EACH FAMILY MEMBER AS END

What human capabilities are at issue, when we think of the family structure? As the case of Salema Khatun shows us, they all are: life, health, bodily integrity, dignity and non-humiliation, associational liberties, emotional health, the opportunity to form meaningful relationships with other people, the ability to participate in politics, the ability to hold property and work outside the home, the ability to think for oneself and form a plan of life – all these things are at stake in the family, and the shape of the family institution influences all these capabilities, for both women and men. The family is indeed a home of love and care, and we should not ignore these capabilities when we assess what different family structures contribute. But we should also remember that the family has a tremendous influence on the other capabilities. Indeed, it influences them pervasively and from the start, since children are usually born into such groupings, for better or worse. On this basis, the family has an especially great claim to be regarded as what John Rawls has called the "basic structure of society," an institution, that is, to which principles of justice most especially ought to apply, if our goal is to promote justice for all citizens. In a similar way, my capabilities approach suggests that public policy should devote particular attention to any institution whose influence on the formation of capabilities is profound, since a bare minimum of social justice will involve bringing citizens up to a threshold level of capability.

When we look at the family, whose capabilities do we look at? Here we must repeat: we look at *each person*. Here, as in the case of religion, a *principle of each person's capability* should guide us. It is not enough to ask whether the family promotes a diffuse and general kind of affection and solidarity. We must ask in detail what it does for the capabilities of each of its members – in the area of love and care, and also with regard to the other capabilities. Such a focus on the individual as the basic political subject, characteristic of the liberal tradition, has sometimes been held to slight the worth of love and care as political goals. But really, it does no such thing. If this tradition urged people to be egoists, putting their own concerns first and those of others second, or to pursue a solitary conception of the good, in which deep attachments to others play no role, then we might well accuse such a theory of indifference to the intrinsic value of love and care. But liberal individualism, whether in its Kantian or its Millean version, really involves none of these things;[6] indeed, all the major liberal thinkers have in their different ways emphasized the intrinsic worth of love and care. For Adam Smith, for example, failure to appreciate this worth was the primary defect of Stoic moral theory. For John Rawls (responding to Schopenhauer's critique of Kant), the model of moral impartiality that is provided through the Original Position, including its Veil of Ignorance, is intended as a model of the virtue of fraternity;[7] and the Rawlsian account of moral development gives a prominent role to attachments in the family.[8] My own view, similarly, has given capabilities for

6 See my "The Feminist Critique of Liberalism," in *Sex and Social Justice*.

7 Rawls, "Kantian Constructivism in Moral Theory," the Dewey Lectures 1980, *The Journal of Philosophy* 77 (1980), 530–32; cf. TJ, 147–9 on Schopenhauer, and the reasons for preferring the Original Position/Veil of Ignorance construction to the combination of benevolence and knowledge. For a perceptive discussion of Rawls's model, and a response to some feminist criticisms, see Susan Okin, "Reason and Feeling in Thinking About Justice," in *Feminism and Political Theory*, ed. Cass R. Sunstein (Chicago: University of Chicago Press, 1990), 15–35, originally in *Ethics* 99 (1989). See also my "Rawls and Feminism" forthcoming in *The Cambridge Companion to Rawls*, ed. Samuel Freeman (New York: Cambridge University Press).

8 See TJ, Part 3, Chapter 8; see also Okin, "Reason and Feeling," for some valuable criticisms.

love and affiliation a central role in the political conception itself, as central social goals.

The *principle of each person as end* does entail, however, that the separate person should be the basic unit for political distribution. The basic political principles mandate that society secure a threshold level of the basic goods of life to *each*, seeing *each* life as deserving of basic life support and of the basic liberties and opportunities; that we do not rest content with a glorious total or average, when some individuals are lacking, whether in liberty or in material well-being. As I have argued, such a principle is especially urgent when we think about the lives of women in the family. For all too often, women have been denied the basic goods of life because they have been seen as parts of an organic entity, such as the family is supposed to be, rather than as political subjects in their own right.[9] All too often, too, they have been seen as reproducers and care givers, rather than as ends in themselves. In concrete practical terms, this has meant that too few questions have been asked about how resources and opportunities are distributed within the family. Vasanti and Jayamma have both suffered, in different ways, from an absence of concern for each person as end. Vasanti was treated as an adjunct to her husband, there for pleasure or for abuse, but not there when important decisions about reproduction needed to be made; Jayamma was treated as the domestic manager of the household, but not as an end equal in rights and opportunities to the males of the household. For both, an emphasis on individual rights and entitlements, far from removing opportunities for love and care, would seem essential in order to promote more fruitful and less exploitative styles of caring.

Instrumental and male-focused ways of valuing women are amazingly persistent, even in lives that are elsewhere characterized by profound moral reflection. Any reader of the *Autobiography* of Mahatma Gandhi, for example, is likely to be struck by the strange combination of a rare moral depth and radicalism, which questions not only colonialism but also the entire foundation of the Hindu social order, and attitudes toward his wife that are extremely traditional and male-

---

9 For a more extensive version of this whole argument, see "The Feminist Critique of Liberalism."

centered. Although Gandhi repents of his personal jealousy and his
sexual demands on his wife, he never shows the slightest sign of thinking that she might also be a sexual agent, or that one of the things
wrong with his sexual demands was their extremely egocentric character. And even when, by his own account, he attains a purer and more
harmonious relationship with her, he continues to praise her, above all,
for conventional wifely traits of obedience and reverence, rather than
for any traits that would suggest that he respected her as a source of
agency and worth in her own right. Seeing this moral intransigence
even in one so morally outstanding, should we not believe all the more
in an approach that insists on treating each and every person as an end,
not simply as an adjunct of the ends of others?

We can see the importance of this principle from another angle if we
consider two different approaches economists have taken to the family.
In Chapter 1, I described the approach of Gary Becker, who assumed
for purposes of descriptive modeling that the family was an organic
unit held together by altruism; the head of the household took thought
for the interests and privileges of its members, seeking to maximize the
utility of the unit as a whole. My objection in Chapter 1 was that this
approach is not individual-focused enough, even for purposes of description and prediction (as Becker has now acknowledged), much less
as the basis for a normative approach. Conflicts regarding resources
and opportunities are ubiquitous in families. For this reason economists
have increasingly turned to a different, more individual-focused strategy, modeling the family as a *bargaining unit*.[10] According to this approach, it is not denied that the members may be linked by bonds of
love and cooperation; they may pursue shared ends, and view one another's well-being as among their very most important ends. But they
are seen to be distinct individuals, to some extent also in competition
with one another for scarce resources.

Used descriptively, such an approach can tell us what conditions
strengthen the bargaining power of different family agents, and can

10 See Sen, "Gender and Cooperative Conflicts," in I. Tinker, ed., *Persistent Inequalities*
(New York: Oxford University Press, 1991), 123–49; Bina Agarwal, " 'Bargaining' and
Gender Relations: Within and Beyond the Household," *Feminist Economics* 3 (1997),
1–51; Shelly Lundberg and Robert A. Pollak, "Bargaining and Distribution in Marriage," *Journal of Economic Perspectives* 10 (1996), 139–58. Agarwal makes some
persuasive criticisms of standard bargaining models, arguing for a plural-valued, richly
qualitative bargaining *approach*.

help us to predict what changes, public or private, will alter those relations, and in what ways. (I shall imagine such an application below.)
A normative approach based on such a descriptive/predictive model
would be a model of a *fair* bargain, in which the interests and rights of
each member are respected. (In Chapter 2 I argued that a suitably
norm-laden form of contractual proceduralism could get us to most of
the same conclusions reached by the capabilities approach, although I
argued that in some ways an approach through the central capabilities
is more informative.) What we need, then, is not an approach to the
family that wraps up the conflicts in a hazy glow of love (as to some
extent Becker's account does), but one that permits us to see the conflicts where they exist, and to define our norms on the basis of this
adequate understanding.

Focusing on each person as the basic political subject does not slight
the worth of love and care as basic political goals. But feminists have
made another argument against liberal person-centered approaches.
They have argued that approaches modeled on the idea of contract or
bargain neglect the value of women's love and care as moral abilities
and sources of moral perception. Because such approaches do not incorporate emotion and imagination into their own structures, they may
possibly lead us to undervalue the worth of those abilities in the political realm, as sources of discernment of the correct political course.

To some extent, again, the criticism oversimplifies the liberal tradition. Some liberal thinkers, for example Mill and Adam Smith, give the
imagination a very high degree of importance in charting the correct
political course; and Smith's account of the role of emotions in the
reasoning of the judicious spectator remains the best account we have
of a productive political role for the emotions. On the other hand,
liberals in the Kantian tradition, perhaps influenced by Kant's own
highly noncognitive conception of the emotions, do exhibit the problem
the critic has described. Both Rawls and Habermas, in their different
ways, attempt to model the procedure of political choice in a way that
dispenses with strong emotion – although in some respects Rawls presents an abstract model of the moral sentiments through other de-

11 Again, for pertinent discussion and criticism, see Okin, "Reason and Feeling." On
   Rawls's definition of "considered judgment" in terms of the absence of strong emotion,
   see TJ, 47.

vices.[11] Their mistrust of the emotions and the imagination is one factor that motivates their preference for proceduralism over intuitive arguments focused on the plurality of necessary goods. And even though Rawls notes that imagination is among the "natural" primary goods, he does not make the social basis of its development an important social primary good.[12] His otherwise compelling account of moral development also makes too little room, one might feel, for the civic role of the emotions and the imagination.[13] By contrast, the capabilities approach defended here, in addition to allocating a prominent place to imagination and emotion in the capabilities list, also relies methodologically on these abilities. Imagination about the necessary components of a truly human life, and emotions of loss and longing associated with the imagining of these central goods, play a (suitably constrained) role in the creation of basic political principles. And the approach continually directs its user to imagine how resources go to work differently in different lives – an exercise that requires a rich contextual imagining of particular lives and circumstances, seeing how general goals and aims are differently realized in different concrete conditions.[14] To the extent, then, that feminists have made cogent criticisms of some liberal thinkers along these lines, the view defended here responds to what is valuable in that critique.

If love and imagination are important both as social goals and as moral abilities for *each and every person*, this already suggests some reform of the family structure: for we see not only that women need to acquire the so-called male abilities of choice and independent planning (as argued in Chapter 1), but also that males need to acquire at least some skills traditionally associated with women's work and the female sphere. They could of course try to acquire these skills in school only, while living in families in which males show a lofty indifference to particular needs and concerns and women do all the nuanced responding and caring. But such a solution is likely to prove unstable. Males

12 Rawls, TJ, 62.
13 See Okin, "Reason and Feeling."
14 I rely on the view I have defended elsewhere, that the emotions have a cognitive dimension and can be valuable guides in the social choice process. See *Poetic Justice: The Literary Imagination and Public Life* (Boston: Beacon Press, 1997); and *Upheavals of Thought: A Theory of the Emotions* (Cambridge: Cambridge University Press, forthcoming).

will be unlikely to work hard at things they have learned to denigrate as female, and they will be unlikely to take such skills seriously, as things they should use in their political lives, if they don't see their fathers using them at home. If, by contrast, they see their male parent caring for them and are asked to take on some of this work themselves in the home, they will be more likely to think of the skills involved as important, and to develop and use them in the outside world. If we think these skills politically important, this gives us reason to care about how the family deals with them with regard to all, not just some, of its members.

The principle of each person's capabilities has one more striking entailment. It is that the family as such has no moral standing within the core of the political conception. It is persons who have moral standing. We are interested in the family as a locus of persons' development, association, expression, education, and so forth. But we insist that it has no force qua organic unit. If politics decides to recognize certain groupings as enjoying a special status, my approach does not forbid this, here as in the case of religious groups. But the moral question behind the political choices should always be, "What does this do for people, thinking of each person as an end?" And thus the protection of the capabilities of persons will rightly enjoy a strong measure of priority over the interests of any group as such. In the case of religion, I held, drawing on the tradition of U.S. free-exercise law, that the rightful bearer of moral claims is not the religious body as such, but the person, seen as a bearer of religious rights and capabilities. This would not prevent us from supporting a group that was in danger of ceasing to exist, as the Amish parents maintained in *Wisconsin v. Yoder*. But the reason we might support such a group is that it is necessary for people's capabilities to worship as they choose, not because the group has any standing in and of itself.

Similarly in the case of the family: we focus on each person as bearer of a variety of associative rights and liberties and as a potential enjoyer of affiliative capabilities. This focus should guide us when we ask which groupings of people, if any, deserve special protection in a political structure. Even where the capabilities of love and care themselves are concerned, the appropriate goal of public policy is the capabilities of citizens to form such relationships, should they choose to do so. Such a focus on people and their choices has clear implications for public policy in matters of marital consent, marriage rights, the abolition of child marriage, the provision of public support for child care, maintenance after divorce, and other related issues. We ask always: What would it be to treat each citizen as an end, promoting the full range of the human capabilities?

III. THE FAMILY: NOT "BY NATURE"

Political approaches to the family, both liberal and nonliberal, frequently exhibit a set of related defects: (1) They treat the family as existing "by nature," failing to recognize the role of custom and society in constructing family institutions. (2) They treat the family as a "private" sphere set over against the "public" sphere, failing to recognize the role of laws and institutions in shaping the family as an institution and in denominating certain groupings of individuals as families. And (3) they treat women's propensity to give love and care as existing "by nature," rather than recognizing the role of custom, law, and institutions in shaping the emotions. Approaches that make these errors are bound to approach the job of framing political principles with too restricted a sense of what political principles have done in this sphere, and what they might do better. Although these defects are familiar topics of feminist criticism,[15] these criticisms have not always been taken to heart by theorists of justice in the liberal tradition; so it is useful to recapitulate the main points that have been made, beginning

15 All three errors were criticized by Mill, as we shall see; for other valuable general critiques of naturalism about women's role, see Susan Moller Okin, *Women in Western Political Thought* (Princeton: Princeton University Press, 1979), and *Justice, Gender, and the Family*; Catharine MacKinnon, *Toward a Feminist Theory of the State* (Cambridge, MA: Harvard University Press, 1989). On the family, see especially Frances Olsen, "The Family and the Market: A Study of Ideology and Legal Reform," *Harvard Law Review* 96 (1983), 1497–1577, and "The Myth of State Intervention in the Family," *University of Michigan Journal of Law Reform* 18 (1985), 835–64; and Martha Minow, "All in the Family and in All Families: Membership, Loving, and Owing," in D. Estlund and M. Nussbaum, eds., *Sex, Preference, and Family: Essays on Law and Nature* (New York: Oxford University Press, 1997), 249–76. For one excellent recent attack on the myth of the "private sphere" as an excuse for not protecting women from violence, see Reva B. Siegel, " 'The Rule of Love': Wife Beating as Prerogative and Privacy," *The Yale Law Journal* 105 (1996), 2117–2207. On women's roles as givers of care and their relationship to justice, see the excellent collection of essays in Virginia Held, ed., *Justice and Care* (Boulder, CO: Westview Press, 1995), and Diemut Bubeck, *Care, Gender, and Justice* (Oxford: Clarendon Press, 1995).

with critiques of the very common claim that the patriarchal family is "natural."

The family, and women's place in it, have often been thought to exist "by nature." To cite just one notorious example, in 1871, upholding a law that forbade women to practice law in the state of Illinois, Justice Bradley of the U.S. Supreme Court wrote:

The natural and proper timidity and delicacy which belongs to the female sex evidently unfits it for many of the occupations of civil life. The constitution of the family organization, which is founded in the divine ordinance, as well as in the nature of things, indicates the domestic sphere as that which properly belongs to the domain and functions of womanhood. The harmony, not to say identity, of interests and views which belong or should belong to the family institution, is repugnant to the idea of a woman adopting a distinct and independent career from that of her husband . . . The paramount destiny and mission of woman are to fulfill the noble and benign offices of wife and mother. This is the law of the Creator. And the rules of civil society must be adapted to the general constitution of things . . . [16]

Justice Bradley's claims both that women's traditional role in the family is assigned by God and that it derives from "nature" – claims that are consistent given that he evidently understands the natural order in teleological religious terms. Similar religious-teleological views about woman's "nature" can be found in the Hindu tradition that shapes the lives of Vasanti and Jayamma. The Laws of Manu and other sacred texts typically portray women as by nature dependent and made for obedience, with a primary duty to serve men: "the scriptures have enjoined this dependency of love."[17] Islamic traditions ascribe to male and female a single nature; nonetheless, women's duties of modesty and subservience have been interpreted in subsequent traditions as strongly asymmetrical to men's.

The appeal to "nature" is a slippery form of argument, since the term "nature" is far from univocal. To say that relation R exists "by nature" might mean one of four things:

16 *Bradwell v. Illinois*, 83 U.S. (16 Wall.) 130 (1873).
17 *Vyas Samhita* sl. 19, 20, cited in Roop Rekha Verma, "Femininity, Equality, and Personhood," in *Women, Culture, and Development*, ed. Nussbaum and Glover, 433–43, with many more related examples.

1. *Biology*: R is based on an innate endowment or tendency.
2. *Tradition*: R is the only way we know; things have always been this way.
3. *Necessity*: R is the only possible way; things cannot be any other way.
4. *Norm*: R is right and proper, the way things should be.

As John Stuart Mill pointed out in his essay "Nature," and also in *The Subjection of Women*, appeals to nature in political argument frequently slip from one of these claims to another, without argument. Thus, from the fact that things have always been a certain way, it is all too quickly inferred that this way is grounded in biology, or that it is the only possible way, or that this way is right and proper. But of course none of these inferences is legitimate: custom does not reliably track biological foundations, and our failure to conceive of another way may be due to a want of imagination or experience, rather than to the inherent impossibility of alternative ways. Clearly the longevity of a custom does not show that it is right.

Similarly, from the fact that a relation is grounded in a biological tendency nothing follows about either inevitability or rightness, although such connections are frequently drawn. We often resist our biological tendencies, providing good vision for the nearsighted, teaching the control of aggressive tendencies, and in general molding behavior in accordance with an independently justified set of moral and social norms. We can move nonfallaciously from number 1 to number 4 only if, like Justice Bradley, we have already understood the biological in a religious or otherwise normative sense, as the way things should be. But such understandings of nature are highly controversial within the major religions, and surely cannot serve as the basis for a political overlapping consensus.

Where the structure of the family is concerned, however, we need not even get very far into those refinements of argument, since it is utterly implausible to claim even that the organization of the family has a fixed *customary* nature. Justice Bradley appears ignorant of the lives of poor families in his own society: Myra Bradwell was hardly the first woman in Illinois to work outside the home. Indeed, the American family has long been characterized by enormous diversity of structures, reflecting the diversity of Americans' ethnic and geographical origins.[18]

18 See Minow, "All in the Family," for an excellent discussion of this issue.

For our purposes we can observe this variety by focusing on Vasanti and Jayamma, seeing how custom and law have constructed very different ideas of family for two women in nominally a single society and religious group.

Vasanti's life has been defined by long-standing Hindu customs of dowry, exogamous marriage, and patrilocal residence. Married as a very young girl, she took up residence in her husband's home, leaving her own home behind and bringing dowry with her – the same pattern that produced the tragic case of Salema Khatun. Vasanti was lucky: her own family rescued her from abuse and helped her out. The high cost of dowry makes this uncommon, since a daughter who returns home either will be another mouth to feed all her life, or will involve the family in the double expense of a second dowry. These customs construct a family structure in which sons are prizes to their mothers, the mothers' main hope of care and sustenance in old age. Daughters, by contrast, are not prizes, since they will soon live elsewhere, and represent a heavy expense.

This customary pattern is prevalent in many regions of India; it is strongly linked to female malnutrition,[19] child marriage, the sufferings of young widows, and other hardships of customary female life. The birth of a girl child is rarely greeted with joy, and proverbs impress on her early that her life will be one of hardship. "A girl child born," goes one proverb, "to marriage or death she is already gone."[20] She is a "treasure possessed by strangers" and "travels on another's boat."[21] From an early age, she is told of the hardships that await her in the marital home, in proverbial sayings such as "O what fun in the house of the in-laws / Blows of the broomstick every third day."[22] Because

19 See Amartya Sen and Sunil Sengupta, "Malnutrition of Rural Children and the Sex Bias," *Economic and Political Weekly* 18 (1983); Sen, "Family and Food: Sex Bias in Poverty," in Sen, *Resources, Values, and Development* (Oxford: Blackwell, 1984) (hereinafter RVD), 346–68; Pranab Bardhan, "On Life and Death Problems," *Economic and Political Weekly* 32–34 (August 1974), 1293–1308; Kumudini Dandekar, "Why Has the Proportion of Women in India's Population Been Declining?" *Economic and Political Weekly* 9 (October 18, 1975), 1663–87.
20 From *Together We Forge a Path*, publication of the Mahila Samakhya Project, Andhra Pradesh.
21 Bengali proverbs cited in Jasodhara Bagchi et al., *Loved and Unloved: The Girl Child in the Family* (Calcutta: Stree, 1997), 17. Bagchi gives an excellent discussion of the history of criticism of this view in the writings of Bengali reformers Rammohun Roy and Iswarchandra Vidyasagar, as well as in fiction written by and about women.
22 Bagchi, pp. 17–18.

she is viewed as already a member of some other household, there is little incentive to invest in her education; even if there were such incentives, early marriage quickly terminates the education process.

These customs have been strenuously protested from at least the early nineteenth century. In Bengal, for example, Ishwarchandra Vidyasagar took up the cause of female education, starting one of the earliest nonreligious schools for girls along with philanthropist John Drinkwater Bethune. He wrote that early marriage immerses a young woman in a "sea of suffering," preventing the development of her body and mind.[23] Many reform-minded people shared his sense of the wrong done to women by such customs; thus changes in customary patterns began to be seen. And yet, 150 years later, the custom of exogamous early marriage is still strongly linked to many types of discrimination against the girl child, and it is still the case that the very existence of a girl child is viewed as an occasion for sadness and a sense of loss,[24] rather than as an opportunity to develop a human being's capabilities.

Efforts to change these ideas and customs face an uphill struggle, since they are so pervasive. Thus on a recent visit to the Sitamarhi district in northern Bihar, I attended a play about dowry perfomed by young girls in an education project run by a local NGO. Playing both male and female roles themselves, the girls told the story of how a young bride and groom successfully resisted parental pressure to marry with dowry; they insisted that it was a bad custom, and the groom successfully got permission to marry without taking any money. Performed for the entire village, this play had quite an impact. And yet: in the next village, only a ten-minute ride by jeep, a village in which there is no NGO operating, women said that dowry was bad, but could never be changed. It is just the way things are. Given the tenacity of this pattern, Vasanti's life is in many respects unusually favored: she had no abusive in-laws to collaborate in her husband's abuse, and her own family was (somewhat atypically) willing to take her back – though not, of course, to grant her equal inheritance rights in her father's estate.

Such customs may often seem like fate. But we have only to look to a different region of India to see how small a role any kind of natural

23 Cited in Bagchi, 7–8. Bagchi here cites from her own more extensive study of Vidyasagar, published in Bengali as *Vidyasagar o kanyashishu* (Vidyasagar and the girl child), special number of *Eksathe*, April 1992.
24 See Bagchi, 8–9.

inevitability plays in the construction of this kind of family life. Kerala has had, since at least the eleventh century, a tradition of matrilocal residence and matrilineal inheritance, sometimes in connection with plural transient marriages for women, as male labor migrated with the season. These customs have been under assault ever since the arrival of Jesuit missionaries in the seventeenth century, who taught that this structure was not in accordance with morality (although at the same time they strongly supported the education of women and opposed customs of caste hierarchy). More recently, contact with the rest of India has made dowry increasingly popular among middle-class Keralan families; the number of informal common-law marriages has also declined, as has female polygamy. And yet female-friendly customs exhibit a striking tenacity, constructing different expectations and roles for young women.[25] The birth of a girl child is usually not viewed negatively, as it is in much of India; nor is it assumed that the girl child will leave the home, failing to support her parents' old age. Jayamma's life is not atypical. She did not move away when she married, nor did her daughters have to leave her. The daughter who married a lower-caste man did leave, but eventually moved back, and later shared the house with her (though quarrels caused the partitioning of the kitchen!). The elsewhere-conventional idea that sons will support a mother in old age is reflected in the national policy that was invoked to deny Jayamma her widow's pension; but Jayamma's sons actually followed Keralan convention when they behaved in a rather offhand and indolent manner toward their mother, leaving her real support to the daughters. Although Jayamma had a monogamous marriage, she is relatively unaffected by norms of female modesty and reticence that prevail in many parts of India. She seems to have somewhat disapproved of nonmarital sexual relationships her daughters have had at various times, but her eye was more on the caste of the men involved than on issues of sexual purity. The general social tolerance of such relationships again reflects Keralan traditions of female independence.

Thus the idea that "family" is a single entity even from the point of view of custom and habit is somewhat absurd, even when we confine

---

25 What follows is based upon discussion with Sardamoni, a leading historian of Kerala, most of whose scholarly writings are in vernacular languages.

our gaze to India; such extreme contrasts are commonplace. But if one can make any generalizations at all about such a complex nation, we can also say that in some respects most Indian families do differ from their U.S. and European counterparts. Such constrasts are risky, because they can easily oversimplify both sides; but if one bears in mind their rough-and-ready character, and the existence of tremendous variety on both sides, they may still be useful.

What American rhetoric means by "the family" is, typically, a heterosexual couple (paradigmatically, at least in the recent past, a working father and a housewife mother), rearing its children in relative privacy and dwelling in its own home, paradigmatically a separate dwelling place. This family norm is the creation of modern Protestant values; it has never been ubiquitous in the U.S., despite political rhetoric that invokes it nostalgically as the universal custom of our past.[26] Not even Ozzie and Harriet were Ozzie and Harriet, as a recent biography of the show-business family shows: they were hard-working professionals whose lives had little to do with the conventional middle-class norms they represented on TV. Nonetheless, such paradigms have been exhibited publicly as norms, and at least part of the population has conformed to these norms. In India such a pattern has never even been exhibited as a norm. The household unit is not portrayed in such an exclusive way, focused on the married couple and their children. Typically the extended family, or at least some parts of it, plays a central role in the daily life of the family, in the rearing of children, and so forth. Children do remain close to their mothers for a time; but even then the mother does not spend much time alone with her young child, fostering the romantically intense type of exclusive intimacy that is common in American child-rearing practices. She is more inclined to introduce her child quickly to larger groupings, the extended family and the village.[27] Whereas American mothers spend a lot of time focused on the faces of their young infants, eyes meeting eyes, faces rapidly responding, Indian mothers from a variety of social classes tend to carry the child on the hip, making much less eye contact as they carry the child around with them in a larger social setting. From the begin-

26 See Minow.
27 See Stanley J. Kurtz, *All the Mothers Are One: Hindu India and the Cultural Reshaping of Psychoanalysis* (New York: Columbia University Press, 1992), a study of Indian child-rearing practices.

ning, then, the child is introduced to a wider world and a larger set of concerned adults.

The construction of the family dwelling place exhibits related differences. It goes without saying that in poor families where five or six people share a single room, there is no such thing as the privacy of the individual in the middle-class American sense – although poor people will frequently seek solitude for the purpose of defecation, walking considerable distances from their dwellings.[28] Lower-class dwellings are often not even fully closed to the elements, and typically one observes a flow of people through the house when one visits. But patterns of family dwelling differ from the U.S. norm in all social classes. In all classes, the home is simply more porous: even in upper-middle-class families, visitors drop in unannounced, there is a constant ebb and flow of people through the house, and the sense that one should not visit unless one has telephoned is (frequently, along with the telephone itself) absent. Homes are also more open to the out-of-doors, and animals such as lizards and toads are a common feature of indoor middle-class life. These structural differences make the family a subtly different thing.

Central to the self-definition of the modern Western (and perhaps especially American) family is the idea that the meaning of one's life is to be found primarily in a relationship of romantic love with a single person. Even feminists who criticize marriage as traditionally practiced frequently hold onto this romantic norm, translating it to a reformed marriage, or a nonmarital heterosexual relationship, or a same-sex relationship. Such a goal is far less common among Indian than among Western women, and that too shapes the family structure by shaping choices and ways of life within it. Martha Chen's extensive study of Hindu widows all over India showed that almost none expressed the desire to remarry, and many were glad to be done with life with a man. Even when marriage itself is prized, its raison d'être is typically not taken to be romance. Not surprisingly, in a culture where arranged marriages are still the norm, romantic love is frequently understood as a potential threat to, rather than as the goal of, marriage.[29] Neither

---

28 See Gulati, *Profiles of Female Poverty*.

29 The stories in Bardhan's anthology bring this out again and again – occasionally by displaying the fate of the exception, as in Tagore's "Haimanti" (see chapter 2). See also Vikram Seth's *A Suitable Boy*, a vivid depiction of the skepticism of middle-class Hindu culture about romantic love.

Jayamma nor Vasanti spoke of love as a goal of their lives, and neither of them appeared to be searching for romantic love. Even Jayamma's daughters, who had premarital affairs, seem to have been looking for pleasure and independence, rather than for romantic love in the Western sense. Stanley Kurtz's study of Indian child-rearing practices concludes that some of these differences derive from differences in the mother-child relationship: the middle-class American mother constructs an intimate relationship of individual responsiveness with her child, whereas a typical Indian mother is less likely to romanticize the relationship, more likely to attend to the child as one among many people and tasks in her world.[30]

Indeed, one can often observe that energies Western people (including many feminists) pour into the search for and the nurturing of a romantic relationship frequently are used, among Indian women, for the creation and sustenance of groups of mutual support among women. Vasanti, rather than dating, is content to focus on her friendship with Kokila and the network of support for domestic violence victims that they have established. She speaks with pride of the fact that, although Indian women are typically isolated and disunited, they have learned through groups like SEWA to help each other and other women outside their group. The women of the women's collective in Andhra Pradesh spoke repeatedly, and with much enthusiasm, of the sense of self-worth and the happiness they derive from the women's collective, which is clearly their primary affective relationship, and in the context of which much of their child-rearing activity is carried on. This same structure is evident throughout South Asian women's movements. Entirely typical is this statement made to Martha Chen by Mallika, a young Bangladeshi widow who participated in a literacy project for women run by the Bangladesh Rural Advancement Committee:

The group helped us and taught us many things. I have learned how to live unitedly. Before if any rich person abused or criticized, we could not reply. But now if anybody says anything bad, we, the 17 members of the group, go together and ask that person why he or she passed this comment. This is another kind of help we have gotten. Before we did not know how to get together and help each other . . . Each one was busy with their own worries

30 See Kurtz, *All the Mothers*.

and sorrows, always thinking about food for their children and themselves. Now we, the 17 members of the group, have become very close to one another.[31]

These structures should not be ignored when we talk about "the family." For the women who are a part of them, they are the locus of a large part of child-rearing, and a primary source of emotional support.

If "the family" is evidently not "by nature" even in the sense of being uniform, then it seems obvious that no particular form of it is necessary and inevitable; given the variety we observe, it seems unlikely that its Western nuclear form is uniquely founded on biological tendencies. Such biological tendencies as exist can be expressed, over time, in many different ways. Still less do we have reason, without an independent normative inquiry, to think that any particular form of this institution is the right and proper one, "that which properly belongs to the domain and functions of womanhood."

IV. THE FAMILY AS CREATION OF STATE ACTION

So far nothing has been said about the role of law and the state. Such variations as I have described might in principle have had origins utterly separate from state action, in religious and cultural traditions. But in fact it is clear that the shape of the family structure and the privileges and rights of family members are in many respects artifacts of state action. When the Hindu legal system gives girls property rights unequal to those of boys, this shapes the Hindu family (as is often mentioned when any attempt is made to change these laws).[32] Laws making it possible for a man to return a departed wife forcibly to the conjugal home, securing what is called the "restitution of conjugal rights," are a salient source of women's vulnerability to unwanted pregnancy and to domestic violence. Government again influences domestic violence when it fails to enforce laws against it, treating the home as a "private" realm in which the police should not meddle.[33] It influences it again when it allows dowry abuse to continue unregulated, or fails to enforce

31 Chen, *A Quiet Revolution*, 216.
32 See Bina Agarwal, "Bargaining," and, on protests against change, *A Field of One's Own.*
33 See Siegel, " 'The Rule of Love.' "

laws against dowry violence. The fact that marital rape is not illegal in India again shapes the structure of the family, by telling women that they may not invoke the aid of law enforcement in this intimate domain. Laws regulating sex discrimination and sexual harassment in employment also shape the family by shaping the options available to a woman should she seek outside employment. Laws regulating child labor and making education compulsory shape the lives of children and the nature of parents' control over their children.

Up to this point, the family looks analogous to other voluntary institutions in society that seem to have their own existence apart from the state, but that are constrained externally by state regulation. Religious institutions are not state artifacts, in the sense that a given religion typically keeps its identity across national boundaries; what it is to be a Roman Catholic has an elaborate definition that is independent of any particular nation in which that religion finds itself. But the state nonetheless regulates that church, saying what it is permitted and forbidden to do, giving it tax benefits as a charitable organization, and so forth. By establishing rules for acquiring these benefits, and by restricting the church in other ways through laws of general applicability, the state influences the shape of the Roman Catholic Church and to some extent affects the privileges and rights of its members. And yet it would seem wrong to think of the church as itself a creation of state action.

So too with universities: they may be founded independently of the existence of any state (as were some of the early American universities); and the definition of what it is to be a member of a university is independent of law. Nonetheless, once a university exists within a state, the state will regulate and constrain it in various ways, all relevant to determining the privileges and rights of its members.

The family, however, is the artifact of state action in a much more direct sense than are these voluntary organizations. For there is really no entity, "the family," into which the state either does or does not intervene. People associate in many different ways, live together, love each other, have children. Which of these will be given the name "family" is a legal and political matter, never one to be decided simply by the parties themselves. The state constitutes the family structure through its laws, defining which groups of people can count as families, defining the privileges and rights of family members, defining what marriage and divorce are, what legitimacy and parental responsibility are, and so forth. This difference makes a difference: the state is present in the family from the start, in a way that is less clearly the case with the religious body or the university; it is the state that says what this thing *is* and controls how one becomes a member of it.[34]

To see this more clearly, let us consider the rituals that define a person as a member of an association: in the university, matriculation (and, later, the granting of a degree); in a religious body, baptism, conversion, or some analogous entrance rite; in the family, marriage. Now it is evident that the state has some connection with university matriculation/graduation and with religious baptism/conversion: it polices these rites on the outside, by defining the institution as enjoying a particular tax-free status, by forbidding cruelty or other illegalities as part of the ritual,[35] and so forth. But marriage is from the start a public, state-administered rite. There are state laws defining it, and these laws restrict entry into that privileged domain. The state does not simply police marriage on the outside, it marries people. Other very similar people who don't meet the state's test cannot count as married, even if they satisfy all private and even religious criteria for marriage. (Thus, same-sex couples whose unions have been solemnized by some religious body still are not married, because the state has not granted them a license.) Marriage has not always been a state function, and there is no necessity that it be so. But in the modern world it pervasively is. Even in India, where marriage and divorce are the business of each separate religious system of law, these systems of law are part of the public sphere: they are constituted by the basic structure of laws and institutions in society, people are assigned to them by a system of public rules, and individuals do not have the option to contract a marriage in whatever way they wish, apart from these rules.

All human associations are shaped by laws and institutions, which either favor or disfavor them, and which structure them in various ways. But the family is shaped by law in a yet deeper and more thoroughgoing way, in the sense that its very definition is legal and political;

---

34 See Minow, "All in the Family," with many fascinating examples of how the Immigration and Naturalization Service uses definitions of "family" to restrict immigration; Olsen, "The Family and the Market" and "The Myth of State Intervention."

35 See Chapter 3 on dilemmas involving the use of drugs in religious ceremonies.

individuals may call themselves "a family" if they wish, but they only get to be one, in the sense that is socially recognized, if they satisfy legal tests.

V. WOMEN'S CARE GIVING: "AN EMINENTLY ARTIFICIAL THING"

If it seems incontrovertible that the structure of the family is shaped by history, custom, and law, so much has not usually been granted regarding the feminine abilities of care and nurturance that define woman's role within family structures of widely differing types. In many different types of families, women overwhelmingly do the child rearing and housekeeping, and are expected to give care and support to men, often without return in kind. It is frequently alleged that this traditional function is itself "natural" in one or more of the senses mentioned earlier, and it is often inferred in consequence that there would be something wrong with any attempt to shake up traditional patterns of care giving. We must, therefore, confront this issue to some extent separately from the issue of family structure; our stand on it will affect what we can and should say about the family.

When we talk about love and care, we are talking both about emotions and about complex patterns of behavior, mediated not only by desire, but also by habits and social norms. The tendency for women to focus their energies on care for children and family may well have biological roots; at one time in human prehistory such a division of roles may have had adaptive significance. Evidence concerning the human species is still too thin and indeterminate to say much with confidence, but there is at least some reason to think this may be so. But we should remind ourselves from the start that, insofar as such biological differences obtain, they are differences in tendency only, and they give us no reason to promote traditional roles for women or to fail to promote them for men – any more than the putative linkage of aggressive behavior with maleness (far more convincingly demonstrated – for example, by violent crime statistics everywhere in the world), gives us reason to relax the restraints of the criminal law or to view male aggression with special indulgence. We have plenty of evidence that men are capable of loving and of caring for children, and that women can succeed in the "outside" life of work (as, indeed, poor women always have done, even while they have also cared for children and done most if not all of the housework); so even if there is some differential tendency, it isn't of the sort that prevents us from establishing social norms of functional sharing if we want to. We have to ask who we want to be. Knowing what equipment we have tells us what is utterly impossible; but knowing what is impossible doesn't, in this case, take us very far toward answering our questions about what is best. Equal sharing is plainly possible, since it has been exemplified.

Moreover, we have very strong evidence that Mill is in fact correct: the "nature of woman," as we currently know it, is an "eminently artificial thing: the result of forced repression in some directions, unnatural stimulation in others."[36] This is a vast topic, but we may approach it briefly, using four distinct arguments.

The first is a *conceptual argument*. The emotion of love, and patterns of desire and action associated with caring, cannot adequately be understood simply as impulses. They are best understood as involving quite a lot of thought and interpretation, especially evaluation.[37] Love involves seeing the object in a particular way, and having a variety of beliefs about the object. These prominently include beliefs about the object's specialness or value. Patterns of care also involve beliefs about what things and people are important and valuable, what is right and proper, and a host of other beliefs, many of a normative nature. These are not the sorts of things that are simply there from birth: they have to be learned. That does not mean that there is no biological basis for the learning: the human capacity for language has to be developed, but such training activates innate biological equipment. Nonetheless, as with language, so here: the large role that training must play in order to impart the relevant type of cognitive complexity also gives much room for social interpretation and for cultural variety to work. And this means that all patterns of love and care must be understood as at least in part cultural constructs, which may at least in principle be altered by altering the beliefs on which they rest.[38]

Let us consider Vasanti and Jayamma. As I have suggested, romantic love does not play a big role in what they have to say about their

36 Mill, SW, p. 22.
37 For much more argument along these lines, see my *Upheavals of Thought: A Theory of the Emotions*, forthcoming.
38 See *Upheavals*, chapter 3.

marriages – or even, in Jayamma's case, her children's marriages. That is by itself a significant sign of cultural shaping at the level of the beliefs that go to make up love. And what the two women say about caring shows, in fact, that they have internalized an extensive repertory of normative social beliefs that inform both emotions and patterns of action. In Vasanti's case, we find the belief that it is a wife's duty (or lot) to put up with a lot of abuse (a belief she later rejected); the belief that a husband who selfishly deprives a wife of children has forfeited some claim to regard; the belief that children are a woman's major source of protection in a hostile world. In Jayamma's case, we find the belief that it is the wife's job to perform (or arrange for the children to perform) all the housework even if she works a full day and the husband does not; the belief that it is her duty to care for the husband in illness, but not his duty to care for her in illness; the belief that her income belongs to the whole family, whereas his belongs to him alone. These beliefs are not innate, and certainly we can find many women in the world who do not have them. They are artifacts of a very particular social order. But what love and care *are* is, at least in part, a network of such beliefs. Were they to change, emotions and patterns of conduct would also change. This clearly happened in Vasanti's case, as she abandoned the belief that it was her lot in life to endure abuse.[39] To those who treat love and care as simply instinctual we can first of all say, then, that they have not got the concepts right.[40]

Second, there is an argument from the *pervasiveness of cultural influence*. Experiments with young infants show that babies are treated differently in accordance with their perceived gender – even in cases where there is no actual sex difference, and the same baby has simply been differently labeled. Perceived girls are cuddled and hugged close; perceived boys are more likely to be tossed in the air. Perceived girls who cry are called frightened; perceived boys who cry are called angry. In that way, and in others, the perceived sex of the child becomes an active factor in his or her emotional development.[41] This is of course

39 We see the same shift in Devi's story "Giribala," in which the husband eventually goes too far, when he sells his daughters into prostitution.
40 For a much more extensive discussion of this whole issue, see Nussbaum, "Constructing Love, Desire, and Care," in Estlund and Nussbaum, 17–43, reprinted in revised form in Nussbaum, *Sex and Social Justice*.
41 See the description of experimental work in Anne Fausto Sterling, *Myths of Gender* (New York: Basic Books, second edition 1985).

only one instance of a more general phenomenon: in every area, environment contributes to the development of personality. Scientists writing about the phenomenon of "cloning" seem unequivocally and unanimously to reject the nightmare idea that a genetically identical individual would be qualitatively the same person.[42] Particularly in the area of sex difference we have a great deal of evidence of cultural shaping at an early age. We cannot use such evidence to rule out a biological component in sex difference with regard to love and care; but we can point out that we are still where Mill thought we were – in absolutely no position to know what that component may be, so early and pervasive are the environmental differences.

Third, here as with the family we may use an *argument from cultural variety*. When we observe differences between human communities with regard to emotions and patterns of behavior, this is pretty good evidence, humans being a single species, that historical and cultural factors are at work. And of course we do see wide variation among cultures in the ways they construct gender difference in the area of love and care. We may use, again, the contrasting cases of Vasanti and Jayamma to exemplify part of the range that exists, even within a single nation. These cases exhibit three distinct types of cultural difference. First, we see differences in the behavior thought right and proper: Vasanti has internalized norms of female modesty that make her shrink from taking a job outside the home, and she has learned to carry herself in a subservient and modest fashion – for example, to look down rather than to look people in the eye. Jayamma has no such sense of female deference, and this absence is a function at least as much of Keralan culture as of social class. (We find equally striking cultural differences within a single region: for example, between Hindu women and tribal women in Rajasthan. The former go well beyond Vasanti in deference, the latter are equal to Jayamma in forthrightness and fearlessness.) Second, we see variation in views about which emotions are good and which ones bad. Both women display an indifference to romantic love that strikes Western women as strange. Jayamma revels in her feisty, independent, and extremely combative personality, whereas Vasanti has learned a gentler and softer set of norms; she seems to think it good

---

42 See essays by R. Dawkins and S. J. Gould in Nussbaum and Sunstein, eds., *Clones and Clones: Facts and Fantasies about Human Cloning* (New York: Norton, 1998), and references in the essay by R. Epstein.

to depend on someone tougher than she is, whether male or female, for support. To some extent such differences may be personal; but they also reflect the influence of cultural norms. Third, we observe differences in views about the appropriate objects for the various emotions. Jayamma remains preoccupied with issues of caste in thinking about her daughter's marriages; Vasanti appears to have lost some of those ideas, in the context of solidarity with the woman's movement. Jayamma thinks it inappropriate to be intimidated by anyone; Vasanti once thought that to live in fear of a husband was just a woman's lot in life, although she now rejects that belief. Again, this variety is best explained by social teaching, along with the great difference between the traditional marriage structures in the two societies: Jayamma has always stayed at home and ruled the home, Vasanti left her home behind to become intensely vulnerable in a strange surrounding.

Consider, too, how the two women fashion themselves – their bodies, their movements, their voices – how they show themselves as female. Here we see cultural differences of both caste and region that separate the two women from one another at least as much as they separate them both from a range of Western women. Vasanti's soft rounded body, her quite leisurely and unathletic style of movement, her downcast eyes, her soft voice – all are familiar parts of Indian middle-class traditions regarding women's attractiveness and appropriate behavior. Norms both of propriety and of sexual attractiveness clearly shape a female persona that is less edgy and mobile, less angular and muscular, less confrontational, than the persona of a typical American of similar age and class. Vasanti does not go to any gym, and she would certainly be aghast at the type of bodily assertiveness, immodesty, and gracelessness involved in running in public – *or* working at the brick kiln. Like so many women in the SEWA movement, moreover, she has been brought up to think it bad form to draw attention to herself or talk about herself. SEWA education leaders typically have to spend a whole day on the exercise of getting a woman to be willing to stand up and say her name in public.[43] Vasanti's recent experiences have changed her – but one can also see her upbringing despite the changes. All this cultural conditioning shapes what, for Vasanti, love and care can be.

Not so Jayamma, who appears never to have had any timidity or

43 Personal communication, education office, SEWA, March 1997.

reticence, and who is generally described by others as a fierce individual. Her voice, her bodily self-presentation, and her angular lack of concern with "the feminine" – all are in marked contrast to Vasanti. Obviously, Jayamma has been brought up doing manual labor from childhood, and she has had to become enormously strong to survive. Poverty has given her no option to develop feminine graces. But cultural issues are also likely to be involved.

Once again, these differences within India are linked to differences between Indian and American norms. In India it is still the case that a wiry athletic body is taken to be a sign that one is either a manual laborer or a dancer/prostitute. Middle-class women avoid looking like this, and think it unattractive. On a visit to a red-light district in Bihar with activists from the nonlaboring classes, I found that I was identified by the sex workers as a kind of kindred spirit, because my body type was more like theirs than like that of a (round, sedentary) middle-class Indian woman – and because the stereotype of American women is that they are all sexually promiscuous.

Seeing this cultural variety in norms of love, care, and gender presentation doesn't, of course, tell us that we can change anything easily, should we want to. Some biological problems are easier to fix than some cultural problems; in general, social rather than biological origin is not systematically correlated with greater ease of change, and some social practices can be enormously resistant to change – as can be seen, for example, in attempts to abolish dowry in India and Bangladesh. In both countries giving and receiving dowry has been illegal for some time, and in the mid 1980s tough new laws were introduced to crack down on domestic violence in connection with dowry extortion.[44] Still, the case of Salema Khatun is by no means uncommon, whether in Bangladesh or in India[45] – and in matrilineal Kerala itself, dowry is

44 In India, dowry has been illegal since 1961 (when the legislature passed the Dowry Prohibition Act); in Bangladesh it has been illegal since 1980. Both nations added further criminal penalties; in 1983 India introduced criminal penalties for cruelty by the husband or his relatives in connection with dowry. In 1984, the Dowry Prohibition Act was amended to introduce more stringent punishments, and in 1986 the Indian Penal Code was amended to address the problem of dowry violence: any suspicious death by burns or bodily injury within seven years of marriage, in connection with evidence of cruelty or harassment prior to death, is defined as "dowry death," and the husband or relative is deemed to have caused the death. By thus shifting the burden of proof, the legal system has made convictions more achievable.

45 For one recent study, see Roushan Jahan, "Hidden Wounds, Visible Scars: Violence

becoming increasingly common. Identifying a cultural origin for a practice does not, then, tell us that reform can forge ahead unimpeded; but it does at least dispel the false sense of inevitability that so often surrounds questions of gender and family; and, by telling us what factors we are contending against, gives us a better sense of how we might approach the issue of reform.

VI. POLITICAL LIBERALISM AND THE FAMILY: RAWLS'S DILEMMA

Let me recapitulate. We see that the family both fosters and undermines human capabilities. Our question is, how may law and public policy ensure that it does more fostering and less impeding? We began by noting that the family is neither a single entity nor a natural growth; it is a plurality of complex social structures. These structures house and further shape, in turn, gender roles in the area of care and love that are themselves in many respects social artifacts. But now we need to step back and face the question of the family in a more general way, asking how public policy should address the tension to which the family's existence as a allegedly private sphere of love and care gives rise. On the one hand, we must take seriously the possibility that, in this case as in the case of religion, important values of personal choice will be sacrificed if the family is made too directly the subject of a theory of political justice. On the other hand, we must not lose sight of the obvious fact that the family has a profound influence on human development, an influence that is present from the start of a human life. It thus has a very strong claim to be regarded as part of the basic structure of society, and among those institutions that basic principles of justice are designed to regulate most directly.

A vivid sense of how this dilemma tugs at liberal political thought can be found in John Rawls's recent article "The Idea of Public Reason Revisited."[46] Responding to questions from feminist critics,[47] Rawls

against Women in Bangladesh," in Bina Agarwal, ed., *Structures of Patriarchy: State, Community, and Household in Modernising Asia* (New Delhi: Kali for Women, 1988), 199–227. See also Indira Jaising, "Violence Against Women: The Indian Perspective," in Julie Peters and Andrea Wolper, eds., *Women's Rights, Human Rights* (New York and London: Routledge, 1995), 51–56.

46 *University of Chicago Law Review* 64 (1997), 765–807.
47 Above all, Rawls is responding to Susan Okin's *Justice, Gender, and the Family.*

makes two claims, which are difficult to render consistent.[48] First, he repeats his old claim, first made in *A Theory of Justice*, that the family is a part of the basic structure of society, that is, one of the institutions to which, by definition, the two principles of justice primarily apply.[49] Second, he makes a new claim that his two principles of justice, while they apply directly to the basic structure, do not "apply directly to the internal life of families." In this respect, Rawls says, the family is like many other voluntary associations, such as "churches and universities, professional or scientific associations, business firms or labor unions." Just as principles of justice do not require that principles of ecclesiastical governance be democratic, although they do supply some essential constraints that bear on ecclesiastical governance, so too with the family: such principles do not regulate its internal governance, but they do supply some important constraints on it. Thus, the family need not obey the Rawlsian difference principle, with regard to its internal distribution of resources and opportunities; nor need it obey the priority of liberty, with regard to basic political and religious liberties. On the other hand, the fact that its members are part of a society in which the lives of all citizens are governed by institutions based on these two principles will regulate, in many ways, what can and cannot go on there.

Where the two principles of justice are concerned, what Rawls appears to have in mind is the following idea. Even if society as a whole is governed by the difference principle, inequalities being tolerated only where they raise the level of the worst off, this does not require the family's internal distribution of income and wealth to obey this pattern. Where liberty is concerned, it is a little hard to know what restrictions Rawls's cautious formulation would permit, since any absolute ban on certain types of religious exercise, speech, and political action on the part of a patriarch – at least when we are considering adult female citizens – would seem to run afoul of public liberty principles straight-

---

48 See section 5 of the article "On the Family as Part of the Basic Structure," 787–794. For my own fuller discussion of Rawls's views, see "Rawls and Feminism," in *The Cambridge Companion to Rawls*, ed. Samuel Freeman (Cambridge: Cambridge University Press, forthcoming).

49 See 788: "The family is part of the basic structure, since one of its main roles is to be the basis of the orderly production and reproduction of society and its culture from one generation to the next."

away. But perhaps Rawls is thinking of cases in which one partner says for example, "I'll divorce you if you convert to Judaism," or "I can't stay with you if you vote for Bill Clinton." If public officials restricted liberties of citizens in this way, it would clearly be illicit; in the family (Rawls may wish to argue) such coercive tactics, while unpleasant, are not violations of basic justice, so long as the threatened party can leave and is not physically threatened.

It is of course important to assert that the principles of justice apply to the basic structure taken as a whole, and that this does not directly entail that they apply to each of the institutions that forms part of the basic structure, taken one by one. Thus it is a little difficult to imagine what it would mean for the principles of justice to apply directly to the family *taken as part of the basic structure*, and whether this would be the same as for the principles to apply directly to the family as one institution that is part of the basic structure. Other institutions that form part of the basic structure do not raise this problem, because the basic constitutional structure has no "inside" life to which principles can apply, until it is given shape in the form of more specific institutions that are created only at the constitutional and legislative stages. So we are not troubled by the questions, what is it for the principles to apply to these other institutions as parts of the basic structure, and is this the same as for the principles to apply to each and every one of the institutions? So the family raises a unique question. Rawls's strategy in answering the question is to turn to other institutions: churches and universities.

The difficulty with the parallel between families and universities, as Rawls is aware, is that the family is part of the basic structure; churches, universities, and so forth, are not.[50] That means, in terms of

50 Rawls has nowhere suggested that churches and universities are part of the basic structure, and he probably would be strongly opposed to such an idea. Institutions that form part of the basic structure can be subsidized by the state, and he would appear to be opposed to state subsidies for churches and universities.

An excellent discussion of this whole problem is in G. A. Cohen, "Where the Action Is: On the Site of Distributive Justice," *Philosophy and Public Affairs* 26 (1997), 3–30. Cohen discusses the family and the market as two examples of pervasive institutions in which people cannot help participating and that influence their life chances pervasively and from the start – but which are treated by Rawls as outside the institutional framework that principles of justice directly govern.

Rawls's conception, that the family has been judged to be one of the institutions that dictates people's life chances pervasively and from the start; a university obviously doesn't have this character.[51] Rawls is clearly torn between the idea that the family is so fundamental to the reproduction of society and to citizens' life chances that it must be rendered just, and the equally powerful idea that we cannot tolerate so much interference with the internal workings of this particular institution.

Rawls's solution is to try to make the external constraints tough enough to deliver genuine equality to women as citizens. He denies that there is any such thing as a private sphere "exempt from justice," insisting that law must intervene to protect the equality of women as citizens and of children as future citizens.[52] "The equal rights of women and the basic rights of their children as future citizens are inalienable and protect them wherever they are. Gender distinctions limiting those rights and liberties are excluded."[53] One concrete proposal Rawls appears to endorse, at least for our historical circumstances,[54] is that the law should count a wife's child-rearing work as entitling her to an equal share in the income that a husband earns during marriage and in the increased assets during the time of the marriage, in the case of a divorce. "It seems intolerably unjust," Rawls concludes, "that a husband may depart the family taking his earning power with him and leaving his wife and children far less advantaged than before." On the other hand, Rawls maintains that we should allow traditional gendered

---

51 Churches may, if a child is born into one, and in that sense the case is an intermediate one; but the case remains different from the family, since every child that is born is for years at the mercy of family in all basic matters of survival and well-being.

52 "Public Reason," 791: "A domain so-called, or a sphere of life, is not, then, something already given apart from political conceptions of justice. A domain is not a kind of space, or place, but rather is simply the result, or upshot, of how the principles of political justice are applied, directly to the basic structure and indirectly to the associations within it. The principles defining the equal basic liberties and opportunities of citizens always hold in and through all so-called domains. The equal rights of women and the basic rights of their children as future citizens are inalienable and protect them wherever they are. Gender distinctions limiting those rights and liberties are excluded . . . If the so-called private sphere is alleged to be space exempt from justice, then there is no such thing."

53 *Ibid.*

54 "Public Reason," 793. The proposal was made by Susan M. Okin in *Justice, Gender, and the Family.*

division of labor within families, "provided it is fully voluntary and does not result from or lead to injustice"[55] – words that are honorable but difficult to apply to reality.

Rawls's approach seems to me to stop somewhat short of what justice requires. The family is indeed part of the basic structure.[56] Children are its captives in all matters of basic survival and well-being for many years. Women are frequently its captives out of economic asymmetry. It is difficult to know whether anything children do in the family could be described as "fully voluntary,"[57] and of course this is true for very many women also, especially those without independent sources of material support. Nor is a child's choice to be a member of such a unit at all voluntary, as membership in a university is, or as membership in a church is apart from the issue of family pressure. So more needs to be said about how the dilemma is to be addressed, compatibly with preserving an appropriate degree of space for personal choice in matters of love and care.

The dilemma has a form similar to that of our religious dilemma (with which it is frequently bound up). If we return to our framework there, this will help us to grapple with it, though we shall discover a crucial difference. As in the case of religion, we have on the one side *respect for an intrinsic value*: in this case, the value of the capabilities for love and care; on the other side (at least sometimes) we have the *claim of the other capabilities*, which pushes us toward critical scrutiny of the family and its agents. We now have two orienting principles. With the family as with religion, we must observe the *principle of each person's capability*. We must, that is, ask at every point not just whether love is preserved but whether the *capability of each person* to select appropriate relations of love and care (and the other central functions) is preserved. Love that exists at the expense of the emotional freedom of others does not deserve public protection, any more than religious freedom attained by tyrannizing over the religious freedom of

55 "Public Reason," 792.
56 Rawls seems to waver on this question when, on 791, he writes, "Even if the basic structure alone is the primary subject of justice, the principles of justice still put essential restrictions on the family and all other associations."
57 On 792 n.68, Rawls notes the slipperiness of the idea of voluntariness, as applied to religion, and he states that he describes religious choice as voluntary only from the point of view of "objective conditions," not subjective ones. But even objectively, children's membership in the family is not voluntary.

others. Nor should public action protect an organic unit as such; what it should protect are the emotional and affiliational capabilities of its members.

The *principle of moral constraint* can also be invoked: anything that is cruel or unjust, though it takes place in the family, doesn't deserve to be included in what we value when we value and protect family. The abuser puts himself outside the moral community for which "family" rightly stands, insofar as it belongs on our normative list; he doesn't deserve to be permitted to invoke its name in his defense. Together with this political principle we also have, as in the case of religion, an informal social version of the principle: family, rightly understood, stands for care and love; thus we may question whether abusive actions can ever be called actions defending the family. The police who follow the leads fed them by Vasanti and Kokila are more justly called defenders of family than are abusive husbands and parents.

With all this in place, our analogous principle would seem to be: the state should not intervene in the conduct of family members without a compelling interest, but such a compelling interest is always supplied by the protection of the central capabilities – including, of course, the individual capabilities to choose relationships of love and care.

Here, however, the symmetry with the religious case begins to break down. For, as we have noted, religions have a life outside the state, as do universities; families do not. The family is a social and legal construct in a much more fundamental and thoroughgoing way than are these other organizations,[58] so the dilemma might more plausibly be construed as one between the associational liberties of citizens, on the one hand, and the claim of the other capabilities, on the other. In addressing this dilemma, I am claiming, the state should give family actors considerable liberty of association and self-definition, but within constraints imposed by the central capabilities – which should, insofar as possible, be built into the legal structure that constitutes and regulates the family.

My approach, unlike Rawls's, recognizes this difference and makes it salient. There is no point in urging that the state can regulate the family from without, the way it regulates a private university. Because

---

58 See the discussion in section IV, and Minow, "All in the Family"; Olsen, "The Family and the Market."

of the nature of the state's relation to marriage, as well as because of the pervasive influence of the family on the opportunities and liberties of citizens, the family simply is part of the basic structure of society, and capability-based principles of justice should apply to it directly as a part of that structure, within limits set by the other capabilities, especially the personal liberties (associational, dignitary, and choice-related) of citizens.

This approach differs from Rawls's, although the differences are subtle. Rawls, for all his eloquent criticism of the idea of a private space free from justice, nonetheless begins with the assumption that "the family," understood in a highly conventional way, is to remain a part of the basic structure and to play a basic role in the reproduction of society. To judge both from his remarks in the 1997 article and from the extensive account of moral development in A Theory of Justice, he appears to envisage that unit as a Western-style heterosexual nuclear family, although the later article gives a looser formulation that can admit other nuclear groupings (same-sex couples, for example). He gives this unit, vaguely specified, a high degree of centrality and support, and he never asks what other affiliative groupings of individuals might, for related reasons, deserve state protection and support. Thus, despite his attack on the private-public distinction, he retains the picture of a society of people divided into nuclear home units that has frequently been used to underwrite that distinction. He strongly suggests that the family has a prepolitical form and that politics can regulate it on the outside rather than constitute it from the ground up – although at the same time he insists that a sphere of life is not a "place or space" exempt from justice. Rawls may also retain, in a related way, a distinction between state action and inaction that suggests that the state is not acting when it doesn't interfere with the traditional shape of the family, whereas it would be acting were it to attempt to change modes of family governance.

My approach, by contrast, begins by focusing on the capabilities and liberties of each person, and does not assume that any one affiliative grouping is prior or central in promoting those capabilities. People have needs for love and care, for reproduction, for sexual expression; children have needs for love, support, and education; and people also enjoy a wide range of associational liberties. But at this point my approach urges us to see how different groupings of persons do in promoting these capabilities. Women's collectives of the SEWA type play a valuable role in giving women love and friendship, in caring for children, and in fostering the other capabilities. Conventional families often do less well. Sometimes a women's collective appears to be more truly a child's family than the nuclear home, as when, as often happens, women's collectives protect children from sexual abuse, or arrange for children at risk of abuse or child marriage to be protected through state-run schools. Giribala's children would have done well to have had the support of a women's *sangham*, rather than the nuclear family that isolated them from protection and left them vulnerable to their greedy and corrupt father's schemes. Rawls seems to give state protection to the privacy of families, but not, similarly, to other affiliative groupings. My approach would urge that this choice be a contextual one, asking how, in the given history and circumstances, public policy can best promote the claims of the human capabilities. The only thing that stops state intervention is the person and the various liberties and rights of the person, including associative liberties, the right to be free from unwarranted search and seizure, and so forth. The family has no power to stop this intervention on its own, as though it were a mystical unity over and above the lives of its members.[59]

Similarly, my approach urges us to question whether the distinctions between outside and inside, and between action and inaction, are really coherent.[60] Laws governing marriage, divorce, compulsory education, inheritance – all are as inside as anything can be in the family. Nor should the criminal justice system recognize a distinction between inside and outside, in the definition and ranking of criminal offenses: it should treat rape as rape, battery as battery, coercion as coercion, wherever they occur.[61] To let things take their status quo ante course is to choose a course of action, not to be completely neutral. In short, the

59 In this respect (though not in all respects!) my approach is close to that of Richard Epstein, in his articles regarding homosexual marriage and surrogate motherhood: see "Caste and the Civil Rights Laws: From Jim Crow to Same-Sex Marriages," *Michigan Law Review* 92 (1994), 2456–78, and "Surrogacy: The Case for Full Contractual Enforcement," *Virginia Law Review* 81 (1995), 2305–41.

60 See Cass R. Sunstein, *The Partial Constitution* (Cambridge, MA: Harvard University Press, 1993).

61 This is not to say that the relationship between parties might not have evidential relevance in a criminal trial: for example, the fact that O. J. Simpson was the estranged husband of the victim could have evidential relevance in supplying a motive for the alleged murder.

state's interest in protecting the dignity, integrity, and well-being of each citizen never simply leads to external constraints on the family structure, whatever the appearance may be; it always leads to positive constructing of the family institution. This constructing should be done in ways that are compatible with political justice.

Thus Rawls's position recommends, in effect, accepting certain groupings as given and not interfering with their internal workings, simply policing them by a system of tough external constraints. This approach does not answer the question how the state ought to define which groupings count as families, and what it should consider as it attempts to answer this question. I have argued that there is no reason for the state to take traditional groupings as given: in light of the human capabilities, the state should consider what groupings it wishes to protect, and on what basis. And I have argued further that there is no way in which the state can really avoid constructing the family unit in accordance with some norms or other; so it had better do so self-consciously, with full awareness of the goals in view.

In practical terms, my approach in terms of the promotion of capabilities and Rawls's approach, which views the two principles of justice as supplying external constraints on the family, will often lead to the same answers. Laws against marital rape, laws protecting marital consent, laws mandating compulsory education, laws banning child marriage and child labor, laws ensuring an appropriate material recognition of the wife's economic contribution to the family, laws providing child care to support working mothers, laws promoting the nutrition and health of girl children – all these laws, I think, we would both support as appropriate expressions of state concern for citizens and future citizens. But the grounds on which we would support them are subtly different. Rawls sees the laws as supplying external constraints on something that has its own form, the way laws constrain a university or a church; I see them as contributing to the constitution of an institution that is in the most direct sense a part of the basic structure of society.

Furthermore, my approach, like Rawls's, would permit the state to give conventional family groupings certain special privileges and protections, just as it gives religious bodies certain privileges and protections. It will probably do so in many cases, since the family does serve to promote the rearing of children, as well as to meet other needs of citizens. Thus parents may be given (as recommended in Chapter 3) certain limited kinds of deference in making choices regarding their children. And tax breaks for family units are not ruled out, insofar as these units promote human capabilities. But for me, the reason the state will choose such policies, as in the religious case, is to protect the central capabilities of individuals; the definition of family, and the policies chosen, should be chosen with this aim in view. Rawls does not ask how "family" should be defined, nor does he make it clear on what basis it should have special privileges, although the state's interests in its future citizens would appear to be one such basis.

Most important of all, because Rawls takes the family as given, he does not ask what my approach urges us to ask at all times: what other affective ties deserve public protection and support? It is not at all clear, then, what role women's collectives could play in his account of society's basic structure. In my approach, though all such inquiries should be contextual, a role for such collectives is built in from the start, since the aim is not to protect any institution that is customary, but rather to protect and foster those forms of association that promote human capabilities, within limits set by the associational and other liberties of citizens.

Notice that here, as in the case of religion, I do not give the traditional form of a practice exclusive privileges: I ask what capabilities it serves and then extend privileges, insofar as is practicable, to other similar institutions that promote those same capabilities. In practice, such an approach, as with religion, would usually involve both defining family broadly[62] and also supporting other organizations, prominently including women's collectives, that are important in a given cultural context in promoting the well-being of women and children.

Again, my approach would forbid certain types of interference in the family structure that Rawls's approach would also forbid. For me, as for Rawls, it is wrong for the state to mandate the equal division of domestic labor or equal decision making in the household. But again, our reasons for this shared conclusion differ. Rawls judges that it is wrong to interfere with the internal workings of a particular institution,

---

62 See the proposal in Minow, "All in the Family," who observes that narrower definitions, rather than reflecting social reality, frequently are simply devices to limit immigration.

deemed to exist apart from the state – whereas I judge simply that there are associational liberties of individuals, and liberties of speech, that should always be protected for citizens, in any context. (Rawls might have reached a result similar to the one he does reach by relying on the priority of liberty; but, significantly, he does not use that argument.) It just seems an intolerable infringement of liberty for the state to get involved in dictating how people do their dishes. Indeed, for me, dubious forms of conduct receive less prima facie protection in the family than in a purely voluntary association, since the family (for children at any rate) is a nonvoluntary institution that influences citizens' life chances pervasively and from the start. Furthermore, the state has a legitimate interest in children, as future citizens under its protection, that it doesn't have in adults who elect membership in a church or a university.

In a wide range of areas, our approaches will support different public policy choices. In my approach, the central capabilities always supply a compelling interest for purposes of government action. Thus it will be all right to render dowry illegal in India, given the compelling evidence that the dowry system is a major source of women's capability failure. I believe that Rawls would have a difficult time justifying this law – because he is thinking of the family as at least partly prepolitical, and of dowry as one of the choices it makes in its prepolitical state. For me, by contrast, the family is constituted by laws and institutions, and one of the questions to be asked is whether dowry giving is one of the things it should be in the business of doing. Permitting dowry is not neutral state inaction toward an autonomous private entity; it is another (alternative) way of constituting a part of the public sphere. (As in the case of religion, my approach admits the possibility of loss and even tragedy. If we should judge that the liberty to give dowry is a significant protected liberty, the choice to curtail the practice will have a tragic dimension. I am inclined, however, to think that this is no more a core area of protected liberty than would be the liberty to pass on one's estate to one's children without taxation.)

Again, interference with traditional decision-making patterns in the family will be much easier to justify on my approach than on Rawls's. Consider the Mahila Samakhya project in Andhra Pradesh. This project, funded and run by the national government, is explicitly aimed at increasing women's confidence and initiative, and empowering them in their dealings with employers, government officials, and husbands. There is no doubt at all that the government is attempting to reconstruct the family by altering social norms and perceptions. No community and no individual is forced to join, and this is a reservation I would support. Nonetheless, it seems likely that the project implies more in the way of endorsing a particular conception of family governance than Rawls would consider acceptable. Apart from the content of the teaching, the very existence of the women's collectives as a focus for women's affective lives transforms the family profoundly, making it no longer the sole source of personal affiliation. It seems likely that Rawls would oppose government support for such collectives on that account, considering it the endorsement of one conception of the good over another – for much the same reason that he has opposed government support for music and the arts. For me, the fact that women's capabilities are in such a perilous state, together with the fact that empowerment programs have shown great success in giving them greater control over their material and political environment, gives government a compelling interest in the introduction of such programs.

Or take SEWA. It is not a government program, but let us suppose it were. For Rawls, this focus on giving women access to credit and economic self-sufficiency, together with education in confidence and leadership, would be, I surmise, an impermissible interference by government in the family structure. The very idea that government would support an all-women's bank would be highly suspect. For me, while I think it very important for a program like this to be noncoercive, it seems quite all right for government to act in ways that aim at changing the social norms that shape the family, and at promoting capabilities in those who lack them. For, after all – and this is the crux of the matter – government is already in the business of constructing an institution, the family, that is part of the basic structure of society. It had better get to work and do this job well.

Even in the area of property, Rawls's approach seems to me to offer uncertain guidance, whereas mine offers clear guidance. Property rights in India have traditionally belonged to families as organic wholes, and women have little or no control over the family unit or "coparcenary," which is run by its male members. Demands by women for land rights have frequently been greeted with the claim that this would "break up the family."[63] And certainly the demand, if accepted, would transform the internal governance of that structure. Rawls might or might not hold that the transformation is necessary to make women equal citizens; but the fact that the change in family governance would equalize women's bargaining position in the family would, by itself, supply an insufficient argument for the change. In my approach, by contrast, we get to the conclusion very directly, since control over property is one of the central capabilities that cannot be abridged unequally on the basis of sex. What Rawls would say, at best, is, "This so-called breakup of the family is an appropriate constraint supplied by external justice." What I would say is, "You didn't just find the family lying around, you constituted it in one way, through the tradition of property law; now we shall constitute it in another way, one that protects women's capabilities."

The greatest difference in the two approaches will be in the treatment of female children. It is here, especially, that my approach recognizes the pervasive and nonvoluntary nature of family membership, and gives the state broad latitude to shape perception and behavior in ways that promote the development of female children to full adult capability in the major areas. This means not only the abolition of child marriage and (where practically possible) child labor, but also (where practically possible) compulsory primary and secondary education for all children. Rawls would presumably also favor these changes. It also means encouraging the public perception that women are suited for many different roles in life, and are active members of the political and economic communities, something that Rawls is likely to see as too much promotion of a definite conception of the good. Thus the content of public education should include information about options for women, and about resistance to women's inequality. (One terrible problem India is now having is that government has no money for new textbooks, with the result that outdated images of women are still used in primary schools despite the fact that few educators like them.) In addition to regular schooling, the Indian government also supports special hostel programs for young girls who are at risk for child marriage, to remove

---

63 See a statement by the minister of agriculture quoted in Bina Agarwal, " 'Bargaining' and Gender Relations: Within and beyond the Household," 3.

them from their homes and give them education and job training. Rawls would likely see this as too much state intervention in the family, even if the mothers consent to the girls' going away: after all, government is saying, "I will support you if you leave this dangerous structure." My approach judges that the protection of girls' capabilities warrants this interventionist strategy.

Finally, my approach will also support government efforts to reshape the capabilities of men. In rural Bihar, the NGO Adithi supports sex equality training for male teachers, reasoning that sex roles in the household will not be changed until boys as well as girls seek new divisions of labor. The male teachers I saw were an intensely idealistic and optimistic group. They proudly proclaimed that in every village household young boys would now be seen doing child care, sweeping, and cooking: they had convinced them that these functions were not shameful for a man. Whether they had achieved so quickly the degree of success they narrated, remains to be seen. But this is the kind of effort that my approach might reasonably support, even as an aspect of government action: rethinking the division of labor in the family is a crucial aspect of guaranteeing women's full equality as citizens.

Rawls's approach to the family and mine are very close: both of us define the person as the basis of distribution; both of us see an important role for liberties of association and self-definition; both of us recognize the intrinsic value of love and care. But Rawls remains half-hearted, I think, in his recognition of the important idea that the family is a part of the "basic structure of society," and of important asymmetries between the family and other voluntary organizations. I have tried to show how an approach through the central capabilities would capture that idea, while still valuing family love and the insights this love affords.

VII. BARGAINING APPROACHES AND WOMEN'S OPTIONS

I have argued that any useful inquiry into these matters must be contextual, understanding how the capabilities are realized in a concrete political and historical setting. I shall therefore not make further detailed recommendations at this point. Instead, I shall suggest a way in which we might approach each question as it arises.

When we ask concrete practical questions about the forms of state action that constitute the family structure, helpful guidance is supplied by bargaining approaches to the family, which help us to think clearly about how changes influence the bargaining position of women, vis-à-vis their fellow family members and vis-à-vis restrictive social norms. The government of Kerala accurately foresaw that providing a nutritious lunch in school would strengthen the bargaining position of children, increasing child education and diminishing child labor. The federal government accurately foresaw that introducing women's cooperatives into rural areas would improve women's bargaining position vis-à-vis their husbands, thus diminishing domestic violence and enhancing women's economic contribution. It also foresaw that the new aggressiveness of women would provide a helpful check on the corruption of local and state governments, as women demand health visits, teachers, and regular water service. (It did not, perhaps, foresee the type of resistance that would be forthcoming in Andhra Pradesh, an especially corrupt and lawless province: the federal government employee who showed me around reported that her life had been threatened, and she fully expected assassination attempts. Similar problems obtain in Bihar, a state that in February 1999 was put under national control because of the breakdown of law and order at the state level.) Governments that have instituted literacy programs have accurately predicted that these new economically relevant skills would make women effective bargaining agents in the struggle to define social norms with regard to who may go out of the house and who may not.[64] A good account of the bargaining structure must be complex and flexible, embodying a good understanding of the different capabilities and how they support one another. So informed, bargaining approaches provide useful insight for people who are trying to promote a set of central capabilities.

In the most general way, guidance will always be supplied first and foremost by the ideas of practical reason and of human dignity: the idea that each human being is a maker of a life plan, and that each

---

64 See Chen, *A Quiet Revolution*; Agarwal, "Bargaining." Agarwal persuasively criticizes the narrow reductive character of some bargaining models, defending a more flexible "bargaining approach."

should be treated as an end and none as the mere instrument of the ends of others. These ideas, combined with the rest of the capabilities on the list, provide a set of goals for public action: we aim to create citizens who have these powers and opportunities, as active planners of their lives and as dignified equals.

With these goals in the background, we may advance some general principles that should guide public action.

1. *The importance of options.* In bargaining theory, one of the most obvious principles is that the "breakdown position" of each member of a cooperative bargaining unit is an important determinant of his or her bargaining power.[65] This is a particularly vital principle for any policy attempting to promote equality for women. Women often have very poor exit options in marriage. Vasanti stayed in an abusive marriage for a long time for precisely that reason. She was illiterate; she had no property; she had no marketable skills. She did have supportive relations, and was in that way better off than many women; otherwise she could not have left at all. But her bad breakdown position put her under enormous pressure to put up with whatever her husband wanted to dish out. Something similar is true of Jayamma's relationship with her exploitative employer. He knew that she had no skills and no literacy, and wasn't likely to find a more regular or better-paying job. So he could refuse to promote her, neglect her health care, and in other ways exploit her.

The consequences of this idea for a theory of women's capabilities are significant. For this reflection tells us that increasing women's economic options is an extremely powerful way of promoting their well-being in the family, and more generally. It means that access to employment and credit, land rights, and literacy are important not only in themselves, but also as powerful supports for women's capability in general. If we want women like Vasanti to be free from domestic violence, it is of course of the first importance to have and effectively enforce laws against it, and to take other action narrowly concerned with this issue, such as setting up shelters for battered women (which hardly exist at all in India). But it is at least as important to work

---

65 See Sen, "Gender and Cooperative Conflicts," 135, calling this principle the "breakdown well-being response."

indirectly, improving the exit options. If she can read, if she can get a loan, if she has a self-employment cooperative to turn to, a woman is far more likely to stand up to abuse – or to end it by leaving.

Options have a more general importance, giving women alternatives to marriage before they are married, and giving them alternatives to unsuitable or undesirable employment. In this way, attention to economic options, in combination with a strong attack on the practice of trafficking, is likely to be the best way to address the problem of prostitution. Criminalization has usually made women's lot worse, making women who are ill treated reluctant to go to the police for assistance.[66] Thus, in Bombay the Annapurna Mahila Mandel offers job training to daughters of prostitutes, viewing this as the best way to give them an alternative future. In Andhra Pradesh, similar programs of skills training combat child marriage. In a related way, addressing the problem of child labor requires giving parents economic options (as does the Kerala school lunch program).

2. *The importance of perceived contribution.* Another important determinant of women's bargaining position in the family is their *perceived contribution* to the well-being of the household – which may or may not be the same as their actual economic and emotional contribution.[67] Women's domestic labor is frequently undervalued, as is the labor they expend in caring for children and spouse. Other family members will allocate opportunities and goods to them in accordance with their perceived contribution, rather than their real contribution. In Jayamma's household, for example, there was a certain disparity between perceived and real contributions, which was reflected in the husband's greater control over family income, even when he was not the major producer and did no domestic work. When women do not work outside the home, this disparity is likely to be even greater. As for girl children, the problem is still more complex: there may not only be the

---

66 See my " 'Whether from Reason or Prejudice': Taking Money for Bodily Services," in *Sex and Social Justice.* A vivid case study on this point is supplied by *A Modern Form of Slavery: Trafficking of Burmese Women and Girls into Brothels in Thailand,* a publication of Asia Watch Women's Rights Project, a division of Human Rights Watch (New York: Human Rights Watch, 1993). The criminal status of prostitution under Thai law (which does not even exempt women forced into prostitution) has been, the report argues, a major impediment to Burmese women who are duped into prostitution by promises of jobs as domestic servants.
67 See Sen, 136–7, the "perceived contribution response."

perception that their labor is less valuable than male labor; but, in most of India, there is also the perception (recorded in the popular saying Giribala repeats to herself) that a daughter is "already gone" – that she will help out someone else's family, and not one's own. Furthermore, on the way she will involve the family in the considerable expense of dowry. Jasodhara Bagchi's study of girls in West Bengal shows that the reasons most commonly given for not allowing girls to go to school involve a combination of economic and cultural factors: the family is poor, and the perception is that the girl's education is not valuable to the family (whereas her domestic labor is frequently seen as necessary).[68]

What steps can public policy take to address this aspect of women's bargaining position? Combatting wage discrimination is surely one step: for Jayamma's work would be perceived to be more valuable were she given wages equal to those of male employees. As Rawls and Okin have already pointed out, the divorce law can change perceptions of the worth of a woman's domestic contribution, by considering this labor when settlements are worked out. As Chapter 3 has shown, this is far from being reality in India, but it is a goal to pursue.

More generally, programs targeted at women usually raise their status in the family. Chen describes the way in which the BRAC literacy program increased not only women's real economic options but also, and to some extent independently, the perception of their worth as agents in the family. The fact that they were seen to be learning and acquiring skills made them seem more important than they had seemed before. Similarly in Andhra Pradesh, after only six months in the government women's project the women reported that their contribution was taken far more seriously by their husbands. Seeing them organized into a group, seeing them effectively demanding services from the local government – and just seeing that national government officials came to see not the men of the village, but the women – made women seem like powerful people who can do things. (I couldn't help noticing this reaction myself, as a circle of men formed around the women and me, as we talked sitting on the floor; the men watched from a distance,

68 See Bagchi, 87–121. Bagchi's study points to other problems that make the life of the girl child worse, in particular the more or less complete absence of local libraries, which would make it possible for girls to read at home and to continue reading after leaving school.

taking in the fact that a foreign professor had come to interview their wives and daughters.) Women reported that these factors by themselves have changed men's treatment of them. There was an initial period of suspicion and resentment; but then the men began to respond positively to the fact that the women's collective was getting things done for the village as a whole. Seeing women as active bargaining agents who were winning some benefits for the village, they began to have more respect for them in the home. They asked their opinions more often, there was some decline in domestic abuse, and the men simply took more care about their own hygiene and bodily appearance.

3. *The importance of a sense of one's own worth.* A third factor of major importance in strengthening a woman's bargaining position in the family is her own perception of her worth and the worth of her projects. As Sen has pointed out, a person who doesn't think herself entitled to anything much, and who believes that others have more worthwhile goals than her own, will bargain weakly.[69] As I have argued in Chapter 2, that is a significant problem for women in the family.

How can this inner sense of non-entitlement be effectively combatted? Both government and nongovernment programs typically spend a lot of time talking to women about their rights, about the fact that they are citizens who have a right to claim things from the government, about the importance of their own plans and projects. And of course the very fact that people are attending to them and treating them as important is itself a significant part of effecting change. But there are other, more concrete strategies. Education obviously plays an important role here, and in two ways: as a source of images of worth and possibility, and also as a source of skills that make possibilities real. The video program devised by SEWA and described in Chapter 2 also aims to produce confidence and high aspiration, simply by showing women what other women like themselves have done. And finally, meeting with other women in groups is of the first importance in gaining a sense of strength and effective agency. As a woman in Andhra Pradesh put it, "A single voice is not heard. Together we demanded and negotiated an increase in wages." A woman in the Bangladeshi

---

69 Sen, 136, the "perceived interest response"; see elaboration and examples in Agarwal, "Bargaining."

literacy program said to Chen, "If anybody's mind is depressed, after participating in the meeting, her mind will be refreshed."[70] The importance of this factor cannot be underestimated: for women who have typically been isolated, each in a separate household, finding strength in group solidarity is a major source of changes in self-perception. Bargaining power against domestic abuse is clearly strengthened by the very existence of the group, which can take action against a male who behaves badly; but it is also strengthened by the sense of power and dignity a woman gets in the group, which makes her intolerant of abuses she might have tolerated before.

Indeed, it would appear that in India at the present time, the single most effective way for government to promote women's sense of their worth and their entitlements is to promote women's collectives. The Mahila Samakhya Project is not a very expensive project; it involves a small staff, and relies heavily on local trainees. Its efficiency in getting women to think about their lives has been tremendous. Once such thinking begins, it is difficult to go backward; and so such collectives, once started, have a transformative power all their own. These women's collectives are communities of equality and agency, rather than hierarchical communities that define women as in crucial ways passive before their destiny. Moreover, these new relationships of care lead to positive changes in the family relationship, giving women new strength to bargain against domestic violence, winning them new respect from husbands and sons. The men in Andhra Pradesh, the women reported, have started to bathe more regularly, since they now want to make a good impression on their wives. Clearly there is often a valuable synergy between networks of care outside the family and a positive restructuring of that institution. As the song "Mahila Samiti," ubiquitous in the Indian women's movement, puts it: "In every household there is fear. Let's do away with that fear. Let's build a women's collective."

In short, we are not forced to choose between a deracinated type of individualism, where each person goes off as a loner, indifferent to others, and traditional types of community, which are frequently hierarchical and unfair to women. The fact is that justice and friendship

70 *A Quiet Revolution*, 155.

are good allies: women who have dignity and self-respect can help to fashion types of community that are no less loving, and often quite a lot more loving, than those they have known before.

VIII. TWO DEBATES IN INTERNATIONAL FEMINISM

There are many concrete areas in which we could use this basic framework to comment on directions for social change, and I have already remarked briefly on some of these: prostitution, domestic violence, child marriage, marital consent, child labor.

But let me instead put the framework to work in adjudicating two debates that have recently arisen on the feminist development policy scene in India, and which are typical of debates in international development more generally: what I shall call the "sexuality-versus-employment" debate, and what I shall call the "land-versus-education" debate.

The first is a heated debate between two groups of feminists about the basic goals of feminism. For one group, let's call it group S, the essence of feminism is a critique of sexual domination, and the essence of change is changing socially constructed gender roles. For the other group, let's call it group T, the essence of feminism is a critique of women's economic dependency, and the most desirable change is to give women more economic options. Members of S are likely to focus on domestic violence, sexual abuse of all sorts, sexual harassment, and prostitution as the major ills, and they are likely to criticize a project as insufficiently feminist if its focus is purely economic and doesn't involve a major component of consciousness raising. For example, the directors of the Mahila Samakhya Project told me that their proposals had been criticized by other feminists as lacking a feminist content, on the grounds that the focus of the program is on empowerment through economic options. Members of T, by contrast, are likely to judge that it is counterproductive to talk about domestic violence and sex roles when coming into a village, and far more productive to talk about credit, land rights, and employment. They are likely to criticize members of S for making feminism look threatening and for saying things that have little resonance in the minds of rural women.

Up to a point, one might think that there is just a strategic issue here: one group thinks that the economic approach is less threatening and therefore more effective, the other group thinks that avoiding direct confrontation with basic issues of gender hierarchy head on is ultimately counterproductive. They may not even always disagree about strategy: for members of S might agree that it is strategically wise to open up a dialogue by focusing on nonthreatening economic issues, while holding that the real source of women's inequality lies elsewhere, and must ultimately be addressed.

But in fact the split lies deep: the two groups have different intuitions about the root cause of women's subordination. Members of S typically think that subordination is all about wanting a submissive sexual outlet, and that economic aspects of subordination are posterior. Members of T think that women's subordination is all about men wanting to control income and property and to have willing domestic servants – and that the sexual aspects of women's subordination are posterior.

There are some genuine differences between the two groups. For example, most members of group S would consider lesbianism an appropriate choice for women wishing to resist domination in a male-dominated sexual world, while many members of T are religious or conservative women who believe lesbianism to be immoral, although they are committed to campaigning for women's economic self-sufficiency. (Thus leaders of some organizations aimed at economic empowerment have conservative attitudes about sexual orientation.) Some more conservative members of T also shrink from saying that there is anything wrong with male sexuality as it is, and prefer to avoid talking about sexuality as such. Probably these are the deepest sources of the intense animosity that exists between the two groups – in a nation that is still among the most repressive in the world toward homosexual people of both sexes, where some of the feminist members of S are lesbian and have been badly treated as persons by members of T. (A leader of Mahila Samakhya in Andhra Pradesh, an intense and fiery feminist who routinely put her bodily safety on the line to struggle against corrupt local officials to keep the women's program going, asked me why "sexual perversion" had become so common in the United States – evincing an attitude not uncommon among feminists of the T variety.)

The issue of homosexuality cannot easily be isolated from larger issues about the root cause of women's subordination. Feminists of the S variety believe that binary gender divisions and "compulsory heterosexuality" lie at the root of women's economic oppression, and that any approach that doesn't stick up for lesbian choices is therefore ultimately self-subverting. They would say that the homophobia of India is not just accidentally related to its patriarchal treatment of women: the fear that women can be sexually self-sufficient, and thus unavailable as sexual outlets for men, is what inspires homophobia, so homophobia is patriarchy's reaction to a deep threat. Some feminists of the T variety vigorously deny this, holding that the issue of women's equality within the heterosexual family is utterly unrelated to the morality of homosexual conduct: one may be intensely homophobic and yet vigorously feminist.

It seems reasonable to think that on the issue of causality the S feminists are correct: there is a long tradition in India (as in most of the world) of regarding women as men's sexual property, and the fear that this system would be upset is very likely to lie at the root of many people's fear and hatred of lesbianism. It may well be that in the long run the treatment of women as property cannot be combatted without combatting the system of heterosexuality that has defined women as sexual property. Once again: if even such a morally reflective and exemplary person as Gandhi regarded his wife as a sexual instrument, not as a sexual agent in her own right, we must conclude that these attitudes run very deep, and it is easy to see how any lesbian choice would threaten them. So it would seem that the T feminists are refusing to discuss an issue that may ultimately be absolutely central in understanding women's inequality.

Fortunately, the dispute that began in December 1998 over the screening of the film *Fire*, which deals with a lesbian relationship between two women who have both been oppressed in traditional marriages, has helped to open up this whole issue. Reacting strongly against the attempts of Hindu fundamentalist thugs to close the film down, artists, academics, and feminists of all types got involved in demonstrating for the free-speech rights of the filmmaker. Although differences still existed among the protesters – some insisting that lesbianism is a traditional feature of Hindu culture, some preferring to focus on the film's feminist aspect – it could no longer be denied that there is a strong link between women's subordination in traditional sexual relationships and their interest in same-sex relationships; and the public attention of feminists of all sorts has been newly focused on the discrimination suffered by lesbians in all strata of Indian society. Open conversation about the topic seems to promise a closing of the gap between the two groups of feminists.

Nonetheless, in many respects the entire dispute seems peculiar. Why should we have to say that the subordination of women is about just one thing? Clearly, it has aspects that are sexual and aspects that are economic. Both of these are socially shaped, and each reinforces the other. Men have seen women as their sexual property, and they have also seen them as their economic servants. Giribala's husband wanted her body, but he also wanted her to walk several steps behind him, carrying the lentils. In some cases, the sexual relation of dominance is the primary relation; in Giribala's case and many others, it is probably the economic relationship that is the more prominent source of male interest and control. (Some of these husbands have other sexual outlets and are thus relatively indifferent to the wife's sexual function.) In short, both types of hierarchy are fundamental, and neither can or should be avoided. Understanding one, indeed, would appear to require understanding the other. T feminists certainly should not refuse to re-think habitual distinctions of gender and sexual roles; but S feminists should not deny that economic issues sometimes have their own momentum, and may offer independent explanations for some aspects of women's inequality.

As we think this way, the capabilities approach, together with a bargaining approach, helps us to make sense of what we find. We begin with the idea that both employment-related capabilities and sex-related capabilities (such as bodily integrity, emotional health, and the capacity for sexual expression) are fundamental human capabilities that should not be abridged. The bargaining approach then helps us to think about the many ways in which the two capabilities complement one another. Women who wish to avoid sexual brutality or exploitation in marriage, and to pursue sexual autonomy, can do so far more easily if they are in a strong bargaining position; and access to employment, credit, and land rights are important sources of strength for their bargaining position. At the same time, the perception that women are whorish and childish, so pervasive in Indian traditions at least since the Laws of Manu, does undercut women's search for employment and weaken their bargaining position in the workplace. So attempts to alter those perceptions of female sexuality are important accompaniments to women's search for economic equality. The approach tells us that neither capability should be subordinated to the other, and that public action on both fronts is a legitimate way to promote both sexual and economic freedom.

Concerning practical strategies, T feminists have strong points to make, which S feminists can readily accept. It is certainly less threatening to enter a village saying that you are going to promote better services and to extend new opportunities for credit and employment, than to say, "I have come to change your sex roles." (Does anyone really say things like this?) In order to avoid backlash against feminist programs, it may be good to focus on economic issues, leaving it to women themselves to draw their own conclusions about sexual life in their own way in due course. On the other hand, that doesn't mean being altogether silent about gender roles, particularly where domestic violence is concerned. Frequently women who are otherwise quite ambivalent about employment outside the home will find it an attractive option if they come to think of it as improving their bargaining position against domestic violence: so these links should be discussed, in order to present a more adequate picture of women's options. Vasanti was interested in the loan and the new sewing machine primarily as ways to exit from an abusive marriage: so any approach that cordoned off that issue would not have addressed her concerns. Domestic violence is one of the first issues women typically wish to discuss. When the Andhra Pradesh women (all illiterate) made drawings of their problems, wife beating and child sexual abuse were both absolutely central. So it would seem that even in strategic terms this question should not be marginalized, even early on, although its links to economic issues should also be pointed out.

In short, the capabilities are an interlocking set; they support one another, and an impediment to one impedes others. The same insight helps us address another controversy in international development discussions, which has been implicitly recognized from the start of my argument: a controversy between supporters of women's literacy and supporters of local norms. On the one side is Amartya Sen, who, with Jean Drèze and other supporters, has long stressed the pivotal role of literacy in enhancing women's bargaining position. On the other side are thinkers of various kinds who urge us to defer to local norms, and who cast aspersions on literacy as a value of Western origin.[71] Sen argues convincingly that literacy is highly correlated with access to information about women's lives and with access to types of employment that women had not previously attained. He has also made a convincing empirical argument that promoting female literacy is the single best way to combat population growth; this position has by now been widely accepted in international population discussions.[72] Government can do quite a lot to promote literacy, so this is one good starting point for government action. The counterargument usually takes the form of saying that development projects have frequently gone wrong by being "top-down" in their approach, imposing alien values on people who have their own experienced sense of life. So if the common people are not asking for literacy, it is just wrong to promote it.

This dispute seems more superficial than the previous one: once one considers bargaining positions at all, one can see that literacy is frequently critical in giving women greater access to goods they are already pursuing. Few would deny that working women seek enhanced control over land rights and employment options, and a greater measure of contact with other women who are similarly placed. But if one grants this one need only look at the empirical literature to see that literacy is extremely important in connection with all of these goods. Agarwal has shown that literacy is correlated with the ability to attain land rights; similar arguments can be made concerning credit and specific types of employment. A detailed study of the introduction of a literacy program in rural Bangladesh, Martha Chen's *A Quiet Revolution*, shows that even women initially skeptical about literacy found it

71 For the local-tradition viewpoint, see, for example, the essays in *Dominating Knowledge: Development, Culture, and Resistance*, ed. F. A. Marglin and S. A. Marglin (Oxford: Clarendon Press, 1990); such an approach is invoked to cast aspersions on the idea of making literacy a central goal of public policy in a number of different places. Some activists hold that any value not already represented in the thinking of common people cannot be commended to them. Government actors sometimes invoke this idea – as, for example, when Rajiv Gandhi did so in a speech at Harvard in the late 1980s. Questioned about why his government had done so little to increase female literacy, he replied that the common people have a wisdom that is different from, but no less than, that of literate people.

72 See Sen, "Fertility and Coercion," *University of Chicago Law Review* 63 (1996), 1035–61; "Population: Delusion and Reality," *The New York Review of Books*, September 22, 1994.

an important route to aspects of life they were already pursuing, such as economic security and enhanced status in the family. They also learned the sheer pleasure of unfolding their minds in this way, expressing their newfound delight with reading and the mental development it promoted. Finally, they expressed delight with their newfound solidarity with other women in the literacy group, which had enabled them to build a nonhierarchical community of a type previously unknown to them. Nobody reading this story could reasonably conclude that literacy was being imposed as an alien value: the women did not take it on until they had made sense of it in terms of their own lives and their bargaining position.

Thus supporters of Sen's contention need not deny that many development programs have been crudely insensitive to the wisdom involved in local understandings, in order to continue pressing for literacy as a central public policy issue. Their claim is that even those who would not grant the intrinsic value of this capability – and much supports the idea that it is of intrinsic value – can still agree that its strategic importance is huge, in supporting a wide range of other human capabilities. The field of human capabilities should not be seen as a tragic "either-or," where ideas associated with modernization battle it out against the claims of traditional values; it is, instead, a "both-and," where a capability new to a subordinated group has significance in part for the ways in which it supports the projects that group was already pursuing.

Let me end this discussion by returning to Vasanti and to Jayamma. How did these women encounter love and care in their family lives, and how have they forged new opportunities for care through developing of other capabilities and new forms of affiliation? Jayamma's lot has been the typical female lot of the "double day," where duties of care for children and husband so devour time and energy – after a physically exhausting work day – that there is not a lot of time left for love in the middle-class sense, in which love is associated with play, delight, imagination, and generous reciprocity. Indeed, Jayamma's deprivations in other areas of human capability – especially in nutrition, economic security, and leisure time – have left her a life relatively barren of love, and created a personality that cannot easily respond to others with warmth and generosity. She is a ferocious and triumphant survivor; but traditional norms of care and traditional family structures

– even the relatively woman-friendly norms of Kerala – have worked against love in her life, by robbing her of leisure and imaginative stimulation. This result shows us, once again, that we don't have a tragic choice between traditional family love and the enhancement of capabilities: people love best when they are in other respects flourishing, not when they are exhausted, or struggling to make ends meet.

Vasanti has had, I think, more good fortune in life. First of all, in a culturally uncharacteristic way, her family stuck with her and supported her in hardship, giving her a sense of security that one can perceive in her personality, with its greater softness, warmth, and openness. Her desire to care for a husband has been thwarted, and her desire for children will probably never be realized, given the rarity of remarriage in her cultural milieu. But she does have generosity, mutuality, and love in her relationships with female friends, and one can see that her capacity for resourcefulness, humor, and imagination is very much alive in these nontraditional settings, all the more since she is freed from the fear of abuse that dominated much of her earlier life. Her story is, then, in one way the same as Jayamma's: it points us to the fact that the human capabilities provide essential support for love, even as love is among the major human capabilities.

CONCLUSION

Women in much of the world lose out by being women. Their human powers of choice and sociability are frequently thwarted by societies in which they must live as the adjuncts and servants of the ends of others, and in which their sociability is deformed by fear and hierarchy. But they are bearers of human capabilities, basic powers of choice that make a moral claim for opportunities to be realized and to flourish. Women's unequal failure to attain a higher level of capability, at which the choice of central human functions is really open to them, is therefore a problem of justice.

I have argued that a political approach based on ideas of human capability and functioning supplies a good basis for thinking about these problems, helping us to construct basic political principles that can serve as the foundation for constitutional guarantees to which nations should be held by their citizens. I have also argued that the capabilities framework provides a good orientation for comparative quality of life measurement when nations are compared. In both areas, the approach supplies better guidance than approaches based on utility or on opulence (GNP per capita). The approach, I have argued, also helps us to think well about two of the most difficult issues facing international development today: the legal and political status of religion, and the legal and political status of the family.

The world community has been slow to address the problems of women, because it has lacked a consensus that sex-based inequality is an urgent issue of political justice. Other forms of hierarchy and inequality – apartheid, for example – have been deemed world outrages and have mobilized the international community. The outrages suffered every day by millions of women – hunger, domestic violence, child sexual abuse and child marriage, inequality before the law, poverty, lack of dignity and self-regard – these are not uniformly regarded as scandalous, and the international community has been slow to judge that they are human rights abuses. Recently, however, the mobilization of an international women's community at many levels – from local collectives, to regional NGOs, to government programs, to international agencies and human rights programs – has begun to make real progress in putting the capability failures of women on the of national and international agenda. People concerned with political change often have doubts about philosophy, wondering how such an abstract and remote discipline can possibly be helpful when people are suffering. Why should we fuss so obsessively about getting conceptual distinctions precisely drawn when there is so much practical work to be done? One reply that has already emerged from my argument is that abstract normative theory is playing a role in practice already, in the form of the normative theories characteristic of utilitarian economics. Economists are not trained in normative argument, and frequently they are unfamiliar with the complicated debates about political norms that have unfolded over the years in political philosophy. And yet they routinely offer controversial judgments regarding normative matters, judgments that often reflect tacit assumptions and unargued specifications of core concepts (for example, the concept of "development"). Wherever utility maximization is used as a normative concept in public policy formation, whenever the controversial philosophical commitments of economics (to aggregation across lives, to the commensurability of the valuable components in a life) are simply taken for granted in talking about policy formation, economists are engaging in normative theorizing. I have argued here that the normative approaches characteristic of utilitarian economics are inadequate guides to public policy. Given that they are already on the scene, we need good theory to drive out bad. Good theories of the requisite sort require philosophy, because they require sustained thought about foundational concepts (such as preference, choice, desire, capability) whose delineation has not traditionally been the focus of the social sciences.

But we do not need philosophy only as a counterweight to the philosophical assumptions of development economists. We need it to help us think through our own intuitive ideas, to criticize them, and to figure out which ones we are willing to hold on to. People do not go through life without forming views about the human good and the right, about what has value and what does not, about what choice is, about what justice and mercy and aggression and grief are. They have views about these things and they use them – not least when they enter the political arena. Often these views embed pieces of highly general theory, derived from custom, or religion, or social science. When public policies are chosen, then, they are the product of many people's intuitions and theories, some of them examined, and many of them unexamined. It seems sensible to deliberate about which theories we really want to hold onto, which intuitions are really the most deeply rooted in our moral sensibility. In the absence of such a public deliberation, the most influential views are likely to be those, simply, that are held by the most powerful or rhetorically effective people. This way of proceeding, defective in itself, is especially defective when we consider the interests of the powerless, who rarely get the chance to bring their own ideas about such matters to the table.

Philosophy asks for public deliberation instead of the usual contest of power. It asks us to choose the view that stands the test of argument, rather than the view that has the most prestigious backers; the view that gets all the details worked out coherently and clearly, rather than the view whose proponents shout the loudest. At its best, its conceptual fussiness is profoundly practical: only if things are worked out in all their detail will we know whether we really do have the alternative that can stand up to objection better than another, and sometimes the fatal objection to a view emerges only after considerable probing. It makes sense for public deliberation to take account of these apparently fussy debates, because this is how we think through what we have to do, see what we really want to stand for.

Philosophy often fails to impress people with its relevance, and sometimes this is the fault of philosophers. Philosophy can offer good guidance to practice, I believe, only if it is responsive to experience and periodically immersed in it. Experience, to be sure, is not raw data for theory. We experience nothing without using theoretical categories; in political thought we will learn nothing from the lives we encounter if we do not bring to our experience such evolving theories of justice and the human good as we have managed to work out until then. But our inquiries are also properly shaped by what we find; with insufficient experience we do not even know what questions we should be asking.

Philosophers may or may not use narratives of experience in their work: but they should be able to show that their work responds to the complexity of experience and has been shaped by a mature human being's sense of that complexity. Feminists rightly demand that theories dealing with women's lives show their understanding of women's experience of subordination and exclusion. Much of what philosophers of the past (in all traditions) have written about women, sex, and the family has not shown such understanding. Again, it is right to demand that philosophers writing about poverty show that they have some understanding of the complex interaction of agency and constraint in the lives of those concerning whom they make recommendations. Again, many traditions of thought have approached these problems with either naïveté or callousness. The solution to these problems, however, is not to reject philosophy, or even the tradition; it is to learn from them and move forward, with an even more passionate commitment to inclusiveness, precision, and sound argument.

Sometimes treatises of political philosophy, though profoundly practical in what their arguments entail, are not written in such a way as to engage nonspecialists. This problem can be addressed by a literary division of labor, as theoreticians either write two different types of work themselves, or else form partnerships with writers who show the theory's relation to practical problems. In the present book I have attempted to write for both specialists and nonspecialists, showing enough of the theoretical structure of my approach to engage the specialist philosopher, but including enough concrete narrative and empirical material to engage the nonphilosopher who wants to find out what philosophical argument may offer to international development policy.[1] I hope I have offered something that will help concerned citizens see the range of alternatives on the table, and some reasons why the capabilities approach is a valuable one among them. This approach is not intended as a recommendation by elite specialists to people who have no ideas on the topic. It is intended as – and, I believe, is – the systematization and theorization of thoughts that women are pursuing all over the world, when they ask how their lives might be improved, and what governments should be doing about that.

---

1 In other more specialized theoretical writing I plan to carry these proposals further: see remarks in the Preface.

In that spirit I conclude by returning to the women's collective (*sangham*) in rural Andhra Pradesh. Toward the conclusion of my visit there, after more than an hour in the 110° heat, the women began to sing for me songs they had learned in the women's collective. One, my interpreter explained, was an old women's song that expressed the idea that a woman's life was a life of sorrow. It used to begin: "Woman, why are you crying?" and then the woman would reply, listing all the bad things in her life. The women of the collective, however, had rewritten the song. Now it goes: "Women, why are you crying? Your tears should become your thoughts." And then the woman tells all her plans for improvement in her life.

Here is how the annual report of the collective records the women's plans:

"We want to plant fruit trees in front of our houses."
"We want to start an herbal medicine shop."
"We will build our house ourselves."
"We want to cultivate banjar lands."
"We want to register our Sangham."
"We want to travel. We want to see our office in Hyderabad."
"We want our school to run better."
"Our sangham should become big. We want more women to join us."
"We want to hold meetings at the Mandal [i.e. regional] level."
"Our children need a better life than us. They should learn new things."

Next to this list of plans is a drawing of a child in wedding dress, under a canopy – with a large red X drawn across it. The accompanying story: "Twelve year old Swarupa of Potulbogada village joined the hostel after attending the summer camp. During the vacation her parents tried to get her married. She sought the help of the sangham and together they managed to convince the parents to allow her to pursue her studies."

The capabilities approach is the systematization and theorization of just such thoughts and plans. It is plural because what women strive for contains a plurality of irreducibly distinct components. It is focused on capability or empowerment, even as the women's own thinking is focused on creating opportunities and choices, rather than imposing on any individual a required mode of functioning. To the thinking that is already there it adds a set of arguments linking the capabilities list explicitly to underlying ideas of human dignity that help us test candidates for inclusion; it adds a framing political approach showing how these ideas of capability and functioning will deal with legitimate concerns about diversity and pluralism; it adds arguments linking capabilities to specific political principles that can be embodied in constitutional guarantees. Finally it adds arguments showing very clearly the incompatibility of this approach with other prevalent alternatives. In these ways, it seems to me, the approach can fairly claim to make a distinctive contribution to the practical pursuit of gender justice.

NAME INDEX

SUBJECT INDEX

adaptation, *see* adaptive preferences

adaptive preferences, 114–15, 136–142, 164
"adaptive selves," 164–5
Elster on, 136–9, 164–6
endowment effect and, 143
institutions and, 142–4
liberalism and, 114–15
Mill on, 140–2
Nehru on, 149–50
Sen on, 139—40
"sour grapes" and, 136–9
Sunstein on, 143
see also desire; preference

affiliation, 82–3, 92, 244–5
Adithi, 283
Ahmedabad, 15
Amish, see *Wisconsin v. Yoder*
Andrha Pradesh, 43, 53–4, 113–14, 140, 260, 280, 284, 286, 288, 289, 294, 302
Annapurna Mahila Mandel project, 286
argument from culture, *see* culture, argument from
argument from (the good of) diversity, *see* diversity, argument from
argument from paternalism, *see* paternalism, argument from
Autobiography (Gandhi), 247–8

Bangladesh, 40
Bangladesh Rural Advancement Committee (BRAC), 40n12, 260–1, 287–9
bargaining approaches, *see* family, bargaining approaches and
Bengal, 256, 287
Bengal renaissance, 45
Bihar, 256, 283, 284
Bob Jones University v. United States, 191–2n42, 203–4, 228–9
Bombay, 286
Bradwell v. Illinois, 253
"breakdown position," 285–6
Buddhism, 58, 58n49, 191, 195

Calvinism, 176
capabilities, 70–86
Aristotle and, 13, 72, 73, 76–7
balancing of, 211–2
basic capabilities, 83–4, 198
basis for constitutional principles, 12, 71, 74–5
central capabilities, 78–80
combined capabilities, 84–6, 98, 149n80
functioning and, 13–14, 86–88, 93–5, 105, 153–4, 160–1, 180
human rights and, 14–15, 96–101
internal capabilities, 84–6
intrinsic worth of, 144, 179, 274–5
loss and, 235–8
Marx and, 13, 71–4